Charles Shanabruch received his Ph.D. in history from the University of Chicago and is now executive director of the Beverly Area Planning Association.

D0078458

CHICAGO'S CATHOLICS

Notre Dame Studies
in American Catholicism

The Brownson-Hecker Correspondence
edited by Joseph Gower and Richard Leliaert, 1979

The Survival of American Innocence:
Catholicism in an Era of Disillusionment, 1920–1940
by William M. Halsey, 1979

Faith and Fatherland:
The Polish Church War in Wisconsin, 1896–1918
by Anthony J. Kuzniewski, 1980

Sponsored by the
Charles and Margaret Cushwa Center
for the Study of American Catholicism

CHICAGO'S CATHOLICS

The Evolution of an American Identity

CHARLES SHANABRUCH

UNIVERSITY OF NOTRE DAME PRESS

NOTRE DAME   LONDON

Copyright © 1981 by
University of Notre Dame Press
Notre Dame, Indiana 46556

Manufactured in the United States of America

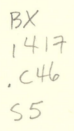

Library of Congress Cataloging in Publication Data

Shanabruch, Charles.
  Chicago's Catholics.

  (Notre Dame studies in American Catholicism ; v. 4)
  Bibliography: p.
  Includes index.
    1. Chicago (Archdiocese—History. 2. Minorities—
Illinois—Chicago region—History—19th century.
3. Minorities— Illinois—Chicago region—History—20th
century. 4. Chicago region, Ill.—Church history.
I. Title.   II. Series.
BX1417.C46S5   282′.77311   80–53071
ISBN 0–268–01840–5

For My Wife

Contents

Preface

THIS IS A HISTORY OF the response of the Archdiocese of Chicago to the ethnic diversity of its members between 1833 and 1924. In recent years, more and more historians and political scientists have recognized the importance of religio-ethnic influences for the development of American cities. Their resulting analyses of party politics, voting behavior, and residential mobility patterns have shed light upon the urban phenomenon. Unfortunately, the role of the Roman Catholic Church, the largest and most influential of the religio-social institutions of the Northeastern and Midwestern cities, has received little attention. To have a fuller picture of the social and political events of the nineteenth and twentieth centuries, its growth and development and changing identity must be considered. Therefore, this examination of the Catholic Church's struggle to maintain unity of faith in the midst of ethnic diversity seeks to elucidate an essential dimension in the dynamics of urban development.

American Catholic historiography generally has consisted of biographies and institutional histories that focus on the unity of faith and only allude to the problems arising from the polyglot character of the Church's membership. Yet the greatest issue that has confronted the Catholic Church in the last century and a half, resolution of the problem of unity in diversity, has attracted the attention of few scholars.

Rev. Thomas T. McAvoy's *The Great Crisis in American Catholic History* and Robert Cross's *The Emergence of Liberal Catholicism* treat the Church's "immigrant problem" from the point of view of "Americanizers," in particular, James Cardinal Gibbons, Archbishop John Ireland, and Bishop John J. Keane. Their studies show how some Catholic leaders in the late nineteenth century tried to alter the immigrants' folkways and identity. From a different perspective, Coleman Barry's *The Catholic Church and German Americans* examines the German-

ix

American endeavor to win a hearing from the predominantly Irish-American hierarchy. Recently, Jay Dolan's *The Immigrant Church: New York's Irish and German Catholics, 1815–1865* and Victor Greene's *For God and Country: The Rise of Polish and Lithuanian Consciousness in America* have further contributed to the understanding of immigrant Catholicism.

In large measure, Catholic historiography has conveyed the impression that bishops encountered the problem of administering to a multiplicity of immigrants in the twenty-year period between 1880 and 1900. This book demonstrates that Church officials were confronted with the necessity of meeting the wants of a diverse flock more than fifty years earlier. Further, the problem did not disappear in the twentieth century. While the national groups that demanded attention changed, the task of melding these miscellaneous peoples into an organized Catholic body persisted.

In addition to enlarging the time span, this study examines more than German-American and Polish-American nationalism. Although the Germans caused the greatest stir in the nineteenth century, and the Poles in the twentieth, other nationalities pressed similarly for recognition. Those other groups that agitated for equality or demanded service are also studied, and the interaction of the nationalities is thus made clearer.

While the setting of this history is local, it is hoped it is neither "parochial" nor antiquarian. By examining the history of a particular diocese over nearly a century, I have tried to trace the growth, direction, and spirit of the Church. The Chicago archdiocese, which was the most cosmopolitan and which became the largest see in the United States, is an appropriate subject for a careful, intensive analysis of the Roman Catholic Church's response to immigrants. The Chicago Catholic experience of achieving unity in diversity, preserving the faith of its immigrants, and progressing toward an American Catholic identity may shed light upon the events in other large industrial cities.

This volume is organized chronologically and thematically. The tenures of the first five bishops of the Diocese of Chicago provide the framework for discussion of the formative years of the Church's local history. The administrations of their archiepiscopal successors, who ruled during the period of greatest immigration, are analyzed separately and at length. The Church's response to the dual pressures of immigrant nationalism and nativism provide the conceptual framework throughout.

Correspondence, reports, and other documents in the Chicago Archdiocesan Archives, the Baltimore Archdiocesan Archives, the

Philadelphia Archdiocesan Archives, the University of Notre Dame Archives, the Richard Edwards Papers in the Illinois State University Archives, the John Dillon Papers in the Trinity College Library, and parochial records are the basis of this study. English- and foreign-language newspapers and periodicals, religious and secular, and privately printed parish histories, anniversary souvenirs, and numerous interviews also contribute to the substance of the work. Secondary sources include monographic studies of Chicago and particular immigrant groups and general social, economic, and political histories of the United States and the nations from which the immigrants came.

I wish to acknowledge my indebtedness to the directors and staffs of the research institutions and archives that I used and to the priests who shared their recollections. To Professor Joseph P. O'Grady of LaSalle College, who offered organizational advice, and to Rev. Andrew M. Greeley of the National Opinion Research Center and Professor John Hope Franklin, who read the study in dissertation form, I offer my thanks. In a special way, I am grateful to Professor Arthur Mann of the University of Chicago for suggesting the study and for his insightful comments and assistance throughout the dissertation's preparation. In the revision process, I benefited from the editorial advice and moral support offered by Professor Emmet Larkin of the University of Chicago. Finally, to my wife, Patricia Bryant, who was both understanding and encouraging, I am profoundly thankful.

1. Trans-National Foundations

IN THE NINETEENTH AND early twentieth centuries, Chicago's Roman Catholic Church was essentially an immigrant institution. Between 1833 and 1879, it grew from a missionary church to a confederation of immigrant parishes and institutions and evolved a spirit and structure that made possible its emergence as a powerful religious and social force. In these formative years the "Chicago Church," which was to become Catholicism's largest diocese, was shaped by the unprecedented growth of the city, the diversity and poverty of its members, the ability and sensitivity of its leaders, and the opposition of its foes. The internal and external pressures that forged its character also conditioned the responses it would make to similar forces in the future.

Tens of thousands of immigrants who came to Chicago in search of liberty, economic security, and a brighter future for their offspring were Catholics. These immigrants were generally anxious to reestablish ties to their religion, which was one with their cultural identity. They therefore gave generously of their time and meager incomes to maintain the clergy and erect churches. The bishops, usually sensitive and responsive to the wishes of their flock, assisted in the creation of parishes. These parishes usually served members of a particular nationality or linguistic group and maintained the Old World language and rites in order to ensure preservation of the immigrants' faith in the period of adjustment to their adopted land. In addition to such "national" parishes, the people built parochial schools to transmit the faith, ensure continuation of their cultural heritage, and defend the young against assaults of the Protestant host society.

Administration of the Catholic Diocese of Chicago challenged the men whom Rome appointed. Some succeeded and others broke under the strain. Lacking a tested model for a rapidly growing, multi-ethnic institution, the bishops had to rely on their own resources. Those with narrow vision and rigid personalities met failure; those with an open

1

mind and flexibility to compromise and share power succeeded. On the whole, successes outnumbered failures, and the Chicago Catholic Church withstood the stresses of growth and the pressures of diversity from within and the demand for conformity from without.

The growth of the Diocese of Chicago was a function of the growth of Chicago. Within the span of fifty years, the city progressed from an inconsequential trading post and fortress to the most important center of Mid-America's economic and social life. Although the swampy plains upon which it rose did not bode well for Chicago's future, its geographic position did. At the southern tip of Lake Michigan, it was ideally situated for commerce. The Great Lakes, the St. Lawrence River, and the Erie Canal connected it with the East and Europe, and the Mississippi River system provided a waterway to the South and West. The lines of travel converged on its site. Thus in 1820 a visitor correctly predicted the location would become "a depot for the inland commerce, between the northern and southern sections of the union, and a great thoroughfare for strangers, merchants and travellers."[1]

Chicago, which was incorporated in 1837, experienced unparalleled growth. In 1830 the settlement had a mere fifty residents, but within the decade it claimed 5,000, and by 1880 that number had multiplied one hundred times. The city's emergence from "one chaos of mud, rubbish and confusion"[2] was equally rapid. By 1840 the city had become the regional center for forwarding surplus farm products to the East, as well as the wholesale distribution center of Eastern goods to rural areas. The need for transportation networks to tap the agrarian hinterland and to create a back-country market became self-evident. In the late '30s and '40s, Americans from the Old Northwest and New England came to Chicago and initiated the first stages of urban development. They were soon joined by an ever-growing number of foreigners from northern and western Europe. All of them came to share in the opportunities promised by its boosters.

Soon, Chicago became a bustling commercial center and shed the last vestiges of a frontier community. The canals that were dug in the 1840s were succeeded by a comprehensive network of rails that further extended its influence. In 1856 the city was served by ten trunk lines with nearly 3,000 miles of track.[3] Lake traffic also boomed. A steady flow of German, Irish, Scandinavian, and French-Canadian immigrants supplied labor and eclipsed the once numerically superior native stock.

The Civil War, rather than retarding progress, established the city's position as the mercantile capital of the northern Mississippi Valley. Chicago became the locus of the grain, lumber, and hog and cattle trades. Although commerce remained supreme, the city broadened its economic base. Livestock trade led to meat processing and derivative industries, such as tanning and leather goods manufacturing. Proximity to the agrarian market gave rise to the farm implements industry and led to further industrialization. Iron production soon took hold along the banks of the Chicago River's north and south branches, and mills were erected to make the steel rails upon which the trade rolled to the city. By 1870 the foundations for Chicago's rise to industrial dominance were laid.

Chicago's development depended upon a constant supply of labor, and this was not wanting. The 1850 population, nearly 30,000, soared to 300,000 by 1870. Most of the new residents came from abroad and reinforced the cosmopolitan character of the city. Germans and Irish still constituted the largest proportions, but other nationalities came in great numbers after the Civil War. Most numerous were Swedes, Norwegians, Poles, and Bohemians. Americans from the Old Northwest and the East continued to flock to the city.[4]

In 1871 Chicago was ravaged by fire, but this only spurred its growth. Wind-whipped flames consumed much of the city's commercial district and many fine neighborhoods, leaving about one-third of its people homeless. Yet the people, in the words of the *Chicago Tribune*, resolved that "CHICAGO SHALL RISE AGAIN."[5] The city's boosters and commercial interests did not indulge in self-pity but immediately set about rebuilding Chicago, on a larger and finer scale than before.

Though the Depression of 1877 retarded progress, it failed to halt the growth of commerce and industry. By the end of the decade, half a million people crowded the site that had been home to a handful of soldiers and Indians half a century earlier. No longer was the shorescape the "fatiguing monotony"[6] described by a traveler in 1823, but a remarkable sight of grand residences and commercial emporiums. Among the most noticeable structures that reached skyward were the spires of the city's numerous Catholic churches.

The first threads of Catholic history in Chicago can be traced to French Jesuit missionaries who sought to convert the Indians to the Catholic faith. The priest-explorer Jacques Marquette wintered near the mouth of the Chicago River in 1674 and preached to the Indians, before moving on to set up a mission for the Kaskaskia Indians. Twenty-one years later a band of Jesuits, led by Fr. François Pinet, established the short-lived Mission of the Guardian Angel to convert the Miami Indians. After four years, the mission closed and the missionaries moved west. In the Chicago area, all the early religious work had focused on the Indians, since no stable French population had emerged to merit the services of a resident priest.[7]

By the end of the eighteenth century, a number of French traders and trappers had settled at the mouth of the Chicago River, but because of the dearth of missionaries in the Northwest Territory they received very infrequent visits. For their spiritual needs, the *habitans à Chicagou* had to journey to St. Louis or other locations that had a resident pastor.[8] By the year of Chicago's incorporation as a village (1833), the Catholic population had grown sufficiently to warrant a permanent clergyman. A group of Chicago Catholics met to discuss their plight and resolved to petition for a resident priest as the only means to conserve their faith. They addressed themselves to Bishop Joseph Rosati of St Louis:

> We, the Catholics of Chicago, Cook Co., Ill., lay before you the necessity there exists to have a pastor in this new and flourishing city. There are here several families of French descent, born and brought up in the Roman Catholic Faith and other quite willing to aid us in supporting a pastor, who ought to be sent here before the other sects obtain the upper hand, which very likely they will try to do. We have heard several persons say were there a priest here they would join our religion in preference to any other. We count almost one hundred Catholics in this town. We will not cease to pray until you have taken our important request into consideration.[9]

Bishop Rosati responded affirmatively and sent a recently ordained Frenchman, John Mary Irenaeus St. Cyr, who arrived May 1, 1833. Of the town's estimated 350 inhabitants, probably 150 were Catholic. Fr. St. Cyr's flock was predominantly French (pure and mixed), supplemented by a few English and Americans.[10]

Ministering to the French- and English-speaking flock was not a serious problem for the young French cleric because he had prepared himself by studying English before his arrival. A month later, St. Cyr reported to Rosati that he was trying to remedy the Catholics' ignorance of their faith. By preaching alternately in French and English, he succeeded in reaching all, including some Protestants who attended Sunday services. One of his goals, he explained, was to "remove prejudice by showing as clearly as possible in what the teaching of the Church consists."[11]

"The most serious problem faced by Chicago's first pastor was the extreme poverty of his flock. Despite severe privations (for want of candles and wine, daily Mass was out of the question), St. Cyr was hopeful because eagerness had been expressed to have a church where the Lord might "dwell continually."[12] Through subscriptions, St. Mary's Church, a small boxlike structure—unpainted, unplastered, without a steeple, and with rough benches and a simple table which served as both pulpit and altar—was completed in October 1833. Because the new congregation had no money for plastering, services were discontinued in winter, when numbing winds whistled through the unfinished walls. This first church reflected the hope and faith of the people, as well as the stark realities of their frontier poverty.[13]

The poverty of the Catholic flock caused the first recorded expression of concern for the linguistic talents of their priests. In 1837 Bishop Simon William Gabriel Bruté of Vincennes, Indiana, under whose jurisdiction Chicago now fell, sent Rev. Bernard Schaffer, a native of Strassburg in Alsace, to work with St. Cyr. Because of the high cost of living, however, the Catholics of Chicago could not support two priests. St. Cyr informed his superior: "It is impossible for two priests to live in Chicago without running into debt. Everything is extraordinary dear, while the majority of Catholics are poor and without means to support their families." St. Cyr noted that one of the priests should minister to the Irish who worked on the canal, but existence of only one chalice and missal between them precluded such services.[14]

To resolve the financial problem, Bishop Rosati ordered St. Cyr to return to St. Louis. When the St. Mary parishioners learned of St. Cyr's recall, they petitioned Rosati to reverse his decision because the removal would "be productive of injurious consequences to the cause of Catholic truth." They stressed St. Cyr's fluency and eloquence in English, while noting that Schaffer's "imperfect knowledge of the English language" made him "unfitted for discharging the spiritual duties of a pastor among an English population."[15] Nonetheless, Bishop Rosati did not give way, and St. Cyr left Chicago in April 1837.[16]

The Church's French phase had been coming to an end. In 1835 the Potawatomi Indians had ceded their Illinois territory and moved west, and the French traders followed. Those who remained behind were soon displaced or absorbed by Yankee and immigrant stock,[17] and the arrival of European immigrants strained the resources of the understaffed frontier Diocese of Vincennes. Writing to his St. Louis colleague in May 1837, Bishop Bruté lamented:

I hear nothing spoken about except emigrants and the cry for priests that goes up on every side. What shall we do, especially as our French priests are, many of them at least, still quite too weak in English? And as for German priests—alas! Where shall we find them? It is heart-breaking.[18]

The priests who were found to work on the frontier occasionally caused their bishops grief. In June, Bishop Bruté sent Fr. Timothy O'Meara, "an Irish priest who came to join us a short time ago,"[19] to Chicago to assist Schaffer. Soon, however, Schaffer died, and O'Meara, who had fled a Canadian diocese because of a scandal, became the pastor of Chicago Catholics. He purchased land in his own name and had St. Mary's relocated upon it. His alleged drinking with the Irish workers who were digging the Michigan Canal caused further concern.

Bishop Celestine de la Hailandière, Bruté's successor, dispatched Fr. Maurice de St. Palais to Chicago in 1839 to take charge of St. Mary's, but O'Meara, supported by the Irish, refused to deed his property to the bishop of Vincennes. However, when St. Palais informed the Irish that they would be excommunicated if they resisted legitimate authority, they submitted. Because he lost the support of his allies, O'Meara signed over the property and resigned the pastorate in June 1840. However, he remained in Chicago and exercised his sacramental powers, against the orders of the bishops, thus causing a minor schism. Only when St. Cyr visited Chicago the following year, and prevailed upon him, did O'Meara retire. Thereafter the Catholics were served by St. Palais and Fr. Francis Fischer, who was sent to minister to the Germans.[20]

The rapid growth of the Catholic population in Illinois and the unhappy incident with Fr. O'Meara indicated the need to establish episcopal authority in the state. In May 1843 the American bishops, convened in the Fifth Provincial Council of Baltimore, petitioned Rome for new dioceses, one of which was to be the Diocese of Chicago. They also proposed appointment of William J. Quarter to head the diocese, which comprised the entire state. Quarter, who was born in Killucine, King's (Offaly) County, Ireland, in 1805, had come to the United States at age 16 to take his ecclesiastical studies at Mount St. Mary's College in Emmitsburg, Maryland, in preparation for missionary work among Irish emigrants. After ordination, he went to New York City, where he ministered to the Irish on the Lower East Side. Because of his good work, the influential bishop of New York, John Hughes, urged Quarter's nomination for the Chicago see. On May 5, 1844, after a tedious journey, the youthful bishop, accompanied by his brother, Fr. Walter, arrived in Chicago.[21]

Bishop Quarter was well aware of the importance of religious practice among the immigrants who made up his flock. "There is no privation so keenly felt by the Catholic emigrant," he noted in a pastoral letter, "as the want of a Catholic church, and the absence of a Catholic priest from the place where they fix their abode, in a new and to them strange land." He therefore pledged: "We shall use our best efforts that they experience no such privations. We shall endeavor that they have, everywhere in the diocese, the consolations of their holy religion.[22]

Ministering to the needs of the growing immigrant communities placed a severe burden upon the new bishop. He faced substantial debt, and interest rates as high as 15 percent. The extreme poverty of his people made matters worse. Shortly after his arrival, he informed the president of St. Louis University: "We are indeed very poor here and I shall have to struggle for some time."[23] Furthermore, he confronted a serious shortage of priests. (The two priests from the Vincennes diocese, who had served Chicago, were promptly recalled upon Quarter's arrival.)[24] To secure the needed personnel, he recruited priests from other dioceses and ordained trained young men who presented themselves to him.[25] To ensure a continual supply of priests, he obtained a charter from the state legislature for the University of St. Mary's of the Lake, which would serve as both the diocesan seminary and a college for young men.[26]

Burdened with these current problems, Quarter also planned for the future. He had come from the East, where the problem of trusteeism (ownership and administration of Church property by a lay board) challenged episcopal authority. Therefore he had a second bill introduced in the Illinois legislature to empower himself and his successors to hold property in trust for religious purposes. Writing to his colleague in New Orleans in 1845, Quarter noted that "this bill, if it passes, will obviate the necessity of anything in the form of trusteeism in this diocese forever. There is not a trustee in the diocese nor shall there be as long as I live."[27] The following month the bill passed, and protected his authority.[28]

Besides securing priests, Bishop Quarter had to provide churches for the ever-growing immigrant communities. Shortly after his arrival, he commissioned construction of a large brick cathedral to replace the new and enlarged St. Mary's Church, erected by the Vincennes priests. The new Cathedral of St. Mary's soon proved inadequate, not only because of its size but also because of its location and the ethnic character of the faithful. Therefore, in 1846, St. Patrick's Church was erected in an Irish settlement on the west bank of the Chicago River to obviate the difficulties of crossing the river and to meet the wishes of the West Side Irish.[29]

When the famine in Ireland brought numerous refugees to Chicago, a group of Irish residents, supported by Bishop Quarter, organized the Hibernian Benevolent Emigrant Society. The society was to familiarize the immigrants with the opportunities and ways of American life, protect them from those who might take advantage of them, and provide understanding in time of bereavement. In a diary entry, Quarter indicated his support and sympathy for the nascent organization:

> Whoever looks into his own heart, be he to the manor born or not, if he has ever wandered from the paternal roof and bade farewell to those that were by him cherished, revered and loved, knows something of the pain that such a separation causes; but if he has left the land of his nativity, friends, and home, and seeks to find a new home and new friends in a foreign land, he knows well how much needed is sympathy, encouragement and kindly greeting, to say nothing of assistance. . . . [I]t is hoped that selfishness has not taken fast hold of the hearts of Irishmen, as to cause them to forget, although they may be now affluent, joyous and happy in the circle of their amiable and kindhearted friends, that they were once strangers and that then a mist hung around every object that met their view because their hearts were sad, that then they would recall in their heart of hearts the one that gave them a kindly word because they were strangers.[30]

The same spirit that animated Quarter's solicitude for his fellow countrymen played on him in his relations with the Germans, who made up nearly a third of his flock. One of his first acts was to bring Rev. Gasper Henry Ostlangenburg from Galena to silence German protest over Rev. Francis Fischer's departure for Vincennes.[31] The Germans had to attend special services at the cathedral, as they had no church of their own. In 1845 Bishop Quarter wrote the Leopoldine Society, a German organization that supplied funds and priests for destitute German Catholic emigrants, and requested money for the erection of German churches. He reasoned:

> The faithful of every nationality gather in one and the same church; this condition does not permit special religious instruction for the German children and people in their own language, and consequently no German priest can exercise a direct wholesome influence over them, which would be possible if they had their own church, in which the sermons and instructions could be conducted in the German language.[32]

In expectation of aid and at the strong insistence of Fr. Ostlangenburg, he constructed two simple German churches: St. Peter's, for the community south of the river, and St. Joseph's, for the colony on the North Side.[33]

Bishop Quarter also tried to secure German priests for the Germans who were scattered throughout Illinois. To the archbishop of Vienna, he lamented that two-thirds of the state's Catholics were in serious danger of losing their faith for want of priests, and asked that every effort be made to meet that need.[34] He also directed that German be taught to seminarians "in order that the students on entering the holy priesthood may be able to preach and hear confessions in this language."[35]

In spite of Quarter's concern for the Germans of Illinois, his efforts seem to have been inadequate. Although no records exist to indicate the exact nature of his failure, it is obvious from the correspondence of his fellow bishops that he did not meet the needs of the multilingual diocese. Bishop Mathias Loras of Dubuque had premonitions of trouble when he wrote Bishop Anthony Blanc of New Orleans in July 1844, confiding it was "unfortunate" that Quarter did not know German, as well as French, because three languages were "necessary" in the Midwest.[36]

When Chicago's first bishop died suddenly, in April 1848, the choice of successor fell to the American bishops, who sent recommendations to the Society for the Propagation of the Faith in Rome, which was administratively responsible for the American Church. Bishop Peter Paul Lefevre of Detroit hoped that an appointment would be made "with the least possible delay" as "the diocese was left in a rather critical condition."[37] More specifically, Bishop John Fitzpatrick of Boston believed a "skilled" man was needed to bring peace and harmony to the heterogeneous group of Catholics in Illinois.[38] Bishop Peter Richard Kenrick of St. Louis, who was most familiar with the Chicago diocese, wrote Bishop John Baptist Purcell of Cincinnati and stressed the need for a bishop who could speak English, French, and German—especially the latter, as the southern portion of the state was heavily German. "I believe," he wrote, "that the exclusive promotion of American Irish subjects will not have a favorable influence either on the discipline of the church, or the reputation for impartiality which is so necessary to cause them to have weight, especially with the German population which in the southern part of Illinois constitutes the principal portion of the Catholics."[39]

The bishops' concern to please the Germans was no doubt heightened by a gathering of German Catholics of Illinois that petitioned the American hierarchy for a bishop who could communicate with them. Fifteen days after Quarter's death, a delegated assembly of German Catholics met in Chicago and commissioned a committee of five to petition the American bishops. Because the German Catholic element was large and increasing rapidly, the committee sought special consideration.

> We humbly ask you . . . to propose such Clergymen, to the Holy Father as candidates for our Bishopric as are acquainted with the German Language, knowing, by SAD EXPERIENCE, how difficult it is for a Bishop to govern the Germans, who knows neither their language nor their character. By doing so, Most Reverend and Right Fathers, you will ever oblige the 35,000 German Catholics of the State of Illinois, and confer a favor which will ever be remembered by your humble servants.[40]

Their petition was supported in substance by several American bishops and was favorably received by Propaganda. Earlier, the latter had indicated that episcopal recommendations for vacant sees take the linguistic ability of nominees into account. Aside from Propaganda's desire to prevent the loss of souls, it had probably been influenced by an unofficial request by the minister of Bavaria that dioceses in the United States that had a large number of Germans be provided with bishops capable of understanding that portion of the population.[41] In accord with this Vatican position, James Oliver Van de Velde, S.J., was selected for the Chicago see.

Van de Velde, born and educated in Belgium, received his seminary training at Georgetown University in Washington, D.C. His experience and education combined to make him a remarkable linguist; he spoke English, Flemish, French, and German fluently and was acquainted with Italian and Spanish. However, Van de Velde did not wish to be elevated, since he would have to sever ties with the Jesuit order. Concerned about the immigrants, Propaganda exhorted him to take the Chicago post: "We have a special interest for the Germans who are in great number in that diocese; it is our highest concern that they be nourished by a shepherd who through preaching can communicate with them."[42] Yet this appeal did not appear to influence his decision, and he submitted the question of his moral obligation to obey the pope's letter of appointment to three theologians. "Their decision," he confided to his diary, "was in the affirmative and he submitted to bear the yoke."[43]

The four churches, chapel, and two parochial schools that had been left by Bishop Quarter were inadequate for the needs of the fast-growing Catholic population. By 1851, membership of St. Joseph's German parish had expanded so rapidly that it was inadequate for the Near North colony. A group of its parishioners organized, obtained property, and collected money to erect St. Michael's Church, a mile farther north.[44] In 1853 the German Catholics on the West Side, numbering nearly fifty families, likewise organized and formed a parish, and St. Peter's German Church, built on Washington Street seven years earlier, was relocated farther south.[45] The increase of Irish immigrants necessitated erection of Holy Name Church in 1850, to replace the small chapel attached to the University of St. Mary's of the Lake, and enlargement of St. Patrick's Church in 1853.[46]

Van de Velde also had to attend to the spiritual welfare of an additional group of Catholic immigrants. In the late '40s and early '50s, large numbers of French Canadians settled in Chicago. The bishop assigned a priest to minister to them in 1849 and accorded them special services at St. Mary's Cathedral. The following year, an entry in the bishop's diary indicated his concern for these newcomers: "The sons and daughters of La Belle France are rapidly increasing in this city — so rapidly, indeed, that their number now warrant and demand a church of their own, where the services may be performed in their own language." A year later, St. Louis parish was established for the French.[47]

Despite Van de Velde's desire to satisfy all immigrant groups, he did not succeed. His most serious failure was with the Irish. Unwisely, tactlessly, he gave a St. Patrick's Day sermon which implied that his Irish listeners, because of their "sinful excesses" with drink, did not truly reverence the Apostle of Ireland.[48] Nor did he get along with the Irish clergy, particularly those who conducted the diocesan seminary.[49] They had had their own way under Bishop Quarter, and found Van de Velde less pliable. The former Jesuit, whose training had taught absolute obedience to authority, would not allow the faculty to do as they pleased. Confronted with the bishop's inflexibility, the priests tried to break him by circulating "false reports" and "engaging in insidious maneuvres [which] incited much groundless prejudice among the people against him."[50] "As soon as communication was reestablished with Rome after the Revolution of 1848, Van de Velde asked to be relieved of his office for reasons of health and his desire to rejoin the Society of Jesus. In response, he was told to bear his charge with patience. When conflicts with the priests worsened, he again sought relief and tendered his resignation. Propaganda referred the matter to the American bishops when they convened the First Plenary Council of Baltimore in 1852, who also refused his resignation, because they feared to encourage dissident clergy. However, they offered to split the diocese in order to relieve Van de Velde of the burden of visiting all Illinois churches. Unsatisfied, Van de Velde went to Rome to persuade the pope personally. Again, his resignation was refused, but the pope offered to work for his readmission to the Jesuits and to transfer him to another diocese. On November 4, 1853, he left Chicago for the Diocese of Natchez, Mississippi. (Ironically, his desire for a congenial climate proved fatal: he died of yellow fever two years later.)[51]

The multilingual prelate's departure again raised problems for the American bishops, who had to suggest candidates to Propaganda. Peter Kenrick, who headed the recently established Archdiocese of St. Louis, which included the Diocese of Chicago, immediately prepared a list of candidates for the post when Van de Velde's transfer was announced. However, not content with his choices, he confided to the archbishop of Cincinnati that none of the candidates was the one "required by the circumstances of time, place and people—the nations are more mixed in Illinois than perhaps any State in the Union."[52] The archbishop of Baltimore, Francis Patrick Kenrick, proposed Anthony O'Regan, but feared that Rome was not inclined to appoint an Irishman to Chicago because of Van de Velde's complaint of "Irish insubordination."[53] Van de Velde, however, encouraged the O'Regan candidacy because he believed that only an Irishman or an American could bring harmony to Chicago.[54]

In 1854 the pope appointed Anthony O'Regan bishop of Chicago and administrator of Quincy,[55] but the Irishman declined, alleging he was unfit for the position. However, when commanded to assume the office, he, like his predecessor, accepted the burden.

Chicago's third bishop was born in Lavalloc, County Mayo, in 1809 and attended Maynooth College. Upon graduation, he had been appointed to the theology staff of St. Jarlath Seminary, Tuam, County Galway, where he taught for ten years and subsequently became its president. In 1849, at Archbishop Peter Kenrick's request, he had come to St. Louis to assume the presidency of Carondolet Seminary, where he won respect for his scholarship, piety, and ability to train seminarians. Neither in Ireland nor America had he had any pastoral experience; his background with theology students ill prepared him to manage the troubled Chicago diocese. O'Regan's anxiety over the responsibilities that awaited him in Chicago caused a "nervous disability" and delayed his installation by more than two months.[56]

On September 3, Bishop O'Regan began a tenure that would be tempestuous. While he seemed to win the favor of the Irish by building three additional parishes for victims of the famine,[57] he was severely criticized by others. Most critical were French-speaking Catholics, who were victims of his insensitivity. Their church, erected on leased land, had become an expensive liability. To remedy the difficulty, the bishop ordered the structure's relocation to another site, unfavorable to the French but favorable to Irish realtors who were his friends. The French were angered by the decision and sought to change O'Regan's mind, only to be rebuked by him. The French pastor left Chicago in anger, and to restore harmony and order O'Regan appointed Fr. John Waldron pastor of St. Louis Church. This appointment only aggravated the French—Waldron's first sermon was preached to them in Gaelic![58]

In St. Anne, a small French village south of the city, O'Regan encountered further difficulties. Fr. Charles Chiniquy, pastor of St. Anne's Church, came into conflict with O'Regan, refused to submit to suspension, and eventually led most of the village's Catholics into schism. Although much of the fault lay with the headstrong pastor, O'Regan's righteousness exacerbated the problem and precluded compromise.[59] O'Regan's correspondence indicates that he was baffled by the French; also, he was fearful of them. His life had been threatened "more than once," he wrote, "and they [French dissidents] are wicked enough to do it."[60]

An equally grave challenge came from some of his Irish clergy. The seminary faculty that had grieved Van de Velde tried to continue its independent course, but was dismissed.[61] When Martin Spalding, bishop of Louisville, gave a retreat for the priests of the Chicago diocese, he had observed their poor quality and advised O'Regan to "get rid of the worst."[62] The Chicago bishop had the same idea, for he had already written to the Society of the Propagation of the Faith in Lyons, asking for priests, as he intended to replace "almost every priest."[63]

Severe financial problems, created by disobedient and irresponsible priests under Van de Velde, were inherited by O'Regan and exacerbated by his inexperience. The banished seminary faculty left him with a $45,000 debt on unauthorized construction projects, as well as the embarrassment of a $30,000 embezzlement.[64] Also, numerous priests solicited money and kept it for their own purposes. So abused was the confidence of the immigrants that they insulted O'Regan's fund raisers. In desperation, he wrote to the Propagation of the Faith, begging for aid to stave off his creditors: "I am every day dragged into the courts of law and in danger of utter ruin." He explained that 40,000 Catholics had but six churches, accommodating a total of 2,000 persons, and lamented: "It is painful to see the poor people kneel outside in the wet and cold around the church. . . . Priests say two masses each but that does little for such a crowd."[65] The only way to preserve the people's faith, he proposed, was to construct ten additional parishes immediately. He admitted, however, that his financial situation left him helpless.[66]

After only one year in Chicago, the "over sensitive" and "easily disheartened" former professor was overwhelmed by the diocese's chaotic state and made painfully aware of his administrative shortcomings. He told Spalding of his intention to resign, but the Louisville bishop dissuaded him temporarily.[67] Two years later he again considered resignation. Writing to the Propagation of the Faith in April 1857, he suggested uncertainty about his future: "For the last nine years this diocese has been grievously afflicted by bad priests, Irish, French, and German. My predecessor was frustrated and tried to resign, he could not live here. I am suffering far, far more and know not what I shall do."[68] Shortly after he wrote this letter, he went to Rome to plead for his resignation. The despondent bishop was relieved of his charge and retired to London, where he spent the remainder of his days in quiet retreat.[69]

Between 1833 and 1857 the Catholic Church in Chicago grew rapidly in membership as a result of Irish, German, and Canadian immigration. This growth, however, was not matched by institutional development. The Church's poverty and inept leaders threatened its mission to preserve the faith. Quarter had the requisite skills to establish the Church on a firm foundation but lacked the opportunity. His successors were well-intentioned but incompetent men who should have been permitted to remain in their bookish worlds. They were, as Bishop Spalding said of O'Regan, "more to be pitied than blamed."[70] To bring order out of chaos, the Church—like the city's governmental and commercial institutions—needed capable, forceful, and diplomatic men. Such a man was James Duggan, the fourth bishop of Chicago.

When Bishop O'Regan left Chicago, with the intention of resigning, Bishop James Duggan, coadjutor of St. Louis, was sent to administer the diocese. Duggan was born in 1825 in Maynooth, County Kildare, and received his early training at the Seminary of Ballaghdareen. In 1842 he responded to Bishop Peter Kenrick's call for recruits and went to Missouri, where he finished his studies at St. Vincent Seminary, Cape Girardeau. After ordination in 1847, he was assigned to the Cathedral of St. Louis. Because of his ability, Kenrick had sent the 28-year-old priest to Chicago in 1853 to administer the diocese until Rome appointed Van de Velde's successor. Although he showed promise as an executive, his age precluded his appointment, but when he returned to Chicago in 1857 he remained, and was officially installed as bishop on January 2, 1859.[71]

Bishop Duggan's chief task was to restore peace and order among the clergy and the confidence of the laity. He institutionalized and delegated his authority instead of personalizing it (as his predecessors had done). In 1859 he established a chancery office to facilitate administration. Equally important, he called a synod of priests to make statutes for the Diocese of Chicago and created a council of consultors to assist with formulation of policy and diocesan development. Further, he soon appointed a vicar general, an assistant who helps administer a diocese by exercising power in the bishop's name, and in 1867 he appointed another, specifically to look after German interests. Through these expressions of trust in the clergy, he brought harmony to the diocese and ordered its administration.

The confidence of the laity was restored. Although Duggan continued to receive aid from the Society for the Propagation of the Faith, he won the necessary trust to build the diocese with indigenous support. Between 1859 and 1869 fourteen additional parishes were established: ten English-speaking parishes and one national parish each for the German, French, Bohemian, and Polish groups. Though only one German parish was commissioned, three of the original parishes built new and enlarged churches.[72]

One of Duggan's major problems was to obtain priests to care for his varied and rapidly growing flock. As a partial solution, he turned to religious orders to staff diocesan parishes; the religious orders could draw upon their Old World and American resources and thus provide not only a certain supply of priests but personnel suited to minister to specific nationalities. During his tenure, Duggan secured Redemptorists and Benedictines to staff German parishes.[73] By sharing his authority with the superiors of these orders—the superiors chose the staff and had direct control over the priests—Duggan brought harmony to troubled parishes. For example, St. Michael's parish had had six pastors within eight years; its parishioners were from numerous German principalities and states and did not share a common German identity. Thus their provincialism had caused serious difficulties for the pastors, each of whom had been identifiable with a specific state or region. When the Redemptorists took charge in 1860, they were recognized and respected by all Germans, whatever their origins, because of the order's prestige throughout the Germanies.[74]

Duggan was also mindful of the new immigrants from Bohemia

and Poland, and he helped them establish their own churches. The first Slavic Catholics generally attended German rather than Irish parishes; the solemn German celebration of the liturgy, as opposed to austere Irish practices, probably made them feel more comfortable. Additionally, many Poles and Bohemians had some familiarity with German-speaking people and their language before they emigrated, and in America they shared the bond of being non-English speaking.[75]

Duggan, however, realized that the Slavic people needed special care. In 1863 he told the bishop of Detroit that there were "many Bohemian families in the city and hardly any of them have made their confessions for years."[76] He asked if Lefevre had a Bohemian priest he might spare for a few days. That same year, the Bohemian Catholics, eager for a church of their own, organized, collected money, and purchased property, and two years later began construction of St. Wenceslaus Church. The foundation of this parish resulted from the initiative and planning of the Bohemian community and the full support of Bishop Duggan. A similar pattern was followed by the Polish colony in the formation of St. Stanislaus Kostka parish in 1867.[77]

Unfortunately, the peace and harmony achieved by Duggan was not to last. In 1866 he began to act arbitrarily, and alienated the most capable of his clergy. It soon became apparent to those closest to him that the bishop's mind was going, but all efforts to persuade him to retire were unavailing. He continued on his irrational course, causing great scandal among the laity and serious factionalism among the clergy. Although the clergy, led by the highly respected Dr. John McMullen (later bishop of Davenport), informed Propaganda of the difficulties, and were supported by the archbishops of Baltimore and St. Louis, the situation worsened before they succeeded in having Duggan removed. Finally, in 1869, he was confined to a sanitarium in St. Louis, where he remained until his death in 1899.[78]

On March 10, 1870, Bishop Thomas Foley succeeded Duggan as coadjutor-bishop and administrator of Chicago. Foley, born in Baltimore of Irish parents, was educated at St. Mary's College, Emmitsburg, and served in the Baltimore diocese. For twenty years he had been pastor of the cathedral and successively held the key posts of chancellor, vicar general, and administrator of the diocese. In these offices he demonstrated sound judgment and gained the experience that his new appointment demanded.[79] He was cognizant of the tension and anxiety that remained after Duggan's removal and attempted to heal the wounds. "Peace be to you," the text of his installation sermon, would be the theme of his administration. "I come here," he told his first Chicago audience, "to teach you that our whole religion consists in this, that we keep peace with God, peace with our neighbors and peace in our own hearts."[80] His gentlemanly manner, tact, good mind, and acute business sense produced confidence and unity among clergy and laity.

The Chicago Fire of 1871 tested Foley's ability. Caught in the fire's path were five of the oldest and principal churches, numerous schools, and various benevolent institutions, representing years of self-sacrificing generosity and deep religious faith.[81] Writing to a fellow bishop, Foley noted, "Our losses are enormous—fifteen hundred thousand dollars," and concluded: "Pray for me."[82] Saddened but undaunted, the bishop directed a reconstruction program and founded thirteen additional parishes.[83] He left the building to the pastors but brought their financial matters under his immediate supervision. Foley, who insisted that all financial obligations be met promptly, made sure that parish debts never increased beyond the means of the parishioners.[84]

The founding of new parishes reflected the increased population of each immigrant group. For the first time in twenty years, construction of churches for the English-speaking fell behind that for the non-English-speaking. Six Irish churches were offset by erection of four German, two Polish, and two Bohemian churches. As under previous administrations, these parishes usually resulted from the efforts of a group of Catholics who desired a parish of their own. St. Adalbert's, established in 1873 to care for Polish Catholics on the southwest side of the city, is an example.

Although the area around Seventeenth and Paulina streets had several Catholic churches, the Poles wanted their own church, with their own priest celebrating the liturgy in their own language. A committee investigated the feasibility of supporting a parish and secured the bishop's permission to organize one. As soon as approbation was granted, money was collected and construction began. Because the newcomers' means were limited, they constructed only the basement, which served as their church until the remainder of the edifice was completed ten years later.[85] Other churches, like St. Procopius (Bohemian), were built because of the overcrowding of an existent parish or, like St. Agnes Virgin and Martyr, because it was a hardship to travel several miles to the nearest English-speaking church.[86]

The desire for parish churches among Chicago Catholics was remarkable, and their poverty did not deter them in realization of their wish. Stables served as churches and boards laid across nail kegs served as pews. One congregation was so anxious to make use of its church that it celebrated Mass in an unfinished structure, and an altar boy's chief duty was to sweep snow from the altar during the liturgy.[87] The first parochial foundations manifested each immigrant group's intense faith, keen desire for community, and willingness to sacrifice.

Chicago's first American-born bishop managed to keep peace with all the immigrant groups except the Bohemians. A conflict erupted between Bishop Folwy and the St. Wenceslaus Society, which held the deed to the Bohemian parish of the same name. After the Great Fire, many of the society's members left the parish because of the destruction and the ingress of new business in the area of their first settlement. They moved to Pilsen, the new Bohemian community on Chicago's West Side, but maintained a strong voice in the running of the St. Wenceslaus Society. When the bishop requested the deed, they refused to give it up, and underscored their claim by seizing the school. The parish, under Fr. Joseph Moliter's leadership, initiated a recovery suit that dragged on for four bitter years. According to one historian, realization that the bishop, not individual parishioners, owned the church led some partisans to abandon the faith. Although the bishop won the lawsuit, the Bohemian community's ties with the Church were seriously damaged. The incident strengthened the already powerful Free Thought and anti-Catholic nationalist element by demonstrating the authoritarian nature of Catholic government.[88]

Division within the Polish community also threatened the Chicago Church, but Foley secured a religious congregation to staff Polish churches and maintain order. In 1871 the bishop conferred with the superior-general of the Congregation of the Resurrection and agreed to give that order the right to conduct all Polish parishes in the city for the next ninety-nine years. Accordingly, Polish parishes would be supervised by the ranking Resurrectionist in Chicago. Because the Resurrectionists closely identified with the peasants, they established organizations that bound the Poles to the Church.

Nonetheless, conflicts arose when strongly nationalistic immigrants of aristocratic origins tried to take control of the Church in Polonia. Frustrated at St. Stanislaus Kostka, they set up their own church, Holy Trinity, but Foley refused both to consecrate the church and assign a pastor, because the people would not turn over the deed to the property. Of primary importance, however, the bishop established a lifeline with the Polish community through a religious order that promised to respect his authority in exchange for the direction of Chicago's Poles.[89]

When Bishop Foley died in February 1879, he bequeathed to his successor thirty-eight churches and numerous parish schools, academies, and benevolent institutions. Also, he had increased the number of clergy by encouraging six additional religious orders to come to Chicago. In 1870 Chicago had 39 diocesan and 11 religious order priests; ten years later it had 38 diocesan and 47 religious order priests (see tables 11 and 12). But most important, he gave his successor a relatively peaceful, well-ordered diocese that boded well for the future. The unsettling problems caused by dissident priests, financial mismanagement, and immigrant rivalry had lessened under his guiding hand. While Foley relied upon the talented Irish for the key administrative positions of chancellor and vicar general, he included Germans in his advisory council and respected and supported the goals of his Continental brethren. His eulogizer, Bishop Patrick J. Ryan, noted that Foley's first Chicago phrase, "Peace be to you," delivered nine years earlier, "was a benediction then—it has proved a prophecy."[90]

While the Chicago Catholic Church struggled to bring order and harmony to its ministry to its rapidly growing, heterogeneous flock, it had to contend with external forces, such as anti-Catholicism and anti-foreignism. Anti-Catholicism was a consistent and important element of the Catholic experience in America. Throughout the Colonial period, British subjects who came to America manifested their no-popery traditions by enacting discriminatory laws, designed to make sure Catholicism would not take root. In the early years of the Republic, a wave of toleration swept the nation, but anti-Romanism was not washed away. Although the inherited antipathies were not always obvious, they were nonetheless constant, according to time and place. This prejudicial spirit occasionally combined with social and economic frustrations to produce violent outbursts, such as the Charleston convent fire of 1834 and the Philadelphia riots ten years later.[91]

Allied to anti-Catholicism was anti-foreignism. Many Americans viewed immigrants as a serious threat to the nation because newcomers accepted lower wages than natives and because the financial drain of supporting alien paupers was said to portend economic crisis. Further, their foreign traditions, "intemperance," and seeming propensity for criminal behavior menaced societal institutions that provided stability, order, and tranquility. Many immigrants, especially the Irish, who were unfamiliar with America's political system, fell prey to political bosses and appeared to jeopardize the continuance of free and democratic government and legislation for reform.

In periods of crisis, prejudicial and ethnocentric sentiments became the basis of organized campaigns. When shaken by a loss of confidence, the natives espoused a negative nationalism, directing their hostility toward Catholics and immigrants. Rather than consider "Romanists" and foreigners as minority irritants, the natives regarded them as enemies of the American way of life. The first of several nativist outbursts that were to affect the Catholics of Chicago occurred in the 1850s, when sectional tensions threatened to sunder the Union. Native Americans, anxious about the nation's welfare, organized the Know Nothing party to safeguard the country against the perceived undemocratic practices and foreign allegiances of the Catholic Church and the unassimilability of the immigrants.

Although many Chicagoans participated in the nativist cause, the city's campaign marched to its own drummer. Chicago, which was settled by industrious Yankees, appears to have been too busy to involve itself seriously with early no-popery movements. Many Chicago Protestants even attended Catholic services until they could build their own churches, and sent their children to Catholic academies.[92] Thus in 1844, the year that anti-Catholicism sparked riots in Philadelphia, Bishop Quarter expressed amazement at the cordial treatment afforded his charges. He wrote to the bishop of New Orleans:

> I am happy to inform you that a spirit of great liberality exists towards Catholics in all parts of the State and in the city a word exasperating or painful to the feelings of Catholics I have never heard uttered. Indeed, the citizens appear *all* like the members of one united and well organized family where each one consults for the benefit and advantage of the whole.[93]

The cooperation and tolerance testified to by Quarter seem to have disappeared as the number of immigrants increased and these newcomers began to exercise influence in the city's politics. Bishop Van de Velde's first pastoral letter, written in 1849, urged that Catholics be united among themselves and merciful and charitable to their persecutors.[94] In the first two years of the succeeding decade, hundreds of Irish, German, and French-Canadian Catholics arrived in Chicago and caused greater concern for the nativistically inclined. Churches, a seminary and university, academies, parochial schools, orphan asylums, and a hospital were tangible witness to the growth of the "alien Church." In addition to brick and mortar manifestation of Catholic prosperity, the *Western Tablet,* a weekly Catholic newspaper (which went to press in January 1852) generated anxiety. "Under the direct sanction and approval" of Van de Velde, it was devoted to the interests of the Catholic Church.[95]

The *Western Tablet* prospectus stated its intention to "represent and defend, in a consistent and dignified manner, the proceedings of our Catholic brethren." Editorially, the paper promised to enlighten Catholics in their faith, defend that faith should it come under attack, and preserve among its readers "respect and veneration" for the laws and Constitution of America. In the very first issue, the editor criticized Protestant journals that attempted to excite the public on grounds that the Catholic Church was hostile to civil and religious liberty.[96]

The conflict between the Catholic Church and nativists rested upon the issues of public schools and the alleged threat to American social and political institutions resulting from the allegiance of Catholic immigrants to a foreign authority. Most of the nativist sentiment was expressed in the press and from the pulpit and platform, but the principals in the battle of words were the *Western Tablet* and the *Chicago Tribune.* Prior to its purchase by J. C. K. Forrest and Henry Fowler in 1852, the *Tribune* had shown little intolerance, but the prejudices and political affiliation of the new owners transformed it into a nativist organ. Similarly, the *Literary Budget,* a monthly edited by William Weaver Danenhowes, consistently and forcefully attacked Roman Catholicism. Chicago's other newspapers tried to maintain neutrality for reasons of political expediency.[97]

The first conflict involved the "common" schools and the funding of Catholic education. Development of a state system of education in Illinois was largely the work of New Englanders who saw religion and education as common partners. The Calvinistic belief that education is the handmaiden of religion prompted transplanted Yankee preachers to lead a campaign to secure an education for every child. Their interest in education, though due in large measure to religious conviction, was accelerated by nativist feelings toward the Catholic Church and its "design" to conquer the West. Through their work, the theories of nonsectarian religious training in the common-school movement and the state's right to educate were developed.[98] As the common-school movement reached its peak in the '50s, the Catholic Church sensed danger, and reacted.

The American Catholic bishops, meeting in successive councils, endorsed and supported religious education and informed parents of their moral responsibility for the religious education of their children.[99] "It must be your care," the bishops wrote in 1843, ". . . to let the precious inheritance descend without diminution. You must, therefore, use all diligence that your child be instructed at an early age in the saving truths of religion, and be preserved from the contagion of error."[100] Because the nonsectarian religious training proposed by the common-school advocates failed to meet the bishops' criteria, Catholics built their own schools.

By 1852, Chicago Catholics had seven schools and academies that provided religious education for 900 students; however, because most Catholics were oppressed by poverty, the figures left much to be desired. Many parents, through indifference or neglect, failed to send their children to school. The *Western Tablet* took these parents to task for causing their children to "grow up in ignorance, — to run about the streets, and contract low and vicious habits, which must finally render them a nuisance to society, a disgrace to their religion, and a curse to their own careless and guilty parents."[101] Worse yet, some parents sent their offspring to the public schools, where anti-Catholic teachers taught them to feel ashamed of their faith.[102]

The Catholic experience with public schools, where no religion was taught or their religion was reviled, prompted a lengthy letter by "Philaleteas" (probably a pseudonym of Bishop Van de Velde), [103] who said that religion is an *"essential"* branch of education, without which there can be "no *real education.*"

> The system of public schools supported by taxation as established in many states of the Union, and chiefly in this city, is entirely at variance with the notions which the members of the Catholic Church entertain of a *good education,* and no Catholic who has regard for the principles of his religion or the dictates of his conscience, can, without a formal violation of his duty as a Christian parent, permit his children to attend the schools that are established on this system. . . . We Catholics look upon the system now pursued in our public schools not only as unfit for the education of our children, but we regard it as unjust and unconstitutional, and as either godless or sectarian, as unjust, because we are forcibly taxed to support schools to which we cannot send our children, without action against our religious convictions, — as unconstitutional, because it infringes the sacred rights of our consciences, and thus deprives us of that religious liberty which is guaranteed to us by the federal Constitution, and either as godless or sectarian, because it excludes all religious principles, thus leading to indifferentism or practical infidelity, or what is more common, because it generates and fosters a spirit of pros- elytism almost exclusively directed against the principles of Catholics, tending to misrepresent the dogmas of faith, and to revile their religious practices.[104]

Having explained why public schools were unsuitable for Catholics, the writer boldly turned to the touchy question of tax support, a subject that had inflamed passions in New York a decade earlier. Van de Velde resented the fact that the Catholic minority, subjugated to the Protestant majority, did not receive the equivalent of the taxes the former paid. To his mind, Catholics were coerced by the controlling majority, who exercised a pretended or assumed right over their consciences and purses which was repugnant to the spirit and letter of the Constitution. The bishop explained:

> We are forced by compulsory taxation to pay for the schooling of the children of others, and have to impose a voluntary tax on ourselves to educate our own. The civil or municipal authorities have no right to claim the child from its parents, for the purpose of training it in a manner which the parent disapproves and condemns; for we honestly and conscientiously hold and maintain that parents have an inherent right to educate their own offspring . . . that they hold this right from nature and nature's God, and that this right is secured to them by the fundamental laws of the country; and that, therefore, as far as we are concerned, it is the right and duty of Catholic parents to choose the teachers that will faithfully execute their wishes with regard to this to them most important object. Hence, we further maintain that such teachers should receive from the general and special fund a pro rata salary or compensation in proportion to the number of children that attend their respective schools. . . . We do not wish to interfere with, nor define the rights of the other denominations; but we consider ourselves bound to define, to maintain, and to defend our own.[105]

Following the lead of its protector, the *Western Tablet* constantly reminded parents of their duty to protect their child from the "spiritual murder" that lurked in the "nurseries of heathenism, vice and crime."[106] The danger of the common school resulted from its permissive milieu, where no check was placed on the conduct and language of boys and girls. "A moral malaria," the editor cried, "freighted at every respiration with contamination of the character and death of the soul," was bred in the public schools because they took no cognizance of man's fallen nature, nor did they, like the Catholic Church, have the mission, jurisdiction, and power to repress and prevent evil.[107]

In response to the *Tablet*'s broadside, the *Chicago Tribune* editorialized that no person, whatever his faith, if "honest and enlightened," could be opposed to popular education and intelligence, unless he feared his faith were in error. The schools were to provide general education, and the home and the pulpit were the proper instruments for religious instruction. The *Tribune* editor warned Catholics that they were courting disaster:

> Hostility to public education wherever it exists is a war upon the liberties and rights of the masses. Our public school system may require slight amendments, but it has been too long and fully tried to be now condemned. It is entrenched in the affection of the people. It is one of the pillars of their freedom. Opposition to it is vain, and will recoil on its authors.[108]

The *Tribune* also scoffed at the Catholic proposal to share the tax dollar with all denominations that desired their own schools. It said that money distributed in proportion to the taxes paid by each group would result in serious inequities that would penalize the poorest children, and contended that schools placed in sectarian hands would produce narrow-minded, bigoted citizens.[109]

After several weeks of heated argumentation, the *Western Tablet* despaired of the *Tribune*'s desire to know the truth.

> We begin to suspect that the *Tribune* has been so thoroughly inoculated with the Anti-Popery virus that it is utterly deaf to reason, blind to glaring fact, and insensible to the plainest claims of candor, honesty, and fair-dealing in all matters pertaining to the Catholic Church.[110]

Even though the *Tablet* ceased discussion of the school question, Catholic dissatisfaction with the common-school ideal did not change. In 1855 the common-school advocates obtained passage of a law forcing denominational and private schools to submit to direct state supervision or forfeit public funds. By 1857, two-thirds of the private and church schools either ceased to exist or became public schools under the law.[111] Catholics had lost their first battle on the question, but again, their dissatisfaction with the common-school ideal was unchanged.

While some Chicago Catholics and the unofficial weekly paper, the *Western Catholic*, protested the discrimination inherent in the public school system,[112] Van de Velde's successors did not speak publicly on the matter lest they inflame quieted passions. In 1875, Bishop Foley confidentially expressed his views to his Cincinnati colleague:

> With regard to the school question. My own opinion is that it is too much to fight the opposition at the polls. It will take a long time to lead the American voters to a fair consideration of our claims on the school fund. We will get it eventually, but later than the present generation. Some friends of the Catholic side are bad and

indiscreet, and apt to put their foot in their mouths every time they say a word on the Catholic school question. We Catholics are agreed on what is right, necessary, and desirable for the education of our children. But we can not always get that which is just right off. We have to talk, pray, agitate and fight a little, and when God is pleased, he grants us what is good for us, but in His own time and way. So many of our Catholic papers say things about the public schools, which were better unsaid. Let us leave the public state schools, to those who choose to use them, and let us build and form our own schools for ourselves. We have to pay for both it is true, but nothing good is cheap. We have many advantages under our government which are not enjoyed elsewhere and we can afford to suffer something.[113]

His position carried the day, till the Catholic school system was threatened by state control.

The editorial war over the common school abated in 1853, but a related polemic continued to rage: Could Catholics be true Americans? Having given up hope of converting Catholic immigrants to the Whig party, the *Chicago Tribune* began to bait Catholics and "foreigners." In September of that year the *Tribune* noted that the pope had placed the United States under the protection of the Virgin Mary, and warned its readers of the growth of the Catholic Church and the dangers of "encroachment." The paper portrayed the Catholic Church as the "unrelenting enemy of the gospel and the best interests of man" and stated that Catholic doctrines were "inimicable to our Republic and cannot exist in harmony with them; . . . they are like oil and water, they cannot amalgamate, and one must obtain the ascendancy over the other."[114] It also played on the theme of priestly interference in democratic governments and said that foreign voters were led like sheep. Episcopal and papal intervention in the constitutional governments of South America showed what was in store for North America if great caution were not exercised. The pledge of loyalty and obedience to the pope, taken by all bishops, indicated that Catholics, since they owed allegiance to a foreign authority, were not free to be true Americans.[115]

A riot involving Irish laborers, working on the Illinois Central Railroad tracks at LaSalle, Illinois, provided the *Tribune* an opportunity to enlarge upon the alien, Catholic "threat." When a contractor decided to lower wages from $1.25 to $1 a day, he enraged the workers,[116] and many quit; but when they went to collect their pay, the contractor, claiming a bookkeeping error, told them they would have to wait. The angry men would not, and in the ensuing violence a laborer and the contractor were killed. Thus it was obvious to all, the paper editorialized, that the Irish were "imbued with a fondness and passion for riots and rows" and, as a group, were listed in police records for criminal action twice as often as any other nationality group. This alleged Irish disrespect for the law was not a racial trait, however, but a consequence of their Catholicity.

The *Tribune* explained that their riotous behavior could be traced "with certainty" to the influence the Catholic priesthood exercised over the Irish in the United States. In Ireland the law was the enemy of the people, and priests, who were their friends, stressed allegiance to Church codes at the expense of civil law, whereas in America the law was the friend of the people. Nonetheless, Old World notions prevailed because priests continued to treat obedience to civil codes in a "trifling manner." Native Americans' expressions of antipathy were justified because the priests continued to tell the Irish that their allegiance and obedience were due not to the statutes and institutions of their adopted land but to the mandates and instructions of their clerical superiors.

> They have taught them, in very truth, that instead of being Americans and freemen of the nineteenth century, they are serfs of the Church and liege men of the Pope. To them the civil law is synonymous with tyranny, and freedom from restraint is the only liberty they can comprehend, whilst the only duty they faithfully and implicitly discharge, is implicit and slavish obedience to the Church.[117]

In conclusion, the editor said the paper was not antipathetic to all Irish people, for Irish Protestants were an "intelligent, . . . noble, law abiding, and virtuous people, . . . the very last to join any riotous demonstrations." If the Catholic Irish hoped to be happy, virtuous, and respected, like the Protestant Irish, they had but to throw off the influence of their priestly directors, the cause of their disgrace.[118] Although the *Tribune*'s logic was dubious, its attitude toward Catholicism was clear.

The nativist daily also attacked the Catholic position that the pope is simply the spiritual head of Catholic Americans. Granting the pope is a bishop, not a temporal ruler, the *Tribune* argued that his authority over his subjects could turn them against free schools and free thought and thus destroy the basis of democracy and independence. The paper's readers were told: *"No free government can exist where the dominion of the Bishop of Rome over the minds and consciences of men remains unbroken."*[119]

Incensed, the *Tablet* denied the *Tribune*'s charges and stated that Catholics had a rightful home in America. The editor appealed to history, pointing to America's discovery by a Catholic and the patriotic deeds of Catholics in the War for Independence. Constitutionally, Catholics possessed the same rights and privileges that other Americans enjoyed, and he promised: "We [the *Western Tablet*] shall endeavor to assert, maintain and defend those rights." He hoped that this course would not give offense to anyone—but come what may, he would stand by his pledge.[120] Only a few issues of the paper (after this assurance was made) are extant but it seems that the *Tablet* remained true to its word.

The *Chicago Tribune* continued to bait Catholics and to publish nativist propaganda. Ribald tales of the confessional and convent provided interesting reading and further ingrained and fortified prejudices. The Know Nothing forecast, that the anticlerical uprisings in Europe would cause the pope to flee to America and undertake to establish a new Holy See in the Mississippi Valley, was repeated by the editor, who called on all Protestant Americans "to prepare for this struggle which sooner or later must be fought between Popery and Liberty, between light and darkness, between the spirit of evil and the genius of good."[121]

Although the advertised struggle between popery and liberty never reached the Mississippi Valley, conflicts between proponents and opponents of slavery and abolition, popular sovereignty and free soil, and open saloons and temperance did, and to garner strength for their cause, advocates of abolition, free soil, and temperance often catered to nativist sentiments. This political turmoil, which consumed Chicago in the 1850s, reflected the political pattern throughout the country.

In the gubernatorial and presidential campaigns of 1852, the Whigs and the Democrats played for the votes of the newly arrived by stressing the anti-Catholic and anti-immigrant bias of their opponents.[122] In succeeding years, nativist sentiment was organized and assumed a greater role in Chicago politics. The Know Nothings organized a lodge in 1854 and worked to restrict Catholic and "alien" influence.[123] They were supported by the *Tribune*'s policy of misrepresenting Catholic doctrines and institutions and pointing out the failures of immigrants. During the senatorial campaign of 1855, the paper opposed the Irish-born Democratic candidate and praised the Republican candidate's opposition to "foreign rule and Jesuitical priestcraft" and commitment to the doctrine that "Americans should and must rule America."[124] Its editorials claimed that foreign-born convicts, "with scarcely an exception," were Catholics and that the "Filthy Beggers" who swarmed in the streets were "all-ALL-ALL CATHOLICS!"[125]

The mayoral campaign of 1855 was the climax of the nativist struggle for power. Prior to that year, the city's mayoral contests had been nonpartisan affairs. However, the defeat of a temperance candidate in the 1854 election, by immigrants who held radically different views on drinking, led to a fusion of antisaloon and nativist interests. The Maine Law Alliance, a temperance group that wanted a statute similar to one in effect in Maine, which forbade the sale of liquor except for medicinal purposes, and the Know Nothing element, which tended to agree with the temperance advocates, joined hands. Clearly, there was cause for union: Chicago had 675 liquor establishments, and of this number the Irish and Germans owned 625![126]

When the *Western Tablet* opposed the Maine Law Alliance, stating that true temperance could not be brought about by law but must be voluntary, "springing from and fortified by religion to which the grace of God is attached, from which comes humility and the thorough reformation of the heart,"[127] the *Tribune* scoffed. To wed the Know Nothings more closely to the temperance crusaders, it asked:

> Who does not know that the most depraved, debased, worthless and irredeemable drunkards and sots which curse the community are Irish Catholics? . . . Who does not know that the influence of the Church of Rome is always directed in favor of drunkenness? Look at her allowed and countenanced funeral wakes, her bacchanalian festivals, her drunken and besotted Priesthood! . . . Let us hear no more of "the Temperance of the Catholic Church." As well might we speak of the piety of the Devil and the moral regeneration of Lucifer.[128]

The *Tribune* backed Levi D. Boone, a leading physician and alderman, and the rest of the temperance ticket. Even if this was a Know Nothing ticket, the paper argued, it should be elected because it was the best ticket in many years. The nominally Democratic ticket, headed by Isaac L. Milliken, was condemned because it was backed by the "Irish, Jesuitical, Foreign Domination and American Proscription Party," led by Bishop O'Regan. O'Regan's goal, the *Tribune* contended, was to establish a city government which would "give American citizens the same privileges which Jews enjoy under the reign of the Sultan of Turkey."[129]

Boone and six of the nine temperance aldermen won and gave the Know Nothings cause to celebrate. Their victory was remarkable in that there were fewer native Americans than immigrants in Chicago. Three factors seem to have given Boone his 345 plurality in the 6,027 votes cast. (1) Many Germans stayed home, to avoid voting for Milliken, who was friendly to the immigrants but "pro-Nebraska," while Boone, a staunch "anti-Nebraskan," was anti-immigrant and pro-temperance. (2) Native laborers, who competed with the Irish for jobs, saw the election as an opportunity to register their anti-immigrant sentiments. (3) Scandinavians and Jews supported the temperance ticket.[130]

The hostile nature of the campaign disturbed Catholics and gave them cause for concern. The *Western Tablet* lamented the racial and religious nature of the campaign and predicted civil strife if such venomous politicking continued[131], but its fears never materialized for the Know Nothings soon split over slavery and faded rapidly as a political force.[132] As nativist power receded, the *Western Tablet* discontinued publication. The departure of Van de Velde, who staunchly supported Chicago Catholic journalism, also led to the paper's termination.

Catholic reaction to nativist assaults is puzzling and leaves much room for speculation. Of the available episcopal correspondence relative to the Chicago diocese, not one letter mentions the city's no-popery campaign. Correspondence for the years 1850 through 1855 dealt with the internal problems encountered as a result of refractory priests and the poverty of the laity. It would appear that the bishops and clergy were too disorganized and preoccupied with their own problems to busy themselves with the taunts of the nativists. Possibly the Irish, who dominated the Chicago Church, were not greatly alarmed, because of their unfamiliarity with the American ideal of freedom of religion and their previous experience of a much harsher brand of anti-Catholicism. Although legally American citizens, they and their German coreligionists were basically foreigners, trying to establish a "foreign" Church in their adopted land. It is revealing that the loudest voice of dissent was the *Western Tablet,* which was edited by James Mulligan, a native American of Irish descent, who later, during the Civil War, organized an Irish brigade to prove Irish loyalty.[133]

More important than the nature of the Catholic response to nativist hostility and discrimination was the effect the latter had on the development of Chicago Catholicism. The Know Nothing campaign made Catholics aware that they were not accepted by the American mainstream and that their loyalty was suspect. It also made them wary of "reformers"—educational, temperance, and otherwise—and they learned they had to build schools to ensure that their children would grow up in the faith, as the nonsectarian state schools would neither support nor respect their religious beliefs. Politically, Know Nothingism forced Catholics to look to the Democratic party for acceptance and advocacy in future struggles with nativism. Finally, their experience with anti-Catholic bigotry confirmed the separateness that accompanied their alienation as immigrants and became an impediment to future relationships with native Americans. Suspicion, defensiveness, and an "isolationist" tendency were passed on to succeeding generations of Chicago Catholics and imparted to new immigrants.

2. Archbishop Feehan, 1880–1902

ON THANKSGIVING DAY, 1880, the Right Reverend Patrick Augustine Feehan, former bishop of Nashville, arrived in Chicago to continue the work begun by his predecessor Bishop Thomas Foley. The well-planned welcome was dampened as the special train bearing the archbishop-elect was more than two hours late. The calcium lights that were to brighten his way had burned out, the military escort had disbanded, and hundreds of well wishers and curious onlookers had drifted away because of the numbing cold. Therefore, when Bishop Feehan alighted from his car that cold night, he saw little of the city and few of the people he was to serve for the next twenty-two years.[1]

Had Bishop Feehan been able to see Chicago more fully that bleak November night, he would have been amazed at the phoenix that had risen from the ashes of the world's most devastating fire (in 1871) and understood the literal meaning of Chicago's "I will" spirit. The flames had indeed proved purgative; as weak businesses went under, large and well-established companies sprang back and ensured Chicago's hegemony over the Mississippi Valley. In the 1880s and 1890s, Chicago's economic empire expanded as railroad tracks, radiating from its heart, extended its financial and commercial grip on its hinterland. The ability to tap resources of grain, lumber, and livestock made it the Midwest's core city. By 1890, Chicago was the nation's second manufacturing city in gross value of products.[2]

To fuel the economic empire, hundreds of thousands of people streamed to the growing metropolis on the shores of Lake Michigan. Within ten years of the fire, Chicago counted more than half a million inhabitants, and by 1890 it had passed the million mark, becoming the nation's second city. In the succeeding decade it recorded 1,698,575 residents. The lure of the city, its promise of wealth, adventure, and an end of rural isolation, drew thousands of Sister Carries and their male counterparts from the farms of the Old Northwest. To these native rural–urban migrants were added thousands of European immigrants, who sought to escape economic, social, and political instability and to create a new and better life for their families in America. Between 1880 and 1900, Chicago's foreign-born population increased from 204,859 to 587,112, each year drawing more heavily from eastern and southern European countries.[3]

Chicago's growth and economic prosperity produced a class of aristocrats, headed by the likes of Marshall Field, Potter Palmer, George Pullman, Philip D. Armour, and Cyrus McCormick, who lived in baronial luxury along the city's lakefront. While this elect few resided in granite and marble mansions, reminiscent of European lords, hundreds of thousands of Chicagoans lived in foul and crowded tenements. Native newcomers were usually able to secure a decent position and establish themselves in respectable districts, but the alien arrivals received the unskilled jobs and lived in overpopulated slum homes that surrounded the business district or industrial sites along the north and south branches of the Chicago River. Bessie L. Pierce observed: "Because they could find no other place to live, newcomers of the lowest income bracket flocked into . . . run-down houses, shacks and even barn lofts, places 'unfit for habitation by a civilized people.' Overcrowding and filthiness were their lot and custom."[4]

The city's growth created serious problems; sanitation, transportation, education, and recreation were in urgent need of attention. Industrial disease, "sweating," child labor, infant mortality, and crime were only a few of the problems that confronted the city. Aldermen, whose duty was to cure the city's ills, prostituted their public trust to line their pockets. For example, in 1882 C. C. Thompson of the Chicago Chamber of Commerce observed: "If you want to get anything out of council, the quickest way is to pay for it—not to the city, but to the aldermen."[5] "Reform" would succeed only when it paid.

Despite the crippling social problems that beset America's commodities center, there were signs that the great mass of humanity would not be scarred by urban disorientation. Individuals, societies, and institutions responded to the confusion and human suffering and attempted to bring order out of chaos. Each left its mark on the city—Jane Addams' Hull House, Ada C. Sweet and the Chicago Women's Club, and the religious denominations, motivated by Christian awareness of the implications of the Gospel. Although these humanizing forces brought much good to the mass within the city, it was never sufficient.[6] It was on such a metropolis that Patrick Augustine Feehan left his imprint, after more than two decades of exhausting service and effort.

Feehan was born in Killenaule, County Tipperary, on August 8, 1829—the year of Catholic Emancipation. When he was 8, his parents, Patrick and Judith Cooney Feehan, sent him to the village school. Soon, however, the boy was sent to live with his maternal grandparents in nearby Clonmel, where he attended a private school. Whether this move was prompted by financial difficulties at home or because of the poor quality of instruction in his village is not clear. At age 16, Patrick went to Dublin's prestigious Castle Knock College, where he earned high honors for scholarship. Two years later he entered Maynooth College Seminary under the sponsorship of Archbishop Paul Cullen of Dublin. Here, too, he distinguished himself.[7]

In 1850 the seminarian's family left Ireland for America. Two years later, Patrick, having received the deaconate, went to St. Louis in response to Archbishop Peter Kenrick's call for priests. The redoubtable Irish-American prelate assigned the "very talented and distinguished" young man to Cardonelet Seminary to teach classes until he was of canonical age for ordination.[8] On November 1, 1852, Feehan was ordained and subsequently assigned to the seminary faculty. The following year he became assistant pastor of St. John's parish in St. Louis. When Anthony O'Regan was appointed bishop of Chicago in 1854, Feehan succeeded him as president of the seminary. After four years of teaching and administering the seminary, the young priest became convinced that his proper sphere of activity was parish ministry. He requested another assignment, and in 1857 was made pastor of St. Michael's parish in St. Louis. Two years later he was transferred to Immaculate Conception parish, where he remained until 1865.[9]

Feehan's zeal and ability were conspicuous and led to his elevation when the Nashville episcopate became vacant. Archbishop Kenrick wrote to Rome, suggesting the appointment of Feehan because of his learning, piety, and ability to win respect and cooperation.[10] On November 1, 1865, Feehan was raised to the rank of bishop and charged with the monumental task of restoring his war-torn diocese. The Nashville diocese, which comprised the entire state of Tennessee, had been a highway for both armies and the theatre of some of the Civil War's bloodiest engagements. The few churches that existed before the war had been ruined. Undaunted, the young bishop reconstructed and further developed his diocese. In 1864 the diocese had only 12 priests to staff 10 parishes and numerous missions; by the end of his fifteen-year administration it had 27 priests and 29 churches. Feehan recruited priests from Ireland and secured the Congregation of the Precious Blood's German priests. Because of his concern for education, the number of schools and academies increased from 7 to 18. Also, a college and a second orphanage were established during his tenure.[11]

The Tennesseans respected their bishop and were saddened to learn of his translation to the newly created Archdiocese of Chicago. Before his departure, a group of prominent laymen paid him tribute and thanks for bringing peace, order, and financial stability to their once impoverished diocese. "Under . . . discouraging circumstances you entered upon your high office," a spokesman declared, "and while studiously avoiding all demonstration and public notice you have quietly, patiently and understandingly pursued the good work, until today you have the proud satisfaction that Providence has blessed your labor and that the diocese is in a healthy and prosperous condition and practically out of debt."[12] These qualities were the reason why Rome called this bishop to assume the momentous task of guiding the Chicago archdiocese.[13]

The few who endured the cold on Thanksgiving night in 1880 saw a well-built man over six feet in height. His head was large, with a broad noble brow and prominent features. His face was fine in outline and full of character, and his blue eyes were expressive, warm, and kindly. The new archbishop, according to a reporter, "impresses the beholder with a sense of highly-cultivated power tempered with exquisite gentleness, and he looks every inch a prince of the church, whose sway would be directed by love rather than authority."[14] In time, everyone would learn more about this man and his abilities.

Archbishop Feehan, austere, pious and scholarly, avoided public attention whenever possible. William J. Onahan, an influential Catholic politician, noted that Feehan had confided to him that he was no good outside the sanctuary.[15] When not attending to Church functions, he both worked and relaxed in his library at the episcopal residence he had built on a 25-acre, beautifully foliaged plot adjacent to Lincoln Park. He loved to read his fine collection of books or work in his flower garden. "Flowers," he was fond of saying, "are like the sunshine to a child. They bring a little of God's free world into the cramped city life."[16]

He was a gentle and nonaggressive man, who intensely disliked controversy; for this reason, some people believed he was a weak man, who did not have the courage of his convictions.[17] Peter James Muldoon, who served Feehan as chancellor before becoming his auxiliary bishop, disagreed: "His courage was not the showy ephemeral kind, but constant, clear, certain and persevering to the end."[18] From the material available, it appears that Muldoon's contention is closer to the truth—as illustrated by Feehan's management of the archdiocesan paper.

In 1900 the *New World*'s board of directors—priests appointed by the archbishop—told its capable, talented editor, William Dillon, that he must give up his law practice and devote full time to the paper, or resign. The editor tendered his resignation, but when the board of directors had nearly completed arrangements for a new editor, Feehan intervened. He sent for the editor; congratulated him on making the paper the best and most respected American Catholic weekly; and told him that if he would continue to edit the paper, he would be free to do as he pleased regarding his practice of law. Further, the archbishop gave the editor a $1,000 annual raise, which was paid out of "his own resources" (his only condition was that this arrangement be strictly confidential). The editor's commentary on Feehan's actions was: "He very seldom interferes, but when he does, his will is law."[19]

A dominant trait of the archbishop was his strong Irish allegiance. Although fifty of his seventy-three years were spent in America, he had deep and abiding love and concern for his homeland and urged his fellow countrymen to feel likewise. A well-worn St. Patrick's Day speech that his biographer found among his papers captures this spirit; he traced the history of Ireland in order to counter those who scoffed at the Irish by traducing their history, and concluded:

> Oh! Surely Ireland has a history. She has much in which we can glory, she has enough to explain the enthusiastic devotion of her children, and we, though at a distance, should not be cheated out of our recollections; today at least we can recall the memories of our native land. We can hear the sound of our fathers' voices from their Irish graves and though that sound be but an echo that we gather from the ruins of the tomb, still we love to hear it and it reaches to our soul and enkindles in them a love for Ireland and a devotion to her traditions and her faith. And hence, this day should be for us not only a national, but also a religious festival. And before you leave the temple, will you not pray to the God of your Fathers, that you in your day may be worthy of these who are gone before you? Oh! I trust in God, there are no recreant Irish here!
>
> Pray not alone for yourselves, pray for your children who will take your places, that they too may be worthy of their race; that

they may never blush for Ireland; that Ireland may never have cause to blush for them. Oh! Wherever they may be, may they so uphold the honor of the old land, that she might clasp them to her bosom and with pride claim them as the children of her children.[20]

Archbishop Feehan's administrative capacity was challenged to its fullest by Chicago. By 1902, 132 churches and numerous charitable institutions relied on him for leadership. His success came from conservative, prudent judgments and his ability to inspire faith in his office. His role was compared to the sun, whose centripetal force keeps the planets from sliding into the void.[21] The "go-ahead spirit" of the city, which had created innumerable social and political problems was not reflected in Feehan's administration; by controlling his priests, but without resorting to extreme authority, he saw to the orderly yet swift development of his diocese. Like a general, he surveyed the field, weighed the chances, costs and results, and left the execution of detail to his priests. In this way he exercised control but did not destroy personal initiative.[22]

Fiscal conservatism was a hallmark of Feehan's administration. While many persons, captured by the hope of making quick fortunes, invested foolishly, he invested Church funds in real estate—and watched its value increase. When a group of faithful requested permission to establish a parish, he demanded that they prove their ability to pay for the church and support its pastor. He also decreed that whenever new parishes began, one building, capable of serving as church and school, be erected till such time the parish could afford to build a regular church. Prevention of large debts was not the only goal. The school, like a magnet, attracted additional families to the parish and thus further built up the congregation. Through wise business strategy, the value of Church holdings increased to an estimated $44 million by 1902.[23]

Archbishop Feehan's great legacy to Chicago Catholics was one of the nation's most extensive school systems.[24] As a scholar and teacher, he appreciated education, but as a pastor he understood the necessity of building a comprehensive system of religious instruction to safeguard the faith of his flock. The policy of erecting a combination church-school building helped ensure the future of Catholicism. "Fill the schools now," he often declared, "and the churches will be filled in the future."[25] For this reason, he, with his suffragans, worked for repeal of a law that threatened to place his school system under state control.

In addition to education, Feehan attended to the needs of the poor and neglected. Sensitive to the plight of orphaned and dependent children, and aware of their vulnerability to proselytizers, he directed the construction and operation of a large diocesan orphanage and training school in Des Plaines, where the city's Catholic orphans received physical care, guidance, and education, as well as religious instruction. Homes were established in the business district for working boys and girls where they could find security and religious direction, in a city where too often the young fell into vice. For girls who had gone astray, the diocese, through the work of the Sisters of the Good Shepherd, provided a home for rehabilitation. Eleemosynary (charitable) work, which had its beginnings before Archbishop Feehan's administration, was expanded and broadened under his care.[26]

While the physical growth of Church institutions indicates the archbishop's business sense and religious zeal, it also reflects his mastery of public relations and personnel problems. The success of any institution, whether profitable or charitable, depends on the smooth and harmonious working of the staff; as chief administrator, Feehan gained the confidence and cooperation of his workers through firmness, justice, and respect for their talents and individuality. He had problems, but he did not experience the extreme hostility that had disrupted the administration of some of his predecessors. The peace and order that he achieved was commented upon by the *Catholic Home Journal*: "The absolute harmony that prevails among the clergy is one of the highest tributes that can be paid to the wisdom of Archbishop Feehan in the matter of Church government."[27]

The secret to his success was real respect for the judgment of his priests. By permitting them wide latitude in their parishes, he gave them a sense of independence and importance, and in return he received their support for his diocesan programs. One observer testified: "As the Constitution of the United States guarantees to every man equal rights so does the Archbishop guarantee equality of rights to his priests."[28] Archbishop Feehan was much like a professional Irish politician; he weighed the power and strength of his constituency and, in acting, respected it, without jeopardizing his position. His administrative family was Irish, or of Irish origin, but his advisory council for diocesan policy contained representatives of the chief immigrant groups.[29]

As in Nashville, Chicagoans respected and admired their first archbishop. The satisfied clergy were like ambassadors of good will and the customary visitations by the unassuming leader cemented the warm relationship he cultivated. In twenty-two years he visited his parishes frequently; he confirmed nearly 200,000 persons, ordained 250 priests, laid 80 cornerstones and dedicated 100 churches.[30] These visits and religious occasions were opportunities to demonstrate his concern for the welfare and interests of the people, as well as to let the people relate to him as their spiritual leader—as manifested on three special occasions. On a return from Rome in 1883, priests and laity honored him with a parade in which 30,000 persons marched and 100,000 lined the streets. A greater and more elaborate display of respect was made in 1890 when Archbishop Feehan celebrated his silver anniversary as bishop. And when he died, hundreds of thousands of Catholics of every nationality expressed regret—and gratitude for his kindly work in their behalf.[31]

Archbishop Feehan's burdens and responsibilities in the fast-growing archdiocese, coupled with his disinclination for publicity and controversy, prevented him from assuming more than local prominence. His brilliant suffragan, John Lancaster Spalding of Peoria, and Archbishop John Ireland of St. Paul were the acknowledged leaders of Catholicism in the Midwest, whereas historian Thomas T. McAvoy called Feehan one of the "many fine bishops who were good shepherds of their flocks, building churches and schools, and making every effort to provide plenty of capable, active priests to carry on the sacramental ministry of the Church and the teachings of Christian doctrine."[32]

Even though Feehan was not an "acknowledged leader," his successes in Chicago had attracted such national attention by 1892 that the *New York Sun* considered him a serious contender for a cardinal's hat.[33] Even in his declining years the speculation persisted. In 1901, when a reporter asked Apostolic Delegate Cardinal Martinelli about Feehan's chances for the red hat, he diplomatically replied: "The work of Archbishop Feehan in the Chicago Archdiocese is great and has certainly attracted the attention of all the Church. As to any future questions I can only say I am no prophet."[34] That this honor was never conferred upon him probably made little difference. "Archbishop Feehan," the Memphis *Catholic Journal and News* wrote, "unlike some other prelates, had no ambition to be the central magnet in an episcopal galaxy; he craved no honor of high position." The desire for power, it noted, never "burned his surplice."[35]

As early as 1895, speculation on the archbishop's health began to surface; however, such rumors were denied by the official Catholic paper, which called such stories the product of "inventive genius."[36] Despite protestations of his "perfectly good" health, Feehan realized the need to slow down; thus he requested that Alexander J. McGavick be appointed his auxiliary bishop, to perform many of the wearing ceremonial duties.[37] When health problems soon forced McGavick to retire, Peter J. Muldoon, a former chancellor, was appointed to take up the work. In Muldoon, the tired prelate found a tower of strength and a source of consolation during his last year, one of serious illness and agitation. On July 12, 1902, the physically weak and work-worn builder of Chicago Catholicism suffered a heart attack and died.[38]

The death of this shy and unobtrusive leader was marked by ceremonies of solemn grandeur and eulogies laden with high praise. Cardinal Gibbons, Archbishop Ireland, and Bishop Spalding (as well as twenty-three other archbishops, bishops, and abbots) came to Chicago to pay their respects and participate in the funeral service.[39] Most important, Chicago's Catholics registered their sorrow at the passing of one whom they loved.

> Thousands of grief stricken people formed an unbroken procession [the *Chicago American* observed] threading their way continuously around the bier, their heart-broken sighs and sobs . . . breaking the solemn silence of the scene. Men and women, bending under the weight of the years, inmates of various institutions which were fostered by the Archbishop, blended their tears with those of devoted nuns, monks, and priests and laymen of every nationality.[40]

The procession of young and old, rich and poor, English speaking and non-English speaking, all under one roof, was not only a sign of his success but the realization of his first Chicago prayer.

When Archbishop Feehan first addressed his Chicago flock (November 28, 1880),on his installation at the Cathedral of the Holy Name, his text was: "Another parable He proposed to them, saying, 'The kingdom of heaven is like a grain of mustard seed, which a man took, and sowed in his field; which is the least indeed of all seeds; but when it is grown up it is greater than all herbs, and becometh a tree, so that all the birds of the air come and dwell in the branches thereof.' "[41] Indeed, the parable was appropriate for the work he undertook. Feehan fostered the growth of a truly *catholic* Church, a supranational Church, in which all nationalities could find haven and solace in the harsh, unfamiliar soil of urban America. When Feehan came to Chicago, there were 38 parishes: 22 "territorial" and 16 "national" (9 German, 3 Polish, 3 Bohemian, and 1 French). In 1902, when he died, 94 additional parishes, serving a vastly increased population of a more cosmopolitan nature, were in existence: 41 territorial and 19 German, 15 Polish, 5 Bohemian, 3 French, 3 Lithuanian, 3 Italian, and 1 each of Croatians, Solvenians, Slovaks, Dutch, and Negro.[42] During his tenure, the number of parishes rose by nearly 250 percent; even more significant, however, was the increase in national parishes. In 1880, 42 percent of the city's parishes were national, but by 1902, 52 percent were national.

Archbishop Feehan did not seek to make the Catholic Church in Chicago predominantly "foreign"; he merely responded to the fact that many members of his flock were from Europe. He knew that Catholic faith and doctrines are universal and well defined, allowing little room for personal interpretation, but that its expression may vary according to customs and traditions. Each immigrant group had special devotions, expressions of belief, and liturgical practices, as well as emphasis on particular doctrines, and if they were to continue to relate to God, it must be in their own manner. A Pole could not become an Irishman, a Lithuanian a Frenchman, or a German an Italian—not even upon entering a church. From experience, he learned that the national parish was one of the foundations on which an immigrant and ethnic community developed and, at the same time, an extension of the community's character.

Thus the network of territorial and national parishes depended upon the pastors and curates, who represented the archbishop at the parish level. Lacking a sufficient supply of American-born priests to staff the churches, Feehan had to recruit clergy from abroad. As in Nashville, he drew upon surplus priests in Ireland to staff the territorial parishes. Also, religious orders were brought to the diocese and given charge of parishes, and immigrant priests who followed their flocks or relatives to America were enlisted. In 1880 there were 85 priests: 39 diocesan and 46 others, belonging to seven religious orders. Ten years later the number had increased to 198, with 135 diocesan and 63 religious; and by 1900 it rose to 275, with 177 diocesan and 98 religious, belonging to eleven orders.[43]

Theoretically, Feehan had absolute control over the diocese. In the chancery, which handled administrative and personnel matters, he placed trusted and capable men who implemented his policy decisions. Through his chancellor and vicar general, he could reward priests by appointing them to comfortable, prestigious parishes, or punish them by assigning them to rural and/or poor parishes. Another key to his administration was the Archbishop's Council, an advisory group, which was composed of influential clerics, chosen by the archbishop to advise him on policy matters. Unlike the chancery personnel, who were Irish or of Irish descent, this body was representative of the ethnic composition of the archdiocese; the Irish predominated, but Germans and Slavs were represented. In 1890 the council had 3 Irish, 1 German, and 1 Bohemian. Ten years later, the council membership reflected the changing composition of Chicago—2 Irish, 1 German, 1 Bohemian, and 1 Pole.[44] Through this advisory body he was able to learn of the needs and concerns of his flock, and he had spokesmen who could represent his wishes to the diverse elements of his diocese. Because Feehan's linguistic ability was negligible, the German, Bohemian, and Pole were vital to maintenance of unity. Thus the advisory council was a practical and essential tool for dealing with the dual system of national and territorial parishes.

The need for priests, in turn, caused Feehan to share his authority with the superiors of religious orders. By their constitution, religious orders are independent of the head of the diocese in matters of discipline and dependent upon a bishop only for the right to minister within his jurisdiction. When Feehan entrusted a parish to a religious order, he understood that he could not choose its personnel; but obtaining the resources of a religious order ensured that his flock, and especially immigrants, would have priests. In 1900, religious orders supplied the staff for 7 Polish, 5 German, 2 Bohemian, and 1 Italian parish, as well as chaplains for 2 German hospitals. Like a political leader, Feehan dispensed power and privilege for the overall benefit of his organization.

Feehan's administrative system was not novel; it existed in Chicago before he came. He built on foundations already laid, and made modifications and adjustments as the situation dictated, but nowhere was flexibility more needed than in the complex system of territorial and national parishes. Nowhere was the need for responsiveness greater than in preserving the oneness of faith among Chicago's Irish, German, Polish, Bohemian, Italian, Lithuanian, and other immigrant Catholics.

The Irish, who spoke the language of the host country, administered the territorial parishes and "constituted the bone and sinew of Catholicism."[45] The foreign-born Irish population rose from 44,411 in 1880 to 73,912 by 1900 and, with the second generation, numbered 180,991.[46] Bessie L. Pierce has observed that "their cohesiveness was pronounced and despite the absence of a language barrier, they remained a strongly unified part of Chicago's cosmopolitanism."[47] They were united by a common tradition and the attacks of old-line Americans, not only for their religious faith but for their attempts to control political patronage. Religious festivals, especially St. Patrick's Day, demonstrated that their Irish identity was wed to Catholicism. English rule in Ireland had made Catholicism and nationalism one, and this union was intensified by a revolution in devotional practice that occurred in Ireland after the famine and was carried to America by tens of thousands of emigrants through the succeeding decades.[48] Irish identity and the Catholic Church were joined in Chicago by the nativists of the 1850s and strengthened by the new immigrants.

Although the Irish lived in every ward of the city, they tended to cluster on the South and Southwest sides, close to the lumberyards and stockyards, where they found employment. As members of the Irish community prospered or felt the pressure of new immigrants, they moved from their cramped and dirty neighborhoods to the open areas farther south and west, and some to the north. When they moved, they still tended to settle together, bound by their shared experiences, interests, and religion. Wherever they settled, they built churches. By the end of Archbishop Feehan's tenure, 63 of the city's 132 churches were Irish dominated.[49]

The Irish in Chicago developed a strong sense of nationalism and maintained it. Although Irish immigration to Chicago continued to be large until 1890, the American-born Irish predominated by that year. Despite the changing character of the community, the Irish did not lose their identity; they intensified it. Thomas N. Brown, in *Irish American Nationalism, 1870–1890,* suggests that the Irish in America developed a strong nationalistic spirit to counter their sense of inferiority, loneliness, and alienation, as well as their poverty and Anglo prejudice.[50] For them, an independent Ireland would lead to respectability and, they hoped, bring a measure of acceptance broader than that in smoke-filled rooms, where politicians bartered for power and votes.

Manifestations of Irish consciousness and nationalism were everywhere present (and supported) in the '80s and '90s. Visits by Michael Davitt, M.P., William O'Brien, M.P., John Redmond, M.P., and numerous other Irish leaders elicited manifestations of concern for Ireland's future as well as financial generosity.[51] Prior to the defeat of the Home Rule Bill of 1892, the city's Irish supported nationalist movements. However, the failure of Charles Parnell's Home Rule movement caused many Chicago Irish to turn their attention to the revival of Gaelic culture, and the Gaelic League established schools to teach the ancient Irish tongue and literature. Women met to relearn near-forgotten handcraft arts. The young organized around music, dance, and sport and efforts were made to have the history of Eire taught in all parochial schools in which the Irish predominated.[52]

While some Irish appear to have merged with the American mainstream, the majority clung to their Irish identity and, through a revival of culture and tradition, sought to overcome their sense of inferiority by focusing on the best of Irish culture. These activities had

the support of the Church, as expressed in the archdiocesan newspaper, and the cooperation of pastors, who opened church buildings
for this activity. But in spite of their intense interest in things Gaelic, the
Irish failed to build lasting monuments that manifested their
nationalism—their churches sufficed.[53]

Before Archbishop Feehan's arrival, German Catholics ranked
second in numbers (and would continue to) as a result of a new wave of
German immigration during the 1880s. During that decade, the city's
German and Austrian foreign-born element increased from 76,661 to
168,082, and, combined with 159,000 American-born of German
parentage, composed 29.8 percent of the city's population. By 1900,
Chicago's German stock had increased to nearly 450,000. Of this
number, roughly 35 percent were Catholics from the southwestern
provinces of Germany and Austria.[54] In 1892, Washington Hesing,
publisher and editor of the *Illinois Staats Zietung,* had estimated there
were at least 143,000 German Catholics in Illinois.[55] Although no exact
figure is available, German Catholics constituted the largest and most
important non-English-speaking element in the Catholic Church.

German Catholics could be pleased with their "marvelous" development and growth.[56] In 1880 they had 9 churches, and by 1890
had added 13 more in response to the needs of the increased population. When the Irish archbishop died, they held 28 churches, less than
half as many as their English-speaking coreligionists but 40 percent of
the foreign-language parishes of the city.

The Germans clustered throughout the city, with the largest
concentration on the North Side, where they reproduced their culture
and institutions and erected statues and named streets after famous
Teutonic poets and artists. As a group, they were prosperous, making
their livelihood in various business ventures and semiskilled trades.
Their community life was enriched by organizations devoted to preservation of their culture: concert groups, singing societies, dramatic
and athletic clubs, as well as numerous mutual benefit societies.[57]

Despite their bond of the German language and pride in Teutonic
culture, there was no unity. Social and religious differences divided the
German community into groups, the largest of which were Protestant
and Catholic. The Catholic Germans came from the southern regions
of Germany while the Protestants came from the northern sections,
where life and traditions were different. They also carried with them
traditional post-Reformation animosities, most recently manifested in
Germany by the *Kulturkampf.*[58]

As Germans, they were very aware of their Catholicism; as
Catholics, they were very aware of their German identity. German

Catholic immigrants felt compelled to build their own churches and institutions because their English-speaking coreligionists could not appreciate the close bond in the German soul between practice of the faith and traditional customs, which was deeply rooted in the centuries-old Catholic culture of the German fatherland. Without their own institutions, Catholic immigrants might turn to German Protestantism. Thus, caught between the misunderstanding Irish and the (at times) hostile Protestants, they established their own religio-social life. Churches with German patron saints; German priests, preaching and administering the sacraments in German; parochial schools, conducted by German nuns and laymen, became a necessity. Hospitals, such as Alexian Brothers and St. Elizabeth's, ministered to their sick, and Angel Guardian Orphanage cared for the parentless. The latter institution was supported by the sale of burial plots in German Catholic cemeteries and an annual collection in German parishes on Pentecost Sunday.[59] In response to their peculiar situation, they created institutions that served them from birth to interment.

Because of the continual, heavy flow of German immigrants in the last two decades of the nineteenth century, the national character of the parishes remained constant. Many priests and members of religious orders who fled Germany because of the *Kulturkampf* came to Chicago and infused the parishes with new blood and German Catholic awareness.[60] The Germans had great concern that their language and culture be maintained in the church, school, and home and that the American-born not forsake their heritage.[61]

Their desire to preserve the mother tongue is illustrated by St. Peter's parochial school. In 1870, 1,200 families made up the parish, but because of the railroads and the settlement of "questionable elements" (non-German immigrants), the parish was reduced to 30 families by 1896 and the once prosperous school had only 85 students: Germans, Irish, Italians, Lebanese, and Negroes. Even though the ethnic character of the school had changed, the German children were still taught German.[62]

While the Germans remained the dominant non-English-speaking element in the Church, the Poles, whose population multiplied dramatically after 1880, assumed the second position. Although nineteenth-century U.S. Census figures for persons of Polish origin are inaccurate (they were classified as Russian, German, and Austrian), knowledgeable estimates give some idea of the growth of the Polish population. The estimated 1873 population of 20,000[63] increased to about 52,000 by 1890,[64] and to 107,667 by 1900.[65]

The wave of Polish immigration was the product of economic, political, religious, and social factors, combined with the belief that emigration to America could solve their Old World problems. Because Poland was partitioned among the Russian, German, and Austrian empires, no simple reason explains the migration. Overpopulation of the Polish villages, failure of the land to support the population, insufficient industrial development to absorb surplus farm workers, and low wages but high taxes were the chief economic reasons for leaving. Russian political despotism and Prussification, linguistic and religious, made American liberty attractive. Finally, the status of the Polish peasant, which once made a life of poverty bearable, was adversely changed by severe economic dislocation.[66]

The Polish immigrants, overwhelmingly Catholic, were similar to, yet quite different from, their Irish and German coreligionists. Like the Irish and most Germans, they were peasants who, no longer able to make a living at home, came to America because of its heralded opportunities, but they differed in their intentions. Most of the late nineteenth-century Poles came with the resolve to return home as soon as they could earn enough money to ensure a new life as a farmer or shopkeeper. William I. Thomas and Florian Znaniecki's classic study, *The Polish Peasant in Europe and America,* demonstrates that few Poles who came before the Great War planned to settle permanently. Their hope was to return home after a few years and, with their savings, "settle on a higher economic and social level. America was the land of opportunities for advancing in the old country."[67]

They also differed in their conception of the immigrants' relation to the homeland. Some Poles came with the goal of establishing another Poland in America, where their culture and race would be preserved. Although most of the immigrants were poor and illiterate peasants, unfamiliar with Adam Michiewicz's Polish messianism (a belief that the Polish nation would rise again, as Christ had risen after the crucifixion), a few clerical leaders were profoundly influenced by it. A letter to the Polish paper *Dziennik Chicagoski,* by Rev. Stanislaus Radziejewski, urged Chicago's Polish immigrants to isolate themselves, preferably on farms, where they could "create a new fatherland which would eventually join hands with the Old Country in as close ties as possible."

> It is important that the Polish people do not perish, meaning those leaving the Fatherland and the future generations. It is not in our power to restore Poland, but it is our duty to see that Poles continue to exist, because if a majority of Poles should become

Germanized, Russianized, or Americanized, then God, even if He should desire it, would not know for whom or from what to restore Poland. To insure that all Poles sailing across the ocean remain forever Polish, our advice is to form groups of Polish colonies, so that the Poles may live for each other only, and not permit any strangers to enter their fold. If our people cross the ocean in a haphazard manner, if they intermingle with other nationalities, if thousands of Poles settle among millions of strangers, then everything about them will be strange and additional new generations will be lost to our nation.[68]

The majority of Poles, led by Resurrectionist priests, who dominated the community, did not believe in Polish messianism, but they endeavored to re-create the Old World in Chicago. Once in America, Polish peasants found support from a group that maintained the social bonds and attitudes of the Old World. Until they were accepted by the host society, they needed the support that such a group could provide. Thus societies sprang up to meet the physical, social, and intellectual needs of the newcomers. However, those societies were secondary to the parish.[69]

According to Thomas and Znaniecki, the Polish parish, the "most important Polish-American institution," had much more significance than can be ascribed to its external form and official purpose; it was much more than a religious association for common worship under the leadership of a priest. The sociologists observe:

> The unique power of the parish in Polish-American life, much greater than even in the most conservative peasant communities in Poland, cannot be explained by the predominance of religious interests which, like all other traditional social attitudes, are weakened by emigration, though they seem to be the last to disappear completely. The parish is, indeed, simply the old primary community, reorganized and concentrated. In its concrete totality it is a substitute for both the narrower but more coherent village-group and the wider diffuse and vaguely outlined *okolica*. In its institutional organization it performs the functions which in Poland are broader and more complex than those of a parish or of a commune in the old country.[70]

"Religious character," though important in itself, does not fully explain the erection of numerous Polish parishes. Purely religious needs could have been satisfied, at much less expense, by using existing parishes and making occasional visits to a Polish priest for confession and spiritual guidance. Whenever possible, Poles refused to join Irish or German parishes, and built fifteen Polish parishes and expanded three existing ones at great personal cost. By establishing their own parishes, they created not merely a place to attend religious services but a community center. In Chicago, Poles established several colonies, clustered about their churches and parochial schools.[71]

The parish, the heart of neighborhood life, was also a source of community cohesion. Around the parish, Poles organized their social, educational, charitable, and religious societies and institutions. Economic enterprises were attracted by the population concentrated about the parish, and the areas adjacent to church buildings were soon sites of small businesses that catered to Polish tastes and traditions. Businesses and Polish-American societies were encouraged by the religious leaders, since they stabilized the community and made it more self-sufficient and self-contained, and thus they strengthened the Church's role in the community.[72] If a business was not Polish owned, efforts were made to ensure that Polish-speaking clerks were employed, so that Poles might secure employment where community money was spent.[73] Thus by looking after its own, the Church ensured its existence.

Ninety-five percent of the Poles were Catholic,[74] and shared a common language, but these former peasants were not intimately united by "nationality"; their identities were rooted in their villages or districts. On a wider scale, Poles from the Austrian, Russian, and Prussian provinces had different experiences and interests, which had to be submerged before there could be unanimity.[75] The common experiences of emigration, language, and religion were sources of potential unity, but they were never fully utilized. Parish and societal rivalries and misunderstandings were constant concerns that turned the community in upon itself. Only when a challenge came from outside the community did there seem to be an expression of solidarity.[76]

Another Slavic group that settled in Chicago in this period was the Czechs, from Bohemia and Moravia, who had suffered political and economic hardships under Austro-Hungarian rule, and when conditions became unbearable they had emigrated. The failure of small farms to support the rapidly increasing population, low wages for industrial workers, and heavy taxation caused thousands of them to emigrate.[77] In 1880, Chicago had 11,887 foreign-born Czech residents; in 1890, 25,105; and in 1900, 36,362. With those who had been born of Czech parentage, they numbered 112,683, or 6.6 percent of Chicago's foreign stock.

The immigrants and their offspring settled together and formed a close-knit colony in the Sixth Ward, known as Pilsen. Mark Ridpath, an author and educator who surveyed Chicago's ethnic communities in 1890, wrote:

> Here they constitute a community by themselves. . . . Of the 54,000 Bohemians in Chicago fully 42,000 have their residence in Pilsen, where they form a foreign nationality with which few other ingredients are mingled. The explorer here hears only the Bohemian tongue, and must journey square after square before he finds other than a Bohemian face. It is essentially a foreign city of no small proportions set down in the midst of a greater city.[78]

The streets of Pilsen, lined with Bohemian provision stores, clothing shops, restaurants, and other businesses, were a re-creation of the homeland. As pressure for housing by neighboring immigrant colonies increased, the members of the Pilsen community moved farther west, but maintained their Czech identity.[79]

Unlike the Irish and Poles, Czech Catholic immigrants found the issue of religion divisive. In the Czech provinces of the Austro-Hungarian Empire, 96 percent of the populace was nominally Catholic, but in the United States, more than 50 percent gave up that faith. The founders of the first Czech community were anti-Catholic nationalists from Bohemia, who condemned the Church for its role in suppressing the 1849 revolution. The Czechs who followed them to America were urged to give up their Catholicism as a sign of their loyalty to the Czech "nation."[80] Czech Free Thinkers (as they labeled themselves) stressed national identity, and they established schools, organizations, and newspapers to this end.[81]

In Chicago, the Free Thinker effort to win Catholics to their side had limited success because of strong clerical leadership and the conservative nature of the more recent Moravian immigrant peasants. To counter the nationalists, the Bohemian clergy, led by the Bohemian Benedictines, waged an all-out battle to preserve the faith of newcomers by providing churches, schools, and parish organizations that welded Catholics together. The parishes gained strength and importance with the increase in Moravian immigration—Czechs of agrarian background, who had not been exposed to the nationalistic criticism of the Church that had affected the earlier immigrants from industrial areas, where provincialism had given way to nationalism.[82] Between 1880 and 1893, five new churches were founded to meet the immigrants' religious and social needs.

Lest new immigrants fall victim to Free Thinkers' journalistic assaults on the Church, the Benedictines responded in kind. They founded the Bohemian Benedictine Press in 1889 and issued the weekly *Pritel Ditek* (The Children's Friend), which was followed by the semiweekly *Katolik* (The Catholic) in 1893 and the daily *Narod* (the Nation) in 1894.[83] (The choice of the title *Narod* reflects the Benedictines' concern to show there was no conflict between religion and nationalism.) Together, parish and press arrested the influence of the Free Thinkers and established a strong Czech Catholic community. In New York, only 25 percent of Czechs retained their faith, while in Chicago about 50 percent remained in the Catholic fold.[84]

Like other groups, the Bohemians were concerned that their children retain their religion and culture. The Free Thinkers had their own schools, where children were taught that God is an invention, the Bible is uninspired, churches are an obstacle to human development, and priests are enemies of enlightenment, truth, and freedom.[85] Catholic children therefore had to be prepared to deal with this element of the community, and a thorough education was considered the only solution. The parochial school was likewise the key to maintaining Czech culture, which, for the immigrants, was one with religion. "It is almost self-evident truth amongst the Bohemian Catholics," an observer wrote, "that without a Bohemian Catholic school the coming Bohemian generation will be lost to the Bohemian nationality as well as their Catholic faith. A child that is ashamed of the language of his parents is not far from being ashamed of the faith of its parents."[86] For this reason the Czechs supported parochial elementary schools and a college–high school, as well as an orphanage.[87]

In 1902, 117 of Chicago's parishes served the Irish, Germans, Poles, and Czechs and 14 other parishes ministered to seven different language groups: French-Canadians and French, 4; Italians, 3; Lithuanians, 3; and Dutch, Slovenes, Croatians, and Slovaks 1 each. Catholic Negros also had a parish, St. Monica's (established in 1885), which was similar to a national parish for it had no boundaries and its members were always considered separately, despite their use of English. (Fr. Augustus Tolton, America's first Negro priest, was its pastor.)[88]

With the exception of the French speaking, all these immigrants were relatively new to Chicago, having come in sizable numbers only after 1880. Most of them attempted to seek out their countrymen and lay the foundations of their respective communities. Until a sufficient number was able to support a parish, they attended services in other national parishes, or did not practice their faith. In general, those who practiced their faith tended to relate with other national groups that were culturally or linguistically similar; the Dutch on the North Side used German churches, Lithuanians attended Polish parishes, and Croatians, Slovenes, and Slovaks on the West Side went to Czech churches.[89] Italians were the exception.

The Italians, who were to form an important segment of the Chicago diocese in the first decades of the twentieth century, began community building only in 1880. Overpopulation and economic reorganization had displaced millions of Italian peasants, so that thousands of *contadini* came to Chicago from Sicily and southern Italy, intending to better their lot and then return home. Between 1880 and 1890, the Italian population of Chicago increased from 1,357 to 5,685, and in the following decade to 16,008.[90] Most of these immigrants settled in one of three colonies—in the vicinity of Grand Avenue, west of the river, in the 17th Ward; in the 22d Ward, east of the river; and in the strip running westward from the south edge of the Loop. They became heirs to the homes of the more prosperous Irish, German, and Scandinavian immigrants, who were moving to better surroundings.[91]

Italians were dissimilar to other Catholic immigrants in their relationship with the Church. Instead of organizing societies to obtain priests and build churches, Italian newcomers tended to wait for priests to organize them into parishes. They had never struggled to preserve their faith, and Catholicism was not an integral part of their national consciousness as it was for the Irish and Poles. In fact, the Church's role before 1870 in opposing the unification of Italy had produced an anticlerical reaction. Also, though the Italians were deeply religious, their Catholicism (as Rudolph J. Vecoli has explained) was a fusion of Christian and pre-Christian beliefs and practices that "did not conform to the liturgy and doctrine of the Church." A spirit of *campanilismo* dominated their religious behavior; that is, the customs of the village were integrated into their practice, and priests were regarded with suspicion but tolerated, because they performed the necessary baptismal, marriage, and funeral rites.[92] A New York priest noted in 1888 that "the Catholic Church is to the mass of Italians almost like a new religion."[93] Finally, their temporary or transient intention vis-à-vis the United States was not conducive to religious regularity or the financial commitment necessary for building churches.

American bishops who were unfamiliar with Italians were troubled by their apparent indifference to the Church. When they met at the Baltimore Plenary Council of 1884, they discussed the problem of Italian "leakage" but found no solution. Through their spokesman, James Cardinal Gibbons, they explained to the cardinal-prefect of Propaganda that one of the major causes of religious indifference and apostacy was the inadequate religious training of emigrants before they left. Those already in America, he said, were in need of dedicated, learned, and morally upright ecclesiastics who would devote themselves *"wholly and perpetually . . .* to the spiritual care of the Italians."[94]

In Chicago, episcopal concern for Italians was evident as early as 1876. In that year, Bishop Foley welcomed Italian members of the Servite order to Chicago and encouraged them to begin a mission among the Italians, with an ultimate goal of forming a parish. Because of the small number of Italians, however, a parish was not founded until 1881. Rev. Soseneus Moretti, O.S.M., spent three years organizing the North Side Italian community before he was able to say Mass in its new church. From this parish, Assumption of the Blessed Virgin Mary, the Servites tried to minister to all the Italians in the city.[95] Since they were not able to reach all the Italians, others tried to take up the slack. In 1898 three zealous Irish women, who had worked with the Negros at St. Monica's parish, responded to the call for volunteers to aid the Italians on the West Side. With the help of some Sisters of Mercy, they set up Guardian Angel school, and within two years of their humble beginnings had a thriving Sunday school with thirty-five teachers.[96] The declining German parish of St. Peter's, at Clark and Polk streets, gave a special eight-day mission for its Italian members and provided free education to the poor.[97]

One of the most ardent workers was Rev. Edmund M. Dunne, later chancellor of the Archdiocese of Chicago and bishop of Peoria, who became the pastor of Guardian Angel parish, the first Italian parish on the West Side.[98] Educated in Rome, he was familiar with the language and problems of the poor immigrants who crowded into the foul and run-down tenements near Hull House. Dunne conceived of his work among Italian immigrants as a missionary venture that merited the support of all Catholics, lest Jane Addams' settlement house succeed in its supposed intention to "draw our children from the Church."[99] Because Dunne needed financial support for his work, he published a letter in the *New World,* emphasizing brotherly responsibility:

> My dear friends, is it no concern of ours whether a notable portion of our Catholic brethren remain faithful to their religion or apostatize or drift into infidelity? Shall we step aside in order to let well-meaning non-Catholic philanthropists wrest from the Church's bosom a considerable number of those who belong to her by birth? As loyal Americans, can we remain indifferent while in the most congested neighborhood of Chicago, children are

growing up in the gutter like social weeds, to become afterwards perhaps a menace to our Garden City? Charity begins at home, and we have here in the Italian colony of Chicago a vast missionary field to cultivate, a variegated collection of sickly plants, both physical and moral, that need our special attention.[100]

Fr. Dunne's request was supported by *New World* editorials, which explained the necessity of financial aid and sought to lessen racial antipathy toward Italians by shattering stereotypes. The initial response was regarded as encouraging, but enthusiasm for the Italian cause soon waned. To help with the work among these new immigrants, a permanent and committed group of persons, as recommended by the American hierarchy, was desperately needed.[101] Bishop Feehan's successor would see to their needs.

Nearly as numerous as the Italians were the Lithuanians, who also had three parishes. They left their homeland for reasons similar to the Poles', and began to arrive in Chicago in significant numbers after 1890. The early immigrants settled on the Northwest Side among the Poles, because many of them spoke Polish and most shared the same religion. However, as the number of Lithuanians increased, just prior to the Columbian Exposition, they were attracted to the South Side by the availability of unskilled jobs in the stockyards. Soon they established two colonies near their work. Between 1892 and 1905, the Lithuanian population increased from 4,000 to 22,492.[102]

Lithuanians prized their religion and, once in America, desired to have their own parishes. Although the early settlers attended services in the Polish parishes, they promptly set out to establish their own. In 1886 they organized the St. Casimir Benefit Society to raise funds to maintain visiting priests, who ministered to them in their native language. Six years later, the newer but fast-expanding colony in Bridgeport, which had been swelled by packing plant workers, secured a priest and erected St. George's Church. Until other Lithuanian national parishes were established, it drew its membership from all over the city.[103]

When the number of Lithuanians increased so that they could form their own colonies, they became self-conscious and, more and more, asserted their ethnic distinctiveness. Some of the first arrivals had Polonized their names by adding *ski* or *wicz,* taken up the Polish language, and followed Polish leadership, but soon they were counseled to be proud of their "beautiful" names, rich language, and ancient race.[104] The parish school, which later became the greatest preserver of language and culture, initially caused serious problems for the pastor of St. George because he had to use Polish nuns as teachers. When the editor of *Lietuva,* an ardent nationalist, objected, saying "What is good for the Polish schools is not good for the Lithuanian school," the pastor found Polish nuns who could speak Lithuanian, and eventually obtained Lithuanian sisters who ensured transmission of his parishioners' language and culture.[105]

At the turn of the century, Lithuanians, Poles, Germans, Irish, Bohemians, and other national groups made strenuous efforts to keep their cultures alive in Chicago. Poorly paid immigrants and their children contributed large portions of their income to build churches, schools, and service institutions and devoted much time and energy to the numerous activities and organizations affiliated with their parishes. For all these groups, the parish, if not the center, was an extremely important element of their lives. In the parish, in the face of adversity, the newcomer and his progeny found solace, priestly guidance, companionship, and part of the Old World in the midst of an alien society.

Archbishop Feehan, who understood the interrelationship between faith and nationalism, encouraged the formation of national parishes to prevent leakage. Although the jurisdictional, personnel, and financial problems attendant to the tripling of the number of parishes were great, he held the system together by his flexibility and adaptability. He placed loyal and capable men in the chancery, selected a "balanced ticket" for his advisory council, shared his authority with religious-order superiors, and encouraged initiative on the local level.

However, despite his efforts, Feehan encountered formidable challenges because of the alien character of the Church's membership. His structure of governance, while preserving immigrant culture, opened the door to the growth of blind nationalism. Some groups exerted pressure to obtain special recognition and power within the Church—at times to the detriment of its catholicity. Also, the conservative and foreign character of the Church prompted nativists and reformers to question the Americanism of the immigrants, their religion, and institutions. The parochial school, the focal point of parish life, came under the strongest attack.

3. Nativism

THE DEATH OF GENERAL Philip Sheridan in 1888 evoked sadness and hope among the Catholics of his adopted city, Chicago. Because this Civil War hero, a Catholic and an Irish-American, held the esteem of all citizens, he demonstrated that a Catholic might be called to the highest position of rank and authority if he were, as the *Catholic Home* editorialized, "first and last, an American citizen." Stirred by the praises sung to the deceased general, the *Home* noted:

> We commend the example of General Sheridan to those who are disposed to think that the American people are prejudiced against Catholics on account of their religion. The truth is, the American people care not whether a man be a Catholic, Jew, Turk, or infidel, provided he be an honest man and attend to his own business.[1]

In 1888 there seemed little reason to believe that a man's religion would hinder him in his plans for public office. Catholics, furthermore, were taking a greater part in Chicago's government than ever before.[2] Shortly after the November elections, *Home* stated that the spirit of Know Nothingism, which had engulfed the city before the Civil War, was dead, never to rise again, and predicted that any society of bigots which attempted to "rake out of the ashes of oblivion the un-American spirit of intolerance which characterized that disgraceful period of our history will be the scorn of every true American citizen."[3]

Prognostication is always risky. Only the week before pronouncing the death of Know Nothingism, the editor of the *Home* had taken the Republican party to task as "narrow, sour, and bigoted" and the "legitimate successor of the Know-Nothings who tarred and feathered priests and burned convents." He also argued that the anti-Catholic *Chicago Tribune* was no better; it had moderated its criticism of the pope and Chicago's Catholics only because election time was at hand.[4]

54

Although this criticism of the Republican party and its organ reflected the political leanings of the *Catholic Home,* which was directed to an Irish readership, there was good reason for concern about proscription and discrimination.

As the loss of confidence prior to the Civil War had nourished nativist traditions, so did the period between the Haymarket riot of 1886 and the Spanish-American War, when Americans sought the causes of events which seemed to jeopardize the nation's future. This period of history, if not traumatic, was at least a serious challenge to the Chicago Catholic Church's respectable identity in the Garden City. For the first time in forty years, Catholics faced the assaults of not just a few fanatical cranks but a large number of the citizenry. They were to see their treasured institution, the parochial school, again come under attack, as well as feel discrimination in their political, social, and economic life. The traditions of anti-Catholicism and anti-foreignism blended in Chicago, where the ever-growing Catholic Church was predominantly foreign in constituency. Disillusioned and anxious Americans perceived their religious convictions, Old World traditions, and New World behavior as a threat to the future well-being of the United States. To meet the crisis, the fearful waged an emotional campaign to save the flag, the Constitution, and "the little red schoolhouse."

Industrialization, urbanization, and the concentration of capital destroyed old and familiar relationships and created new problems that caused Americans to question their country's ability to maintain its equilibrium. They had been able to pride themselves on the nation's lack of basic socio-economic cleavages and rigid class structure because continuous economic growth and westward expansion had dissolved restraints on the individual. However, in the 1880s, many Americans awoke to the realization that the nation's horizons were permanently contracting. Strikes and mass boycotts in the second half of the 1880s, and violence, crime, squalor, corruption, and chaos in the major cities, where foreign-born elements congregated in unassimilated masses, impelled native Americans to look for the causes of this rending of the social fabric. In this period of massive and recurring discontent, when monopoly and plutocracy cast darkening shadows over the prospects of American society, and the opportunity to escape westward seemed to diminish, John Higham finds the rebirth of nativism as a significant force in America.[5]

The people most affected by social and economic change were not strikers, or those whom they struck, but those who fell between these contending forces. Small businessmen, nonunionized workers, and white-collar personnel were, by their very "in betweenness," most shaken. They sought to recapture a lost homogeneity and to preserve the ideals by which they lived and which, they believed, made them true Americans. In their search, they turned to patriotic societies, such as the Order of United American Mechanics, the Junior Order United American Mechanics, and the Patriotic Order Sons of America, or they formed new ones. Through these societies they preached against plutocratic capitalists and foreign radicals of the likes of anarchist Johann Most.

Playing on the theme of "imported" radicalism, they also lashed out against the "despotic Romanist threat." Despite the temperate leadership of Cardinal James Gibbons nationally and Archbishop Patrick Augustine Feehan locally, some of these patriotic groups predicted imminent danger if "foreign clerical tyranny" were permitted to continue. For the "in betweens," who sought the comfort of homogeneity, the common school was idealized as the surest means of imparting appreciation of American values and conformity. The rapid multiplication of parochial schools, which taught allegiance to a foreign authority and preserved the immigrant's Old World identity, was viewed as a challenge to the little red schoolhouse. Even though the Catholic conviction that the state should contribute to the upkeep of Church-related educational systems could not be realized under the Constitution, nativists believed such systems were a menace to America. As one patriotic leader noted: "According to the principle under which they [Catholic children] are educated, they will vote every time to support the Roman Catholic Church against the state."[6] Self-righteously, Chicago's patriotic societies agitated for the preservation of American ideals and institutions through the common school, more rigorous naturalization laws, and immigration restriction.

The Catholic Church, through its leaders, both clerical and lay, responded to the charges of un-Americanism in word and deed. The first significant conflict was a result of passage of a controversial compulsory education law.

When the American Catholic hierarchy met in plenary session in Baltimore in 1884, it took up the question of leakage (loss of membership) and recommended a comprehensive system of education as one solution. In America, no tradition supported maintenance of the Catholic faith, and competition with other sects and a growing spirit of materialism were taking their toll. To preserve the faith, the bishops urged a complete educational program and (in their pastoral letter) explained their goal to the laity, who would have to support it. "In days like ours," the bishops wrote, when error is so pretentious and aggressive, everyone needs to be completely armed as possible with sound knowledge,—not only the clergy, but the people also, that they may be able to withstand the noxious influence of popularized irreligion.[7]

Expanding on the educational theme, they stated that civilization must rest on sound popular instruction. In their mind, a "sound" education develops what is best in man and makes him "not only clever but good." The American practice of relegating religion to home and church could only train a generation that divorced religion from the "practical business of real life" and thus threatened American civilization. Without religion, they held, morality would soon decay, leading to degeneration of the body and the mind; all that would remain would be the amoral Darwinian struggle for existence. Lest their motives be misinterpreted, the bishops declared that their support of denominational schools was not antagonistic to the state but, on the contrary, "an honest endeavor to give the State better citizens, by making them better Christians."

The pastoral letter acknowledged that the public schools, as organized, could not give a Christian education because it did not lie within the state's province to teach religion. However, friends of Christian education followed their conscience when they sent their children to denominational schools, where religion has its rightful place and influence. To this end, the bishops called not only for the multiplication of Catholic schools but the perfection of those already existent. Unequivocally, the pastoral letter stated: "No parish is complete till it has schools adequate to the needs of its children, and the pastor and people of such a parish should not feel that they have accomplished their duty until the want is supplied." A pastor without a parochial school was likened to a general without an army.[8]

Archbishop Feehan convened the first Archdiocesan Synod on December 13, 1887, in the Cathedral of the Holy Name, to promulgate the directives of the Third Plenary Council and to formulate a diocesan constitution based on its decrees. In the matter of education, the synod adhered to the Baltimore rulings by making it incumbent upon a pastor to "act energetically" in establishing a parish school.[9] All parents were directed to send their children to the parish school, unless they could show "sufficient cause"—and obtained the archbishop's approval—for doing otherwise.[10] Finally, a board of examiners was appointed to ensure that the diocesan regulations were carried out. The commission was divided territorially (North Side, West Side, South Side) and linguistically (German, Polish, Bohemian) to guarantee communication and understanding.[11]

The archbishop, with his pastors, exhorted parents to send their children to parish schools so that the gift of faith might be preserved.[12] Feehan's belief that the Catholic school was the best means to fill churches in the future was explained by the *Catholic Home:*

> A public school system that leaves religion and morality out of its course of training might be good enough if there were no hereafter, no heaven to be won, no hell to shun, no soul to be saved or lost and if man's first duty in life were not to love and serve God and thus secure his eternal salvation. Here is the starting-point and fundamental principle of education for everyone who believes in God and in the revelation of our Lord Jesus Christ. To surrender this principle to the secularists is a practical denial of religion and logically leads to atheism.[13]

Chicago's Catholics, stimulated by the common-school movement of the 1850s, early valued parochial education. In 1880, twenty-nine of the city's thirty-one parishes had schools, with total enrollment of 16,713 children. Increased immigration during the '80s strained the ability of parishes and schools to accommodate the growing population, but progress was made. By 1890, sixty-two of eighty-one parishes had schools, with a total enrollment of 31,053.[14] Under the direction of Archbishop Feehan, clergy and laity endeavored to carry out the directives of the Third Plenary Council and the diocesan constitution.

Catholic parents honored the bishops' joint pastoral mandate of 1884 and the continued exhortation of the local clergy, not solely to ensure the eternal salvation of their children but also to preserve the cultural traditions that were bound up in their religion.[15] Immigrant parents confidently sent their children to the parish school because it was administered by their own priest and conducted by religious men and women who, unlike public school teachers, had received their training in Old World ways. These teachers could be trusted to inspire godly fear and wholesomeness, and love of the homeland, as well as to foster the language of their ancestors, which was often the parents' only medium of communication. The parish school served to cushion alienation between generations, which resulted from immigration, by teaching children to appreciate the sometimes unfathomable ways of their parents. The importance of the parochial school is perhaps best exemplified by the Polish experience. In 1886 the *Chicago Tribune* stated that as little as 10 percent of Polish children went to public schools, "and then only after they have attended the church school and learned the principles of creed and patriotism in the mother tongue."[16]

While Catholic parents sacrificed to build parochial schools, other forces were working to impede their success and, if possible, destroy their schools. Some native Americans, sensing danger as a result of widening social chasms, urban chaos, and the rending of familiar patterns of life, believed that Catholic "superstition," ultramontanism, and authoritarianism created a peril for America. To these persons the parochial school was a threat—it subjected young minds to un American and possibly "radical" tenets and promoted allegiance to a foreign power. It was in this atmosphere that the Illinois legislature passed a compulsory school bill with provisions that threatened the independence and continued growth of parochial schools.

In 1889 a second compulsory education law, referred to as the Edward's Law (after its author, Richard Edwards), put Catholic education on the defensive. The first compulsory education law (passed in 1883), contained inadequate provisions for fulfillment of its intent, and within a few years its failure to improve school attendance became apparent; therefore the friends of compulsory education did not hesitate to declare for more effective legislation. The Chicago School Board, spurred on by the Chicago's Women's Club, established a special committee to investigate the problem of nonattendance. The Committee on Compulsory Education, supported and advised by Chicago reformers, drafted a bill that was submitted in the lower house in January 1889.[17]

Almost simultaneously, Richard Edwards, Republican state superintendent of public instruction, heeded advice in Governor Joseph Fifer's inaugural address, drafted a similar compulsory education bill, and had it submitted in the upper house. Edwards, an apostle of universal education in the Yankee minister tradition, was born in Wales in 1822, grew up in Ohio, and embarked on an educational career. His early years were spent teaching and administering "normal" schools in Massachusetts and also as an agent of that state's board of education, which was under the direction of Horace Mann. At Mann's suggestion, Edwards had gone to the Midwest to crusade for popular education. In 1862, after five years of normal-school work in St. Louis, he went to Normal University in Normal, Illinois. For the next fourteen years he taught and served as president of that institution. In 1876 Edwards tendered his resignation to become pastor of the Owen Lovejoy Congregational Church in Princeton, Illinois, where he remained until he went to Knox College, in 1885. The following year, at the behest of universal education advocates, he ran for, and won, the office of the superintendent of education.[18]

Increased crime rates by the jobless young, unscrupulous sweatshop practices, and desire for an informed electorate were given as reasons for the passage of an educational reform measure.[19] However, as the legislative session neared adjournment, both bills merely gathered dust. Then, on May 23, 1889, the Chicago school board's Committee on Compulsory Education, led by Frederick W. Foch, Jr., a German Lutheran, began to lobby for passage of its bill and obtained a modified version of the Edwards bill. Cajoling and conniving, the Chicago committee set a record for the fastest passage and signing of legislation ever recorded. On May 24, Governor Fifer signed "An Act concerning the Education of Children," and congratulated Foch and his protegés for their assistance.[20] Many legislators did not seem to realize the scope and implications of the bill they voted into law, but they would soon be made aware of them.

The law, intended to ensure every youth a minimum education, contained two controversial clauses. First, every person who had a child between ages 7 and 14 was compelled to send the child to a public day school for at least sixteen weeks of each year, under penalty of paying a fine of $20, which would go to the public school in the city or district in which the offender resided. Almost as an afterthought, the law provided an exception:

> But if the person so neglecting shall show to the satisfaction of the board of education or of directors that such child has attended for a like period of time, a private day school, *approved by the board of education or directors of the city, town or district in which such child resides,* or that instruction has otherwise been given for like period of time to such child in the branches commonly taught in the public school . . . that shall not be incurred.[21]

The second controversial stipulation was that, for the first time, parochial as well as public schools were required to teach the elementary subjects of learning in the English language. According to the law, "no school shall be regarded as a school under this act unless there shall be taught therein in the English language, reading, writing, history of the United States, and geography."[22]

Prior to passage of the bill, some resistance to the English-language provision was registered. A quiet attempt was made in the interests of private schools, where instruction was given in foreign tongues, to have the words "in the English language" struck from the bill.[23] The use of foreign languages in the schools had been a problem for a long time, and the rise of nativist tendencies caused many to suspect the loyalty of parochial schools, even though English was generally used for the enumerated subjects. On this issue the legislators held fast, as the opposition did not show enough strength.[24]

Although the opposition to the Edwards Law has been viewed as a reaction of Lutherans and Catholics to the English-language clause, a more fundamental issue was involved.[25] The *Catholic Home,* Chicago's only English-language Catholic paper, had early taken note of Superintendent Edwards' school bill and warned all patrons and friends of parochial and private schools to alert themselves to its scope and spirit. While the bill awaited action, the paper called on all pastors to take immediate action, as it would be easier to prevent mischievous legislation than to remedy it. The editor stated his views on the purpose of the bill and its supporters:

> It means State control; of all schools, private and parochial as well as public. This compulsory school law is the entering wedge whereby the State is to force its way into every schoolhouse in the State, and subject its management and its pupils to the despotic control of State agents and State machinery.

Those who supported the bill were characterized as "tinkerers" possessed with the spirit of state paternalism, "the meanest type of tyranny," who sought to invade the private schools and exhibit their contemptuous disregard for the rights of parents and conscience.[26]

The failure of Catholics to act on this warning could be attributed to the lack of time necessary to organize and lobby effectively. In time, however, the arguments expressed in this editorial would provide the basis of the Catholic protest. In neighboring Wisconsin, the Bennett Law, which was similar in nature to the Illinois law and enacted the same year, fomented a heated controversy that further alerted Chicago Catholics to the implications of the Edwards Law.[27] The new right of school districts to judge the competency of private educational institutions did not pose a serious threat in Chicago, where Catholics were the predominant religious group, but the principle of the state's right to dictate to and control parochial schools was perceived as dangerous because the Illinois legislature was largely Anglo-Saxon Protestant. Catholics were aware of the growing sentiment that blamed their institutions for impeding assimilation, and they acted to safeguard them by a show of strength.

In the verbal battle between supporters and opponents of the law, the Catholic position rested on a principle. If the Catholic campaign were to succeed, it must enlist the support of all Catholics and friends of private schools, as well as avoid feeding anti-Catholic and anti-foreign feelings. The language issue affected Germans, Poles, Bohemians, and other Continental groups, but it was not fully appreciated by the Irish and more assimilated Catholics. The heart of the Catholic position rested on parental rights, a theologically defensible position which could draw the support of all Catholics and mesh with the tenets of German Lutherans. The only resolution of the school controversy would come, the *Catholic Home* believed, when the fundamental principle of the God-given duty of parents to see to their children's education was recognized and respected. To this end, Catholics stressed that the education of a child is delegated by God to parents and that, as it is a duty, it is also a right. For the state to interfere with this right is a contravention of God's will.[28] The fundamental error of the law was the false supposition that children belong to the state.

Thus the Catholic position stood on principle and not on the issue of language. The *Catholic Home* admitted the state's right to legislate the use of English and counseled Catholics not to protest the language provision. It warned an influential Wisconsin German Catholic paper that it was standing on a "very narrow platform" when it decried the language clause of the Bennett Law:

> If there is no principle involved, other than the requiring of a certain amount of instruction in the English language, those who are not German will find it hard to understand the attitude of opposition the Germans have assumed. We are sorry to see in a German Catholic paper the foolish statement that "the learning of English leads to immorality and infidelity." We are entirely unwilling to believe that the faith and morality of the German Catholics are so bound up with the German language as to be lost when translated into English. It seems to us a mistake to make an issue on the mere question of language.[29]

As in Wisconsin, Illinois Catholics found the issue of parental rights a uniting bond with German Lutherans, who conducted more than 200 schools, enrolling nearly 20,000 students, and who were unwilling to submit passively to the threatening power of the new law.[30] Shortly after the passage of the compulsory school law, the Illinois District of the Lutheran Missouri Synod issued a conciliatory statement recognizing the state's unquestionable right to safeguard adolescents and promote the common good through compulsory attendance. But it added:

> The ready concession of this right, however, does not obligate us to approve of such of its regulations for the extension of the common educational program as would be inconvenient and oppressive for us or endanger our religious liberty.[31]

The district held that its schools were maintained in the interest of the state as well as the church, and thus it would be unfair to disturb or destroy them.[32]

Quick to see a potential ally, the *Catholic Home* supported the Lutherans as clearly within their rights to resent and oppose state paternalism. The editor wrote:

> Our Lutheran friends . . . are entirely in the right when they say to these busybodies, "hands off! These are our schools! We will educate our children as we prefer; our right to educate them is not derived from you, is independent of you—comes to us from a source higher than you."[33]

Throughout the controversy, the *Home* continued to defend the Lutherans and commend them for their work in protecting constitutional liberties.[34]

The Catholic position was assaulted for confusing the state's right to demand compulsory education with the belief that the state could dictate a citizen's creed. Joseph Medill's *Chicago Tribune* made light of Catholic logic and pointed to the protection in matters of religion afforded by the Constitution.[35] The paper held that the safety of the people is the supreme law—and not the "natural right" of parents to spoil the lives of their children, or "liberty of conscience" that sets the whims of the individual above the law. The state, it said, must protect the child from ignorance so that he or she could become an intelligent, Americanized citizen.[36] The nativist *Tribune* feared that Catholics had set out to destroy the public school system by multiplying and expanding their parochial schools.[37] It warned the Catholic hierarchy that continued peaceful relations between Catholics and other Americans were jeopardized by the formers' insistence on parochial education. The episcopal directive that parents withdraw their children from the public school, so they could be "un-Americanize[d]," the Republican paper counseled, must be rescinded.[38]

When the Wisconsin bishops issued a lengthy pastoral letter, denouncing the Bennett Law as unnecessary, offensive, and unjust, the *Tribune* was quick to respond.[39] The prelates were taken to task for setting themselves above the law and the Church above the state, at the pope's direction. The paper considered their pastoral letter a species of foreign meddling in American domestic affairs.[40] By making a political issue of the law, the bishops raised the question whether the politics of the state were to be run by Rome:

> In Illinois and Wisconsin a contest between the supporters and enemies of the American free schools, between the right of Americans to make their own laws and the claim of an Italian priest living in Rome that he has the power to nullify them, can

have but one termination—the defeat of such arrogance and presumption.[41]

However, the *Tribune*'s assumption that Catholic "arrogance" would be crushed was premature. Catholic voters allied with German Lutherans and set out to bring about the repeal of the compulsory education law. The struggle was intense, as reformers, friends of compulsory attendance, and nativists joined to thwart the demands of the advocates of private schools and parental rights. A major shift in Illinois party politics was the result.

The great majority of Chicago Catholics were loyal Democrats because of the party's tradition of accepting their alien background and religion. Indeed, Catholics formed the backbone of the Chicago Democratic organization. German Lutherans, however, tended to align themselves with the Republican party, whose pre–Civil War abolitionism and postwar conservatism reflected their ideals and interests. Since 1856, the Republicans, supported by German Lutherans, had held sway over Illinois politics, but the compulsory school law threatened to disrupt this traditional alliance. Both parties saw the political opportunities and dangers created by the Edwards Law and tried to take stands that would ensure electoral victory.

When the Democratic State Central Committee met in March 1890, it was informed that Germans who had previously supported the Republican party would vote Democratic if the committee would include a platform plank supporting repeal of the Edwards Law. The *Tribune* observed that it would be foolhardy for Democrats to make an issue of compulsory education since they would lose two votes for every one they gained. It reasoned that the Democrats already had all, or most, Catholic and many German votes, but would lose the support of Anglo-Saxons. For this reason, Medill's paper anounced that the Republicans would be happy to have the Edwards Law as an issue.[42]

Republican smugness soon vanished, with the Democratic mayoral victory in Milwaukee, where Lutherans supported an anti-Bennett Law Democrat endorsed by their clergy. "How long this queer mixture of oil and water will stay together," the *Tribune* editorialized, "it is impossible to guess, but the time will come when the Lutherans will discover that they are merely catspaws of their old antagonists."[43] Because the Republican paper was unwilling to accede to a similar alliance in Illinois, it promptly alerted German Lutherans to the danger of cooperation with Democrats and acquiesced to an amendment of the hated law. The editor stressed that it was unreasonable to blame Republicans for the compulsory attendance law since the bill had been passed by German Lutherans and German Catholics, Republicans and Democrats alike.[44]

On April 14, 1890, thirty-five Chicago-area Lutheran congregations declared against the new power granted the school boards. This
was soon followed by a meeting of the German Lutheran District of
Illinois, which toughened its opposition and circulated pamphlets
critical of the hostility toward private and parochial schools and the
infringement of individual conscience.[45] Shortly afterward, the
Tribune's hard stand on the compulsory education law gave way to
support for the Lutherans' "reasonable" demand for amendment, and
went so far as to encourage prompt action by a special legislative
session. The Republicans wanted to dispose of the law as a political
issue.[46]

The Illinois Democratic convention, assembled in Springfield on
June 4, 1890, adopted a plank that upheld parental rights in educational matters. While granting the state the right to demand compulsory education, the convention declared:

> To determine and direct the education of the child is a natural
> right of parents. There arises out of this parental right the duty to
> provide education. . . .
>
> For the education of his child one parent may select the
> public, another may select the private or denominational school
> . . . and for doing which he need offer neither excuses nor
> apology.
>
> The public and private or denominational schools are in law
> neither related, nor are they subordinate to the other, nor need
> they be antagonistic.[47]

When, later that month, the Republican convention assembled in
Springfield, it also declared its opposition to "any arbitrary interference with the rights of parents and guardians to educate their children
in private schools." Its platform called for immediate repeal of sections
of the law which provided for state supervision of private schools.[48]

But the special legislative session failed to amend the Edwards
Law, and it became an election issue in the fall. Democrats blamed
Republicans for the law, demanded its repeal, and nominated Heinrich Raab for superintendent of public instruction. They believed that
Raab, a German-immigrant educator from Belleville, Illinois, who had
been elected to that office in 1882 but declined renomination in 1886,
would attract the German vote and be inoffensive because of his
commendable record for freedom from partisanship as an administrator.[49] The Republicans stressed the need for an amended compulsory school law, renominated Richard Edwards, and declared the
sacredness of the public school system.

Religion and ethnicity became important factors in the election of

1890. Quakers, Baptists, and Congregationalists saw the Lutheran and Catholic advocates of parental rights as enemies of the common-school system, and their organizations pledged support to the public schools.[50] In September 1890, several patriotic orders, including the American Protective Association (which later became the chief nativist organization in the country), joined hands in forming the Committee of One Hundred to preserve the little red schoolhouse. The committee, which claimed 18,000 supporters among its member societies, assailed the Catholic and Lutheran school systems for impeding Americanization and fostering alien attachments.[51] "The public school is the chief Americanizing institution of this country," Rev. H. G. Jackson of Chicago Centenary Church declared in a sermon. "There the plastic mind of the youth receives the impressions of love and loyalty that make of him a patriotic defender of his country's liberties. The public school is the child of the State, and no church whatsoever should have a word to say respecting its government."[52] The Sunday before the election, numerous Protestant congregations were warned of the Catholic threat to the common school and were urged to vote to protect the system—and by implication the Republican ticket.[53]

Richard Edwards, who was slated for reelection, took to the stump to defend himself and explain his commitment to the public school system. In an address, "Stand by Our Free Schools and Our Flag" (delivered at Carrollton, Illinois, on October 18, 1890), he called attention to the positive effects of his law and asked for support, lest the law be changed. The year prior to the passage of the law, Illinois school enrollment had decreased, he explained, but the year after its enactment, public school enrollment increased by 16,454 and private schools by 6,729 new students. For this reason, he felt he could call on all friends of education to support this concept of compulsory education, though emendation of particulars was justified. He then attacked the critics who, he believed, were using opposition to the controversial law to disguise their real intent—destruction of the public school system:

> Opposition to this law is born of opposition to the free school. I do not affirm that all who have been led into this opposition by designing men are enemies of the free schools, but I do affirm that the animating principle of this opposition comes from that source. I do affirm that the scheming managers of the movement are enemies of the free schools. And I, therefore, affirm that the free schools are in danger. This opposition is a blow aimed at our educational system. It comes from men who would say to the families of the land, "If you want to educate your children, you

must pay for it to some private corporation or some private person." It comes from those who are distressed because they are compelled to pay a school tax, especially, when the money is used for education of some other persons' children. There are men in our land who are not favorable to the idea of general intelligence. There are men who dislike to see the people sufficiently well educated to be their own guides in politics and religion. These are opposed to the free schools, and they are availing themselves of this senseless clamor against the compulsory education law to do what they can to break up our system.

Against such, my friends, may I not appeal to you? Stand for the free school system. Stand for that universal intelligence that makes the people fit to rule. Stand for the culture that uplifts the entire race and does not tend to give power to a class.[54]

While Protestant ministers and Republicans supported Richard Edwards, Catholics and Lutherans supported candidates pledged to repeal. Although Archbishop Feehan made no recorded announcement, some of his priests used their pulpits to assail the Edwards Law, and the *Catholic Home* waged its battle for parental rights.[55] Less than a week before the election, at a banquet honoring the archbishop's twenty-fifth year in the episcopacy, Judge Thomas A. Moran praised the thorough education given to 43,000 youths in the diocese's schools and congratulated the jubilarian for the success of the educational system. He then commented on the school question. Those who believed that Catholic schools were in some manner dangerous to American institutions did so, he believed, "out of an abundance of their ignorance, and . . . bigotry against the Catholic faith," and no amount of reasoning would convince these "fanatical . . . enemies of religion and morality." He assured the guest of honor that Catholics were cognizant of the issues and ready to preserve what they had created:

> The intelligent and patriotic Catholic citizen has reached the conviction that securing to the rising generation the education that is imparted in these schools is the surest guarantee of the permanent preservation of our free institutions. To preserve civil liberty a people must have and practice the virtues, which exist only where morality is based on religion.
>
> Our people have made sacrifices for the establishment and maintenance of these schools. They will continue to support, increase and preserve them; they know how to resent and how to prevent any impertinent interference with the control or management of these, their schools, no matter from what direction

that attempt is made, and however specious may be the pretext for interference.[56]

The German Lutherans waged a more organized campaign to defeat Richard Edwards. The school committee sent circulars to all German Lutheran pastors, stressing the urgent need to defeat the Republican candidate and to support Heinrich Raab. Candidates for the state legislature who were known to support repeal were listed and recommended.[57] In Chicago, the Lutheran Evangelical School Committee sponsored a mass meeting and demonstration at the Second Regiment Armory Hall, highlighted by impassioned speeches against the school law and the playing of German melodies.[58] The Democratic candidate stumped the city, attending as many as three protest rallies a night to condemn the law and its author.[59]

The election proved that parochial education interests were unanimous in their opposition to Richard Edwards: Raab won by a plurality of 35,000.[60] John W. Cook, president of Illinois State Normal University, writing his friend and mentor Richard Edwards, lamented that the most important education legislation in twenty years had not received adequate support. "Was there ever," he exclaimed, "so senseless a Campaign! Prejudice and race feelings have seemed to exclude every atom of reason. Talking to a stone wall was a highly profitable employment when compared with a conversation with the average German on the subject of compulsory education and your relation to it."[61] Similar sentiments were voiced by other partisan friends. George P. Brown, of Public School Publishing Company, said the Republican campaign had not been vigorous enough, and defeat came because of the unity of Germanism, ecclesiasticism, Raab's cries "for the Fatherland," and ignorant foreigners "who were voted by the priests like sheep."[62]

The election also affected the composition of the state legislature: Republicans maintained control of the senate but the Democrats prevailed in the house of representatives.[63] As a result of this split in the 1891 General Assembly, the Edwards Law was not repealed. The repeal proposal, approved in the Democratic controlled house, failed in the senate because it did not stipulate the teaching of certain subjects in English. The senate bill, which called for the simple repeal of school board jurisdiction over private schools, was killed in a house committee.[64] Neither party would compromise; hence the issue would have to go before the electorate again in 1892.

The *Tribune* was angered by the Democratic "demagogues" who played for the immigrant vote by bartering away American institutions. "They want American children to be taught exclusively in

Bohemian, German, Italian, Hungarian, Russian, French, Spanish, or Arabic by teachers employed by priests belonging to those nationalities, who are seeking to perpetuate foreignism, alienism, and un-Americanism in this country."[65] Republicans railed against Democrats because they had voted against their bill, and claimed that the Democratic opposition was attempting to keep the sectarian issue alive for the 1892 campaign.[66]

Although the Committee of One Hundred lost the election in 1890, its animating spirit remained vital. One driving force, stimulating concern for preservation of the common school, was Rev. Oliver E. Murray of the Wabash Avenue Methodist Church. Murray, an English immigrant, born of a Romanist father, whom he hated, and a Protestant mother, whom he loved, lamented that he had not been born in America.[67] In a series of "Americanist" lectures, presented each Sunday afternoon with a different "patriotic" leader presiding,[68] he gave play to his anti-Catholic hostility and his desire to be considered an American patriot. In these lectures he warned his ever-growing audience to stand prepared to defeat the "black Pope," a "chameleon of circumstances,"assuming all garbs and speaking all languages and "exceedingly active in this land."[69] The little red schoolhouse became as potent a symbol as the flag and the American eagle. With the fervor of a revivalist, Murray asked his listeners to lay down their lives for its gentle yet essential influence, on which American liberty depended.

For Murray and his followers, Catholicism was first and last a dangerous evil that threatened the nation's destiny. The Methodist preacher's special Washington Day address, "The Spirit of Washington," was remarkable for its staging, showmanship, and message. Standing on a flag-bedecked platform in the church sanctuary, with a model of a little red schoolhouse mounted on a pedestal that was draped in red, white, and blue bunting, he warned his audience of the dangers of Rome. He showed them a large cartoon of the Statute of Liberty, lighting the globe from New York Harbor; at the statue's feet were the Constitution and Washington's "I can not tell a lie" hatchet, and behind the statue the great, gaunt arms of Pope Leo XIII stretched from across the ocean, holding a gigantic papal tiara that threatened to descend and extinguish the Goddess of Liberty's light, as one might snuff a candle. His audience perceived the relationship between Liberty's enlightening torch and the "sacred model" at the speaker's side. Never would they permit the flickering tapers of Catholicism to replace the steady flame of American democracy, emanating from the common school.[70]

Through his revivalistic addresses, the publication *The Patriot, an Advocate of Americanism,* and the National American Patriotic Union,

Murray gave his followers a mission and sense of fellowship. He introduced his magazine as a résponse to a "long-felt need" to give Americans "just recognition" because "beggars from across the sea, talking foreignism, receive every attention."[71] NAPU extracted a pledge from its members to promote patriotism and defend American institutions, in return for a sense of importance. And for his work, Murray was able to glory in the sobriquets "bigot," "hypocrite," and "know-nothing," bestowed upon him by the *Catholic Home*.[72]

Murray was buttressed by other Protestant ministers who preached on the common-school issue with religious zeal. Rev. David Benton, pastor of Lincoln Park Congregational Church, warned against the persistence of national identity fostered in parochial schools. "Men cannot," he stated, "think American thoughts in other than the American language. It cannot be done in any foreign language — in any other than the language of liberty."[73] Similarly, the pastor of the Ada Street Methodist Episcopal Church, in a service for Grand Army of the Republic members, denounced legislators who threatened the common school. Pointing to a model of the little red schoolhouse hanging from the belfry, he declared: "We do not object to sectarian teaching. Neither do we plead for a common religion, but we do plead for a common school with one common language."[74]

In 1892, Illinois Democrats again played on the school question, and selected for their spokesman and gubernatorial candidate John Peter Altgeld, a German-immigrant judge and defender of working people. Early in the campaign, Altgeld blamed Governor Fifer and his Republican supporters for the odious law, and continued to hammer on this issue. The Democrats contended that the only way to repeal the law was to follow the example of their Wisconsin neighbors, who by electing a Democratic majority, had disposed of the Bennett Law.[75]

As the election approached, the Catholic bishops of Illinois took counsel together over the problems raised by the Edwards Law and decided to issue a joint pastoral letter to clarify the Church's position. They defended the right and necessity of parents to provide their children a Christian education, according to the directives of the plenary council of 1884. The bishops acknowledged that they represented a minority view, and stated that

> in our country those who believe that Education is essentially religious, seem at present, to be a minority; but we are persuaded that all christians, who have seriously meditated on the subject, know that we and those, who in this agree with us, are right. The arguments of our opponents are arguments of expediency; but

when there is a question of the highest human interests, what is true and right is also the most expedient.

Illinois Catholics were commended for their faith and generosity, despite their grave inconvenience in supporting two school systems. Archbishop Feehan and his suffragan bishops noted that there was no escape from the double burden of law and conscience. However, they hoped the day would come when Catholics would be free from the unjust tax that was levied against them.[76]

Finally, the bishops condemned the Edwards Law as "an insidious and unjust law, under which the pretext of zeal for popular education, is really a violation of our most sacred rights, as men and citizens." They explained that freedom of worship implies freedom of education, and that to violate one was to void the other. Those who favored this violation of the Constitution, they said, were "unworthy of the support of enlightened and fair-minded voters." "Let us use all right and honorable means to have it repealed, and let the designing and bigoted be taught that the West is not a field in which their labor will bear fruit."[77]

The pastoral letter also announced establishment of the *New World,* a weekly Catholic newspaper, as the official medium of the bishops of Illinois, through which priests and laity might be informed of the developments of the Edwards Law struggle, as well as other matters touching on the Church. In its first issue, the *New World* carried the text of the pastoral letter on education. Throughout the fall, the paper sustained the position of the bishops and supported the Lutherans.[78]

Illinois Lutherans had also taken cognizance of the issues in the forthcoming election. In the 1892 session, the Illinois District of the Missouri Synod resolved to support only candidates who pledged themselves to repeal or modification of the compulsory education law. Its school committee examined the platforms of both parties in detail and found that Republicans and Democrats alike supported repeal of the public supervision of private schools. But because the Republicans were again backing Richard Edwards, the author of the hated law, and because Governor Fifer had publicly attacked the principles upon which objections had been raised, and had criticized parochial schools, the committee declared in favor of the Democratic party and its candidates as the safest and best course.[79]

The *Chicago Tribune* saw its party's chances for electoral victory slipping away, and worked desperately to secure votes. It assured Catholics that they had no need to fear, for the next legislature would repeal the law ("which was passed innocently enough, receiving the votes of both parties, but which turned out to contain some provisions which were the work of educational cranks"), and it pointed to the Republican platform, which promised to protect parochial schools. It would not consent, however, to the bishops' protest against taxation, because it meant abandonment of the century-old policy of separation of church and state.[80]

While the *Tribune* tried to garner support from the more Americanized Catholics, it simultaneously wooed the Lutherans. Its editorials told Lutherans that because their official position was to oppose the Edwards Law, but not to avoid paying taxes, they had little in common with Catholics. It flattered them by adding that "Americans generally would be gratified if the leaders of the Roman Catholic Church instead of reviving memories of old and bitter controversies, would take a leaf out of the book of the disciples of Martin Luther, and pay school taxes, not with a protest, but with pleasure and as a patriotic duty."[81] The *Tribune* also warned them that they would suffer grievously at the hands of the Democrats, who were tricking them into wasting their vote.

The Republican effort failed; Lutheran ministers supported the Democrats from the pulpit. All Germans, Catholic and Lutheran, were called on to unite for a common cause.[82] In a leading article, the *Illinois Staats Zeitung* claimed that God was on the side of the Democrats: "Now, God's helping hand reaches to you, you Christian, in the Democratic Party. Do you not see it? O German Man, O German Christian—seize without delay, even with joy this helping hand of God."[83]

The Democrats scored a great victory at the polls. The combined efforts of German Lutherans and Catholics swept their entire slate into office and captured both houses of the general assembly. Chicago's predominantly German-populated wards, which had gone Republican in 1890, gave Democrats 60 percent of the vote. Less dramatic but equally telling returns in the Polish wards showed a 10 percent increase in the Democratic vote, giving Altgeld 72 percent of the ballots.[84] The *Chicago Tribune* attributed the success of the entire Democratic ticket to the unfamiliar "Australian ballot," which was first used in this election. Many voters, it believed, were afraid to spoil their ballot by splitting their vote, and therefore voted straight Democratic. Altgeld defeated Fifer by more than 19,000 votes, while Grover Cleveland gathered a 26,000 plurality. Their margin of victory came from Cook County, where Altgeld had a plurality of 30,389 and Cleveland 32,000.[85] It was the first time in forty years that a Democrat was governor of Illinois.

Postelection analyses of the Republican defeat varied, but the school issue seemed to have been a crucial factor. In an interview, the defeated governor stated that the national issue of the tariff and labor unrest were the major causes of the loss; he admitted there had been some German defection, but maintained it was not as great as supposed.[86] Nevertheless, there were others who thought the Edwards Law issue was the deciding factor. A prominent German Lutheran explained that three-fifths of the German Lutheran voters were Republicans, and nearly all of them voted for Altgeld. H. C. Zuttermeister, a member of the Lutheran school committee, declared:

> I am a Republican and have always voted the party ticket until this time. There was no excuse for bringing the school question in it at all. We warned the Republican party two years ago the questions must be settled or it would become an issue in the state campaign of '92.[87]

While Republicans lamented that German Lutheran preachers and teachers had mistakenly become missionaries of the Democratic party,[88] Catholics and Lutherans rejoiced in their victory. The *New World* editorialized that parental rights had been safeguarded and that secularists who would "snatch the child from the mother's bosom have been rebuked."[89] The *Illinois Staats Zeitung* called the election results "majestic," as the rights of parents would be protected.[90]

The new, Democrat-controlled assembly promptly repealed the Edwards Law. "An Act concerning the Education of Children," signed by Governor Altgeld on June 17, 1893, stated simply that parents must send their children to "some public or private school."[91] Gone were the English-language stipulation and the dominance of the local school board. Parochial schools were again free to develop.

The struggle to repeal the Edwards Law demonstrated the power of ethnic and religious factors in the political arena, as politicians often used ethnic and religious differences to play one group against another. However, the attack on the institution wherein ethnic and religious differences converged produced a vigorous reaction that ignored traditional party alignments. German Lutherans united with their former foes because they shared a mutual dedication with Catholics to a parent's right to preserve religion and national pride and ensure continuity between generations through parochial schools. That the Catholic–Lutheran alliance did not endure after repeal of the Edwards Law only serves to emphasize the force generated by the convergence of religious and ethnic interests. Illinois politicians would again play on group differences, but they were careful not to support legislation against immigrant institutions that were religiously affiliated. Politicians feared that immigrants' churches and schools would again become "political seminaries."[92]

Ironically, in the battle to preserve their national identity the immigrants were Americanized. Instead of submitting to the state, they resisted and learned the ways of participatory democracy. The repeal campaign schooled them in the need for vigilance, organization, and exercise of the franchise. It gave them experience in political organizing and coalition building and demonstrated that their diversity need not be an impediment to unity. Finally, the election of immigrant Altgeld and the repeal of the Edwards Law proved to them that they had a say in shaping their destinies and, thus, served to inspire greater loyalty to their adopted nation.

The Catholic Church also benefited from the repeal campaign. In Chicago, the Church had not been a monolith but a loose confederation of national churches, bound by a common faith. Most of its members had viewed themselves as German Catholics, Irish Catholics, Polish Catholics, and the like, and Archbishop Feehan used the discriminatory law to forge a unity based upon their Catholicity. Instead of focusing on the possibly devisive language issue, he stressed parental and religious rights. By fostering cooperation among all nationalities, he established himself as a leader, strengthened respect for his office, and gained the loyalty of his heterogeneous flock. What might have been a disaster for Chicago Catholicism became the first major step in creation of a supranational Catholic identity. But the repeal of the Edwards Law did not end nativist activity; rather, it stimulated hostility.

When the political and economic turmoil of the '90s convinced more and more people that America was coming unglued, the American Protective Association was seen by many as a ready and attractive vehicle of salvation. Avoiding the complex social and economic problems of the day, APA focused on "true Americanism" and attacked Catholicism as a "foreign enemy." By 1895 this Chicago-headquartered organization claimed 2.5 million members.[93] In Chicago, the APA, though associating with the common-school alliance, had played an inconspicuous part in the fight to save the Edwards Law. After the election of 1892, however, it became the dominant anti-Catholic force by publicizing "the Catholic menace."

Although the numerical strength of the Chicago membership is uncertain, there is no doubt about APA's intent: limitation of Catholic influence in politics. When Democrat Carter Harrison made his successful bid to recapture the mayoralty in 1893, he was opposed by APA because most Catholics supported him, but in this election its opposition had little impact.[94] However, when John Patrick Hopkins campaigned for the seat left vacant by the assassinated Harrison, anti-Catholicism boiled to a fever level. In the two weeks prior to the election, Hopkins was attacked from Protestant pulpits and smeared in an avalanche of campaign literature that played on the "Romanism" issue.[95] Hopkins won by only 1,290 votes.[96]

Catholic reaction to APA was unity in the face of adversity. Shortly after the Hopkins victory, the *New World* pointed out that suffering for a common faith had drawn all Catholics closer together.[97] And it was Archbishop Feehan's newspaper that assumed the task of cementing Catholic unity by exposing bigoted foes and their falsehoods, strengthening Catholic awareness of their rights, and counseling Catholics to abstain from behavior that evoked antipathy.

The *New World*'s policy of neutrality in partisan politics was tested by APA's alliance with the Republican party. When the nativists used the Republican platform to decry Catholicism, the paper trod carefully so as not to create anti-Catholics among deeply committed Republicans. However, it called upon the Republican party to clear itself of the suspicion of being allied with the "bastard Americanism" of the APA.[98] The *New World* even clashed with Archbishop John Ireland for his defense of the Republican party and his declaration that the party was not required to repudiate APA doctrines.[99]

The anti-alien sentiments of the Know Nothing period had not fully disappeared, and the Haymarket bombing of 1886 reignited the smoldering anti-foreignism. Although fear of socialists, communists, and anarchists had generally faded by 1892, all immigrants, because of their foreignness, had become suspect. Although numerous Catholics were thoroughly American, the Chicago Church was essentially "foreign" and thus viewed as a possible menace. After passage of the Edwards Law, Catholics grew exceedingly sensitive to anti-foreignism and regarded it as a covert variety of anti-Catholicism. The *New World* responded to allegations of disloyalty by citing demonstrations of Catholic loyalty and pointing out the material benefits that had accrued to the nation, and Chicago in particular, through the honest energy of immigrants.

When reformers and nativists expressed concern that many immigrants were easily swayed by national group interests and ignorance of the American democratic system, the *New World* shared their concern. It agreed that remedial action had to be taken, but opposed additional and stringent naturalization legislation. "What is necessary for citizenship," the editor argued, "is moral integrity, devotion to the principles of the republic; and these do not depend upon the place of one's birth or one's education."[100] Rather than take extreme measures, he asked that the courts prosecute ward heelers who violated the laws.[101] Consistently, the archdiocesan paper counseled Catholics to be good citizens, supported such reform measures as direct election of senators and civil service, and decried the "audacious unblushing defiance of public opinion and all sense of decency" exhibited by Chicago aldermen.[102]

As more and more Americans lost faith in America's ability to assimilate the growing number of eastern and southern Europeans, restrictive immigration legislation was proposed. Senator Henry Cabot Lodge (of Massachusetts) sponsored a literacy test bill that required that all immigrants, 16 years of age or older, be able to read. The literacy requirement was devised to discriminate against Slavic peoples, Italians, and Jews, without admitting racial bias. The Catholic Church, whose ranks were swelled by the new immigrants, attacked the Lodge bill as "unjust and discriminatory" and "narrow and un-American."[103]

Catholic optimism contrasted with nativist pessimism. The *New World*'s conception of America, presented in a feature article, "American Citizenship," was "a nation of many nationals." It embraced the melting pot theory, stating that a new national type was being formed by the union and assimilation of different races and families of different cultures and characteristics. From the beginning, and particularly from the formation of the national government, constant emigration from all the countries of Europe had produced a balance of differences. The writer admitted that emigration might have brought criminal, anarchistic, and pauper elements, but "amid all the dross there has constantly predominated the pure gold of industry, sobriety, and integrity and the vast majority were imbued with a spirit of true civilization and guided by the principles of religion and morality."[104]

Chicago Catholicism's response to the nativist outburst of the 1890s indicated that, despite the host society's continued prejudice, the Church had changed. In the Know Nothing period, its reaction to bigotry had been hysterical and vituperative. By comparison, its response to the APA and immigration restrictionists was moderate and mature. Generally, inflammatory rhetoric and wholesale condemnations were replaced by irony and reasoned explanations. Instead of denying Catholic failures, errant behavior was acknowledged and wrongdoers were chastised; instead of hiding internal dissension and differences (such as the disagreement with Archbishop Ireland's Republicanism), they were openly discussed. Chicago Catholicism was no longer insecure. Through strength of numbers, wise leadership, and increasing success in the marketplace and the political arena, it had become self-assured.

More than revealing a matured Catholicism, the nativist episode helped consolidate the emerging supranatural Catholic identity. The Edwards Law, the organized prejudice of the APA, and immigration restrictionists caused people to retreat to the security of their parishes and communities, but such rejection made them conscious of their identity both as immigrants and Catholics. For this reason, nativism, rather than weakening Chicago Catholicism, strengthened it by reinforcing the immigrants' relationship with their Church.

Ironically, when anti-Catholicism was at its height, the most serious threat to Chicago Catholicism, the centripedal force of immigrant nationalism, was least pronounced. Between the passage of the Edwards Law and the decline of the APA in 1895, when American Catholicism's claim to catholicity was most challenged, Chicago Catholicism faced no major problem with nationalism. However, the question of meeting ethnic groups' demands for recognition persisted.

4. Immigrant Nationalism

ARCHBISHOP PATRICK AUGUSTINE FEEHAN confronted the problem of his successors: unification of an ethnically diverse membership. This task was made more difficult by the rapid increase in the number and variety of his constituency between 1880 and 1900. America's Catholics took little part in the development of a sense of national identity. With the exception of the descendants of Maryland and Virginia Catholics, they did not share America's cultural traditions. The democratic and individualist imprint of Protestantism that shaped the country's life was foreign to Catholic newcomers. Moreover, Catholics did not have a sense of unity, common to most Americans; they did not view themselves as American Catholics but continued to see themselves as Irish Catholics, German Catholics, Polish Catholics, Bohemian Catholics, and the like. Their sole source of unity was theological; a common faith and sacramental practice held them together. As a voluntary organization composed of heterogeneous elements, the Church faced the challenge of becoming American enough to be accepted by the Anglo-Saxon Protestant host and yet Catholic enough to preserve the faith of its immigrant members.

Many Catholics who had endured the hostility of the host society because of their religion and origin (or lineage) wondered if it were not time for the Church to become more American and less European. They were not willing to deny the authority of the pope but they questioned the existence of national parishes, which encouraged and reinforced alien national consciousness. Men like Archbishop John Ireland, Bishop John J. Keane, Fr. Isaac Hecker, and (to a lesser extent) James Cardinal Gibbons wanted to make the Church more American. These men, referred to as "Americanizers," were possessed of missionary zeal toward non-Catholic Americans, who they believed could be converted if the Church were "deforeignized." Also, they were acutely aware of the anti-Catholic and anti-foreign sentiment

78

which jeopardized the peaceful growth of their Church. Thus, in their dual desire to convert and to be accepted, they sought to Americanize the Church.

The Catholics whom they sought to Americanize reacted defensively to the suggestion that they give up the culture that embodied their religious traditions. In fact, they agitated against the predominantly Irish-American hierarchy, claiming its goal was "Irishization" rather than Americanization. Instead of consenting to the Americanizer's demands, they asked for fairer treatment and proportionate representation in the Church's power structure. Because this was a time of heightened nationalism in Europe, the most recent immigrants were more reluctant than ever to part with their new-found identity.

In the nation's most cosmopolitan city, Patrick Augustine Feehan, the Irish-born and -trained archbishop, encountered deep-rooted anti-Catholic and anti-alien sentiment, on one hand, and strong nationalist feelings on the other. His see, from its earliest times, had fostered respect for the cultural traditions of its diverse membership as a means of preserving the faith. Nationalism, he discovered, was a way of life among Chicago Catholics, who settled in cohesive groups and maintained their ethnic ties into the second and third generations. He soon learned that the continuous flow of immigrants constantly reinforced Old World identity.

In the twenty-two years that Archbishop Feehan directed the physical and spiritual development of Catholic Chicago, he had to deal with nativist, Americanizing, and nationalist pressures. His response to the latter determined the character of the archdiocese, shaped the Church's relation to the host society, and manifested his attitude toward Americanization. Four incidents, involving nationalist aspirations and ambition, demanded his attention: the threatened condemnation of Irish nationalist societies, German nationalist sentiment in Church affairs ("Cahenslyism"), Polish nationalism and the establishment of a schismatic church, and resistance of the Irish-born to American-born Irish leadership.

Two convictions carried the prelate through his vexatious Chicago tenure. First, he believed that a man's love for his mother country was wholesome. "The love of the son for his mother," Feehan was fond of saying, "does not preclude his love for his wife. On the contrary, if he is a good son, he will be a good husband."[1] Second, he held that America's greatest danger, which threatened to debase its flag and its institutions, was not foreignism but the corruption of morals. If adults and children could be preserved in their fear and love of God, no one need be anxious for the nation's destiny. "A good Catholic," he often remarked, "is always a good citizen, for he is obedient to law, believing that all just authority comes from God."[2] He maintained that the good citizenship of his fellow immigrants and their offspring depended upon fostering strong ties to the Church and the society that evolved around it. His mission, therefore, was to make the Catholic Church a dynamic part of the lives of all its members.

For the Irish, the experience of prejudice and bigotry at the hands of the Know Nothings was disillusioning. To rationalize their failure to be accepted into the American mainstream, these immigrants and their descendants turned on the hated English, who had kept them poor, illiterate, and unskilled. They told themselves that the English were to blame for their disgraceful social ills, both in the homeland and in America. From awareness of American prejudice, the realities of poverty, and the sense of alienation and loneliness that affected the immigrants sprang Irish-American nationalism, bent on freeing Ireland from British domination. As Thomas N. Brown explaidddd, the formal content of their nationalism owed much to the thoughts and traditions of Irish heroes, "but it was from life in America that it derived its most distinctive attitudes: a pervasive sense of inferiority, intense longing for acceptance and respectability, and an acute sensitivity to criticism."[3]

Irish nationalism provided the immigrants, and especially second-generation Irish-Americans, with opportunities for leadership and prestige and a rationalization for the pain of nonacceptance in American society. Numerous societies sprang up, dedicated to the dream of an independent Ireland. These societies, however, had a significance beyond their goals. They offered companionship to all, and business and political opportunities to some, but more important, they transformed a rootless nobody into a somebody. Thus, in the minds of many members, these organizations tended to assume greater consequence than pursuit of Irish freedom.[4]

Chicago's Irish population suffered from a sense of inferiority and a deep-felt need for acceptance and respectability. The scars of the nativist onslaught in the 1850s persisted, as did the poor condition of the Irish in the city's society. Surely, some of Chicago's Irish were acquiring the promises of the American dream, but their general lot was discouraging. By 1880 they still stood on the bottom rung of society, compared with the other major groups, the Germans and native Americans. In the upper ranks of the professions and business they were poorly represented; only 5 of 161 doctors, 30 of 494 of the city's leading lawyers, 6 of 222 members of the Board of Trade, 2 of 42 bankers, and 4 of 44 building contractors were Irish or of Irish origin.[5] With the passing of the frontier stage in the city's development, the gap between the sons of St. Patrick and the elite widened and further separated them from the respectable society to which they aspired.[6] Their position in society was reflected in a want ad that appeared in the *Chicago Tribune* the day Patrick Augustine Feehan became Chicago's first archbishop:

> WANTED—A GOOD COACHMAN: SINGLE MAN; neither Irish or colored will do. Give addresses and name and references.[7]

Ireland's record of unbroken defeats and submission to English domination was a sorry stigma borne by Chicago's Irish, who lived in a society that viewed self-government as a sign of a responsible people. If they could rid themselves of the stigma of being a dependent and landless people, they believed they might be more acceptable to Americans. John Finerty, editor of the Irish paper the *Chicago Citizen* and a one-time congressman, wrote that "all other foreign elements in this country, with, perhaps, the exception of the Poles, have strong governments behind them, and they are held in more respect than the Irish who have no government of their own to boast of."[8] Similar feelings were expressed in Finerty's paper by Matthew Brady, a Liverpool-born Irishman:

> Shall the Irish remain slaves to a tyrant's arbitrary will in Ireland, or wandering over the earth, be the miserable subjects of the scurrilous jokes and insulting wit of ignoble, unmanly, brainless, monkey-like dudes, so poor in manhood, spirit and intelligence as to be unfit for higher uses than to keep flies off us in summer time,—shall we, I ask, remain thus miserably circumstanced from paltry craven fear to make any sacrifice necessary to restore to us our plundered inheritance?[9]

Chicago's Irish-American nationalism was rooted in the Irish history of oppression and the practical and psychological needs of people striving for acceptance. At the same time, it met the need for friendship, personal advancement, self-respect, and a sense of identity. The identity it fostered, they contended, was not inconsistent with their love of America. They reminded Americans that they desired for Ireland the same thing the United States had achieved a century earlier: independence from British tyranny. Accordingly, to be a good American, one had to sympathize with the Irish nationalist cause.[10]

Although the high-water mark of Irish nationalism in Chicago was between 1880 and 1890, the movement began earlier. During the Civil War, the Irish who served in the Union and the Confederate armies learned the skills necessary to end British rule of their homeland. Through the Fenian Brotherhood, a secret society of international proportions, they attempted to realize their dreams. Supported by deteriorating Anglo-American relations, the American branch of the Fenians laid plans to aid an Irish uprising and wrest Canada from English control.[11] In this effort, Chicago's Irish manifested financial generosity and a willingness to sacrifice their lives. Despite Bishop James Duggan's initial condemnation of the Fenian Brotherhood for its secretiveness and espousal of the violent overthrow of legally constituted authority,[12] the society flourished in Chicago. A large fair was held to collect funds to support the cause, more than 1,000 men joined the society and drilled twice a week, and an "Irish navy" was organized to sweep the Great Lakes of British commerce. In June 1866, Chicago's Irish community sent more than a thousand men and two vessels to aid in the assault on Canada.[13] The Fenian invasion, however, was unsuccessful because of disorganization and factionalism.

The military failure, lack of continued United States support because of a change in diplomatic policy, and factionalism forced the Fenians to bide their time. However, improved conditions in Ireland after the island's uprising of 1867, the subsequent decrease in Irish immigration, unfavorable American political conditions, and the American Catholic hierarchy's condemnation of the Fenian movement in 1870 worked to its demise.[14] Nevertheless, since Irish-American conditions did not significantly improve, the basic ingredients of nationalism remained.

In the 1870s the recently formed Clan-na-Gael sustained the embers of radical Irish nationalism and gradually became the dominant nationalist force in America. Like the Fenian Brotherhood, the Clan sought the "complete and absolute independence of Ireland by the overthrow of English domination by means of physical force."[15] Its work was preparation rather than immediate war, as vivid memories of Fenian failures proved a moderating force.[16] When conditions worsened in Ireland and Anglo–American relations again deteriorated, Clan-na-Gael was ready for action.

In the next decades, Chicago became the center of radical Irish nationalism under Alexander Sullivan's leadership of the American branch of Clan-na-Gael. Sullivan was an ambitious lawyer-journalist-political hack who, despite probable (but unproven) murder and theft, worked his way into the society's inner councils.[17] In 1881 he was elected to the chairmanship of the Clan's national executive committee and used his influence to found the Irish National League of America two years later. Through the INLA, which was composed of the Ancient Order of Hibernians, the Catholic Total Abstinence Union, the Irish Catholic Benevolent Union, and nearly all other Irish-American fraternal and benefit societies, the Irish hoped to bring attention to their aspirations. This new organization was run by a powerful central committee whose objectives were self-government for Ireland, development of Irish industry, injury to British manufacturing, and revival of the Celtic language and art. Sullivan, however, wanted to make the League an instrument of Clan-na-Gael radicalism.[18]

Sullivan met opposition within his organization, but he found his severest, most powerful critics in the Church hierarchy. On the whole, the American and the Irish hierarchies opposed Irish revolutionary societies on the grounds that their oaths conflicted with one's duties to God and country and their revolutionary goals were opposed to the Church's teaching on a just war.[19] Many conservative bishops, especially Archbishop Michael Corrigan of New York and Bishops Bernard McQuaid of Rochester, Richard Gilmour of Cleveland, and Francis Chatard of Indianapolis, sought the condemnation of secret societies. However, the more liberal prelates hesitated to act for fear of alienating a large number of Irish Catholics who were sympathetic to the Clan. Archbishop Ireland and Cardinal Gibbons were reluctant to condemn the Clan and other secret societies, but these organizations' staunchest defender was Chicago's Archbishop Feehan.[20]

Unlike the prelates who supported Charles Stewart Parnell's constitutional independence movement, but combated Clan-na-Gael influence, Archbishop Feehan maintained friendly relations with the radical nationalists. Approvingly, he reviewed Irish nationalist demonstrations at St. Patrick's Day parades and was frequently in the company of Alexander Sullivan at important events, and occasionally dined at his home. This benevolent attitude was also extended by priests of the Chicago see; priests of Irish birth and descent were ever present at nationalist rallies and supportive of their activities. The most noted was Rev. Maurice Dorney, the popular and powerful pastor of St. Gabriel's parish in the stockyard district. He was a trusted friend of Sullivan and influential in the inner circles of the Clan. Dorney's most publicized work was to deliver papers defending Charles Parnell to the special parliamentary committee investigating charges that the Irish leader was involved in revolutionary terrorist activity.[21]

The *Western Tablet,* Chicago's unofficial Catholic newspaper, supported Alexander Sullivan and the cause of Irish freedom. The editor endorsed a free and equal union with England, according to Parnell's plan, but should England refuse, he favored "a combination of the whole Irish race to wrest by physical force complete independence from her."[22] Because Sullivan's Clan financed and directed bombings in London that endangered life, the *Western Tablet* suggested an alternative: setting London ablaze! Recent fires, the editor rationalized, had shown that property could be destroyed without loss of human life.[23]

Whether Archbishop Feehan agreed with violent tactics is unknown; however, he never openly condemned them. When he returned from Rome, where he and other American prelates laid plans for the Third Plenary Council, he was welcomed by Henry F. Sheridan, a Clan member, who spoke for the Ancient Order of Hibernians. Aware that the forthcoming council was to consider condemnation of the Order, Sheridan addressed Feehan:

> We come to you in a sincere and filial spirit to speak words of warm affection based on our knowledge of your personal character. With the objects of our organization you have always shown a generous sympathy, inspired by a thorough understanding of our aims and perfect familiarity with our methods. When in other portions of this country, the Ancient Order of Hibernians has been misunderstood, misrepresented or clouded, it has always found you a discriminating stanch [*sic*] and steadfast friend; for you informed yourself of its character, and neither calumny nor ignorance has swayed your fidelity to our convictions.

Sheridan explained the good work that AOH encouraged for home, religion, and society, but stressed the society's weekly military drills that readied members to protect America and to free Ireland. "The God-planted instincts of resistance to tyranny are as keen in your heart as in ours. The duty in the sight of God and man to aid those of our race who are still under the cruel clutch of the malignant and hypocritical power is as fervently felt by you as by us. If it should be in the decrees of the future that . . . our swords are ever to leave their impatient scabbards to rise under the great standard of our isle of saints . . . we should confidently turn to Your Grace for the blessing upon our hopes which you could not withhold." The Hibernian leader concluded by pledging the allegiance and affection of the society to the archbishop.[24]

Within the year, Archbishop Feehan reciprocated the Irish nationalists' pledge of loyalty by defending the Ancient Order of Hibernians at the Third Plenary Council. At the meeting, Francis Chatard and other bishops decried the AOH's strong ties to radical Irish groups and its resistance to ecclesiastical authority. As the debate neared its close, the friends of the society feared that it might be condemned, but the usually silent archbishop of Chicago rose and delivered an eloquent defense.[25] Recalling the incident, Archbishop Ireland said:

> We were spell-bound, for we never dreamed that he possessed such power of explanation, refutation and sarcasm. Near the conclusion of his plea, he turned to the accusers of the Irish organization and told them that they neither understood the faith nor the loyalty of the members they had been accusing, and defied them to prove by a special committee of investigation the charges preferred. He was like an enraged lion defending its offspring, and as he shook his head in denunciation his flowing locks gave truth to the comparison.[26]

Feehan's defense was effective. His eloquence and reasoned argument created a stunned silence that led to tabling the condemnation. In private session, it was agreed that a committee, which included Archbishop Feehan, should inquire into the nature and character of the society and report to the council. In effect, the threat to AOH was checked.[27] But Clan-na-Gael was in a more precarious position because it was a revolutionary secret society. When the conservative bishops demanded its condemnation, Feehan, Ireland, and Gibbons resisted. Even after the murder of Dr. Patrick Cronin, an anti-Sullivan Clan member who had publicly accused the radical leader of political ambition and misappropriation of funds, the society escaped condemnation.[28]

Alexander Sullivan's implication in the murder of Dr. Cronin caused serious problems, not just for Clan-na-Gael but for all of Chicago's Irish Catholics. Although Sullivan was not indicted (for lack of evidence), several of his associates were convicted. The sensational coverage of the trial produced adverse publicity and cries of un-Americanism. The *Chicago Tribune* declared that Clan members were "disloyal to American principles and institutions" and violated "the fundamental duties of American citizens" because their oath to secure an Irish republic meant more to them than their oath of United States citizenship.[29]

The *Tribune* played the role of defender of the Catholic Church, saying her leaders did not know what transpired in the inner sanctums of the secret society and suggesting that Archbishop Feehan would now withdraw his approval. It also intimated that he should send Fr.

Maurice Dorney to a quiet country parish where he could give no
further scandal.[30] The *Catholic Home,* which replaced the *Western
Tablet,* did not accept the *Tribune*'s "kindness" toward the Church
uncritically; rather, it regarded the *Tribune*'s defense as a ploy to force
Archbishop Feehan to make a statement of condemnation.[31] But the
prelate remained silent, and neither withdrew his approval of the Clan
nor removed Fr. Dorney from his parish.

In this episode of intense Irish-American nationalism, Feehan
rejected the position taken by the conservative American prelates and
the Irish hierarchy, who held that a free Ireland must only come
through constitutional means. He also ignored the sentiment expressed in the city's newspapers and the demonstrations of civic-
minded Chicagoans who denounced the Sullivanite course of action
and the Clan as a threat to American society.[32]

Since Feehan never explained his action, his behavior is open to
conjecture. Bishop McQuaid contended that his Chicago colleague
(with Archbishop Ireland and Cardinal Gibbons) failed to condemn
the Clan because he feared to lose the favor of the Irish.[33] This
explanation is worthy of consideration in light of the strong nationalist
feelings in Chicago and Feehan's disinclination toward controversy
and confrontation. Yet the fact that Feehan put himself "on the line" at
the Baltimore council of 1884 demonstrates that he did not always
avoid conflict. In light of his nationalist feelings, friendship with the
leaders of the movement, and reasoned defense of Irish societies, his
action (or inaction) was, in effect, his defense of militant Irish nationalism. He was aware that condemnation could mean taking sides in
an already factionalized movement. The Church's role, he seems to
have believed, was to preserve and foster the faith, not to alienate the
faithful because of questions of political expediency. A condemnation,
dictated by the anti-Catholic *Tribune,* would have led to disaffection
and jeopardized the growth of Chicago's Catholic Church.

While Archbishop Feehan stood with Archbishop Ireland on Irish-
American nationalism, he parted company with him on the Americanization of other national groups. Unlike the Irish, the other Catholic
groups were handicapped by the language barrier (although most
immigrants learned English so they might get on in the marketplace).
They endeavored to preserve their languages. For them, language was
the soul of their national identity: a link with the past and the surest
means of expressing their innermost sentiments, especially among
themselves, their families, and their Creator. When the immigrants
came to America, they sacrificed to re-create the precise forms of their
Old World churches, but soon sensed that they were treated as

second-class citizens, even within the Church, because they were not English speaking.

The Irish controlled the hierarchy in the American Church and in many instances discriminated against non-Irish, and non-English-speaking Catholics, as non-Americans. A story published in *Courrier de l'Illinois* and reprinted by a Chicago German Catholic paper expressed the alienation of foreign-born, non-Irish Catholics:

The American Paradise

A jolly good fellow, French Canadian by birth, arrives at the gate of Paradise and knocks. St. Peter, a bunch of keys in his hand, opens the little window in the door and inquires:

"Who is out there?"

"It is I, Jean-Baptiste," answers our man in his mother-tongue.

"What do you wish?" asks St. Peter, also speaking in French.

"Good St. Peter, with your permission I would like to enter into the Paradise of Our Lord."

"How have you deserved it, Jean-Baptiste?"

"I have raised fifteen children, I have been a good citizen all my life, and have always done my duty."

"You seem to be a Canadian."

"You are right, Great St. Peter, I am a native of Grand Metis in Quebec."

"Do you come directly from there?"

"No, Great St. Peter, I came by way of the United States."

"Ah! is that it? That changes the matter. Jean-Baptiste, my friend, I am sorry for you but this is not your Paradise here. There appears to be a new and very small one, prepared especially for a new Church, the name of which I do not know. I think they call it the American Church. Go there and ask for St. Patrick, the patron of Ireland. He has a key to it and can do more for you than I."

"Thank you very much, Great St. Peter."

The window closed and Jean-Baptiste wended his way to the American Paradise.

Arriving at the gate he rapped. St. Patrick, a key in hand, opened the window in the door:

"What do you want?"

"Grand St. Patrick, avec votre permission, j'aimerais a entrer dans le paradis americain." [Great St. Patrick, with your permission, I would like to enter the American Paradise.]

"What do you say?"

"Grand St. Patrick, avec votre . . ."

"Talk the 'United States,' I do not understand French!"

"Je ne peuz pas, Grand St. Patrick; J'ai toujours fait mes devoirs en francais . . ." [I cannot, Great St. Patrick; I have always fulfilled my duties in French . . .]

"You do not talk English? Then you are not an American and there is no room for you here, get out!"

Down banged the window, and Jean-Baptiste, very much embarrassed, returned to the Paradise of Our Lord.

"What Jean-Baptiste" — said St. Peter in French — "you are still here? Why are you not in the American Paradise? There ought to be room enough there, for not many enter it."

"I will tell you, Great St. Peter," answered our friend. "St. Patrick won't let me in because I do not talk 'United States.' If there is no Canadian Paradise, Good St. Peter, open for me the gate to yours."

The case was complicated. St. Peter went to consult with the Lord, who decided:

"Open the great gate for Jean-Baptiste; he was a good father, a loyal citizen, a faithful Christian, and it is not necessary to speak English in order to enter the Kingdom of Heaven."[34]

The German-Americans, the largest non-English-speaking group, were most agitated by second-class treatment. In the United States, these immigrants developed a new identity: German-Americanism. They tried to preserve the culture of the fatherland and hoped to influence the development of the American nation with their rich heritage. Contrary to the accusations of their critics, they did not seek to Germanize America. When faced with Yankee boasting and nativist ravings, they took comfort in the cultural and economic achievements of the German people. The unification of Germany (in 1871) heightened their identity and consolidated their position in American society. Focusing on the past, they resisted Americanization, lest assimilation destroy their recently created identity.[35]

Within the Church, German Catholics found that their parishes were often deprived of parochial rights, that their clergy were mistreated and not proportionately represented in administrative positions, and that their special concerns were unappreciated. To secure fair treatment at the hands of the Irish-American hierarchy, appeals were made over the heads of domestic officials. Their agitation for acceptance in the American Church was not solely a matter of injured pride but a desire to preserve the Catholic faith. Second-class status humiliated German Catholics and gave cause for some to turn Lutheran, since they revered Germanism.

In 1886 Fr. P. M. Abbelen, vicar general of the Diocese of Milwaukee, presented a memorial to the Propaganda, stating the grievances of the German Catholic minority and the offenses of the Irish Catholic majority. Abbelen explained that the want of sympathy toward Germans threatened their perseverance in the Catholic fold, and he begged the Roman authorities to define and decree that all German churches, and those of other nationalities, be "placed on equal footing with the English (Irish) and . . . be entirely independent of them"; that all European immigrants be assigned to a church of their own language; that bishops and priests "be admonished . . . not . . . to seek to suppress and root out the language, manners, the customs, the usages and the devotional practices of the Germans," and that bishops who were ignorant of the German language but governed a mixed diocese appoint a vicar general to care for Germans. He did not ask for perpetuation of a German national church in America, but that the painful transition from one nationality to another not be hastened and forced at the expense of the Catholic faith, which was interwoven with German culture.[36]

The American hierarchy, led by Archbishop Ireland and Bishop Keane of Richmond, Virginia, responded to the memorial immediately. They explained that the conflict was not with the "Irish Church" but "between the English language and the German language." The German clergy, they emphasized, by trying "to preserve intact the German spirit among the emigrants and their descendants . . . and to give a preponderant position to German influence in the Church in America," threatened the mission of converting American Protestants. Moreover, "the Church will never be strong in America; she will never be sure of keeping within her fold the descendants of emigrants, Irish as well as others, until she has gained a decided ascendancy among the Americans themselves." The frequent American charge that the Church was a foreign institution and a menace to the nation, they contended, could only be eliminated by more rapid — but not dangerous to the faith — Americanization.[37] Although many of the conservative bishops, such as Gilmour and McQuaid, did not favor rapid Americanization, they opposed the "dangerous precedent" of letting nationalities legislate American Church affairs from Rome.[38]

German Catholic behavior gave Americanizers cause for alarm. The year after Abbelen's Roman venture, the German clergy organized the Deutsch-Amerikaner Priester-Verein as a means of uniting German Catholics in public manifestations of their faith and common interests. German Catholic resistance to the Edwards and

Bennett laws, which threatened the practice of their language and (indirectly) their faith, was a source of embarrassment to the Americanizers. Additionally, most German Catholics embraced conservative positions on Church–state relations, education, and labor organizations that were at variance with Archbishop Ireland and his followers. These differences, as well as conflicting interests, had become, as one historian notes, "a keg of ecclesiastical gun powder."[39]

The charge was touched off in 1891 by a memorial prepared by the St. Raphael's Society, an organization dedicated to the physical and spiritual welfare of European emigrants. The document, referred to as the Lucerene Memorial, claimed that the Catholic Church had sustained the loss of 10 million faithful in the United States. To remedy the situation, the society suggested that separate churches be established for each nationality; priests of the same nationality be appointed to these churches; religion be taught in the national language (even when the number of immigrants did not merit a separate parish); separate parochial schools be established for each nationality; equal privileges be granted to foreign priests; and "whenever it is possible, have in the episcopacy of the country where they emigrate, several bishops who are of the same origin."[40] The memorial was signed by thirty-five delegates from five nations and was delivered to the Propaganda by Peter Paul Cahensly, secretary of the society and a member of the German legislature.

When the news of Cahensly's mission reached the United States, the Americanizers were enraged. They incorrectly claimed that the Priester-Verein was using the German government to intervene in domestic matters. The Americanists, especially John Ireland, used the memorial in a sensational manner to consolidate the Americanization movement.[41] Although the pope, through his secretary of state, supported the American hierarchy's right to select bishops, the German position was not condemned. The Cahensly incident sorely strained the Church's claim to catholicity.

In Chicago, too, German Catholics were conscious of their national identity and sought to maintain their culture against the pressures of Americanists. The increased immigration of the 1880s swelled the membership of existent parishes and led to the establishment of new ones. Their parochial schools, which taught the German language and imparted religion in that tongue, flourished. *Katholisches Wochenblatt* served adults and *Katholischer Jugend Freund* entertained and informed the young. The parish, the center of social life and basis of identity, supported the maintenance of Germanism.[42]

The Edwards Law and the Americanizers alarmed the German

community and welded it together in the desire to preserve its traditions and language. Anton C. Hesing, editor of the *Illinois Staats Zeitung*, expressed the importance of the German language to Archbishop Feehan on the occasion of his silver jubilee in 1890. Speaking in his native tongue, as the "representative of the German Catholics," he declared:

> Our German language is to us the treasure that is inseparable with our being. We are better citizens, better men and better Christians if we give expression to our noblest feelings in our own tongue unhindered. It is the tie that holds us together, and it presents our duties to our country, and even to our God and Church, more forcibly to our souls than any other language, for its euphone even, touching our souls leads us to prayer and all that is good. This treasure cannot and shall not be torn from us. For it and for the preservation of our German parishes and parish schools we stake our best powers. Upon these two rests our steadfastness in the faith and our loyalty to religion and the Church. With our language we sacrifice the very essence, the peculiar character of which—the soul, from which alone emanates true piety—suffers injury. We desire to be faithful American citizens; we desire to remain devoted children of the Catholic Church, but we also desire to find an unhindered expression of the soul in our own language.[43]

Although all Germans were not as attached to their language as Anton Hesing, they were proud of their culture. Because an increasing number of German-American Catholics were more comfortable with English, Arthur Preuss established the *Review* in April 1894 with two objectives: (1) to communicate German ideas and sentiments to persons ignorant of the German tongue and (2) to counter English-speaking Catholics who, through their so-called American press, "misrepresented and assailed" German Catholics. Begun as a monthly, the *Review* soon had a supporting readership that permitted Preuss to publish weekly.[44]

Preuss used the paper to attack chauvinistic efforts at Americanization and to defend "the equal rights of all nationalities represented in the great amalgam called the American people." His harshest criticism was reserved for Irish prelates and journalists who contended that "Irish," "American," and "Catholic" were synonymous terms. Each nationality, Preuss argued, had "an original and indestructible right" to maintain its identity and freely develop alongside others. "The suppression of any nationality, in general, or in any of its legitimate branches of development," he wrote, "is a violation of the order established by God himself and will bring about its own punishment." As a community, the Church stood higher than any nationality and was commissioned to unite all nations, to place them in brotherly relation, to create one great family of nation: *"eine grosse Volkerfamilie."*

In doing so, the Church was directed to deal justly with the peculiarities of the different nationalities by accommodating herself to them. "The Church cannot, therefore," Preuss wrote, "identify herself with the opinions, customs, idiosyncracies of any one nationality. She cannot be Italian, French, German or American; nor can she show a preference for any one people; least of all can she attempt to aid one nationality in imprinting its stamp on another." "It is her duty," he added, "to take each nation as she finds it, and to elevate it, to ennoble it [as] best she can." From its diversity, the Church was enriched because each nation could learn from the others and appropriate to itself foreign traits and institutions worthy of imitation.[45]

From this theology flowed the *Review*'s condemnation of Americanizing elements and its defense of German Catholic requests for reasonable considerations. The paper considered the Americanist charge that Germans were attempting to Germanize Catholicism in the United States "a d--d barren ideality," evolved by the "fertile though morbid brain of a chauvinistic prelate who demeaned himself as if he and his followers had an exclusive patent on American patriotism."[46] Preuss explained that German Catholics did not ask for the appointment of bishops or demand that priests learn German—rather, those who were appointed to rule should harbor no prejudices and ill feelings toward them, but treat *all* the faithful, whose eternal welfare had been entrusted to them, justly and kindly. If an episcopal leader could not speak German, German Catholics asked that he try to learn a "smattering" of the idiom, or appoint German vicar generals, or "establish some other reliable channel of communication." It was only reasonable, he argued, that in sees where Germans were numerous they should be represented in the episcopate. For German congregations, a German or German-American was demanded; and in parishes in which Germans were numerous, a German-speaking pastor who was willing and able to preach occasionally, and attend regularly to sacramental wants, was asked. Finally, Germans must be respected and be free to develop uninhibited.[47]

Although this English-language German paper criticized Archbishop Ireland and numerous Irish-dominated diocesan newspapers for their misrepresentation of German-American Catholicism and for Irish chauvinism, it did not berate Archbishop Feehan. Even though

Feehan did not speak German, Chicago's Germans found him to be an ally most solicitous for their welfare, as illustrated by the growth of St. Aloysius parish. When the Germans who moved into the Humbolt Park section of Chicago had asked for their own church, he promptly met their request. Later, he supported the militantly German pastor's plan to build a complete German community.[48] Germans were given a voice in the archdiocesan administration through their consultor and the school committee. The controversial Deutsch-Amerikaner Priester-Verein held its first meeting in Chicago in 1887, with the Irishman's approval, and the work of the St. Raphael Society won his blessing and support.[49] He even defended Preuss's *Review* when numerous critics tried to muzzle it.[50] Finally, the archbishop's staunch defense of parochial schools, the chief means of transmitting German culture, won for him the abiding respect and loyalty of Chicago's German Catholics.[51]

For his even-handed treatment of the Germans, Feehan won the accolades of the most nationalistic of that race. Washington Hesing, the publisher of *Illinois Staats Zeitung,* praised him for his fairness and declared that if the favorable and prosperous condition of the German Catholics of Chicago were to deteriorate, it would be their own fault. Arthur Preuss wrote that Feehan proved himself "a truly Catholic prelate, guided by principle and zeal, regardless of national consideration."[52]

The problems of discrimination faced by German Catholics were shared by their Polish coreligionists. Like the Germans, Chicago's Poles desired to preserve their national identity and resisted Archbishop Ireland's plans for accelerated Americanization. Tens of thousands of Polish immigrants settled in Chicago and swelled the Church's membership with deeply religious people. They crowded into tenements and boarding houses near their places of employment and built churches to serve their spiritual and social needs. Through these churches and affiliated societies they kept alive their Old World ways, developed a new sense of nationalism, and endeavored to pass this on to their children through parish schools.

For those who wished to preserve the Old World in Chicago, there were internal and external obstacles. Within Polonia, two contending forces vied for power and control of the community at the expense of religious unity and national solidarity. One group, composed of and led by educated and aristocratic Poles, desired to use America as a base for freeing Poland. The other faction was composed of simple, deeply religious Poles of peasant origin who placed their trust in religious leaders rather than in the formerly aloof nobles. Nationalists wanted to use the churches to unite the people and work for an independent Poland; priests, however, saw the parishes as an instrument to meet the religious and social needs of Chicago's Polonia.

The nationalists, who originally sought to segregate the Poles to protect their identity and culture, soon came to the conclusion that they must enter the American mainstream, achieve respectability and power, and use it as a lever to free Poland. The instrument for organizing Poles for this latter purpose was the Polish National Alliance, which was formed in Philadelphia in 1880 and established in Chicago a year later. PNA's outspoken impatience with clerical "conservatism" and its willingness to accommodate to American ways led to serious differences with the clergy and its organizations, the Polish Roman Catholic Union. Founded in 1874, PRCU sought to preserve Catholicism among future generations of Polish-Americans, maintain the national impulse of American Poles, aid parochial schools, and support other work that fostered Polish culture.[53]

The conservative peasant element, referred to as the "churchgoers," was dominated by Rev. Vincent Barzynski, C.R., who came to Chicago in 1874 to assume the pastorship of St. Stanislaus Kostka parish. For a quarter of a century he shaped the growth and development of Polonia's religious and community life. Barzynski, entrusted with great power, was relied upon for counsel in Polish matters by Archbishop Feehan, who was not familiar with the Polish language and traditions. With near complete control, the Polish-born and -trained Resurrectionist directed the foundation of parishes, convents, schools, religious and fraternal societies, and charitable institutions and imprinted upon them his motto: "For God and Country." In his desire to build a community-parish as a fortress against the forces of materialism, socialism, anarchy, and atheism, he relied upon, and fostered, strong religious and ethnic ties.[54]

Because Barzynski placed the Church before, not equal to, the independence of Poland, he was criticized by nationalists and others who sought to exercise leadership in Polonia. The former opposed the churchgoers' efforts to preserve alien traditions, to the exclusion of American ways. But Americanization, the conservative element believed, would destroy the foundation of the community-parish and all that was dear to them. To weaken the impact of nationalist criticism, Barzynski used the pages of *Dziennik Chicagoski* (a daily newspaper he controlled), *Narod Polski* (the weekly organ of the Polish Roman Catholic Union), and the economic and social pressure that accompanied his position as a Church leader.[55]

To break the hold of "clerical rule," the Polish National Alliance

initiated an unsuccessful campaign to have Polish taught in the city
schools. The PNA believed that instruction in the Polish tongue in
public schools would lessen the attraction of Church schools and
provide the children a more liberal education. *Dziennik Chicagoski* was
quick to attack this proposal. PNA's plan, Barzynski's paper argued,
would endanger the enrollment of parochial schools and, consequently, destroy morals, patriotic feelings, and respect for Polish
ways.[56] It contended that public schools were sufficient for Americans;
however, they were inadequate for Polish children. Not only were the
public schools permeated with Protestantism, the editor said, but the
spirit, language, and mixing of nationalities were in every respect alien
to Poles.

> Even if the Polish language were taught in the public schools, the
> child educated there would not grow up to be a Pole. The
> surroundings would deaden his Polish national spirit and would
> make him an average American. How can a Polish child learn the
> history of Poland there? Who will teach him to honor Polish
> heroes? Who will inculcate in his breast the true Polish spirit and
> love our fatherland? Nobody. . . .
>   So everybody understand that if he wishes his child to
> become a good Pole and a Catholic, the child should be sent to a
> parochial school; if he wants him to become an American, indif-
> ferent to religion, often times without any sense of duty, let him
> send the child to a public school.[57]

Clearly, Palonia's internal conflict indicated that the Polish clergy,
dominated by Fr. Barzynski, would not tolerate a weakening of ethnic
ties. For them, religion and nationality were synonymous. One
strengthened the other.

Even more threatening to Polonia was the campaign of
Americanizers, such as Archbishops Ireland and Keane, who agitated
for a more thoroughly American Catholic Church. In the face of this
external attack, nearly all Poles, including those of the Polish National
Alliance, pledged themselves to resistance. *Dziennik Chicagoski* first took
up the fight and soon other papers joined it. The *Polish Courier* warned
its readers that they must guard their names and nationality by
supporting their churches, schools, and religious societies: "We must
and should do our utmost to protect and prolong the life of Polish
Catholic churches. It is our life, our backbone; without it we are lost."[58]
PNA's organ, *Zgoda*, also took up the fight; it urged all Poles to defend
their rights and their native language, and condemned the
Americanist "demand" that all sermons be preached in English:

Polish people are greatly opposed to this form of Catholicism compelling Polish Catholic people to listen to sermons spoken in the English language, when the majority of older people do not understand it. If this request is fulfilled, the Catholics will demand that the Germans, Italians, and all other nationalities do likewise. The question was raised by Archbishop Keane against the Poles. For what reason? Are the Polish parishes getting too rich? Are they expanding too fast or it is that the Irish want to dominate the Catholic world? Can't the Polish Catholics have as much freedom as the other nationalities? Isn't the United States a land of freedom? It is, but that is not the reason the Irish should have more preference than any other nationality. . . . Let the Polish people run their schools and churches the same way they are run in Poland, within the rules and the laws of the pope and the Bible. For this cause we will fight and continue fighting if necessary.[59]

Rev. B. M. Skulik, of St. Hyacinth's Church in LaSalle, Illinois, also tried to explain the importance of Polish national parishes to English-speaking Catholics. In an awkwardly phrased letter to the *New World,* Fr. Skulik argued that the national schools and churches kept the Catholic faith alive, provided consolation amid poverty, and helped Poles become good and honest citizens. "If the Polish schools should be suppressed," he wrote, "the Pole will . . . be deprived of their faith, their nationality, and would become agitators, a barbarous tribe of anarchists. What the Poles are, their civilization, honesty, patriotism and whatever good you may find in them, they owe their Catholic Church and pastors."[60]

Polish clerical resistance to Americanization was accompanied by schisms which threatened to destroy the traditional allegiance between Poles and Roman Catholicism. Rev. Francis Hodur, of Scranton, Pennsylvania, formed a schismatic church when his bishop proved unsympathetic to Polish needs, and soon found adherents in other urban centers. Chicago, too, had an "Independent" movement, led by Rev. Anthony Kozlowski, the ambitious assistant of St. Hedwig's parish. In 1895 Kozlowski, coveting control of the parish, rebelled against Vincent Barzynski's manipulation of parish affairs[61] and led 1,000 of the parish's 1,300 families in founding an independent church, the Independent Polish Catholic Church in America.[62]

Feehan viewed Kozlowski's church as a serious threat to Catholicism in Polonia; so he issued a circular, appealing to Kozlowski's followers that "they should not bring this stigma and disgrace, not only on religion, but upon the Catholic land whence they have come, and on themselves and their children." Further, he said, Kozlowski had no official jurisdiction in the Archdiocese of Chicago.[63] Feehan exercised restraint, giving fatherly admonition and "kindly advice,"[64] but when this course failed, Feehan, supported by Polonia's clergy, excommunicated Kozlowski for grievously violating the "laws and discipline of the Catholic Church and the Archdiocese of Chicago" and "contumaciously" persisting in "schismatical behavior."[65]

Kozlowski's success in winning adherents had disrupted the religious and social peace and unity in Polonia and forced the clergy to act.[66] Within three years the Independent Polish Catholic Church in America claimed 17,000 members.[67] Equally important, Kozlowski was consecrated a bishop by a member of the Old Catholic Movement in Europe and thus secured perpetuation for his church. The schismatics played upon the absence of Polish representation in the American Catholic hierarchy, produced statements that showed unjust and arbitrary treatment of Poles, and denounced the Polish Catholic clergy as traitors to Polish nationality. Their charges that Polonia's churches would have to use "the Latin or Irish tongue" and that the Polish language was to be banned from the schools were taken seriously. In July 1901, Chicago's Polish clergy met at St. Stanislaus Kostka Parish Hall and resolved to work for unity in the community and to silence their critics, Irish and Independent. In an open letter, they called for "the full support of every true-blooded Pole" in defense of their language and nationality. They also sent a letter to Pope Leo XIII, requesting that he ask priests of other nationalities to end their "bitter and hard feelings" toward Poles.[68]

Two months later, the Polish Catholic Congress met in Buffalo, New York, and discussed the American hierarchy's inattention to Polonia's needs. Rev. Casimir Sztuczko, C.S.C., pastor of Chicago's Holy Trinity parish, served as secretary of a committee that drafted a communique to Apostolic Delegate Sebastiano Martinelli and the nation's hierarchy. Written in the name of the Polish Roman Catholic clergy and laity, the letter explained that Poles were "unhappy and distressed" because the Independent movement "engendered strife, caused scandals, degraded the image of Polonia, and inflicted irreparable religious, moral, social, and economic harm." Despite the clergy's endeavors, the letter continued, the schismatics continued to win adherents because they could point to the poor treatment afforded Poles. The proposed solution was simple: a Polish bishop to counteract the Polish Independent bishops. "We are convinced," the committee wrote, "that Auxiliary Bishops would . . . elevate the tone of both clergy and laity, be establishing [sic] unanimity and uniformity where hitherto differences and discord prevail."[69]

Archbishop Feehan made no public statement regarding the Polish request for an auxiliary bishop; however, his concern for the Poles is certain. Quietly, he secured priest and sisters to staff their churches and schools. For example, he brought the Sisters of the Holy Family of Nazareth, an order committed to work with Polish exiles, to teach, and he encouraged them when they established a hospital.[70] He did not force himself upon the Poles, but let them settle their own problems. Acknowledging that interference by an "outsider" would worsen matters, he did not take sides in the rivalry between the Polish National Alliance and the Polish Roman Catholic Union. He relied on Fr. Barzynski and, later, his Polish consultor, Fr. Francis Lange of St. Josaphat's, to deal with Polonia's problems. Only when his authority was directly challenged, as with Kozlowski, did he intervene. That he did not respond to the petition of the Polish Catholic Congress is partially explained by the problem he simultaneously faced, as a result of his appointment of an Irish-American auxiliary.

Archbishop Feehan's most serious difficulties arose not because of German or Polish ecclesiastical ambition but because of his own Irish-born and -trained pastors, who were critical and, at the same time, jealous of their American-born cousins. Even when Irish nationalist sentiment was at its peak in Chicago in the 1880s, a definite division between Irish immigrants and Americans of Irish descent was acknowledged. The immigrants frowned on their American relatives and called them "narrow backs" and "spurious Irishmen."[71] In the Church itself, similar divisions caused Archbishop Feehan deep pain and sorrow, when he was least able to deal with the problem due to failing health.

Numerous Irish-born and -trained clergy, "serenaded" to Chicago by Feehan, held important pastorates in the city and outlying areas. Their Irish training and experience were reflected in their pastoral work; they ruled their parishes and parishioners like baronial lords in social and economic affairs and demanded near-Jansenistic behavior in religious matters. They had brought to America conceptions of iron-handed domination and rigid pietism, at a time when the second generation was discarding such ideas as inconsistent with American social and religious experience. Like the immigrant German and Polish clergy, they feared that the loss of Old World ways would cause degeneration and loss of the Catholic faith. Bound by common experience, visions, and aspirations, the Irish-born clergy sought to perpetuate Ireland in America. To this end, they worked to promote their members to influential positions and limit the influence of the "Americans."[72]

Although Feehan was a Maynooth graduate and an ardent Irish nationalist, he did not aid his fellow countrymen in their mission to re-create the old order in Chicago. His American and episcopal experience made him aware of the need for a loosely run, pluralistic administration—one that did not espouse a particular nationalistic conception of Catholic religious behavior. Whatever his precise reasons, he came to rely on American-born priests to help administer the archdiocese. After the late 1880s, he appointed American-born priests to the chancellorship. When he became ill and could no longer administer the sacraments, he chose Alexander J. McGavick, a young Illinois-born and -trained priest to aid him.[73] The Irish priests, resenting Feehan's reliance on native clergy, believed he had been duped by an American conspiracy. When McGavick became ill and incapacitated, the Irish priests realized they had to take action to prevent the archbishop from choosing his former chancellor, Peter James Muldoon, as his next auxiliary bishop.

Fr. Muldoon, born in Stockton, California, and educated at St. Mary's College, Kentucky, and St. Mary's Seminary in Baltimore,[74] was a certain choice because of his capable work as chancellor. Initially, the Irish priests, led by Revs. Thomas F. Cashman, Thomas Pope Hodnett, and Hugh P. Smyth (respectively pastors of St. Jarlath and Immaculate Conception parishes in Chicago and St. Mary's parish in Evanston), tried several legitimate and acceptable means to block appointment of their "bête noire."[75] When these efforts failed, they resorted to falsehood and deceit. In January 1901 a letter, signed by more than a score of Irish priests, was sent to the apostolic delegate, charging Muldoon with grave immorality and drunkenness. Letters were also sent to Cardinal Gibbons, who was suspected of supporting the Muldoon candidacy, and to Bishop Spalding of Peoria.[76] They hoped that their charges would quash Muldoon's appointment, but their plan failed; the former chancellor was nominated and scheduled to be elevated on July 25, 1901. To assure the priest-protestors that the full weight of Rome was behind the decision, the apostolic delegate was designated to preside at the ceremony.[77]

As a last resort, several priests, led by Hodnett and Cashman, decided to take their case directly to Martinelli and to the public. On July 20, Jeremiah J. Crowley, a County Cork cleric who had come to Chicago in 1896 and served as assistant at Nativity parish till appointed pastor of St. Mary's Church (Oregon, Illinois) three years later, pleaded their case to the apostolic delegate. To show the gravity of the accusations, Crowley resigned his pastorate in protest when the delegate dismissed the charges. Simultaneously, Crowley sent a letter of resignation to Feehan, outlining the reasons for his actions.[78] What

made the matter so serious was that Cashman arranged to have the
letter printed in the *Chicago Record-Herald* two days before the ceremony.

Crowley's letter indirectly charged several priests, including
Chancellor Francis J. Barry, Bishop McGavick and Bishop Elect Mul-
doon, and directly charged nine other priests of specific immoralities.
Crowley boldly wrote his ecclesiastical leader:

Most-Reverend Sir:

I . . . hereby protest the appointment of your nominee, Rev.
Father P. J. Muldoon for auxiliary bishop of Chicago. The
reasons have already been forwarded to Rome, but I have a moral
certainty that they were intercepted or purloined, because if the
holy see were in possession of the very grave charges, Muldoon's
appointment would never have been sanctioned. . . .

Those men you champion, though of Irish descent and of unde-
niable Irish names, are also known to you for having unreasonable and fierce antipathy to the people and the priests of that
nationality in particular and to those of foreign birth in general.
They referred to them as "Micks" and "Biddies," "Frog-eaters,"
"Dagoes," "Polacks" and "German Plugs," and on every occasion
are discriminated against, though they are indebted for their
education to these generous loyal Catholic people. In a word, with
your knowledge they are using language and pursuing methods
that are calculated to the absolute disintegration of your archdiocese.

And you are now going to cap the climax by making their leader
and boon companion P. J. Muldoon a bishop of the holy Catholic
church? For twenty years you have ignored the intelligent, influential and loyal Catholics of your diocese. You gave them no
recognition whatsoever, save as sources of revenue. You habitu-
ally spoke of them with contempt and strenuously opposed every
suggestion that pointed toward their recognition. Hence, to-day
it is universally recognized both by the laity and clergy that your
archdiocese is in a state of chaos and that all ecclesiastical discipline is broken.[79]

The letter received considerable play in the press and was circulated widely by Crowley and Paul E. Lowe, Cashman's close friend.
Muldoon's only comment to reporters who quizzed him on the protest
was that the Holy See's decision satisfied him that he was free of the

charges and that he would pray for his friends and enemies alike. Chancellor Barry declared there was no validity to the "scurrilous indictments" and suggested that the writer must be "crazy." Further excitement was aroused by Crowley's announcement that his life had been threatened by friends of Muldoon and Barry and the rumor that the bishop-elect was to be murdered.[80]

Muldoon was elevated to the auxiliary bishopric without incident, but the matter did not end. Fr. Crowley rescinded his resignation, only to find that the archbishop had accepted it and would not return the pastorate unless Crowley made reparation and apologized for defamation. Unwilling to abide by Feehan's conditions, and disobediently, he returned to his Oregon parish, to continue his duties. When Crowley refused to obey, Feehan became incensed and obtained a court order barring him from the Oregon parish. Only when the sheriff served the injunction did Crowley submit.[81] However, he declared his intention to have a hearing in an ecclesiastical court in order to justify his behavior and prove his charges against Muldoon, Barry, and associates. In October 1901, Martinelli commanded Crowley to submit to Archbishop Feehan or be excommunicated. He refused and was excommunicated.[82]

The open bitterness and hostility of the Irish priests and the serious nature of the charges were a deep embarrassment to all Catholics in the United States. In 1901 Bishop Spalding, senior suffragan of the archdiocese, reluctantly wrote Mieczyslaus Cardinal Ledochowski, prefect of the Propaganda, stating that Feehan was no longer capable of governing, that finances were in a chaotic state, and that "good" priests were discouraged and the laity demoralized. The cardinal-prefect immediately commanded the apostolic delegate to make a full investigation of the administration of the Chicago see, with consideration to naming an apostolic administrator who would be charged with the power to govern. The most serious charges directed at Feehan—intemperance, financial mismanagement, and lax discipline—were not substantiated, and the matter of a special administrator was dropped as inexpedient and inopportune.[83]

The Irish priests sought to take advantage of the American hierarchy's embarrassment over the scandalous news emanating from Chicago. In October, as the apostolic delegate conducted his investigation, they sent telegrams to the leading secular newspapers in New York, Boston, Cincinnati, Philadephia, and St. Paul in the name of Feehan's official organ, the *New World*. Their brief telegram stated that Rome had decided the forthcoming conference of American bishops was to retire Feehan because of his feeble health, and they suggested that the papers interview their archbishops on the matter. In this way they hoped to catch the archbishops off guard and secure compromising statements that would force them to retire Feehan. However, little attention was given to the purported retirement because the archbishops refused to comment or speculate on the matter until they received official notice. By their circumspection, the prelates saved Feehan from further pain and defeated the Cashman-Hodnett conspiracy.[84]

In March 1902, Jeremiah Crowley revived tensions. He demanded a pastorate, but rejected Feehan's conditions for reconciliation: retraction and an apology to the maligned priests.[85] Previously silent about the controversy surrounding his appointment, Muldoon finally spoke out. He admitted that his policy of ignoring the assaults (as "unworthy of notice") had failed. "It has come to such a stage," he informed reporters, "that it is my duty, for my honor as a man, to make answer to these attacks and charges." The young bishop explained that the problem was "the old story of the Irish priests against the Americans."[86] To back his position and shed light on the sordid and mysterious charges and efforts to discredit himself, Archbishop Feehan, and other native priests, he produced an affidavit, written and signed by Paul E. Lowe, the layman who had fronted for Cashman and Hodnett.[87]

To silence the men who still backed Crowley, especially the pastors of St. Jarlath's and Immaculate Conception, Archbishop Feehan issued a warning of immediate suspension to any priest in the diocese who financially or morally aided the insubordinate priest.[88] While Feehan did not eradicate the source of tension by his threat of suspension, he reasserted his authority and effectively silenced his critics. The Irish clique caved in under the threat of suspension and left Crowley to fend for himself. Crowley appears to have been taken advantage of by his Irish colleagues, but due to pride and self-righteousness he refused to submit, and eventually became an anti-Catholic lecturer.[89] Rather than retaliate against his severest critics, Feehan allowed them to retain their pastorates, lest they create new problems or effect a schism.[90] Although open conflict ceased, the bitterness engendered by the Irish clergy's struggle for recognition and power continued to influence the development of the archdiocese, even after Feehan's death.

In the twenty-two years that Archbishop Feehan presided over the Archdiocese of Chicago, he always felt the pressure of opposing interest groups. On one hand, nativists and Americanizers lobbied for the Americanization of the immigrants and their religious institutions. On the other hand, strong nationalistic elements sought the maintenance of their language and deeply rooted traditions. The task of weighing the needs of each group and deciding the course of action most beneficial to all fell to him. His position was very difficult, for no matter what course he pursued, not everybody would be satisfied. Although the Americanists may have questioned his moderation and conservatism, they could not but stand in awe at the marvelous work he accomplished with such diverse elements. The theoretical questions that drew the attention of Archbishops Ireland and Keane were a luxury for a man who faced the practical problem of preserving the faith of scores of thousands of immigrants.

Archbishop Feehan, aware of the strong national loyalties of his constituency, realized that denationalization, if engineered by the Church, could adversely affect religious loyalty. When he dedicated a new German church on the South Side in 1895, he took the occasion to remark that the word of God was preached in fifteen languages in Chicago's Catholic churches and that the spread of the faith in the city was the most convincing proof that diversity of language was a help, not an obstacle, to the Church's growth in America.[91] He knew that the tenacity of old prejudices and old ways could not be rudely interfered with, lest the wheat be destroyed while tearing up the cockle. He knew that the immigrants' languages, as Archbishop Patrick J. Ryan declared in his eulogy for his Tipperary friend,[92] were "hallowed by a thousand satisfying associations . . . [and] their old customs and wise laws [were] often the accumulated wisdom of centuries." The Philadelphia prelate praised the prudent, slow progress that marked Feehan's work in creating a truly Catholic and truly American people of his polyglot flock.[93]

Under Archbishop Feehan's administration, the Catholic Church grew rapidly in numbers and diversity but slowly in a sense of unity. The immigrant groups maintained their nationalist loyalties, whether German, Polish, Irish, French, or Bohemian. As an administrator, Feehan had serious shortcomings; he tended to drift with events instead of directing them. His shy and retiring nature and abhorrence of confrontation, referred to by his critics as timidity and weakness, led him to watch and intervene only when his authority was challenged. That a man of greater assertiveness might have produced a more unified development of Chicago's polyglot archdiocese is questionable. The traditions of ethnic diversity were well established before he came, and the waves of newcomers ensured their perpetuation. Feehan's contribution was to accommodate the Chicago Catholic Church to the needs of the people, so that, as he prayed at his elevation, "all the birds of the air might dwell in its branches."

"With no liking for controversy," the *Chicago Inter Ocean* eulogized in 1902, "he succeeded in a field where controversy had been rife for years. Not aggressive himself, he dominated aggressive men." "Coming from a field where the question of nationality had been of little importance, he became popular in a field where nationality was most important."[94]

To his successor, James Edward Quigley, he left the formidable task of cultivating that field.

5. Perfecting the Coalition

THE IMMIGRANT CHARACTER THAT shaped the development of the Catholic Church in Chicago, from its origin until the death of Archbishop Feehan, persisted in the first decade and a half of the twentieth century. The immigrant and ethnic ghettos remained. When inhabitants of the oldest immigrant settlements relocated, they were replaced by more recent immigrants, who reproduced similar patterns of social and economic life. Even when the children of the older immigrants moved to more comfortable and healthy surroundings, they took many elements of the immigrant ghetto with them. In both the new and the old sections of the city, the spire of the Church cast its shadow of influence.

Immigration data clearly indicate that Chicago was the destination of tens of thousands of immigrants. Between 1891 and 1900, 132,000 immigrants came to the bustling metropolis, and in the next decade 291,700 immigrants arrived.[1] In 1910, immigrants and their offspring numbered 1,693,918 and constituted 77.5 percent of the city's population. Although Chicago remained thoroughly foreign in character, the origins of the immigrants changed. Arrivals from northern and western Europe decreased and immigrants from eastern and southern Europe increased.[2]

In the first decade of the twentieth century, additions to the foreign-born Irish and German populations were relatively small. By 1910, nearly two of every three persons of Irish or German stock were born in America.[3] The significant change was their departure from the old immigrant settlements. As the immigrants and their children gained experience, learned skills, or obtained an education, they moved upward socially and economically, and outward to neighborhoods which bespoke their better conditions. Not all Germans and Irish improved their status, but most of them had begun, or completed, the change.[4] However, their improved status did not mean the end of

105

old relationships. When the circulation of the *Abendpost* and the *Illinois Staats Zeitung* declined, despite the increase in German stock between 1903 and 1915, the ties of ethnicity still bound them together. German boys played with German boys, and the same held for the Irish. For these upwardly mobile people, the immigrant institutions remained, until full acculturation and assimilation were effected.[5]

The Bohemians appear to have progressed much like the Germans and Irish. When they came to Chicago they took the unskilled, arduous jobs, but, through keen appreciation of education, hard work and thrift, improved their lot. They too began to move out of their crowded settlement, Pilsen, and established new communities farther west. Although not as closely knit as Pilsen, these settlements appear to have been as exclusive (if not more so) as the newer German and Irish neighborhoods.[6] While the Bohemians had proportionally more foreign born among their population than the two previous groups, less than 50 percent were of Continental origin.

In the first decade of the twentieth century, the wave of "new immigrants," from eastern and southern Europe, reached full force. Poles, Lithuanians, and Italians predominated, but numerous Croatians, Slovaks, Serbs, Hungarians, and Slovenes also arrived. They added to the settlements that already existed and formed new communities. In 1910, more than 230,000 Poles resided in Chicago, of whom nearly 54 percent had been born in the partitioned territories. They generally resided in the cramped and dingy quarters northwest and southwest of the Loop and near the steel mills in South Chicago, where they found jobs that did not require special skills. Most were former peasants, suspicious by nature, who seldom ventured beyond the ghetto; its shops and community institutions obviated the need to mix with other people, except at work. The same held for the Lithuanians, who were different only in that nearly 80 percent of the population was foreign born.

Immigration from southern Italy, Sicily, and the Austro-Hungarian Empire in the first decade of the century also contributed to the city's pool of unskilled, near-destitute population. Sixty percent of Chicago's 75,000 Italians were foreign born. They too lived apart. Colonies representing various provinces of Italy replaced the recently vacated German, Irish, French, and Swedish settlements. Here they set up shops, established Old World institutions, and ventured forth only to secure work. Serbs, Croatians, Slovenes, Slovaks, and Hungarians tended to settle on the West and Southwest sides and in South Chicago, where their unskilled labor was in demand. The census data for 1910 record that 8,505 of the 10,083 Serbo-Croatians, 4,635 of the 6,336

Slovenes, 9,507 of the 13,253 Hungarians, and 9,321 of the 13,093 Slovaks were of foreign birth.[7] Between 1900 and 1915, these newest immigrants developed institutions to ease their transition from rural Europe to urban America.

The death of Archbishop Patrick Augustine Feehan in July 1902 provided Chicago's clergy an opportunity to influence the selection of their next superior. Shortly after Feehan died, Bishop John Lancaster Spalding, as senior suffragan of the archdiocese, appointed the controversial auxiliary bishop, Peter J. Muldoon, administrator, until such time as an archbishop was installed. Spalding, according to Bishop James Ryan of Alton, Illinois, had little choice: either appoint Muldoon or admit the terrible state of ecclesiastical affairs by rejecting the natural appointee. It was not, Ryan wrote the auditor of the apostolic delegate, that Muldoon was personally responsible for the "stench in the nostrils of the better class of people and clergy" of Chicago, but he was victimized by an ambitious clergy.[8] The question in the minds of the laity and clergy was whether Muldoon would be nominated by the irremovable rectors and diocesan consultors, whose duty it was to suggest episcopal candidates to Rome.[9]

On July 24, according to the procedure outlined by the Third Plenary Council of Baltimore, Bishop Spalding called the consultors and irremovable rectors together for the balloting. Before the election, the voters swore to set aside all personal feelings and motives and to be guided by the Church's welfare. Three choices were made: *dignissimus,* "most worthy"; *dignior,* "more worthy"; and *dignus,* "worthy." Their three selections (or *terna*) were respectively Bishop Spalding, Bishop Muldoon, and Bishop Quigley.[10] In the afternoon, the suffragans of the archdiocese, Bishops Spalding, Ryan, and John Janssen of the Belleville diocese, studied and discussed the priests' *terna* and submitted their own. They agreed with the morning voters only in the *dignissimus* designation; for the second and third positions they chose Bishop George Montgomery of Monterey and Los Angeles and Fr. Daniel J. Riordan, pastor of St. Elizabeth's parish in Chicago and brother of the archbishop of San Francisco.[11]

The selection of Spalding to head the *terna* was not startling; he was greatly admired for his intelligence, poise, and renown as a writer, speaker, and educator. More surprising was the selection of Muldoon as *dignior*; he had just weathered the storm of character assassination and, at 36, was young for such an assignment. However, he was greatly respected for his administrative ability, which was reflected in the prosperity of his West Side parish, St. Charles Borromeo, and recent work as Feehan's chief administrator and vicar general. Additionally, he was esteemed by the immigrant clergy and laity. The thoroughly German pastor of St. Aloysius parish, Aloysius Thiel, had previously said of Muldoon: "He, if any man, thoroughly knows our cosmopolitan archdiocese and all the peoples that form its parts. And to judge from his past I take it for granted that all of them are not only known to him, but also dear to his heart."[12]

According to the *Chicago Daily News,* Muldoon's selection was the result of his "exceptional . . . cosmopolitan backing [which] was felt throughout the voting."[13] The *New World* declared that both Spalding and Muldoon were acceptable "in a very exceptional degree" to Chicago's various nationalities.[14] The third choice, James E. Quigley, was regarded as a manifestation of the Chicago priests' desire to strengthen the Buffalo prelate's candidacy for the see of New York, left vacant by the death of Archbishop Michael Corrigan.[15] They little expected their vote of confidence to have a bearing on the selection of Chicago's archbishop.

While Chicagoans awaited Rome's action on the *terna,* they were not aware of the political jockeying and intrigue that would accompany the ultimate selection. Rev. Hugh Smyth, the irremovable pastor of St. Mary's in Evanston and an anti-Muldoonite, informed Rev. Dennis O'Connell, the influential friend and advisor of Cardinal James Gibbons, that Muldoon owed his choice as *dignior* to four voters who were indebted to him for their position, and two others who feared appointment of a strict disciplinarian.[16] When Bishop Spalding sent Cardinal Gibbons the result of the voting, he noted that the bishops of the province and the "intelligent and religious priests and laymen of Chicago" believed that appointment of Muldoon would be "an irreparable calamity."[17] Michael Cudahy, the meat packer, one of Chicago's most prominent laymen, also wrote Gibbons, opposing Muldoon, and pleaded for the selection of Spalding.[18]

Resistance to the Muldoon candidacy was also registered outside the Archdiocese of Chicago. Achbishop John Ireland of St. Paul wrote the Propaganda to call attention to the importance of the Chicago appointment and stated that selection of the auxiliary bishop would be a "grave disaster for religion" because he was "young, inexperienced, with very ordinary talents, with little public esteem among Catholics, and no influence among Protestants."[19] Ireland declared that the decline in the morals and moral condition of the Chicago clergy under Feehan had to be reversed, and he contended that appointment of Muldoon, who was supported by the guiltiest faction in the recent scandal, would condemn Chicago to mediocrity.[20] Similar sentiments were forcefully expressed by Patrick W. Riordan, archbishop of San Francisco and a former Chicagoan. Both men recommended that Spalding be appointed to cure the ills of the "grievously" afflicted Chicago Church.[21] Cardinal Gibbons also supported the Spalding candidacy. However, he praised the virtues of Muldoon, but noted that the extreme situation created by the previous year's disorder demanded that another man be selected.[22]

Nearly five months after the submission of the *terna,* word reached Chicago that James Edward Quigley had been recommended to the pope. Why had the discussion taken so long, and why did the cardinals engage in "extremely lively" debate and bear "traces of extreme excitement" as they left their meeting?[23] Why had the two candidates, most familiar to Chicagoans, been passed over for an outsider? One paper conjectured that Spalding, who was considered the certain choice, was opposed by the former apostolic delegate, Cardinal Martinelli, because of his liberalism and recent outspoken criticism of Catholic University of America. No one could have known, or would have guessed, that Spalding was rejected because his appointment would have caused great scandal and irreparable damage to the Church in America: his estranged lover had threatened to make public her former relationship with the candidate.[24] Nor were Chicagoans aware of the strong opposition to Muldoon's appointment.

Although wonderment was expressed at Quigley's selection, Chicago Catholics readily accepted Rome's decision as the will of God. Bishop Muldoon told a reporter that Quigley's appointment gave him "great personal pleasure" because he was a personal friend and a devoted and energetic churchman, capable of strong and vigorous leadership. Despite the desire to see their man selected, the Muldoon supporters expressed willingness to bow to Rome's choice and pledged their fealty to the new superior.[25] The laity also registered their gratification. The appointment was agreeable to them because of Quigley's reputation as a "strong personality" and able administrator. They also hoped that his being an outsider would help him rise above the factions.[26]

The appointee was not jubilant over the news from Rome; he wished, instead, to remain in Buffalo. The previous summer, when Quigley learned of his position on the *terna,* he let it be known that he was grateful for the compliment, but hoped to remain where his dearest friends resided and his life blended with his work. Furthermore, he declared that Chicago required a man thoroughly familiar with the archdiocese, because it would take an outsider at least five years to familiarize himself with the post. The bishops of the New York province besought Rome to permit Quigley to stay in Buffalo, and the candidate himself wrote, asking that he be permitted to continue to work in his diocese. Both petitions were weighed and dismissed; the welfare of Roman Catholicism's fourth largest archdiocese was paramount.[27]

James Edward Quigley was born in Osawa, Ontario, Canada, in 1854 of immigrant parents who left Ireland in the famine time. When he was an infant, his parents moved to Lima, New York, then to Rochester, and when he was 10 they settled in Buffalo. Since James was the first son, Mrs. Quigley desired to offer him to God, as was a tradition in her family. As an adolescent and a young man, he studied with the Christian Brothers at St. Joseph's College and with the Vincentians at the Seminary of Our Lady of the Angels (now Niagara University). Only once did young James question the vocation his mother encouraged. When he was 16, he took the West Point admission exam and was accepted; he decided, however, to serve the Church. After completing studies with the Vincentians, young Quigley went to Europe for advanced training. He attended the University of Innsbruck, Austria, then entered the College of the Propaganda, Rome, where he concluded his collegiate studies in 1879 and received his Doctor of Theology degree, *summa cum laude.* Shortly afterward, he was ordained and returned to the Buffalo diocese. He served his apprenticeship both as pastor and administrator. Between 1884 and 1886, he was rector of the cathedral, counselor to the bishop, president of the diocesan school board, and synodal examiner. When the Right Rev. Stephen V. Ryan died, Fr. Quigley was appointed his successor, and was consecrated bishop of Buffalo on February 24, 1897.[28]

During his tenure, Bishop Quigley exhibited attributes that qualified him for the archbishopric of Chicago. He was respected as a defender of authority in Church and state and regarded as a "rigid disciplinarian both among the laity and clergy."[29] Skillfully, he brought harmony and order out of the turmoil that had existed before his appointment and struck a crushing blow at the socialists who were infiltrating Buffalo labor unions. Yet, despite his reputation, Quigley was not a harsh man. He was devoted to his people and ever solicitous for their welfare, and in return he won their affection. Besides being a capable administrator and sensitive pastor, he was a cosmopolite. His European training, direction of Buffalo's heterogeneous flock, and linguistic ability—he preached in German, Italian, and English and was versed in French and Polish—suited him for the Chicago see. Furthermore, one Chicago daily reported, he had "always taken a deep interest in the welfare of immigrants."[30]

On March 10, 1903, James Quigley arrived in Chicago and was welcomed by thousands of Catholics who lined the streets between the train station and the episcopal residence. That night the 49-year-old Irish-American was formally installed as archbishop of Chicago and delivered his first address to Chicago's Catholics. He explained that he assumed the burden of office in response to God's will, and could, with the help and cooperation of the laity and clergy, fulfill his divinely commissioned task. However, he said he accepted full responsibility and would bear the consequences of any mistakes he might make. What was clearly implied, but not stated in his address, was a call for the unity and respect which had escaped his predecessor. "I shall seek," he maintained, "the counsel of others, and in the multitude of counsel may find the right, *but I must decide for myself*. Whatever I do I shall do in justice and charity." He had recognized the warm welcome of the official greeters he encountered that afternoon, and noted: "You have promised me your reverence and obedience, I hope I shall have your love also."[31]

If the city's second archbishop did not win the love of his flock, he won its deepest respect. He was not gregarious, but "stolid" and "solemn," uncomfortable with levity and conscious of the dignity of his office. He kept his own counsel, and even his closest associates knew little of his personal thoughts and feelings. They came to know, however, that he cared for them. To many of his priests he was like a father, thoroughly interested in their welfare and ever willing to listen to their personal and parochial concerns.[32] The day after his installation, he let it be known that he was the people's servant. He established office hours, from 9 a.m. to 2 p.m., for "any and all" who wished to see him, and promised to install a phone so that persons who lived at a distance could make sure he would be there before they started out.[33]

The theme of service characterized his administration, and eventually led to his premature death on July 10, 1915. Even a partial listing of his work in these twelve years bears witness to his sense of stewardship. He fostered charity work, induced the Jesuits to found Loyola University, and the Vincentians DePaul University,[34] so that Chicago would be "the principal educational center of the western hemisphere," and reorganized institutions for the care of dependent children and established training and industrial schools for them. He gave a chapel and cemetery to Cook County for use by poor-house inmates professing the Catholic faith. He established parish boards (or layman trustees) in each parish to supervise parish finances, and he divided large parishes, believing that smaller churches and schools would give the people a greater sense of participation. He turned the episcopal summer home that his predecessor had built (adjacent to the home for dependent children at Des Plaines) into a hospital for children. Cathedral College, a preparatory seminary, was initiated in 1904 for young men interested in the priesthood.

Quigley's influence was also felt beyond Chicago. He helped found and head the Catholic Church Extension Society of the United States to care for Catholics in rural areas; called the first missionary congress of the Roman Catholic Church ever held in America (in 1908); and he sheltered, and caused convents and monasteries to be founded by, religious orders which were persecuted in Europe. He also sent trusted priests to revolution-torn Mexico to investigate the conditions of the Catholic people and clergy, arranged shelters and schools for the refugees in the United States, and directed the work of securing justice for Mexican Catholics through the State Department in Washington, D.C.[35] All the accomplishments of Archbishop Quigley were manifestations of his sense of mission and belief that Catholicism must extend to all aspects of life. "The religious progress of the faithful in his care," Bishop Paul Rhode, Quigley's auxiliary, pointed out, "was his great thought, to the exclusion of all else."[36] This conviction was most manifest in his dealings with the special needs of the diverse population of his archdiocese.

Although Quigley did not enunciate a philosophy of the Church's relation and responsibility to immigrants, his appointees did. Bishop Muldoon, who had served as Feehan's vicar general and was retained in that office by Quigley, believed that Church officials should treasure diversity as a mosaic, because cultural differences reflect the various features of Christ himself.[37]

A more thorough statement of the Church's mission among the immigrants was made by Rev. Edmund M. Dunne, D.D., who was chancellor from 1905 to 1910, when he became bishop of Peoria. Dunne, who distinguished himself as a student in Belgium and Rome and as a devoted minister among Chicago's poor Italians, epitomized the Church's mission to all nations. He spoke Latin, German, Italian, Polish, and modern Greek almost as fluently as English, and had a reading knowledge of several other languages.[38] According to Dunne, the Church was guided by well-defined principles in her dealings with immigrant members, even if they were not always consciously set forth. He summarized the principles to which the Church "steadfastly" adhered: "(1) The immigrant must be kept faithful to his religion; (2) through his own language as long as necessary; (3) he must at the same time be made a good American citizen."[39]

The "cardinal principle" of preserving the faith of the immigrant, who often had lived in lands where Catholicism was the state religion—where it was rooted in his daily life and regulated all his habits, where the environment was impregnated with Catholicism—caused America's bishops and priests to exert themselves "in every way to put within reach of their flock every facility for the profession and practice of their faith." To this end, the Church had the responsibility to use the potent appeal of the immigrants' language and ceremonies of worship and devotion. The goal of the Church, Dunne explained, was not the conformity of newcomers to an American mold:

> It never was the Church's policy to obliterate the racial characteristics of her children coming here to enjoy liberty and advantages. No nation on earth has a monopoly of all those qualities that go to make up civilization. Each can learn from his neighbor and nowhere was there greater opportunity for the exercise of mutual forbearance in toning down antagonistic tendencies, for the display of the finer traits of national character for the benefit of others, than in our cosmopolitan American commonwealth.

The Church did not seek, Dunne continued, indefinitely to perpetuate national characteristics, because segregation into national units was not in the best interests of the common country or the immigrants themselves. The immigrants' usefulness as members of the Church and the Republic depended on their "amalgamation" with the people at large; but, he added, "their progress is conditioned by their absorption into the American nation."[40]

A convinced cultural pluralist like his chancellor, Archbishop Quigley respected all nationalities. Ministering fairly to the Archdiocese of Chicago, which boasted a membership of "more Irish Catholics than the city of Dublin, more German Catholics than the city of Berlin, more Polish Catholics than the city of Warsaw, more Bohemian Catholics than the city of Prague, more Italian Catholics than the city of Pisa,"[41] was a great challenge. Yet he met the challenge and did not alienate any nationality.

The former Buffalo prelate was a realist, aware that the gradual dissolution of ethnic exclusiveness, as witnessed among the Germans and Irish, would have to take its own course. As a churchman, he wanted to make sure that Catholicity was an integral part of the processes of adaptation and acculturation. The *New World* editor reflected Quigley's mind when he commented on the diversity and the exclusiveness of the city's Catholics:

> Undoubtedly temporary segregation has its advantages; it protects, to some extent, religion and race. It is impossible, however,

that such a status should continue. The friction resulting from association with other races will gradually disintegrate these colonies. . . . The importance of having all these nationalities touch at certain points with the great Catholic body is apparent.[42]

Slowly, through a common faith, the power for good, latent in the ethnic communities, would be united to bring about a more Christian America.

During Archbishop Quigley's tenure, twenty-six territorial parishes were established for the Irish and other Catholics who used the English language. The chief change in most of the new parishes and in the older parishes, which had served a near-rural population on the city's edges only decades before, was the parishioners' economic condition. Although the flow of Catholics from the poor, working-class districts had begun earlier, the change became more noticeable in the first two decades of the twentieth century. People without "evidence of great wealth or pinching poverty" moved from the industrial and commercial districts to comfortable residential areas, like Lake View and Rogers Park on the North Side, Woodlawn, Englewood, and even Kenwood and South Shore on the South Side, and Garfield Park and Austin on the West Side.[43]

Despite their new mobility, the Irish brought traditions, customs, experiences, and attitudes that set them apart and fostered rather cohesive ghettos. The parishes they established became the center of their new environments—an anchor that ensured continuity with their former life. The parish provided groups of like-experienced individuals a place to meet and an educated community leader.

With the move from the first settlements and the reduced number of new immigrants, the Irish seemed to be on the verge of losing their ethnic identity. Although the Ancient Order of Hibernians continued to exist, the "more American" societies, like the Knights of Columbus and the Catholic Order of Foresters, successfully competed for members. Lest the young lose their Irish identity, a campaign was begun to teach Irish history in their schools. The Irish History Society of South Chicago and the Ancient Order of Hibernians, supported by Archbishop Quigley and his newspaper, launched the drive. The importance of Celtic history was explained by the *New World*:

If there is any greatness in the Irish character it is the outgrowth of Irish life and Irish ideals, and if the Irish-American is not to degenerate into a creature without distinction and individuality, he must know the history of his people. The race of strongest and highest character is the one that will model and shape American life, and aside from our duty as Irishmen it is our highest duty as Americans to give all that is beautiful and best in us to the land in which we have found a home.[44]

The young would become not only better men and women, and better citizens, but better Catholics, because Ireland's history was one in which nationality and religion were closely intertwined.[45] By 1909, after more than five years of work, Irish history was taught in twenty-six of the territorial parish schools.[46]

The revival of Gaelic culture continued to attract attention in the new century. Societies fostering Gaelic language, song, dance, art, literature, and sports still met; but by 1910 the number of announcements carried by the *New World* had decreased, pointing to lessened enthusiasm.[47] Chicago's Gaelic revival ran parallel to the same movement in Ireland and helped to finance the mother country's revival. To further the work of the Gaelic League of Ireland, Chicagoans established the Douglas Hyde Fund, and the ever-generous Quigley contributed $100.[48]

Chicago's Irish were anxious that their trans-Atlantic cousins win freedom, but they were critical of nonparliamentary means. Thus, while they encouraged the revival of cultural nationalism, they objected to physical-force nationalism. Cherishing the vision of a free Ireland, the city's Irish lent moral and financial support to John Redmond, M.P., in his endeavors to win independence. Redmond received consistent and strong backing from the *New World*, which informed its readers of Irish political events, demanded Home Rule, and encouraged its readers to support the cause. Sinn Fein, heir to Clan-na-Gael, was respected for its intention but criticized for its lack of realism. When in May 1914 it appeared that Home Rule was certain, the *New World* rejoiced that "the dream of a century has come to pass in Ireland."[49]

Chicago's Irish still clung to their Irishness and, simultaneously, sought the host society's respect. They denied that they were, as the *Chicago Inter Ocean* suggested, "too Irish," and declared that if they were good citizens they deserved the respect and rights accorded all Americans.[50] As they moved up the economic ladder, they became more sensitive about the image of their race. The *New World* called upon Irishmen to "mercilessly expose [the] outrageous injury to their race" caused by persons who, when charged with crimes, assumed Irish names.[51] Further, they were asked to protest the mockery of vaudeville's "Paddy, Pigs, and Potatoes" caricatures and to boycott stores that sold postcards that boldly and deliberately insulted the children of

Eire. "We do not believe," Quigley's organ editorialized, "that Catholic Irishmen should waste time resenting trivial things, but we do believe that there are some things they should not let pass. No race in America has any right to insult people of another race. Caricatures of this kind are distinctly un-Christian, un-American, and unwise."[52] The archdiocesan weekly supplied its Irish readers with past and present information that fostered pride, but cautioned them not to ignore their shortcomings—intemperance and lack of intellectuality.[53]

Serving the people as they emerged from the old ghettos were more and more American-born priests of Irish descent. Bishop Quigley, in his desire to have a native clergy, founded Cathedral College as a preparatory seminary. Unlike Feehan, Quigley did not call upon Irish seminaries for his priests, but twelve of the first sixteen Cathedral College alumni had Irish surnames.[54] Chicago's Irish would find that their priests were one with them in the process of adjusting to and meeting the problems of American life.

German Catholics were also moving out of the older districts and relocating farther north and south. Unlike the Irish, however, they did not build many churches—only two were established during Quigley's tenure, and both of them in his first two years.[55] The almost complete cessation in founding German national parishes in the new century reflected the sharp decline in immigration and the acculturation of native-born German Catholics. Andrew J. Townsend, a historian of Chicago's Germans, hypothesized that the decrease in national parishes "lies in the fact that the German Catholics were more Catholic than German and found that they could worship well in English-speaking Catholic churches."[56]

The parishes near the city center, such as St. Francis Assisi, St. Joseph's, St. Peter's, and St. Boniface, became victims of commercial ingress or the pressure of new immigrant groups. Between 1905 and 1915, the zealous pastor of St. Joseph's found it impossible to stem the progress northward, beyond the parish bounds, because his parishioners sought homes in better residential sections. In 1886 the parish records listed 258 baptisms and 54 weddings, but by 1906 only 75 baptisms and 26 weddings.[57] The same situation developed at St. Francis Assisi, on the southwest edge of the Loop. The influx of non-Catholics sealed the fate of the parish and "no human power could alter it."[58] St. Boniface, the first German parish on the Northwest Side, prospered until the turn of the century but suffered because of the expanding pressure of the Polish community and the destruction of housing for factory expansions. In 1901, 1,200 children attended the parish school, but fifteen years later only 200.[59]

The two new parishes, St. Gregory's on the far North Side and St. Clement's on the northwest edge of Lincoln Park, were indicative of the change taking place in Chicago's German community. St. Gregory's, built in 1904 as an exclusively German-speaking parish, soon had two of its three Sunday sermons preached in English, and according to the parish chronicler, this proved an invitation to the Irish. Because the Irish came to the church in great numbers, the parish rapidly lost its reputation as an exclusively German parish.[60] In 1905, St. Clement's began as a bilingual parish, but after seven years found "there was little call for and much less need for continuing the use of the German language." It was made a territorial parish in 1912 to serve all the local residents, including a considerable number of Irish.[61]

Societies and newspapers also marked the acculturation of second- and third-generation German Catholics. If indeed some church societies, like the Catholic Guards (Katholische Garde von Amerike), retained the language at the old parish of St. Michael's, where the newer immigrants continued to settle, others did not.[62] The staunchly German pastor of St. Aloysius parish failed in his efforts to have the church societies' meetings conducted in German.[63] Even solidly German parishes like St. Michael's made concessions to change. In 1909, for example, its parishioners produced the play *More Sinned Against than Sinning,* billed as a "drama of Irish life." At the 1914 meeting of the Diocesan Union of Illinois, composed of young men's societies of the German churches of the state, the question of opening membership to societies of all nationalities was seriously considered. Such an "important and radical change," the representatives decided, should not be made until each society had an opportunity to discuss the matter.[64] However, entertainment of such a change was, in itself, a significant departure.

Change was coming fast. In 1909 the German Central Verein published *Central Blatt and Social Justice* in English, lest the younger generation cease to recognize traditional German Catholic ideals. The *Central Blatt* explained that the society's leaders desired that the "beautiful German Catholic spirit continue to live in the American people," and that the spirit of Christian progress, preached by Ludwig Windhorst and Bishop Wilhelm von Kettler, have an impact on American minds. To reach the younger generations of German-Americans, to win the appreciation and respect of Catholics of other nationalities, and "to have a shaping influence on the non-Catholic American mind and ultimately the destinies of the nation," they accepted the need to use English.[65] The circulation statistics of Chicago's two German Catholic weeklies demonstrate the realism of the *Central Blatt*'s accommodation. In 1903 the *Katholisches Sonntag* and *Katholisches Wochenblatt* had, respectively, 12,000 and 5,630 readers; in 1908, 12,000 and 5,300; but by 1915 only the latter paper existed, with a readership of 5,000.[66]

The changes in the German parishes were not the result of an Americanizing campaign by Archbishop Quigley. On the contrary, he did all in his power to meet the needs of German Catholics. He supported them in founding a new cemetery, spoke to their national societies, and attended their celebrations.[67] More significant, he appointed Rev. Aloysius J. Thiele, pastor of St. Aloysius parish and advocate of institutional growth, as his vicar general to the Germans in 1909. One of Thiele's first acts was to go to Germany to recruit candidates to study for the priesthood, because there were not enough vocations from the Chicago diocese to care for the spiritual wants of the people. In 1910 he returned with ten young men, five of whom eventually became priests.[68] Quigley also entrusted the appointment of priests to his German vicar general and in this way gave the German clergy a voice in their own affairs.[69]

For the Germans who were becoming more American, Quigley also made accommodations. The *New World*, which had been a thoroughly Irish paper,[70] began to take cognizance of the numerous German readers who sought Catholic news in English.[71] Thomas O'Hanan, who had studied literature in Germany and served as editor of the archdiocesan weekly between 1910 and 1915, added more coverage of German events and German Catholic societies, and wrote feature stories on German culture and artists, such as Goethe and Schiller.[72] Not only did this please Germans, it informed the Irish of German culture and provided a basis for unity.

The bitter relations between the Irish and Germans in the 1890s, which had prompted the *New World* editor to ask "Will anyone tell us why it is that the Irish Catholics and the German Catholics cannot get along together?"[73] mellowed in the early years of the new century— though the relations, to be sure, were not wholly amicable. Msgr. Martin F. Schmidt recalls that many German priests of the Archdiocese of Chicago were highly critical of Irish behavior and the apparent favoritism accorded them by Quigley, but they did not act on their antipathies. Paradoxically, the nationalism that had caused problems earlier proved one of the greatest sources of unity for the Irish and Germans. Because Germany was threatened by cordial Anglo-American relations and the Irish still bore a centuries-old prejudice toward Britain, they found unity in their mutual antagonism. In 1910 the *New World* rejoiced that the sons of St. Patrick and the sons of St. Boniface were joined by a "pact and union" through the intermediary of the Ancient Order of Hibernians and the Central Verein.[74] Both the Irish and the German people were able to agree with Professor Munsterberg, who, addressing Chicago's Germania Club in 1914, declared that *England* was not the mother country, but all of Europe.[75]

In this period, both of these Catholic groups retained many of their traditions, conceptions of themselves as Irish and as German, and a desire to live with their own people, but through contact, mutual concerns, and the gradual process of Americanization they improved their relations. (This same process affected the French,[76] who were older immigrants but few in number.) The changes that were taking place among the Irish and Germans were a blessing for Archbishop Quigley. Because their allegiance to the Chicago Church was assured, and interethnic tension decreased and communication increased, he had to give only minimal attention to their needs. If he had had to divide his attention among these older groups and the recent immigrants from eastern and southern Europe, his ability to lead would have been jeopardized. With the certainty that the largest and most prosperous of his flock were secure in the fold, he was able to devote almost all of his pastoral attention to the newer groups, whose allegiance to the Catholic Church in Chicago was not yet secure.

The desire to preserve Old World ways, which absorbed the energy of Polonia in the last two decades of the nineteenth century, continued into the twentieth. In fact, these efforts seem to have redoubled. The immigrants feared they were losing their children to American society. They asked themselves who—if their children jettisoned the rich culture and spirit of Polishness—would carry on the tradition. The imperative to secure the attachment of the young to their parents' heritage became a recurring theme in Polonia's newspapers.

Narod Polski, official organ of the Polish Roman Catholic Union, faced the problem of keeping the Polish nationality alive. In a strongly worded plea to parents, the editor shamed his readers by praising the bravery of Poles who resisted Prussification. He pointed to the failure of Poles, living in America, who neither did battle for the oppressed homeland nor gathered their young under the standard of God and country, but limited their Polishness to staged performances, lectures, and political speeches. "In the race for the dollar and in the battle of existence," the paper said, "we forget our fatherland, and do not try to retain the Polish spirit in our children." Because of this failure, the youth—"the flower of our nation"—were slowly drawing away from the fatherland and the older generation, stealthily joining "English" organizations, and amusing themselves "in American fashion, in alleys and halls of the lowest kind." They were no longer willing, the paper lamented, to join Polish or Church organizations, and even worse, were ashamed of their names and extraction.[77]

Parents were charged with instilling patriotism and perpetuating their nationality. To this end, *Narod Polski* counseled parents to demand that Polish be spoken at home and that national culture and customs be made an integral element of family life. Additionally, societies for the young were encouraged to preserve the language and culture and to provide a place for expression and enjoyment of native traditions. Marriage to persons of other nationalities, even if the spouse was a Catholic, was strongly discouraged, because it made a person "indifferent to his nationality" and the children of such a union were "lost to the Polish race."[78]

The situation was especially grave for the young. In an editorial titled "Americanization," the Polish National Alliance organ *Dziennik Zwiazkowy* explained:

> He who supposes that we Poles here in America are not threatened with the loss of our national identity is gravely mistaken and shortsighted. It is true that loss of national identity does not threaten Poles who were already in their middle ages when they came from Poland and settled here. But loss of national identity threatens our children, born here or brought here in their childhood by their parents. We will not lose all our young people in the foreign sea, but we are losing a large percentage of them, and if we do not pay more attention to this fact, in a few score years we will lose half our young people, who will cling to foreigners and will be forever lost to the Polish cause.
>
> Americanism penetrates into Polish homes through doors and windows. It does not appear in so brutal a form as Germanization and Russification in Europe, but because of this it is all the more dangerous. Americanism soothes us, lulls us to sleep, tempts us with various little tricks, but it is systematically trying to pour all races, all nationalities, into one mass.

All Poles were urged to join Polish organizations as the strongest "shield against Americanism."[79] Those who did not preserve their nationality, *Narod Polski* declared, "were Irishmen of Polish descent."[80]

The rapid growth of national parishes and schools illustrated the Poles' commitment to their culture and faith. During Archbishop Quigley's tenure, the number of Polish parishes grew from eighteen to thirty-three. When Holy Innocents' (formerly a Protestant church) was consecrated in 1905, Fr. Skuminski, who spoke on the occasion, noted that the Polish people now had few excuses to make; they could now attend this Polish church and forget about the German church they had been attending for years. And they *did* attend the church. Within three years, the original membership of 144 families grew to 800. "The Polish families are buying out the properties of the Swedes and the Germans," one paper reported, "and have intentions of making this neighborhood surrounding Holy Innocence [*sic*] parish strictly Polish." The frame church soon became too small, so that in 1910 construction was begun on a brick edifice which seated 1,700. The six-room school building that was part of the original purchase also reflected the growth of the parish: within two years, six rooms had to be added, and in 1914 a new building and assembly hall were commissioned. Although the growth of Holy Innocents' was remarkable, it was not uncommon.[81]

The Poles had great faith in the ability of their schools to preserve the Polish spirit, and despite enormous sacrifices and continued conflict over administration of the schools,[82] these working-class people built new schools, added classrooms, erected high schools and academies, and even attempted to found a Polish university in Chicago. Between 1900 and 1910, enrollment in Polish national schools increased from 12,276 to 21,276, and in the following decade jumped to 35,862. By 1915, Polish schools accounted for 27.7 percent of parochial school enrollment.[83] The reason for the success of the Polish parochial schools was simply put by *Dziennik Chicagoski* on the occasion of the blessing of a school cornerstone: "The only refuge for preserving the consciousness of Polish origin among our children [is] Polish parochial schools."[84]

Poles, like their German coreligionists earlier, came under attack because they segregated their young. However, they argued that the schools taught English and that their children did very well upon graduation.[85] Two important events reassured them of their Americanism. In 1908 Vice President Charles Fairbanks spoke at the dedication of the new St. Stanislaus Kostka school,[86] and on March 10, 1912, President William H. Taft addressed the pupils of three Polish parochial schools at Immaculate Conception parish in South Chicago. The president told his audience he recognized that "you are all striving to be better boys and girls and better Americans and better Poles."[87]

Building parishes and schools filled the need to preserve the Polish spirit. However, Poles continued to desire understanding from, and representation in, the hierarchy of the Catholic Church in the United States. When the Polish memorial of 1901 to the American hierarchy bore no fruit, the Polish clergy did not abandon their demand for a Polish prelate. Wenceslaus Kruszka, a Ripon, Wisconsin, cleric and historian of Polish-Americans, encouraged them. In 1903, buoyed by the support of Bishops Muldoon and Spalding of Illinois, Quigley of Buffalo, and others sympathetic to the cause, Kruszka collected statistics to impress the Vatican with the numerical strength of Poles in America. Affidavits poured in. Chicago's mayor, Carter Harrison Jr., certified that 250,000 lived in the city. In 1904, after several delays, Kruszka delivered his message and statistics to the recently installed pontiff, Pius X, who promised to accommodate the American Poles.[88]

Not all Chicagoans, however, were enthusiastic about Kruszka's mission and Pius X's pledge. While the Ripon priest awaited the selection of the pope, the *New World* took note of his activities, and summarized the "salient points" of the memorial of 1901, but did not print the entire document for fear it might "provoke controversy—a thing never to be desired in the household of the faith." The paper said that some Poles were losing their faith because of their lack of representation in the hierarchy and the dearth of Polish-speaking clergy. However, it did not mention the contentious issues regarding the discrimination felt by many Polish clerics.[89] The paper followed up the story, and carried Kruszka's message of papal approval, but added that it had heard from other sources that appointment of a Polish bishop was not imminent.[90] The "other source," referred to by the *New World*, may have been the Resurrectionist Fathers, who, according to Joseph J. Parot, believed the unnamed bishop would probably be assigned jurisdiction in Chicago—and feared that a bishop, not of their congregation, would undermine their control of Polonia. Indeed, Rev. Francis Gordon, C.R., heir to Barzynski's *Dziennik Chicagoski,* was a constant critic of Kruszka.[91]

After thorough investigation of the needs of Polish-Americans and the dangers presented by the schismatic Polish churches (Bishop Anthony Kozlowski's churches joined Bishop Francis Hodur's Polish National Catholic Church in 1907), Rome concluded that Polish-Americans needed a bishop. The archbishop of Chicago was "chiefly instrumental" in realization of the Polish dream;[92] he supported the Kruszka petition and set the machinery for selecting a Polish bishop. Because Auxiliary Bishop Muldoon would soon become the bishop of the newly created Diocese of Rockford, an opening was available for a Pole.[93] On August 16, 1907, all the Polish priests in the archdiocese were called to Holy Name Cathedral to vote for an auxiliary bishop. Although Quigley cautioned them that their selection would not head an all-Polish diocese, but would be a bishop to all nationalities in Chicago, they must have been elated.[94]

In June of the following year, word came that Fr. Paul Rhode was to be the new auxiliary bishop. Born in Prussian Poland in 1870, Rhode came to America with his widowed mother in 1879 and attended Fr. Barzynski's St. Stanislaus School. He received his secondary education at St. Ignatius College in Chicago and his ecclesiastical training at St. Francis Seminary in Milwaukee. Rhode's kindliness and capability as a pastor and administrator won the affection and respect of his fellow clergy and the people he served, especially the parishioners of St. Michael's in the South Chicago steel mill district. Both the Resurrectionists and their opponents were happy—not a Resurrectionist himself, Rhode had been under their tutelage at Polonia's mother church.[95] Most important, the people were overwhelmed with joy because "at last their prayers were answered . . . a bishop of our own flesh and blood, of our longing and suffering."[96] The *New World* praised Rome's selection and assured Chicagoans that Rhode's elevation "inevitably will do much to heal ancient wounds."[97]

The appointment of Bishop Rhode was timely. Despite Quigley's regard for Poles, his work in fostering Polish institutions, his presence at Polish functions, and his support of Polish independence,[98] the Poles were anxious to have one of their own recognized in Church affairs. The growth of the Polish National Catholic Church and continued agitation by nationalists and disgruntled clergymen, who considered themselves "plainly abused by the autocracy of Irish and German bishops," had to be considered. That even Quigley could not bridge the gap was made very clear when he, instead of Bishop Rhode, went to St. Casimir's parish to administer confirmation. The parishioners had told their pastor they wanted Rhode to perform the ceremony, but he had ignored their request. *Dziennik Zwiazkowy* published an observer's account and analysis of parishioner reaction:

> They acted entirely indifferent to the Irish Catholic dignitary. Neither the religious nor the national societies came out to welcome the archbishop, as is the custom; only a small handful of people loyal to the reverend pastor welcomed the distinguished ecclesiastical official. Many adults failed to appear to be confirmed, having no wish to receive the sacrament from the hands of a person of another nationality. There were many vacancies in the church, because a large number of children also stayed away; and when the archbishop commenced to talk to the congregation in the English language, half of those present left the church.
>
> This religious ceremony was a total failure because of the anger of the parishioners. Such tactics on the part of the pastor can cause a break in this parish—an occurrence that should be

avoided. We have enough dissension as it is among our heavily oppressed people. The maxim taught by the clergy "He who is a Catholic is also a Pole, and he who is not a Catholic is not a Pole," seems to have lost its effect. This was proved by the behavior of the Polish Catholics in the presence of the Irish dignitary. In this instance we find that nationalistic feelings have taken the upper hand even over religious feelings. The Poles have indicated clearly that they are staunch Poles and that they want everything to be Polish in a Church.[99]

The Polish National Alliance's claim that conservative clerics, represented by the Polish Roman Catholic Union, were isolating themselves from Polish public life was strongly denied.[100] Whether Polish nationalism was more powerful than religious feeling is unmeasurable. It appears, however, that nationalism was constantly increasing, to the point of jeopardizing harmonious relations within the Catholic Church in America. Bishop Rhode's moderate and tactful leadership helped to bridge the gap and perpetuate the Barzynski doctrine of God and country. In a speech to a Polish gathering he warned: "If that which is of Polish origin will remain in America, it will be on the strong foundation of the Holy Faith." This faith demanded allegiance to duly constituted authority, not an emotional response to excessive patriotic propaganda.[101]

The problem of reconciling religion and nationalism, faced by the Poles, was not absent from the Lithuanian colonies on Chicago's South Side. Divisions between nationalists and Catholic conservatives produced serious tensions in Lithuanian parishes. Like the Poles, Lithuanian pastors taught that a good Lithuanian was a good Catholic.[102] To support the Church position, a Catholic daily, *Draugas* (Friend), was published to counter the nationalist daily, *Lietuva*.

The Lithuanian colonies also faced the prospect of being absorbed by the generally larger Polish settlements in the vicinity. A rising spirit of nationalism led the Lithuanians to denounce the Poles as their "eternal enemies" and disassociate themselves from Poles in social and political affairs. In 1909, when it was suggested that Lithuanians join with Poles to erect a statue in honor of the Revolutionary War hero Thaddeus Kosciusko, they rejected the idea. Dr. A. Rutikauskas wrote to *Lietuva*, declaring that Kosciusko was Lithuanian and that the Poles had no right to claim him. The Polish attitude, "What is yours is also mine, but what is mine is not yours," he said, had gone too far. Furthermore, any Lithuanian who cooperated with such a Polish project must be repudiated.[103]

The same spirit of nationalism also caused serious problems in religious affairs. The ever-growing Lithuanian consciousness prompted demands that Lithuanian priests sever relations with Polish priests and that the parochial schools become less Polish and more Lithuanian. Although many young Lithuanian women became nuns, they entered Polish religious orders, in the absence of their own. Archbishop Quigley realized the tension in the situation, and in 1909 brought the Sisters of St. Casimir to Chicago. Founded in Scranton, Pennsylvania, in 1907 to work among Lithuanians, the order carried out its special mission in Chicago.[104]

Quigley also ministered to the needs of the other new immigrant groups in his see. He helped found churches and secure priests (mostly members of religious orders from Europe) to conduct them. In his brief tenure, he founded and staffed numerous national parishes: 4 Slovak, 3 Croatian, and a Slovene, Hungarian, Chaldean, and Belgian (see table 10). His greatest energy in church building, however, was expended on newcomers from Italy.

As archbishop of Chicago, he financed and erected several new Italian parishes. While a student in Rome, Quigley had developed a fondness for Italians and their ways, and later, as a priest in Buffalo, he helped establish that city's first permanent Italian parish.[105] When he came to Chicago, which at that time was receiving thousands of immigrants from Italy, he tried to meet their spiritual needs. Because they lacked a tradition of Church support and, as he reported to Rome, Italians from southern Italy and Sicily were "unexcelled in their ignorance of religion," he assumed personal responsibility for their care.[106] He took the initiative in establishing parishes and securing priests, for he feared they would be lost to Catholicism because of the growing efforts of proselytizing Protestants in the city's "Little Italies."[107]

In 1902, Chicago had only one Italian parish, the Church of the Assumption, conducted by Italian members of the Service Order, and several missions conducted by Servites and Italian-speaking, Irish-descent priests. To remedy the matter, Quigley brought individual priests from the East, such as Fr. Ricardo Lorenzio, who was made pastor of Santa Maria Incornata, and the Scalabrini Fathers, whose special mission was to care for the spiritual and physical needs of Italian immigrants. Having worked with the Scalabrini priests in Buffalo and gained their respect, he persuaded them to come to Chicago, where they were placed in charge of several parishes. The Italians of the Servite Order were also commissioned to expand their work.[108] Within two years, Quigley created five Italian parishes, converted the missions to parishes, and established an additional parish in 1911. Because the Italians were poor and (compared to other national groups) disinterested in church-building, the archdiocese assumed the financial burdens.[109]

Generally, the Italians were slow to mix and to accept American ways. Only at Assumption parish, which was primarily composed of northern Italians, were there signs of adapting to American ways. The church's monthly bulletin, *Calendario Della Parrocchia Dell' Assunta, Chicago,* was published in Italian and English, and special services and missions were held in English for the young.[110] However, the other parishes, because of the recent arrival of their members and the economic and educational level of the Sicilians, Calabresi, and Neapolitans, were slower to accommodate. At times, their apparently superstitious and strange (to America) socio-religious customs even caused embarrassment to the Church. In 1910, Archbishop Quigley issued regulations for the celebration of the Feast of Our Lady of Mount Carmel because some laymen used the procession of statues for their financial gain. He wished to halt further abuses and prevent scandal. He did not, of course, seek to ban their traditional display of devotion.[111]

Unlike other national groups, the Italians did not build schools to preserve their culture. As late as 1910, only one of the ten Italian parishes had a parochial school. James Sanders noted: "This was extraordinary in a diocese where most of the other parishes had schools."[112] The poverty, lack of education, and religious attitudes of the *contadina* from southern Italy, combined with the cultural defense of a tight familial system, seem to have made the erection of schools a luxury rather than a necessity. Thus it devolved on zealous pastors, aided by Irish and German laity, to set up Sunday schools as a temporary expedient. When Rev. Luigi Giambastani, O.S.M., attempted to organize a Sunday school at St. Philip Benizi in 1910, he had to go door to door and "convince parents to send children to mass and school on Sundays." His hard work bore fruit, and by 1912, 800 to 1,000 children attended the parish Sunday school.[113]

Changes in ethnic exclusiveness became apparent in this period, yet the character of the Chicago Catholic Church remained foreign. While the Irish and Germans began to associate with one another, their identity still seemed to be Irish-American Catholic and German-American Catholic, rather than American Catholic. The newer immigrants had not yet reached the point of dialogue and amalgamation.

Thus the selection of James Edward Quigley as the second archbishop of Chicago was propitious. His cosmopolitan training and leadership enabled him to take firm control of the heterogeneous see and perfect the coalition of nationalities bequeathed by Archbishop Feehan. Assured of the allegiance of the Irish and Germans, he was free to direct his attention to accommodation of the thousands of new immigrants from eastern and southern Europe. Guided by the commission to care for the spiritual welfare of his flock, he made every effort to establish parishes and schools wherein the immigrants' faith would be preserved through maintenance of Old World languages and rites. By his pragmatic responses to individual and group needs—whether it was an Italian priest, an order of Lithuanian sisters, or a Polish bishop—he gave all a sense of belonging, avoided serious administrative problems, and achieved his ultimate goals: preservation of the Roman Catholic faith and harmony among his diverse flock.

6. Social Catholicism

ARCHBISHOP JAMES E. QUIGLEY, as he gazed upon the people who crowded Holy Name Cathedral to witness his installation, saw a diverse population—not simply by reason of birth and descent but social and economic condition as well. He was thinking about the needs of these people, especially the poor and the victims of the industrial society. "These are the days," he said, unconsciously paraphrasing Thomas Paine, "that try the souls of men." "Great questions of Faith," Quigley noted, "great questions of society are being worked out. The opportunities for God's Church are incalculable and Her obligations unmeasurable. She must take Her part in the solution of these questions. . . . We, Her representatives and Her children, must take a part in their settlement."[1]

Quigley's concern for the spiritual welfare of Chicago's Catholics, as manifested in special consideration of their national interests, was apparent in his direct interest in the disadvantaged, the poor, the dependent, and the outcast. Under his administration, the multifarious institutions and associations in the archdiocese expanded and multiplied to keep pace with the increased population and the staggering problems of an urban, industrial society. Under his watchful eye, the Chicago Church responded to the social and economic needs of all his flock. But the Industrial Revolution and the "population explosion" so exacerbated poverty that voluntary associations—such as the Church—could not meet the need. For this reason, state intervention was inevitable, for the state was the only institution with adequate resources and the ability to mobilize them.

In America, the philanthropic tradition of providing assistance to the poor changed drastically in the last decades of the nineteenth century. Charity organizations, influenced by social Darwinists, who viewed competition as the law of life, advocated self-help (instead of gratuity) to remedy pauperism. In their efforts to use their resources to best effect, professional philanthropists and charity workers discovered that pauperism was as much a cause as a product of social ills. Consequently, a new conception of poverty evolved that focused on the environment rather than the pauper. With this change a program developed, referred to as "preventative social work," which placed public authority above private initiative and public benefit above personal gain. Less and less, social workers emphasized individual rescue and devoted their energies more and more to a well-publicized crusade for social reform legislation against the forces that spawned misery.[2]

Catholic participation in charity work was motivated by concerns different from those of the new class of "scientific" philanthropists. When Cardinal James Gibbons addressed a session of the Parliament of Religions at the Columbian Exposition in 1893, he stated the Catholic view:

> It is the recognition of the fatherhood of God and the brotherhood of Christ that has inspired the Catholic Church in the mission of love and benevolence. This is the secret of her all-pervading charity. This idea has been her impelling motive in her work of the social regeneration of mankind. I behold, she says, in every human creature a child of God and brother and sister of Christ, and therefore I will protect helpless infancy and decrepit old age. I will feed the orphan and nurse the sick. I will strike the shackles from the feet of the slave, and will rescue degraded women from the moral bondage and degradation to which her frailty, and the passions of the stronger sex had consigned her.[3]

Catholics, therefore, distinguished between their own beneficent activity and that of secular societies and nonreligiously motivated persons. They called their own work "charity" and applied the terms "philanthropist" and "philanthropy" to the secular giver and his gift. The Catholic Church's essential mission was spiritual regeneration: to rescue the fallen and to sanctify and redeem the weak. Individual Catholics were charitable because they wished to demonstrate their love of God and to help their brothers for Christ's sake; philanthropists helped their fellow man for man's sake. Thus, because of the latters' motivation, Catholics viewed such good and well-intentioned work as possessing limited value. Also, Catholics were suspicious of philanthropists because these "do-gooders" appeared to be antagonistic to religion, particularly Catholicism, and because they appeared to make destitution a crime and a disgrace and thus engendered discontent and bitterness.[4] In "Philanthropy or Charity," an editorial in the *New World*, the editor declared that Christian charity is far superior to the short-sighted and inadequate humanitarian impulse, for man alone cannot solve the problems of human existence, no matter what remedies he employs.[5]

Besides manifesting love of God, Catholics engaged in charity work to win their own salvation and to preserve the faith of their coreligionists, as Catholic theology teaches that the giver receives merit in heaven for his generosity on earth.[6] Equally important, especially in Protestant America, charity work countered forces hostile to Catholicism. State, county, and municipal institutions and agencies provided for the dependent and poor, but Catholics distrusted them because they placed Catholics in settings where they might be directly or indirectly proselytized or denied access to the teachings of their religion. Speaking of the charitable activities of one society, the pastor of St. Jarlath's stated:

> 'Tis pleasant to stand on the deck of the grand old Barque of Peter as she securely rides over the years and storms of time, but all honor to those who go down into the dark hold below to dress the wounded and stop the leakage.[7]

As early as the 1840s the city's Catholics, led by Bishop Quarter, engaged in work to help immigrants, the sick, and the orphaned. However, the greatest activity was initiated in the last two decades of the nineteenth century and came to maturity under Quigley's administration. Institutions were built to serve all Catholics, but, like the parishes and the schools, they generally catered to particular ethnic groups. Orphanages, nurseries, hospitals; homes for working boys and girls, the unwed pregnant, and the aged; a temporary shelter for dependent mothers and children; and other charity institutions served Chicago's Catholics. Such organizations as the St. Vincent de Paul Society, the Visitation and Aid Society, and the Illinois Charitable Relief Corps provided aid and relief to Catholics, and especially the young, detained in public institutions.[8] Their work was encouraged and complemented by parish priests, such as Fr. Maurice Dorney of St. Gabriel's, who not only saw to the spiritual well-being of his flock but provided food and rent money to those who had fallen on hard times, and obtained employment for them. At the age of 50, Fr. Dorney obtained a law degree and used his new expertise to give free legal advice to those who were confused by the complexities of the law.[9] In 1905, with good reason, Thomas James Riley, an observer of Chicago's social and cultural institutions, asserted it was "patent that the Roman Catholic Church is unexcelled in charities."[10]

Aside from the numerous forms of direct relief and service provided by Catholic institutions and clubs, neighborhood service centers, referred to as "settlements," were created. The rise of Catholic settlement work can be explained only in relation to Catholic perceptions of secular and religious settlements that sprang up in Chicago. The contrast between them was remarkable.

On September 18, 1889, Jane Addams' Hull House settlement opened its doors to poor immigrants on the Near West Side. This neighborhood center and its staff provided the area's adult residents a place to meet, an opportunity to learn, and a helping hand, and was an advocate in times of trouble. Children also found Hull House a vital institution—athletic, social, and educational activities enhanced their lives. But more than simply providing a community center, the settlement was a locus for social reform. Jane Addams, Ellen Starr, Julia Lathrop, Florence Kelly, Dr. Alice Hamilton, and other women and men used the settlement for social service and as an experimental laboratory for programs in social work, citizenship, and social reform. Hull House, its humanitarian foundress explained, "is an experimental effort to aid in the solution of the social and industrial problems which are engendered by the modern conditions of life in a great city." "The one thing to be dreaded in the Settlement," she added, "is that it lose its flexibility, its power of quick adaptation, its readiness to change its methods as its environment may demand."[11]

Generally, Chicago Catholics did not perceive the world the same way as Miss Addams, nor did they believe that the purpose of a settlement was to serve as a laboratory for social experimentation. Catholic settlement work, such as institutional and direct charity activity, stressed the spiritual dimension of the individual.

Four years after Miss Addams established Hull House, Catholics embarked on the settlement aspect of charity work. In response to the poverty of the Depression of 1893 and the directives of the women's congresses, the Catholic Congress, and the Parliament of Religions of the World's Columbian Exposition, the Chicago Catholic Women's League was founded. Incorporated in September 1893 for "the advancement and promotion of the general good of humanity in accordance with the principles of the Catholic Church,"[12] the league conducted a wide range of activities, including direct relief, protection of unmarried girls who were new to Chicago, and cultural and educational programs. However, its major endeavor was development and support of settlements.

Within three months of the World's Fair, three houses were opened, one in each section of the city and each with a corps of officers and workers. Each settlement—St. Anne's on the West Side, St. Elizabeth's on the North Side, and All Saints (later St. Mary's) on the South Side—would eventually provide a nursery, kindergarten, "kitchengarten," sewing school, library, savings bank, mothers' club, and employment and relief bureaus.[13]

In succeeding years, other settlements were established, most of which served residents of Polish and Italian neighborhoods. St. Elizabeth's Relief Society, organized by a St. Stanislaus Kostka priest, established St. Elizabeth's Day Nursery in 1904 to care for children of working mothers, and later extended the center's activities to educational and health programs. Eight years later, three Polish pastors opened Guardian Angel Day Nursery in the Back of the Yards district to care for children and provide evening classes in sewing, painting, cooking, and primary English for young working women.[14] To serve Italians in the Hull House vicinity, the Guardian Angel Sunday School Association opened a recreational facility for boys in 1910. Soon afterward, the Guardian Angel Center was incorporated, with the goal of improving the "moral, physical, educational and social welfare of the people of the neighborhood."[15] The settlement's seven rooms provided a place for varied educational, social, and recreational activities. Santa Maria Incornata and St. Philip Benizi (Italian parishes) also founded settlements, but they were less ambitious in scope.[16]

Catholic entrance into settlement work was more than a simple response to the social, physical, and educational needs of the poor. It was a concerted effort to duplicate the work of humanitarians at Hull House, the University of Chicago Settlement, the Northwestern University Settlement, and various Protestant institutions in the immigrant ghettos. Catholics maintained a strong and persistent fear that these neighborhood centers posed a serious threat to the spiritual welfare of the newly arrived. In 1903 the *New World* editorialized that the social workers and reformers, though very earnest in their concern for newcomers, "are not apt to reap any remarkable harvest."[17] This declaration indicated confidence that parish priests and Catholic societies would keep immigrants close to the Church. Equally significant, it pointed to the Church's belief that settlements were competitors. This was most evident in the Church's attitude toward Jane Addams and Hull House.

Jane Addams' mission among the poor found little favor in the *New World*. The pioneer of Chicago settlement work was criticized because she sought (and received) too much attention, because she and her helpers threatened the sanctity of the family, and because her activity was tolerant of forces hostile to Catholicism. The archdiocesan paper registered dismay at the "canonization" of Miss Addams by many Chicagoans and the city's papers. The attention paid to "the high priestess of Hull-House," "the Sweetheart of humanity," and the "Saint of Hull House" troubled the Catholic paper.[18] When the *Chicago Record-Herald* featured a series of articles on various nationalities, it stated that the great factor in training all newcomers in citizenship was Hull House, and the *New World* objected to such unqualified praise:

> But really, is Hull House the chief agency for diffusing culture and teaching civilization in Chicago? We do not so believe. When we reflect upon the tremendous number of German Catholic churches and schools, Irish Catholic churches and schools, and Catholic churches and schools for Poles, Bohemians, Italians, Austrians, and even Syrians, we feel obliged to enter a protest for the sake of truth. . . . The Catholic Church . . . is building civilization here after a manner which Hull House does not understand and cannot appreciate. It is a fact visible to God that the Catholic Church in Chicago is doing more to create a snow-white dawn among all races surging into this great, restless, terrible city than fifty Hull Houses could do, and if one but stop and reflect impartially it will be equally visible to man.[19]

After describing the variety of work among Chicago immigrants (three-fourths of whom were Catholic), the editor noted that the Catholic "masses are advancing here as in no other city in the world and the great dawn-building Catholic Church is the cause." It concluded: "There is no uplifting influence like it on all the earth, and at least some part of the good it does ought to be recognized by secularism."[20]

The Catholic weekly, moreover, had no patience with female settlement workers, who were dismissed as "feminine busybodies who neglect their own homes in order to indulge in a little sentiment or gain notoriety by attempting to pauperize whole neighborhoods." The paper stressed that it bore no ill will toward women of various denominations who worked with the children of the poor, but it scorned "the tactless, hysterically emotional, childless female slummers" because they insulted devoted fathers and mothers who were giving "real" parental care to children "whom they have accepted as a sacred trust from their Creator." By giving breakfast to children of the neighborhood, the paper said, settlement workers were taking away the responsibility that belongs to parents. When these "scientific philanthropists" announced that 36 percent of the city's school children did not eat breakfast, the editor declared that it was not true. As a final thrust, he charged that settlement workers were "socialistic amazons," seeking to weaken parental authority.[21]

More serious even than tampering with parental rights was Jane Addams' supposed disregard for the salvation of souls and her tolerance of materialistic, anticlerical, socialistic, anarchistic, and free-love causes.[22] When the Hull House foundress declared that the churches should pay attention to the terrible conditions of the poor "of this world instead of idly contemplating the next,"[23] the archdiocesan weekly counseled her:

> Jane, Jane, if you would but take the trouble to peep into the Catholic hospitals and Houses of Refuge in our country you would quickly learn that Hull House would scarcely form their vestibule. A little humility, Jane, a little humility.[24]

The Church had a dual mission, to alleviate physical want and bring spiritual nourishment. However, Jane Addams—the *New World* explained—"worked the salvation of the stomach of many a 'down and outer' at the loss of his eternal soul."[25] Addams' humanitarianism was doing irreparable injury because there was not "a spark of the spiritual in her work or her whole make up." Hull House theories in education, sociology, and ethics were morally bankrupt because they disregarded the spiritual life. The paper argued that she did not comprehend that there could be no moral regeneration or reform, except from the soul outward. "Miss Addams," it concluded, "imagines that she is binding the wounds and healing the sores of humanity when in reality she is sowing the seeds of discontent which will ripen in the miseries she would fain remove."[26]

The gravest objection the Chicago Catholic Church had to Jane Addams' Hull House was its apparent attempt to lead Catholics— especially Italians, whose Catholicism seemed to be weak—to give up their faith. "For years," the spokesman for the Guardian Angel Sunday School Association explained, "the Hull House Boy's Club and other clubs in the neighborhood of the Forquer Street Mission have been robbing the Mission of the boys who through the efforts of the Association have received religious instruction." The boys were taking advantage of Hull House's congenial atmosphere and recreational facilities and had begun to neglect their religious duties. Thus the catechists pleaded for funds to equip their center in order to retain their students and win back former students. It was absolutely necessary, the association contended, to have a club for Italian boys where their faith would not be endangered.[27]

The *New World* also did battle with Jane Addams because she permitted anticlerical Italians to use the settlement. A number of young men formed the Giordano Bruno Club, named after the monk who was convicted of heresy and burned at the stake (by the civil powers), to study modern Italian literature and history. The members of the club, like many nationalistic Italians, were anticlerical, opposing the temporal power of the pope and clerical influence in political affairs. However, they affirmed the authority of the Church in spiritual matters. Similar to the Irish, whose loyalty to Home Rule did not conflict with their loyalty to the Church, the anticlericals maintained that they could be devout Catholics and yet belong to the anticlerical party.[28]

In the spring of 1908 the Giordano Bruno Club produced an anticlerical play at Hull House that portrayed the life of its namesake. Because the lead character constantly breathed invectives against the pope, bishops, and priests, the *New World* charged the settlement with wronging the Church, causing Italians to lose their faith, and creating a corps of priest-hating anarchists.[29] The editor attacked humanitarian-run settlements as "roosting-places for frowsy anarchists, fierce-eyed socialists, professed anticlericals and a coterie of long-haired sociologists intent upon probing moonshine with pale fingers."[30]

The tension was renewed nearly six years later when the Giordano Bruno Club scheduled another play at Hull House. As soon as the *New World* heard that the club had rented Hull House theatre to produce *Galileo, Galilei* ("a very bitter anti-clerical play"), it dispatched a staff member to meet Miss Addams to verify the report. Informed that the production of plays fostering anticlericalism "would not be tolerated by Chicago Catholics," she replied that the advisability of giving space to the club had already been considered by the settlement's board. Furthermore, she said the institution was absolutely nonsectarian and, as the anticlerical movement was a national issue in Italy, there was no reason why the play should not be presented at Hull House. Nonetheless, she promised to present the matter for reconsideration to the center's board, but the earlier decision was sustained and the play was presented.

The week following the play, Jane Addams visited the *New World* office to explain why the play was permitted. Because the Italian group had contracted with Hull House, she contended that it could not go back on its word. More important, she stressed that she saw nothing objectionable in the play. Furthermore, there was nothing wrong with the club, for, besides presenting anticlerical plays the group read noncontroversial literature, such as Shakespeare. The editor responded to his visitor's three-point argument, informing her that she had insulted a million and a quarter Catholics in order to favor a "few fanatics." According to the paper's report, Miss Addams seemed unwilling to come to any understanding; "in fact she failed to appreciate why we should object to seeing our priesthood being defamed and mocked by falsehoods and misrepresentations on the stage."[31]

An editorial in the same issue, "The Offending of Hull House," further explained Catholic grievances. The editor, James Conwell,[32] noted that he had previously defended Miss Addams, believing her to be unjustly criticized, but now admitted that he had been partially mistaken. Conwell countered her three reasons and protested the club's "un-American purpose." "In the first place," he wrote, "anti-clericalism has no place in America and Hull House in fostering it under its patronage is perpetuating a phase of life which is ugly and nasty and destructive, and no one is deceived by the shabby excuse that anti-clericalism has any part in the life of Italians." Relative to the sanctity of the contract, Conwell contended that, had a play offensive to the Jewish community been protested—for example, a drama depicting Russian Jews practicing ritual murder—it would have been stopped.

> Now we Catholics are over 50 per cent of this community. We are the strongest cohesive force in Chicago. We bear our power with modesty. We are long suffering, but we are not cowards. We don't propose to have perpetuated here in America the decadent viciousness of Europe. We solemnly protest against the transplanting to free America of the lies of our atheistical enemies across the seas. And we protest more mightily and solemnly because the lies against us receive the shadow of decency under the roof of Hull House.

Catholic perceptions of Miss Addams illustrate that Catholics were determined to preserve the faith of the immigrants and were intolerant of those who might weaken the bonds between a Catholic and his parish. The editorial broadsides also indicate that Addams' accusers did not understand her perception of social settlement work or her conception of civil and political liberty.

Catholic involvement in charity work focused on relief for the individual and redemption of the soul. Catholics, it seems, did not grasp that the women of Hull House believed that social and environmental change, more than individual change, was most necessary. Jane Addams' involvement with the Bull Moose party was one of her efforts to bring to government the progressive innovations tested at Hull

House; she hoped to lead the federal government to institute programs and initiate legislation that would better the lot of all people, especially such as those in the tenements surrounding her settlement. The *New World* editor demonstrated his misunderstanding when he wrote that "Jane Addams became a Bull Mooser, simply because the animal has antlers, and horns are used for 'tooting.' "[34]

During the period of ferment referred to as the Progressive Era, when men tried to make government more responsive to society, regulate industry, and induce the state to meet its social responsibilities, Chicago's Catholics participated. However, they appeared to have reservations about the role of the state, especially as related to family affairs. Many reformers viewed Roman Catholicism as a retarding force on the thrust for progress. The *New World* disagreed, and in an editorial responded to its critics:

> One of the odd things of the twentieth-century civilization is that it cannot see that the Catholic church is actually leading in all movements that make for real advancement and universal uplift. There is no denying that she opposes many things erroneously called advance, but she does so because she sees with eyes two thousand years old, yet full of the keenness of youth, that the measures proposed are destructive. Progress that destroys is not progress. It is insanity.[35]

Whether the reform was political or social, the Catholic position challenged the reformers because they dealt with structure and not with the essence of betterment—the individual. The Church taught that the fabric of society can be only as strong as the moral life of its members. Changes in the social order would not come unless individuals were regenerated.

Only religion could bring the ideal order. Pragmatism, the philosophy that equates the goodness or badness of an act with its practical success or failure, was regarded by Catholics as a serious threat to the moral growth of America. Even though, as the *New World* editorialized in 1907, pragmatists might wrap their theory in "fold after fold of the phraseology of Christian ethics, in order to hide its barbaric nudity, and make it acceptable and attractive to uncritical and unreflecting minds," their doctrine was inherently "a pagan shoot." In commerce, its fruits were trusts and strikes; in government, it produced tyranny and absolutism; and in international affairs it begot militarism, universal conscription, crushing taxation, and ceaseless diplomatic intrigue.[36]

Even Protestantism was criticized, because, with the rise of the "social gospel," many ministers became advocates of public reform and led campaigns for better government, and though the values they imparted, the archdiocesan paper explained, were timely, they were not of eternal significance. Instead of crusading against officials, it suggested, ministers should inculcate the principles of Christianity and encourage parishioners to practice parenthood and educate their offspring in the spirit of the Gospel.[37]

Catholicism's primary concern was to strengthen the moral life, especially through the family. Thus all influences that tended to weaken the family were not only criticized but condemned. Age-old moral and social evils (such as intemperance), as well as recent challenges to the traditional family, were attacked. The emergence of the "new woman" was considered a serious threat to the sanctity of the home because many women who received higher educations took up new roles and were no longer contented with household duties and child rearing. The *New World* did not criticize higher education, but "false education" that led college graduates to remain single and defeat God's purpose for them. Thus when a well-born Bostonian feminist remarked that foreign women were conservative, the paper responded that God may have sent the "Irish Marys, Italian Marias and Polish Hildas" to America for the purpose of "saving the country from women graduates of our great universities."[38]

With changes in the social and economic order, two other developments also jeopardized the family: divorce and "race suicide" (family limitation). Catholic doctrine states unequivocally that marriage is indissoluble, and the rising divorce rate in the new century caused alarm. Divorce, Catholics argued, was destroying the nation's moral fabric by wrecking the home and re-creating the decadence of the Roman Empire.[39] Just as disturbing was the practice of controlling the size of families. Catholic opinion declared that a person should not marry unless he or she was ready to assume the responsibilities of parenthood. The declining birth rate, which was attributed to parents' desire for a comfortable life and a good education for the few children they bore, the *New World* believed, was a manifestation of individual selfishness and the moral depravity of society. Even more alarming was the increased number of abortions; a doctor estimated that 50,000 were performed annually in Chicago in 1907.[40] The archdiocesan weekly frequently warned women to gird themselves against the vicious spirit of the age—for example:

> Perhaps never before in the history of modern civilization have such crude and dangerous moral and social heresies attacked the home and its sanctuaries as in this our day. . . . It is because of this

fact that we must arm our Catholic mothers, our Catholic sisters and our Catholic daughters with those virtues that make for the preservation of home and the family—by which they can withstand the reign of evil that besets them on every side and thus give to their hands the victory of valiant women.[41]

Allied to this degeneration of the home, many Catholics believed, was the women's suffrage movement. The argument of the 1890s, that the right to vote would bring women into the "mire" of the political game,[42] persisted. For example, a 1911 editorial noted that women had more moral sensitivity than men but lacked equal legislative wisdom, sound judgment, and statesmanship.[43] Because there was no moral imperative to the *New World*'s position, some Catholic women, especially those of the Catholic Women's League, militantly supported the suffrage cause.[44] When limited suffrage was granted to Illinois women in 1913, the paper promptly instructed them in their duties and exhorted them to vote to counteract secular and anti-Catholic forces.[45] When "foreign" women hesitated to exercise the franchise, Auxiliary Bishop Rhode wrote an open letter, urging them to use their new power.[46]

In the second decade of the twentieth century a noticeable change in the Church's position on social questions occurred. Prior to 1910, the Chicago Church accentuated the prime responsibility of the individual to live a moral life. Problems in society were attributed not so much to the failure of the community to meet the needs of its members as to its members' failure to conform to moral precepts. However, this near-absolute stress on personal salvation gave way to a broadened awareness of the meaning of charity and various tactics for dealing with social ills. In 1911 the *New World*, influenced by recent writings on the social meaning of the Gospel, stated that civil society was established by God for the purpose of making it easier for man to achieve his final end, and the ills of society were of universal concern. All must endeavor to produce such a state of affairs as would enable man to acquire "moderate prosperity" and "comparative security."

However, the paper was not yet willing to advocate state relief, for it feared that such a measure would lead to pauperization and sloth rather than save persons from abject poverty.[47] Nonetheless, its larger conception of society (manifested by an editorial) was a sign of change.

Fr. Frederic Siedenburg, S.J., established the Loyola University Lecture Bureau in 1913 and the Loyola School of Sociology a year later. The latter, the first Catholic undertaking of its kind in the United States, awakened Catholics to social justice questions. Siedenburg, who had come to Chicago at the turn of the century, taught science at St. Ignatius College, but on a sabbatical to study science in Germany he became aware of that nation's progressive system of social welfare and, more important, came to understand the thinking of Catholic liberals who grew up under the influence of the Christian socialist bishop of Mainz, Wilhelm E. von Ketteler. He sought and received his superior's permission to remain in Europe to study economics and sociology. In 1911, after three years of study in Germany and Austria, he returned to Chicago and began a new mission that eventually made him one of the most influential social workers in America. A partial list of his achievements and activities includes director of the National Catholic Welfare Council, president of the Illinois Council of Social Work, and influential member of the National Conference of Catholic Charities, the National Conference of Social Work, and the Illinois Welfare Board.[48]

At the meeting of the Illinois Federation of Catholic Societies in 1913, Siedenburg's topic was "The Church and Social Work." He explained: "Social work means working for society and society is a God-ordained and God-instituted affair." By "society," he pointed out, "Catholics mean an aggregate of individuals working for the moral, intellectual and physical welfare of all concerned." Though his definition of society was all embracing, his radical contribution was the clear relationship he established between moral and intellectual and physical welfare. He concluded by calling on all persons to work for improved conditions as a means of correcting intemperance.[49]

Although no direct link between the establishment of the Loyola Lecture Bureau and the School of Sociology and the *New World* is recorded, the new sense of awareness was quickly appreciated by Archbishop Quigley's organ. Editorials focused more and more on the legislative means of eradicating the social ills that affected the moral development of the populace. Sending children to jail was stoutly opposed, because the young came in contact with experienced and hardened criminals. Illinois's progressive child-labor legislation was praised as a step in the right direction, but farther-reaching laws were advocated to protect children in all phases of work, and though Chicago's progressive juvenile court system was lauded, the paper believed that more case workers were needed. Besides editorials, the paper carried features advocating special studies to provide a factual basis to remedy housing problems, turning empty fields over to the poor and unemployed for gardens, the creation of playgrounds, formation of associations to provide loans to the poor at a fair rate, and regulation of employment agencies that preyed upon unsuspecting immigrants.[50]

From this simple concept of relief, Catholics broadened their vision of society and eventually, if timidly, embraced reform. While cynicism regarding social reform passed, skepticism toward reformers remained. Catholicism's response to calls for reform was dictated by its mission to preserve the faith of the immigrants and the realization that its own institutions and organizations were unable to remedy the social injustice that afflicted its members. A similar pattern of liberal conservatism was witnessed in the Church's response to economic justice, which, because most Catholics were working-class people, received the greatest attention.

Shortly after Archbishop Feehan's death (in 1902), William Dillon wrote a four-part article titled "The Catholic Press and the Twentieth Century," in which he reflected on the educational mission of Catholic journalism.[51] He began by describing the nineteenth century as a period in which scientific and inventive genius had subdued the forces of nature and harnessed them for the comfort and convenience of man. From this progress, however, came an attendant evil—materialism: loss of concern for things of the spirit and the mind. This spirit of materialism, he said, "is more rampant, the power of money is more absolute and unrestrained, in this republic of ours, at the dawn of the twentieth century, than it has ever been before in this world in any age of which we have authentic record." In light of society's materialistic bent, Dillon believed that the work of the new century would be to cure social evils that sprang from man's inventiveness. The chief task of the next generation would be to face and solve the problem of the disparity between the wealthy and the poor. Such nineteenth-century reformers as Edward Bellamy and Henry George had sought to meet the problems of economic disparity by radically changing the economic and social system, and had failed. Dillon respected their honorable "concern and vision" but concluded that they did little more than broadcast "a beautiful daydream," for he believed that experiments with socio-economic systems were doomed to failure because they did not raise the moral standards of the individual and society. The only solution, he maintained, was to implement the principles enunciated in Leo XIII's encyclical *Rerum Novarum,* to which Archbishop Quigley had dedicated himself.

In May 1891, Leo XIII had presented to the world *Rerum Novarum,* which applied Christian principles to the class struggle that grew out of the industrialization of the economically advanced nations. Leo decried the spiritual bankruptcy of economic liberalism—the laissez-faire policy that rejects moral and political intervention in industry— and condemned socialism because it makes the individual subservient to the state and the community. Between these extremes he interposed the Christian ideals of charity and justice, and provided Catholic reformers a basis for waging battle against greedy capitalists and atheistic socialists. He encouraged formation of workingmen's associations as a means to secure a wage sufficient to enable the worker "to maintain himself, his wife, and children in reasonable comfort."[52]

Although Leo's encyclical was primarily directed to Europe's Christian progressives, who were waging a battle against an ever-growing socialist influence, it had significance for America's industrial workers. In the last two decades of the nineteenth century, American capital was arrayed against labor and there was cause to believe that workers might embrace socialism in order to secure redress of their grievances. In a memorial service in 1897 for the "single taxer," Henry George, Bishop John Lancaster Spalding lamented the condition of labor in America:

> We are waging a more remorseless and destructive battle than was ever waged by men who bared their breasts on the fields of conflict to the deadly shot and the thrusts of sabres. . . . Fatally it [economic liberalism] grinds down the weak and helpless. It is the survival of the strongest. Nature knows no pity, nature has no sympathy, nature destroys the weak and uplifts the strong.[53]

A less eloquent but perhaps more touching account was given by a young woman, employed as a railroad cashier, who wrote the *New World* some two years later:

> America is called the land of the brave and free. A land in which such injustice is practiced as is practiced every day here in Chicago has no claim to such beautiful words as brave and free. Coward and slave should be substituted for them.[54]

What was to be the Catholic Church's response to the plight of the laboring man, who more and more fell under the powerful hand of capitalists? Protestantism's response to the brutalizing warfare between capital and nascent unionism and to the injustices of the system that fostered violence and crime among the urban poor was the Social Gospel. Protestant ministers, such as Revs. Washington Gladden and Walter Rauschenbush, endeavored to raise the consciousness of labor and capital and make them aware that they should be partners in creation of a Christian cooperative commonwealth.[55] American Catholicism's response was more traditional; in general, it preached kindness to the poor and patience in poverty. Although some Catholic leaders pushed for social reform along Leonine lines, most remained "subservient to the rich and powerful and indisposed to advance the collective welfare of the laboring poor."[56]

In Chicago, where the labor movement obtained an early and strong hold, ecclesiastical and lay leaders stoutly opposed socialism, communism, and anarchism but consistently defended labor's efforts to organize. Nearly thirty years before Leo XIII's encyclical, at a time when many American bishops sought to prohibit Catholic membership in the Knights of Labor, Bishop Thomas Foley had declared he found no cause for condemnation.[57] In the following decade, Archbishop Feehan supported Cardinal Gibbons' endeavor to prevent the condemnation of the same society.[58] The Chicago Catholic Church, which had an estimated 10,000 members in the Knights of Labor in 1886, supported labor unions. In that year, after the archbishop of Quebec had condemned the Knights, P. J. Conway, Feehan's vicar general, wrote the *New York World:* "We see nothing reprehensible in labor organizations, but feel rather like encouraging them. So far as I know there is not the least clash between their principles and our Church's teachings."[59]

William J. Dillon, who edited Feehan's official paper for eight years, drew on his wide knowledge and experience to champion the principles of a just wage and labor's right to organize. He had been born in New York, where his father, John Blake Dillon, had fled to avoid arrest for his part in the unsuccessful Irish uprising of 1848. When amnesty was declared in 1855, William was taken to Ireland with his family and there received his education. As a student at University College in Dublin, he studied political economy and wrote his thesis on the failure of economic liberalism. In 1879 he was elected to Dublin's Land League committee and worked to create a peasant proprietary and to protect peasants from excessive rent and evictions. For health reasons, he returned to the United States, but continued to manifest his concern for the downtrodden.[60] His former involvement in agrarian-style unionism and his understanding of economics were reflected in his *New World* editorials.

Under Dillon's editorial direction, the paper sided with labor and supported reform legislation to protect workers and break up trusts and monopolies. Rather than simply condemn socialism and anarchism, he worked to alter the conditions that promoted their growth. Aware that the laws of supply and demand accounted for the terrible conditions of most workers, he supported trade unionism. He realized that as individuals, laborers were helpless; they had to take work at any wage or "starve and see their children starve." Organized labor, Dillon explained, was "the only agency that can stand between labor and the degradation and ruin which is the inevitable result of unchecked competition between those who are in desperate need."[61] When large corporations argued that unions infringed on the individual's right to sell his labor for what he saw fit to take for it, Dillon disagreed:

> This sounds well. In the abstract the combine is asserting the absolute right of every man to take his own price for his labor. In practice it is asserting the right of the huge corporation with vast resources to profit to the uttermost by the desperate need of the workingman.

"Justice," he concluded, "is allied to cooperation, not competition."[62]

While defending the worker, Dillon called for restraint and the regulation of large corporations. He admitted that the trusts were a mixture of good and evil. Insofar as they cured the evils of unchecked competition in the sale and manufacture of goods and substituted cooperation, they were good, but insofar as they placed in the hands of a few the power to dictate wages and prices, they were an "insolent and intolerable evil."[63] Thus when Vice President Theodore Roosevelt told a Minneapolis Labor Day rally it was evident that government "supervision and control" of combinations was necessary, Dillon rejoiced that these words came from such an authority.[64]

Unlike many ecclesiastics, who simply condemned socialism and counseled Catholics that happiness would come in the next life, Dillon published and discussed the letters sent to the paper by socialists. He did not tell them they could not be Catholics and socialists at the same time, but he told them that socialism, as presented by its ablest writers, did not guarantee an end to the conflict between capital and labor. Dillon believed that the rights of the individual had to be respected and he contended that modifications in the economic system could resolve the differences, if based on Christian principles.[65]

Dillon won the respect of workingmen for his strong defense of their rights. Their praise was greatest when he took Archbishop John Ireland to task for an article in the *North American Review* which denied that workers on strike had the right to keep men from working in their stead. Ireland maintained that labor's effort to block those who were willing to take a job, at whatever wages offered, violated the sacred right to personal liberty. Dillon explained that Ireland was essentially asserting the right of "capitalists to avail [themselves] to the uttermost of the desperate need of the laborer." The lawyer-editor argued that the St. Paul prelate shirked the question of injustice and invalidated his position:

> You must first determine whether the treatment of the striking

laborers has been just or unjust, before you can say with confidence that the taking of their places by other laborers is, in the true and high sense, an exercise of the right of personal liberty. The right of personal liberty, properly understood, never confers on a man a privilege to aid and abet injustice.[66]

The *New World*'s progressive message did not directly reach non-English-speaking immigrants. In 1892, *Dziennik Chicagoski* acknowledged that the Church, by following the directives of *Rerum Novarum*, might "lead its followers to a gradual but continual improvement of the unbearable social conditions of modern times."[67]

Not until 1901, when the Socialist Party of America was founded, was there a concerted action to counter the socialist campaign among the immigrants. In that year, efforts were made to organize a Catholic labor movement which would educate German, Polish, and Bohemian workers in the principles of *Rerum Novarum*. Theodore B. Thiele, a leader of the German Catholic Federation, explained that the new movement sought to instruct Catholic workers in the principles of Christian labor organization, help them find employment, and assist them when they were in distress. The membership in socialist- and anarchist-dominated unions, he said, necessitated a movement that pointed out the fallacies of socialism and demonstrated the Church's concern for the downtrodden. This movement was not, he stressed, an attack on unions, but an effort to oppose "Socialism and the influence advocates of that belief exert in the unions."[68] The Catholic labor campaign, however, soon faded.

When Archbishop Feehan died in July 1902, and Dillon resigned the editorship of the archdiocesan paper a month later, many Catholics must have been concerned whether the positive thrust of the Church on social questions would persist. Would the *New World* continue to support the rights of the workingman, and lobby for reform, or go the way of Archbishop Ireland, who appeared blind to the needs of labor, and of Archbishop Corrigan, who stressed that the poor should wait for their reward in the hereafter?[69] Would the recently organized Socialist Party of America, led by the charismatic Eugene Debs, lead Catholics to abandon their faith in search of an advocate? Would the Lithuanian immigrant Jurgis Rudkus, of Upton Sinclair's *The Jungle*, become the prototype of Chicago's ethnic Catholics?

Chicago's second archbishop, James E. Quigley, brought to his office the experience and knowledge that suited him not only for preserving the faith of the immigrants but also for ameliorating the social conditions that threatened to erode their commitment to Catholicism. Even before he came to Chicago, his concern for the welfare of Buffalo's workers was well known. When a dock strike paralyzed the inland port in 1899, he had arbitrated the dispute, after all other agencies failed. Further, he had sponsored the unionization movement, so that organized labor took hold and prospered in Buffalo without socialist dominance.[70] In 1901, when German Catholics organized the Christian Reform Society to reduce the influence of socialists by endeavoring to reconstruct the social order according to *Rerum Novarum,* Quigley was so impressed that he planned to extend the organization by creating "circles" in every parish of the diocese, to which workingmen and employers should belong.[71] In a pastoral letter of July 1902, he urged the formation of workingmen's associations:

> The spread of Socialistic principles among the workingmen has convinced the clergy and the thinking laity that the time has come for an organization under the auspices of the Church for the insistence upon the settlement of the social questions according to Christian principles.[72]

In his installation address of March 20, 1903, Quigley clearly indicated his concern for the working class and pledged that the Catholic Church "must and will do" its part in resolving the social problems faced by society. The Church, he firmly believed, was called to brighten the lot of laboring men and women—to raise these people up, to comfort them, and to give them a fuller measure of happiness.[73] Because he was concerned about the influence that socialism exercised upon the working class, he tried to demonstrate that the Church was the workers' friend, a defender of their rights, an advocate of Christian justice, and a counselor in the principles of Christian responsibility. Through the *New World*, Quigley's views on socialism, the responsibility of capital, the rights and duties of labor, and the Church's mission and position on the social question were made known.

Charles O'Malley, a layman and "writer and poet of mark," assumed the editorship of the *New World* in December 1902,[74] and attempted to convey the new archbishop's thoughts on socialism. His flair and style made his editorials enjoyable reading; however, he lacked Dillon's incisive mind and wide experience and, therefore, misread the socialists' appeal. When he tried to demonstrate that socialists were in error, his adversaries accused him of "a monumental ignorance of Socialism."[75] Rather than reasoned dialogue, he relied upon mockery, as in his treatment of a Socialist party platform of 1905 which proposed municipally owned ice houses and coal yards, city-operated and -owned transportation, free medical attention and free food, books and clothing for children under 16 years of age. O'Malley wrote his own platform for the socialists:

1. Free moonshine to aid the delivering of Socialist speeches.
2. Free rain for cooling the heads of Socialist audiences.
3. Free beer for clearing the throats of Socialist speakers.
4. Free wind wherewith the lungs of Socialist orators may be filled.[76]

Socialist leaders like Debs were labeled "ungainly freaks" and parasites "sucking the blood of the man who toils."[77]

In 1905, because of his strident and harsh treatment of Protestants, O'Malley was succeeded by Fr. Thomas Judge, the *New World*'s first clerical editor. Judge focused on anarchism and communism rather than socialism. Emma Goldman, an anarchist speaker who denounced government, law, police, religion, and moral codes, enraged the priest and received his sharpest rebukes. When she was scheduled to give a lecture at the University of Chicago—an institution that was frowned upon because of its faculty's liberality in religious and moral matters—Judge exclaimed that the institution was fostering education "inimical" to democracy and religion, and described Goldman as a "vicious creature whose ambition is to make others as vicious as she is herself; a destroyer, not a builder, and enemy of every established government without the remotest idea or concern as to what would take its place amongst men."[78]

When O'Malley returned to the editorship after Judge's death in 1907, he moderated his anti-Protestant attitude and picked up the threads of his predecessor's crusade against anarchism. The nation, he argued, had been founded as a refuge for the oppressed people of the world, and Americans had a right to expect even anarchists to contribute to the peace of society. The Republic was made and sustained by industrious people, not by anarchists, whose avowed goal was to disrupt and destroy it. Thus when a group of Russian-Jewish anarchists tried to stage a march of the city's unemployed, in defiance of the mayor's prohibition, O'Malley praised the police for suppressing the demonstration and warned the participants that they would find themselves as hated in America as they were in the Old World unless they behaved "nicely" and became good citizens, like their German brethren.[79]

Archbishop Quigley's official newspaper did not focus simply on the shortcomings of socialism but also took to task the abuses of economic liberalism, as outlined in *Rerum Novarum*. When capitalist manipulations drove up coal prices in 1903 and Chicago workers threatened to riot, the *New World* told the industrialists that their greed was doing more to bring about the rule of socialism than all the "strife-stirrers."

Unless, the paper prophesied, those who organized pools, trusts, and combinations ("manskinning machines") introduced the principles of honesty and justice into their dealings, they would bring about their own ruin."[80] It also attacked capital's campaigns to identify trade unionism with radicalism. "Some socialism," it noted, "may exist in unions, but no man truthfully can say that all are pervaded by it or even its spirit. There are too many Catholics in the unions for them ever to become dangerous." Rather, it charged that "flame-spreaders" like D. M. Perry, president of the National Association of Manufacturers and chief lobbiest for anti-union legislation, were a serious menace to the social order.[81]

Although some industrialists praised the Catholic Church for its conservatism (i.e., its opposition to socialism and its advocacy of property rights), the *New World* tried to make clear that its mission was all embracing. "She is against Socialism, true," the paper editorialized, "but for nearly two thousand years her sword has been stretched out against injustice and oppression and inhuman greed."[82] The powerful meat packers, who expended vast sums of money to "defeat the ends of justice" and schemed to circumvent the law by buying legislators, were decried. The mine owners, who, through alliances with law enforcement authorities broke the Western Federation of Miners' strike at Cripple Creek, Colorado, by loading strikers into boxcars like cattle and dumping them in another state, were chastised for their Russian-like autocratic methods. The textile mill owners, whose unjust dealings with employees caused the Lawrence strike, led by IWW organizers, were condemned for their greed and disregard for human welfare.[83] The paper declared that socialism would be better than capitalistic control of the machinery of government because the latter allowed for the feudalistic juggling of the lives and property of the American people.[84]

Charles O'Malley employed his literary talents to denounce the blind rapacity of the lords of the economic order. His poem "The Slums," published in the *New World* on May 2, 1908, also carried a warning:

> Ye, who are gathering millions and stripping the poor
>   of their rights,
> Have ye no fear that God's tempest will topple ye
>   down from your heights? . . .
> Look to the slums that ye make, and tremble in fear,
>   for they
> Shall be a hot whip in His hand, and a terrible lash
>   one day

For out of their depth shall arise the Man of Terror
   and Fate;
And he shall do as God wills, and slay til your
   paths grow straight.

To avoid future bloodshed, government regulation and control of industry were supported and the trust-busting efforts of President Roosevelt lauded. When Congress finally passed more rigorous trust legislation in 1903, the *New World* expressed joy, but cautiously added: "No matter how hostile to the trusts the laws may be, they will never prove effective unless applied. The possession of a hot mustard poultice never cured Paddy Flaherty until he put it on."[85] The paper believed that effectual regulation of trusts, immediately applied, was the only safeguard against Congress's ownership of all trusts in the near future.[86]

While the *New World* called for regulation of capital, it supported the labor movement because it was the surest means by which workers might secure justice.[87] The labor unions—especially the American Federation of Labor, led by Samuel Gompers—were praised for their defenses of workers' interests. Because of Gompers' conservative course and his unionists' rejection of radicalism and defense of private property, the *New World* supported the AFL.

> Is it not the time for the mass of employers to realize that the majority of unionists are the best friends they have? Instead of describing their workingmen as socialists and anarchists, as is only too common, ought they not frankly acknowledge that really the unions are protecting their rights and property? No doubt there is a great deal of socialism rampant in the unions, but invariably it fails when put to a vote. Upright employers ought to see that the craze [of attacking unions] spreads no further. Moreover, they ought to give credit where credit is due.[88]

However, unions were neither unqualifiedly endorsed nor uncritically supported. If unions appeared to violate the public trust and the principles of justice, they were subject to censure. In the first decade of the new century, when constant labor unrest threatened to retard the economy, disrupting services and causing layoffs, higher prices, and violence, the Catholic paper cautioned that strikes be pursued only with sufficient reason. "Sympathetic" strikes, "except in rare instances," were considered unjust to the general public. "Why on earth," the editor asked, "should the peanut-roasters on Adams Street go on strike because someone mistreated the plumbers on the north side? Why should the united white-washers quit work because the market-gardeners are ill paid and have struck for better pay?"[89] Additionally, such strikes violated contracts and reduced public support for organized labor. Accordingly, when Gompers repudiated the tactic of the sympathetic strike, the paper praised his "well made" decision.[90]

Finally, the Church unequivocally opposed violent means to prevent non-union men and scabs from carrying on business as usual during a strike. All men, by reason of their citizenship and religion, were called upon to respect property and human life. In addition, organized labor's dependence on public support demanded peaceful strikes. Therefore, when some of the city's striking teamsters threw egg shells filled with muriatic acid, the *New World* promptly condemned the action and counseled teamster leaders to eschew violence. "*Workingmen,*" the editor declared, "*cannot win unless supported by public sympathy; and resorting to such methods as this unquestionably will cause public opinion to turn against them. Their leaders must hand the acid-throwers over to the law they have outraged or stand prepared to lose their cause, however just it may be.*"[91]

The concern of the Chicago Church for the workers went beyond editorial endorsements, as illustrated by the response to the packinghouse workers' strike of 1904. When the packers lowered wages and refused to accept unskilled workers as members of the Amalgamated Meat Cutters and Butcher Workmen of North America union, more than 30,000 workers struck.[92] Most of the strikers were Catholic immigrants; Irish, Germans, and Bohemians were numerous but Poles, Lithuanians, and Slovaks predominated.[93] Michael Donnelly, the striking union's president, exhorted his men to keep the peace, but he was regarded with suspicion by the newer immigrants. Thus the task of keeping order fell to the religious leaders and settlement workers of Back of the Yards, where most of the men and women lived.

Although the *New World* early counseled Catholic workers to prevent violence and ignore agitators,[94] the peacekeeping task was borne by the priests of the seven neighborhood parishes. They made sure that strikers and their families had sufficient means to endure the long strike that was anticipated and told their flocks to avoid violence. Fr. Dennis Hayes, of St. Rose of Lima parish, admitted that he did not believe in strikes because they seldom accomplished any good, but he realized "the men must keep together to maintain the principles of their union."[95] Rev. M. Pyplatz, of St. Mary's Polish parish, cautioned against hasty action but told his parishioners they were correct in "fighting for their rights." The *Chicago Tribune* lauded the work of the parish priests, who had "organized in an attempt to restrain their congregations from rioting," and noted that "much of the peaceful attitude of the strikes is said to be due to their influence."[96] With the exception of a Bohemian pastor, the priests supported the strike.

One newspaper account declared: "The pastors who labor with the people of the stockyards did not [in their sermons] openly praise the men for striking, but their words clearly leaned to the union's cause, and several of the clergy later admitted that outside of their churches they used their influence to aid the strikers' cause." One such priest was Max Kotechi of SS. Peter and Paul Polish national parish, who preached restraint on Sunday but, the day before, had led a non-union worker to the union headquarters and induced him to join the union.[97] Five Back of the Yards pastors held a meeting to consider means to bring union leaders and packers together for a "peace conference," but ultimately failed.[98] Although the parish priests did not succeed in settling the strike, and the union lost much power, the Church maintained the respect of the workers and proved an important factor in moderating violence.

The Catholic Church maintained the workers' allegiance at a time when dissatisfied Protestant workers were quick to attack their churches as capitalist allies. Unlike Protestant congregations, whose policies were determined by rich donors, the Catholic churches were built by the poor and considered to be their own. Thus when the Baptist Association of Illinois lamented the hostility of workingmen toward Christian churches, the *New World* boasted of Masses attended by large numbers in workingmen districts. It credited Catholic successes to the priests, who reproved rich and poor alike, and the absence of parochial domination by the wealthy.[99] Furthermore, the priests lived among the people, "joying with them in their joy and sorrowing with them in their sorrow." When the poor were wronged, the editor noted, their pastors did not turn against them and side with the oppressor for personal gain; instead, they joined the victims, fighting their battles and suffering with them till they won.[100]

The Church's response to the poor, who constituted the majority of Catholics, was dictated by its mission to preserve the faith and its recognition of the needs and conditions of the working class. The chief threat to Catholic influence was socialism, and Catholicism's responses to it between 1903 and 1910 were largely reactionary. However, a more positive thrust was developed to meet the challenge of the fast-growing Socialist Party of America.

Thomas O'Hanan, who succeeded O'Malley in 1910, was less acidulous and more reasonable in discussing socialism. The Church, he wrote, was opposed to the seizure of property without full compensation to its owners, and to socialism's lack of loyalty to the government;

to its materialism, which implied a rejection of God; and to its refusal to receive instructions on the meaning of justice from the Church. But he pointed out that the Church did not oppose state control of capital, after it had been honestly acquired by the public. Indeed, he said, the Church was sympathetic to socialism's opposition to unjust class discrimination, its concern for the poor who were denied their rights, and its resistance to long hours of labor for women. "It is only where Socialism is dishonest, disloyal, unjust, atheistic, insubordinate and tyrannical that the Church opposes it."[101]

Despite the *New World*'s efforts, socialists were making inroads among recent immigrants who could not read the English-language diocesan paper. Socialism's attraction seems to have subsided among the Irish and German elements, as they improved their socio-economic position, but it had a message for newcomers. Between 1905 and 1915, socialist newspapers increased in number and circulation and used the plight of the bewildered poor to the advantage of their cause.[102] "Hell exists in every working man's home because misery and hunger lead to dissension, quarrels and crime," A. Szturowski wrote in the Polish socialist paper *Dziennik Ludowy,* while adding: "Heaven exists in the homes of capitalists and the priests because there is abundance and luxury."[103] For a successful defense against such propaganda, the Chicago Church had to depend upon the numerous Catholic foreign-language newspapers[104] and the work of parish priests and societies.

In 1912, Bishop Peter J. Muldoon warned Catholics that they must do more than condemn socialism, or their words would come back to haunt them. Speaking to a committee of the Federation of Catholic Societies, which had taken a deep interest in social problems, he declared:

> To my mind one of the most important things resisting the spread of socialistic ideals is the personal service of the priesthood and the laity amongst the poor. . . . It is a democratic society which the church has to deal with here and the ballot means a great deal; but there must be more widespread spirit of consecration for the benefit of all and above all the protection of the weak.

"You cannot," he said, "talk socialism in the parish in which the priest spends much of his time amongst the poor, aiding them in their difficulties and pouring the healing balm of sympathy into their wounds." These words of advice were praised by the *New World* editor as the most realistic way to deal with the threat posed by socialism.[105]

The Catholic campaign to organize and educate the workers, begun between 1901 and 1903 to combat socialism, had not taken hold.

Thus, by the second decade, renewed efforts, enlightened by Fr. John A. Ryan's theological treatise on a just wage, were made to reach the workers at the grass roots level. Ryan's *A Living Wage,* published in 1906,[106] applied the ethical principle that "wages should be sufficiently high to enable the laborer to live in a manner consistent with the dignity of a human being."[107] In 1910, Fr. Peter Dietz organized the Militia of Christ for Social Service to influence labor unions through their Catholic membership.[108] Begun in St. Louis to implement the principles of justice laid down by Leo XIII, the society was extended to Chicago in 1911. The Militia supported social reclamation and opposed class warfare and atheism. In Chicago, it conducted a series of educational lectures in various school and labor halls, featuring Peter W. Collins (author, editor, trade unionist, and anti-socialist) as the principal speaker.[109] Existing societies, such as the Ancient Order of Hibernians, the Knights of Columbus, and Catholic Order of Foresters, initiated lecture programs to expose the fallacies of socialism and to help immigrant workers realize and appreciate the advantages of the American democratic system.[110]

However, the most significant force in the cause of economic justice was Rev. Frederic Siedenburg's work. Siedenburg, like John A. Ryan and Bishop Muldoon, believed that emotional denunciations of socialism bore little fruit. Accordingly, he developed a program that would not only refute the socialist philosophy but "spread the gospel of constructive Catholic practices and principles."[111] His program took definite shape in the Loyola University Lecture Bureau, which gave over 100 lectures in its first year, 1913.[112] He recruited knowledgeable professionals to lecture on social reform. The topics presented in a series of free lectures sponsored by the Ravenswood and Brownson Council of the Knights of Columbus were "The Social Question," "Socialism and Christianity," "Socialism and the Workingman," "Socialism and the State," "Child Labor," and "Education and Social Reform."[113] His Loyola School of Sociology emphasized the economic problems responsible for the plight of the poor. Speakers such as Owen R. Lovejoy, general secretary of the National Child Labor Committee, spoke on the need to end the injustices of child employment and Rev. John A. Ryan lectured on the need for a women's minimum wage law.[114] Through Loyola's School of Sociology, Siedenburg provided Chicago Catholics a ready resource to help improve the lot of the poor and to support economic and labor reform.

During these years, when organizations (locally and nationally) began to mobilize to secure Christian justice for the laborer, Quigley's official organ lent editorial support and publicized their activities. The paper regularly carried articles by Dietz on the need for social reconstruction and the rights of labor,[115] and Siedenburg's activities and lectures were given wide coverage. Legislation favorable to the working masses was defended and supported, and readers were told to write their elected officials to request its passage. For example, the paper called for a federal commission of industrial relations so that labor and capital might be "emancipated from illusion, assumptions, generalities, prejudices, by knowledge of facts." Readers were reminded that they too must be emancipated from their indifference "toward the great problems of social justice and governmental efficiency and exercise their rights by urging congressional action."[116]

The response of the Catholic Church to social and economic reform was conservative, for its primary mission was to preserve the faith of its members. When directly assaulted by forces that competed for the loyalty of its constituency, the Church condemned the opposition but accommodated to the threat by making "Catholic" the opponents' activities. Through these accommodations, the Church slowly embraced reform and accepted the state's role in meeting social problems. The experience of nativist rejection made it impossible for the Church to work hand in hand with reformers, but it *did* work side by side with them, knowing that its continued influence depended upon meeting the needs of all Catholics. By so doing, the Church affected social reforms and union development in Chicago.

7. First American-Born Archbishop

Between 1916 and 1924 the Chicago Catholic Church developed a new identity, more American than hyphenated. The actions and policies of a different type of archbishop, interacting with Chicagoans whose character was changing, resulted in a more vital American Roman Catholicism. Archbishop Quigley's death was a sad event for thousands of Catholics who regarded him as a sympathetic father and advocate. Moreover, his passing was untimely, for the spirit of immigrant nationalism and the possibility that America might be drawn into World War I demanded a tried leader. Once again, Chicago Catholics waited and wondered who would carry on the unfinished work of the able Irish-American who had spent himself on their behalf. This time, however, they had no indication of the candidates, because a recent Vatican decree had strictly forbidden discussion of the balloting.[1]

Immediately after Quigley's funeral, Bishop James Ryan, of Alton, Illinois, convened the irremovable rectors and the diocesan consultors to select a *terna*. Seventeen electors participated and submitted their choices to the bishops of the Illinois Province: Bishop Edmund Dunne of Peoria, *dignissimus;* Bishop Peter J. Muldoon of Rockford, *dignior;* and Bishop Andrew J. McGavick of Chicago, *dignus.* Dunne was selected on the third ballot, after he secured enough votes to overcome the staunch support given to Muldoon. The latter won the fourth balloting easily, and McGavick succeeded on the sixth vote.[2] But after the priests had voted, the bishops of the province reviewed, then rejected, the priests' *terna* and tried to prepare their own.

According to Bishop Muldoon, who unofficially communicated the results to Cardinal James Gibbons, the suffragans "would not agree on the candidates proposed by [the] priests." Furthermore, after fifteen ballots, he declared, the bishops adjourned without making a selection for *dignus,* and significantly, their choices were not men who knew Chicago best.[3]

155

A month later, the apostolic delegate, John Bonzano, wrote Cardinal Gibbons, the venerable spokesman for the American hierarchy, and asked for "whatever information you possess regarding the proposed candidates [for archbishop of Chicago] and your opinion about them," for transmission to the Consistoral Congregation.[4] Gibbons responded that he favored Muldoon because "he is a native of Chicago,[5] is well acquainted with the needs of that Diocese, and also because his appointment to Chicago would be a vindication for him of the unjust persecution against him whilst he was Auxiliary of Chicago." Of Dunne and McGavick he had "nothing" to say.[6]

Archbishop Sebastian G. Messmer of Milwaukee, who also favored Muldoon, took the liberty to address Cardinal Gibbons on the question of Quigley's successor, explaining that he was familiar with the conditions and needs of Chicago, as well as the candidates of the priests' *terna*. In light of this knowledge, he said "there is no other more fitted for the place in every way than Bishop Muldoon." To strengthen his argument, he noted that Quigley had stated that an "outsider" would be a mistake, because it would take five years to understand the diocese. He then explained his preference of Muldoon over Dunne:

> There is no one among the names proposed, Bishop Dunne excepted, who knows Chicago as Bp. Muldoon. You know yourself, that he was Abp. Feehan's right hand long before he was his auxiliary. Again Bp. Muldoon is far more of a public and social man than Bp. Dunne. While the latter has a few who would welcome him among them[,] some of the Diocesan clergy, because he speaks their language quite well, yet I know again that Bp. Muldoon is the choice of the far larger portion and majority of the Clergy and the people. In fact I am told that even his former enemies, the so-called Crowley Crowd, have buried the hatchet and will receive him with glad hearts. There is absolutely nothing to be feared in this regard. That Bp. Muldoon is a much more energetic and active man than Bp. Dunne is a well known fact.[7]

The Milwaukee churchman concluded with a request that Gibbons use his influence at Rome in Muldoon's behalf, and parenthetically commented, "not Apostolic Delegate here, but Rome direct."[8] Gibbons immediately responded that he was in accord with his colleague and had already communicated his preference for Muldoon to Bonzano. In a postscript, Gibbons promised to repeat his choice to Cardinal De Lai, prefect of the Propaganda.[9]

Chicago's Poles viewed the vacancy as an opportunity for the

American Church to give long-overdue recognition to their nationality. The day after Quigley's death, they were startled to learn that Auxiliary Bishop Paul Rhode was to be placed over the Diocese of Green Bay, Wisconsin. Believing that the Poles' nearly 350,000 faithful and 140 priests deserved "equal rights," a committee of Polonia's leaders respectfully petitioned Bonzano.[10] Their letter expressed regret at the departure of Rhode, who had brought Chicago's Poles a "harmony and peace hitherto unknown." The writers implied that the Polish National Catholic Church was a source of imminent danger and they feared "that here in Chicago, deprived of the care of a Bishop from among our own race, who would know us intimately, the interest of our Holy Religion may suffer."

> In general our religious interests are becoming so complex and important from the standpoint of our present and future growth, that we are in conscience bound to humbly pray your Excellency that we be not left without the care and guidance of a Bishop of our nationality, who will understand our needs and aspirations.[11]

The priest-electors of Chicago, who had overwhelmingly preferred an Irish-American;[12] Messmer and Gibbons, who championed Muldoon's candidacy; and the Poles, who sought the appointment of Rhode, were to be disappointed. On November 29, 1915, Rome announced its choice, which did not reflect the Chicago priests' interests or counsel. If the Catholics of Chicago had been surprised at the appointment of James Edward Quigley in 1902, they were more surprised when word came that their new archbishop was to be a young New Yorker who had not yet administered a diocese. Msgr. William Owens, who was studying for the priesthood at St. Bernard Seminary in Rochester at the time of the announcement, recalls that he and his Chicago classmates rushed to the bulletin board when they heard that the appointment had been made. The posted name was "George W. Mundelein," and their first reaction was that someone had misspelled Bishop Muldoon's name.[13] Several Chicago priests expressed similar reactions when newspaper reporters broke the news and recorded their responses.[14]

In public at least, clergy and laity generally registered approval of the choice. Chancellor Edward Francis Hoban said the announcement was a surprise, but that he was pleased because he had heard Mundelein was a capable man. Msgr. Francis Kelly of the Catholic Extension Society, one of the few Chicagoans who claimed to know the appointee, praised the selection because the Brooklyn auxiliary was a "most energetic man" and a builder who, despite his 43 years, had wonderful deeds to his credit. Numerous laymen expressed their surprise and satisfaction, but a sense of disappointment as well. Quin O'Brien, a lawyer, admitted: "I had hoped a westerner would be appointed."[15]

Publicly, the clergy supported the selection, but many were upset that their votes had gone for naught. Shortly after the announcement, Bishop Muldoon wrote Cardinal Gibbons to thank him for the support he had given his candidacy and noted that he was "very happy and contented" to remain in Rockford. However, he expressed dismay because the "Chicago clergy and laity are stunned and feel very, very keenly the voice of Chicago, through her elected officials, [was] utterly ignored." The choice of a "total stranger," when there were several other choices on the submitted lists, Muldoon wrote, put the priests in "no pleasant frame of mind." Such disregard, he feared, "is going to break down respect for legitimate authority."[16]

Muldoon must have realized that the Irish-Americans had counted on a continuation of "staunch" Irish leadership, maintained since 1880.[17] The bond of common descent had been a means of access to authority and a source of hope that a sympathetic hearing would be given to their requests. Thus, besides being opposed to an inexperienced outsider, they had serious "reservations" about a man who was not one of their own.[18]

Mundelein's appointment was a result of knowing the right people and being in the right place at the appropriate moment. Even though he lacked the advocacy of Cardinal Gibbons, he was, as the *New York Times* noted, well known in Vatican circles.[19] Furthermore, he had maintained the friendship of John Bonzano, who had been his mentor at the College of the Propaganda before Bonzano's appointment as apostolic delegate.

On the evening of November 29, 1915, Mundelein received word of his selection and Bonzano's *"congratulazioni vivissime."*[20] When Bishop Dunne made the welcoming speech in the new archbishop's honor, he played on the traditional expression, "We have a new archbishop by the grace of God and the favor of the Apostolic See," by telling his clerical audience: "We have a new archbishop by the grace of God and the favor of the Apostolic Delegate."[21]

If favor played an important part in the appointment, so too did chance. In 1915 the episcopacies of Chicago and Buffalo were vacant. Originally, the pope had provided Bishop Dennis Daugherty, who had administered the Philippines, for the former see and Mundelein for the latter. Indeed, it would have been a natural promotion for both men: bishop to archbishop and auxiliary to bishop. However, when the

Canadian government, at war against Germany, learned that a German-American was likely to be made bishop of the border city, it protested. Rome responded by sending Daugherty to Buffalo and Mundelein to Chicago.[22]

Besides favor and chance, the appointee's early career had demonstrated his remarkable talents. George W. Mundelein was born in New York City, July 2, 1872, of Francis and Mary (Goetz) Mundelein.[23] On one side of the family, he was descended from those who had helped build the first German Catholic parish in the United States, and on the other from a German-immigrant grandfather who had given his life to preserve the Union. Francis Mundelein, a butcher by trade, was never rich, and George knew the pinch of hard times. He had valuable opportunities, however, to learn firsthand the customs, traditions, and even the languages of the various immigrant groups who crowded into the Lower East Side. As a boy, he attended St. Nicholas school and played in the neighborhood where his ancestors had settled generations before. Eager and bright, he attracted the attention of family friends, who provided the financial aid to further the education his family could not supply. He attended De la Salle Institute and then Manhattan College, where he received a bachelor of arts degree at age 17. His exceptional ability did not go unnoticed; upon graduation, he received an invitation to take the entrance examination for the U.S. Naval Academy, but (like Quigley) he chose to serve the Church.

Mundelein's decision to study for the priesthood resulted in another change. Ordinarily a New York resident, pursuing the calling of a diocesan cleric, would have attended the New York archdiocesan seminary; however, because of apparent financial problems, Mundelein took an exam to qualify for a scholarship offered to German-speaking candidates for the priesthood who would serve in the Diocese of Brooklyn. He won the scholarship, and in 1889 began his ecclesiastical studies at St. Vincent's Seminary in Latrobe, Pennsylvania. Under the Benedictine Fathers of the Archabbey of St. Vincent, he acquired his knowledge of theology and philosophy, and his academic record was outstanding. One of his fellow students, who later served as pastor of St. Paul's German parish in Chicago, recalled that Mundelein was "an extremely brilliant" student.[24]

The young scholar's request for adoption by the Diocese of Brooklyn opened new doors for him. Because Mundelein was too young to be ordained upon completion of his theological studies at Latrobe, the Most Rev. Charles E. McDonnell, bishop of Brooklyn, sent him to Rome for further study. Seeing the potential in his young seminarian, and having the benefit of a Roman education himself, McDonnell hoped that Mundelein might gain additional knowledge and insight into the government of the Church, make the acquaintance of some of his influential friends in the Curia, and thus acquire friendships that would be of value in the future. Three years of study in Rome not only provided McDonnell's charge with firsthand knowledge of the workings of Church politics but gave him a deeper sense of the universality and cosmopolitanism of Catholicism.

Upon ordination in June 1895,[25] Mundelein returned to Brooklyn, where he served as the bishop's assistant secretary and ministered to a Lithuanian congregation on weekends. Two years later, the young priest was made chancellor. In this capacity he came into frequent contact with men of prominence in business and finance. Bishop McDonnell rewarded the young chancellor's diligence and ability by obtaining special honors for him. In 1906 Mundelein became the nation's youngest monsignor, and three years later its youngest auxiliary bishop. He also received the distinction of being the first American member of the Liturgical Academy, and later was honored with membership in the Ancient Academy of Acadia, an international society of Catholic literary scholars.

In his brief tenure as auxiliary bishop of Brooklyn, the young Mundelein won a reputation both as a builder and a prudent executive. His most noted accomplishment was erection of the Cathedral Chapel of Queen of All Saints, where he served as rector. This building, the most perfect specimen of Gothic architecture in America (according to some critics), reflected his artistic tastes as well as his business sense, for it was a combination building—church, school, and rectory all in one—that was both utilitarian and esthetically pleasing. He also gained respect as an indefatigable laborer for the spiritual and physical welfare of Brooklyn's aged, poor, orphaned, and dependent Catholics. Education, especially of young men pursuing a clerical vocation, also received his attention. His wide experience, demonstrated talent, friendship with Vatican officials, and circumstance combined to make him the third archbishop of Chicago.

Archbishop Mundelein came to Chicago ready to accept the challenge of ministering to the city's more than 1 million Catholics. "I am going there full of courage, full of hope, full of confidence," he told a Brooklyn gathering. "I am not going to fail, for this is a case where the position was not sought." God would make his mission successful.[26] The day after his installation at Holy Name Cathedral, however, he was given cause to wonder what God had in store for him. The occasion was a banquet at the University Club for introducing him to the prominent

Chicagoans whom he would likely meet in his official capacity. The leading bankers, businessmen, and lawyers, as well as other professionals, and the influential politicians came to make his acquaintance and bid him well. However, the festive spirit that pervaded the luxurious club soon ended, when about 100 of the nearly 300 guests became ill. They vomited, gasped for air, and reeled from the banquet hall or collapsed on the way out. An anarchist, employed in the kitchen, had added arsenic to the soup in the hope of wiping out Chicago's leaders. No one died, for the poisoned soup had been diluted to accommodate 100 last-minute guests. The new archbishop, who was not adversely affected by the concoction, later told a reporter it would take "more than soup to put me out."[27]

The spirit that Mundelein displayed after the "arsenic incident" was but one indication that he was a man to be reckoned with, which he made perfectly clear when he first addressed Chicago's priests. In his concise and straightforward manner, he told them he realized they had not expected appointment of an "obscure bishop" and an outsider, and he acknowledged that, though not enthusiastically, most priests had demonstrated the loyalty necessary for edification of Catholics and Protestants. Furthermore, some of his episcopal colleagues had warned him that Chicago was the "most difficult and thorny portion of the Lord's vineyard," but he was of the firm conviction that the Chicago see was the most promising and fertile portion, promising the greatest and most golden harvest of souls. He came, he told them, not for honor but to work with them, sowing as well as reaping.

Chicago's first German-American administrator told his priests he was not like his predecessor and asked them to be understanding till they got used to his ways and he to theirs. He explained that

> perhaps I am quicker in grasping a thing, and am likely to act more quickly [than Quigley], so don't judge at once that I have not attached enough weight to your case. And if I seem to hurry you when you call, it is not that I am not interested in you, but perhaps because others may be waiting and waiting impatiently. Finally remember I have a bad memory for names and faces, so if I a second or third time ask your name, lay the blame to a leaky memory rather than a cold heart.

Additionally, Mundelein asked for their loyalty. Because he was human, he was liable to err, and thus he depended upon the clergy to "cover up my mistakes, not to expose, to discuss, or to criticize them." As the man in the public spotlight, he stressed that their cooperation was essential.[28]

At a retreat three years later, he expanded on the subjects of loyalty and obedience. Although the archbishop had never undergone the rigors of military training, he admired its discipline and order, and used its vocabulary in his address. He explained that Christ had fashioned his Church on the pattern of an army; through confirmation, all Catholics are soldiers, and the select few, called to the priesthood, become officers by their ordination. Every priest, in his ordination, gives a public pledge of obedience and loyalty to his superior officer, the bishop. This tie, he stressed, is the greatest strength of the organization. Accordingly, all men and women must accept episcopal injunctions; "no individual or group of priests or laymen in the Church . . . may depart from the general discipline laid down by [the bishop]. If they do so contumaciously, that constitutes mutiny, rebellion, treason to the general body of the Church." "In union there is strength," he concluded, "and in dissension there is defeat."[29]

In practice, Mundelein ran his archdiocese like a general. His correspondence shows that he would stand for no deviation from the rules of order he set down. When a man manifested disloyalty by openly criticizing his decisions, he was disciplined.[30] His late-night visits to rectories to see that priests were home, according to his regulations, was a drastic change from the fatherly Quigley, who believed that no one could do evil. For his nocturnal expeditions and, at times, abrasive style, he acquired the sobriquet "the Dutch Cleanser."[31]

Mundelein was pragmatic enough to realize that ambition, as well as fear, is a valuable instrument of control. Like a military commander, he dispensed titles and/or positions of power to subordinates. The archbishop once told a young priest that he had to reward two kinds of men: "the men who do things and the men who enable things to be done." When he needed money for a special charity, Mundelein explained, he went to wealthy parishes to ask the support of the pastors. Speaking with an Irish pastor, he said: "Father, we need $100,000 for an orphanage." The priest replied that he seriously doubted that his parish could afford such a donation, to which Mundelein responded: "Monsignor So and So [a German pastor who had not yet been raised to that honor] gave me $200,000." The Irishman quickly changed his estimation and declared that if a German could manage it, so could he.

Although Mundelein did not directly promise promotions, his ploys were usually sufficient to loosen tight-fisted pastors.[32] The men who staffed his offices were given monsignorships because they did what was expected of them. Unlike his predecessor, Mundelein made extensive use of the ecclesiastical patronage system. When he took office, there were but three monsignors, and by 1928 there were twenty-nine. The percentage of diocesan clergy given honors grew from .7 percent to 3.9 percent. This increase is most striking when compared to the Archdiocese of New York, where 4 percent of the diocesan clergy were monsignors in 1915 and only 3.5 percent in 1928.[33]

The new archbishop also proved to be a capable businessman. When he took charge of the archdiocese, he acquired control of a plant worth some $50 million. By the time he died, in 1939, he had added markedly to the Church's assets. Under his administration, 250 new churches were erected and a seminary, which alone cost $20 million, as well as numerous institutions for the needy, were constructed.[34] He was able to build because he was a very able financier and fund raiser, but new construction was never begun without a feasibility study by his consultors. He was neither a penny pincher nor vulgar, for the buildings he commissioned are remarkable both for quality and good taste.

His financial interest extended to the parish level. Parishes that were no longer self-supporting, because their congregations had moved to better neighborhoods, were converted to devotional centers, with the whole city as their mission. The old French parish of Notre Dame, for example, was assigned to a religious order who used it as a center for special devotion to the Blessed Sacrament. Within a short time the church drew faithful from all sections of Chicago to its services and once again prospered financially.[35] Italian parishes, established under Archbishop Quigley, were still indebted to the archdiocese and their schools were still subsidized by it. Because Mundelein believed these churches should pay their own way, he refused to construct new Italian parishes, despite the petitions he received. He cut off their educational subsidies and turned the parishes over to religious orders who could better manage the financial problems.[36] Other national parishes, unable to make ends meet, were converted into territorial parishes.

Mundelein's careful attention to financial stability quickly led to the consolidation of Catholic charity fund raising. Prior to his coming, each institution raised its own funds. Understanding that numerous fund-raising drives annoyed donors and wasted valuable personnel and fiscal resources in their execution, he established the Associated Catholic Charities. The new program, designed by businessmen, called for one major campaign and disbursement of funds from a central office to the various charitable institutions of the archdiocese. With this streamlined system, money increased significantly (more than half a million dollars annually) and the cost of administration decreased, in comparison to the previous procedure.[37] The archbishop's success bore witness to the words of a New York banker, who, after a meeting with Mundelein, remarked: "The church certainly gained one of the cleverest headed businessmen in the country . . . when George Mundelein became a priest."[38]

The era of parochial autonomy, which had existed in fact, if not in theory, ended with the arrival of Mundelein. In the fashion of the new generation of businessmen, he systematized and centralized all operations in the name of efficiency and order. But Mundelein's methodical and less personal approach to administration was not well received by many. Some of his clergy, unable to appreciate the new regime, criticized him for running the archdiocese like a "German meat market."[39] Yet despite their displeasure with his manner, the clergy could not but respect his thoroughness and administrative genius. A priest who had lobbied for the appointment of Muldoon grew to admire Mundelein because "he is on the job every minute. He thinks big and consequently acts big."[40]

Mundelein's successes in Chicago were respected by his colleagues in the episcopacy. Unlike his predecessors, Mundelein soon became a national and international figure in Church affairs and a powerful force in affairs of state. Nationally, he assumed a leading position in the American hierarchy, and in 1918 his organizational skill led the American bishops to select him chairman of the board of Home and Foreign Missions of the National Catholic War Council and administrator of a nationwide campaign to bring relief to Catholic victims of World War I.[41] His successful work in this assignment won him the respect of European prelates, and the very considerable contributions of Chicago Catholics to Peter's Pence, an annual collection for the personal use of the pope, won him a cardinal's hat. On March 24, 1924, he and his Manhattan College friend, Most Rev. Patrick Hayes, archbishop of New York, were inducted into the College of Cardinals.[42]

His influence extended beyond Church affairs. He counted among his friends Illinois Governor Edward Dunne; Samuel Insull, the utilities magnate; and President Franklin Delano Roosevelt. He swayed others who, because of his position as spokesman for more than 1 million persons, valued his friendship and good offices. Thus Mayor William H. Thompson was compliant, and Secretary of State William Gibbs McAdoo paid him generous compliments. Mundelein was prepared to put his influence to work, as when, in a letter to Acting Secretary of State Frank Polk, he requested special consideration be given to German priests in the Chinese missions. "I shall be very glad," he wrote Polk on March 27, 1919, "to report to the Catholics of Chicago, numbering one million, that my appeal on behalf of interests so dear to their hearts received favorable consideration on the part of their Federal Administration. . . . I need only add that any cooperation on your part will likewise be considered a personal favor."[43] Mundelein realized, of course, that the Wilson administration needed all the support it could muster for its League of Nations proposal.

From his Chicago base, he drew the attention of world leaders for his advocacy or opposition to their positions. In November 1921, Eamon De Valera, the Irish leader, expressed a special debt to the German-American archbishop for taking the leading part in securing the American hierarchy's support for the Irish in their struggle for independence.[44] Others, conversely, raged against him. Mundelein not only spoke out against the fascism of the Detroit "radio priest," Fr. Charles Coughlin, but criticized Nazism and called Adolph Hitler "an alien, an Austrian paper hanger and a poor one at that." Further, he declared that the Nazi officials, especially Paul Joseph Goebbels, minister of propaganda, were "crooked." Hitler's government responded by demanding that the Vatican force him to retract his statement, and had the German ambassador to the United States make a representation of protest to the U.S. State Department.[45]

While much of Mundelein's work was with the practical aspects of administering the archdiocese, gaining respect or a hearing for Chicago Catholics, and serving as their spokesman to the nation and the world, he did not lose his religious perspective and awareness of his mission. His goal was to make Chicago a vital center of Catholicity and to reap a golden harvest of souls. A good deal of ambition and egocentricity may have permeated his work, but he strengthened the allegiance of Chicago Catholics to their Church. The crowning glories of his administration were maintenance of the largest Catholic school system in the world, erection of a magnificent archdiocesan seminary, and hosting the International Eucharistic Congress in 1926, which drew thousands of visitors from the ends of the earth.[46] These accomplishments demonstrated the vibrant faith of Chicago's Catholics.

Changes in the Catholic population of Chicago, if not as dramatic as the differences between Archbishops Quigley and Mundelein, were equally significant for the Church. When Mundelein assumed the leadership of the Chicago Catholic Church in 1916, its distinguishing mark was its immigrant constituency. The rapid growth of the city, which marked Quigley's tenure, persisted. The 1910 population of 2,185,283 had climbed to 2,701,705 by 1920, and to 3,376,438 in the succeeding decade.[47] The constitution of Chicago's population remained foreign, yet it changed, as the number and origin of its newcomers were altered by events in Europe. The four-year immigration record of 129,813 for the period 1911–1914 was never surpassed. The breakdown of familiar lines of communication and transportation during the Great War had a significant effect, for fewer than 20,000 European emigrants came to Chicago between 1914 and 1918.[48] The literacy test, imposed in 1917, further restricted immigration from southern and eastern Europe, and the passage of national-origin immigration legislation in the '20s closed the door to the traditional sources of manpower.[49] Thus Chicago's foreign-born population increased only slightly between 1920 and 1930, from 808,482 to 859,409.[50]

While the foreign-born population increased by only some 51,000, the number of Chicagoans of foreign parentage grew from 1,140,816 to 1,332,373 in the same period. The most significant changes, however, were registered among specific groups. The number of Irish and Germans, by birth or parentage, decreased in each decade after 1910. Meanwhile, the number of foreign-stock Italians, Poles, Lithuanians, and other Slavic races increased dramatically. Between 1910 and 1930 the number of Poles jumped from 203,132 to 401,316, Lithuanians from about 25,000 to nearly 64,000, and Italians from 74,943 to 181,861. Additionally, Southern Negros, few of whom were Catholic, and Mexicans, most of whom were traditionally Catholic, immigrated to Chicago to meet industry's demands for unskilled labor. The 1920 Negro population of 109,458 soared to 233,903 by 1930. In the same period, the Mexican population grew from 1,224 to about 14,000.[51]

For the Catholic Church, the most significant demographic change was the increased number of native-born persons of foreign parentage. The 1920 census recorded more than two-thirds of the persons listed as English, Irish, and German were second-generation. Also, nearly 59 percent of the Czechs, more than 55 percent of the Poles, and 51 percent of the Italians were native born. Only among the relatively small Slavic and Lettish groups, such as the Slovaks and Lithuanians, did the immigrant element predominate.[52] No longer was the Chicago Catholic Church composed primarily of immigrants.

Alterations in economic and social position and group identity were as important as numerical changes for each immigrant group. Education and better jobs contributed to a noticeable rise in status and prosperity, while European events, in particular World War I and the creation of new nations, affected ethnic consciousness and cohesion.

As the Irish continued to climb the socio-economic ladder, they tended to move farther and farther from the central city; however, they did not lose their ethnic identity. Like James T. Farrell's fictional Studs Lonigan, the Irish maintained close ties among their people. Race consciousness was maintained through the turbulent struggle for an independent Ireland, through the Church, and the parish school.

Irish independence appeared assured when the British Parliament passed a Home Rule bill in 1914; however, a clause delaying its realization until after the war changed the "Irish Question." Many Irish accepted the Constitutional Nationalist call to support England in its defense of Catholic Belgium; however, as the war dragged on and on, the Irish became restive. Revolutionary nationalists played on the growing disenchantment and sought to overthrow British rule forcibly. The Easter Rising of 1916 was quickly suppressed; its leaders were captured and (except De Valera) summarily executed;[53] and Chicago's Irish were enraged by the executions that attended the reestablishment of British law and order. The archdiocesan paper chronicled the events leading up to the rebellion and explained that revolt was a "logical" consequence when the ruling population, one-tenth of the whole, defended "rank inequality" and practiced "ill-concealed injustice."[54] On June 3, 5,000 Irish jammed the Auditorium Theatre to hear speakers laud the rebel heroes who followed in the traditions of Wolf Tone, Robert Emmet, and Allen, Larkin, and O'Brien.

When President Woodrow Wilson had asked Americans to enter the war and "make the world safe for democracy," Irish-Americans, who had leaned to the German cause, hoping that a weakened England would produce a free Ireland, rallied to the support of their adopted country.[55] Yet, they still hoped for a free Ireland, and made it clear that Wilson's pledge of self-determination for the oppressed people of Europe ought to include Ireland.[56] When the war ended, they girded themselves to win the battle of the peace. In Chicago, a month after the armistice, 15,000 Irish rallied to demand an independent Ireland and, when Eamon De Valera visited Chicago the following summer, 40,000 cheered him at a rally in Cubs' Park.[57]

During this period, efforts were made to maintain Irish culture and to increase the number of parochial schools that taught Irish history.[58] However, these efforts were not successful. A decrease in

Irish immigrants and the death of Chicago Irish (such as Rev. J. J. Carroll, the Gaelic preacher-scholar and pastor of St. Thomas the Apostle Church) combined to weaken the sense of Irishness.[59] When Ireland acquired her independence in 1922, Chicago's Irish population rejoiced because justice had been done, but with this victory, they seemed to have lost their greatest source of unity and identity.

While the Irish were able to nourish their national identity and, finally, celebrate the realization of a centuries-long dream, German-Americans had been forced to abandon their Germanness. Even before 1915, the German-American community had begun to suffer cracks in the armor it had fashioned in the last two decades of the nineteenth century. Home, church and school, and the press had begun to falter in perpetuating the German language. However, the steady breakup of German-Americanism was temporarily checked by the outbreak of war in Europe. Between 1914 and 1917, German-Americanism was infused with new vigor and the people with renewed cohesion.

In Chicago, German-Americans demonstrated keen interest in the European struggles and openly sympathized with the fatherland. Horace L. Brand, unofficial spokesman for the city's German interests, used his papers, the *Freie Presse* and *Illinois Staats Zeitung,* to counter anti-German propaganda and call for an absolute prohibition of exportation of weapons and munitions, because America's professed neutrality aided England and her allies. In the face of anti-German sentiment after the sinking of the *Lusitania* on May 13, 1915, Chicago's Germans blamed England for forcing the fatherland to resort to extreme measures to preserve freedom of the seas. As the war progressed, they collected funds and supplies for German victims of war, worked to defeat political candidates sympathetic to England, and mobilized to keep the United States out of war. Sadly but loyally, when the United States declared war on Germany in April 1917, they worked to defeat their Continental homeland.

America's entrance into the war unleashed a hysterical cry for "100 percent Americanism," which most seriously affected the German populace of Chicago. Their Germanism had to be differentiated from their Americanism, and the hyphen had to be removed. Sauerkraut became "liberty cabbage," the old and respected Germania Club was renamed the Lincoln Club, German-language newspapers fell on hard times, and efforts were made to prevent the teaching of German in the city's public schools. These and numerous other assaults on their loyalty vitally affected Chicago's Germans. The people who, before the war, had believed that "hyphenism" was in accord with Americanism, generally yielded to the anti-German pressure and gave up or modified their social and cultural life.[60] The prewar German-Americanism did not survive the war.

The flow of German-surname persons to outlying districts and the suburbs continued. More and more, they mixed with other peoples, intermarried, and maintained only a spark of the pride of earlier days. By 1930 the great majority of Germans had ceased to live in specifically German communities, but had scattered themselves in more or less cosmopolitan areas. This widespread dispersion prompted a sociologist to conclude that social unity among Germans had significantly declined and that they had been absorbed into the general life of the city.[61]

Chicago's Slavic peoples also changed significantly in the decade and a half after the beginning of the European conflict. Economically and socially, the Czechs, Poles, Lithuanians, and Yugoslavs adjusted to American life, but because of their numbers and time of arrival, they occupied different places on the socio-economic scale. The Bohemians, who had long resided in Chicago, with their more recently arrived linguistic cousins, peasants from Moravia, were the most successful of the city's Slavic population. The Czechs moved directly west from their Pilsen settlement and established the "California Settlement" (3600 west and 2200 south) and from there moved farther west to the nearby suburbs of Cicero and Berwyn. Thrifty, hard-working people, they were considered materialistic by many because they struggled to acquire the skills to earn a comfortable living and in the process, adjusted so well to America's economic system. Yet their financial success—their involvement in earning the resources to erect decent modest dwellings—did not destroy their consciousness as a community. In their new settlements they founded their old fraternal organizations, their Free Thought schools, *skols* for athletic arts, and Catholic churches and schools.[62]

The Poles, the largest of the eastern European groups, likewise made progress; however, they did not exhibit the same financial success and social mobility as the Czechs. Their early colonies remained thoroughly Polish and supplied the people for the new settlements that sprang up adjacent to them. The main arteries of transportation, such as Archer Avenue on the South Side, Milwaukee and North avenues on the North Side, and Torrence and Commercial avenues in South Chicago, tied the new to the old. Despite their movement, their dispersion "represented the smallest amount of any important group in the city" between 1898 and 1930. Compared to the Czechs, the Poles had not made much progress in economic and cultural assimilation. The influx of immigrants immediately prior to and after the war and the consistent strength of community institutions helped preserve the Old World character of the Polish communities.[63]

Lithuanians in Chicago (relatively few, compared to their eastern European neighbors) manifested similar characteristics of concentrated settlement and maintenance of community institutions. Like the Poles', their communities near the stockyards and the steel mills received thousands of new members, who reinforced the language and traditions. When they moved from their older settlements in Back of the Yards, they settled in the Chicago Lawn region.[64]

Besides their Slavic roots, all of these groups shared a dream: a homeland free of foreign domination. The outbreak of World War I and America's intervention made them acutely aware of their origins and strengthened their sense of identity. Chicago, which hosted the nation's largest Polish, Czech, and Lithuanian communities, witnessed a display of devotion to the mother countries as intense as that exhibited by the Irish and the Germans. The prospect of breaking Austria's domination of the Czech and Slovak peoples became an overriding concern that brought together individuals and organizations that had warred with one another for nearly two generations. The Czech Free Thinkers, who first settled in Chicago, had consistently sought the establishment of a free nation and the end of religious influence, which, they believed, obstructed the growth of nationalism. In 1914, Catholics and Free Thinkers worked independently to give relief to the victims of war and encouraged members of their communities to go to Canada to fight for their homeland; in 1917, when the United States entered the war, their mutual antipathies and distrust gave way to concerted action. The National Alliance of Czech Catholics and the Slovak League joined the Bohemian National Alliance at a meeting in Chicago in 1917. Together, they held rallies, disseminated propaganda, and tried to mobilize all Americans of Czech origin to lobby for American support for an independent Czecho-Slovak state.[65]

Nationalist aspiration also burned in Polonia. The chasm that separated the Polish National Alliance and the Polish Roman Catholic Union was bridged, since the war gave all Poles cause to believe that their partitioned homeland might be reunited. Although Polish socialists viewed Russia as the chief enemy, because it held the greatest portion of Polish territory and administered it barbarously, most Poles believed that unity was contingent upon the defeat of Austria and Germany. In 1914 the Poles in America formed the Central Relief Committee, and two years later established the National Department as the Relief Committee's political arm. Members of both the PNA and the PRCU supported these organizations. Again, ideological and religious differences gave way to the nationalist impulse.[66]

Like the Slavic communities, the Lithuanian colonies also were subject to "endless quarrels and disputes" between ardent nationalists, socialists, and a "church element." Nonetheless, they too managed to work together to raise a "fairly large" sum of money for relief of their war-stricken brothers and sisters in Lithuania. Yet, at the close of 1915, the editor of a nationalist paper lamented: "These lofty deeds were swamped by a sea of disunity and partisan hatreds."[67] Not only did they experience internal tensions, they were split about working with Poles, who had received a specific promise from President Wilson that he would work to reestablish Poland. For Lithuanians, who had been a subject people for 500 years, memories of their historical traditions as an independent nation were obscure.[68] Despite these problems, through the war experience and re-creation of their nation they developed a deeper and more intense consciousness of their Lithuanian identity.

Italians, who composed the other major Catholic group of recent immigrants, also went through a transition in this period. Their early settlements near the Loop, which housed many immigrants, were abandoned because of the expansion of the business district or the desire for more healthy and comfortable environs. As one observer noted of an old settlement: "Many of the people, as they have been able to afford it, have moved further north, especially the young people who marry. They establish their homes north and west of the neighborhood in which they were born, and bring up their families more nearly according to the standards they learned in school."[69]

The city's Italians were not affected as strongly by the events in Europe as other recent immigrant groups. In fact, they seemed disinterested when the Italian government declared war on Austria-Hungary in May 1915. They did not respond to their native country's call to return and fight. Nonetheless, when America entered the war, Italians (as Humbert Nelli noted in his study of Chicago's Italians) "willingly registered and served in the armed forces of their adopted country."[70] Heroic participation in the war gave Italians an increased sense of pride, and the prosperity that followed in its wake provided opportunities for increased esteem through economic success.[71] Just as significant was Benito Mussolini's fascist experiment in government in the 1920s, which excited "patriotism . . . to an extent probably never reached before."[72]

Participation in World War I and the struggle to secure the formation or re-formation of a nation for the relatives left behind heightened the sense of group identity among all newcomers, though not all members of a community embraced it. For those who had been brought to the United States at an early age, or been born here, maintenance of Old World consciousness was a source of conflict. In the Old Country, a child was expected to treat his parents with fear and respect, to assist in familial enterprise, and to share whatever he or she earned — but the Old World village supports did not exist in the New World to foster former ways. Rather, the American experience prompted the young to resist the "strange" mores of their parents, and adolescents to reject them. "The initial dissimilarities of experience," Oscar Handlin wrote in *The Uprooted,* "widened with time as the youngsters ventured out from the home and subjected themselves to influences foreign to their parents."[73]

A 1913 sociological study of daughters of immigrants in the packinghouse district documented the process of generational alienation, which began with adolescents' break from the customs of parent-dominated homes and efforts to be a "conspicuous part of some prevailing custom, fashion, or sentiment." For example, the simple question of whether a daughter might wear a hat became an emotionally charged issue. In eastern and southern Europe, women of peasant origin wore a babushka, rather than a hat, as a sign of their lower status, and after immigration they continued that custom. Their America-reared daughters rejected the notion of caste and placed exaggerated importance on possession of a fashionable headpiece because it signified oneness with all classes and all nationalities. The babushka did not have a place with the hopes and ambitions of immigrants' offspring.

> In this process of assimilation the American girl presents a strange mixture of independence and helplessness, self-assertion and submission, loyalty and rebellion, that confuse, anger and grieve the foreign parent; but neither understands the subtle and irresistible forces at work to produce a situation so difficult and so dangerous for the girls.[74]

Pressure to assimilate increased in the second decade of the century. When the widely heralded Progressive reforms failed to produce their expected results, their frustrated sponsors used the immigrants as scapegoats. The greatest pressure, however, was the growing fear that America might be drawn into the European conflict because of the "divided loyalty" of immigrants. America's stated policy of neutrality demanded national solidarity, but interpretation of that policy begot sharp differences of opinion and accentuated the lack of unity. The demand for conformity, euphemistically referred to as "100 percent Americanism," grew in proportion to the nation's prospects of entering the war. Efforts to enact restrictive immigration legislation were renewed and charges that immigrants were morally and intellectually inferior, and prone to criminality and violence, were widely debated.

The increase of anti-foreignism was wed to anti-Catholicism. Progressives blamed Catholics for impeding social progress. In the South and West and rural North, a growing chorus of fearful persons inveighed against a "papist plot" to subvert the machinery of democracy. In 1915, religion was interjected in Chicago mayoral politics and the city Board of Education considered establishing a quota to limit the number of Catholic teachers in the public schools.[75]

Chicago's Catholics, led by Archbishop Quigley[76] and his official organ, the *New World*, denounced such intolerance and testified to the immigrants' readiness to. assimilate to American culture and ways of living. The Literacy Test bills were vigorously opposed as anti-Catholic and un-American.[77] In 1915, Bishop Paul Rhode served as president of a Polish-American antirestriction organization,[78] and Fr. John Sobesyczyk, C.R., opposed the discriminatory character of the restriction bill at a White House conference. He told President Wilson that the literacy test was "unjust, unfair, unpatriotic, un-American and inhuman" because it was a reversal of "our American ideals of liberty and liberality."[79] The *New World* carried a series of articles by Fr. Frederic Siedenburg, S.J., which provided socio-economic and political reasons for opposing the literacy test.[80] The Catholic position called for appreciation of immigrants' gifts, expressed belief in the benefits of cultural diversity, and challenged discriminatory revisions of immigration legislation.

George W. Mundelein believed the immigrants were becoming loyal Americans but he did not express his predecessor's confidence in cultural pluralism. Furthermore, his vision of what the Catholic Church in Chicago should be differed from his predecessor's; it had been shaped by personal experiences, the changes that were taking place in the immigrant communities, and the resurgence of nativism. Rather than endorse the Quigley model of unity of faith, based upon diversity of expression and decentralization of authority, Mundelein worked toward unity of religious identity, based upon cultural homogeneity and centralization of authority. Rather than perfect the supranational Catholic identity fashioned by Archbishops Feehan and Quigley, he sought to create an American Roman Catholic identity.

The new archbishop's Americanism was similar to, yet different from, that of the earlier generation of Americanizers. With them, he shared the belief that the second and third generations would remain Catholic only if the Church became "more American" in its identity. Also, he believed that the Americanization of the Catholic Church would reduce nativist hostility. However, he did not share the optimistic belief that the Americanization of Catholicism would lead to the conversion of large numbers of Protestant Americans; he accepted plurality of religion as a fact that would never change. He believed that the Americanization of Catholics would provide the cultural unity necessary for the Church to meet the pressures the host society imposed upon it.

To realize his vision for the Church in Chicago, he would minimize its apparent weaknesses and maximize its strengths. To him, the national parish network was both a liability and an asset. It fostered diversity and separateness and, therefore, impeded centralization; however, national parishes were the foundation of the Chicago Church's amazing growth and the essential factor in the fidelity of its immigrant membership. Mundelein, pragmatic and politically attuned, understood that he would not be able to alter the national parish system fundamentally; nonetheless, he was aware that the power of his office could be used to convert national parishes into vital links in his Americanization program. Through new territorial parishes, centralized education and charity structures, and a new generation of priests, he would fashion an institution that could provide Catholics the means to compete as equals in the American economic and political system, without compromising their Catholicity. The United States' involvement in World War I provided the opportunity to actualize his vision.

8. Divided, Then United

WHEN THE REVERED SPOKESMAN of American Catholicism, John Lancaster Spalding, bishop of Peoria, died in 1916, Archbishop Mundelein took the opportunity to point out that devotion to Roman Catholicism did not hinder allegiance to America—that loyalty to a spiritual organization that was international in character did not exclude intense dedication to one nation. "It is rather refreshing," the young archbishop told mourners, "in these days, when we are so often accused by the vicious and ignorant of lack of patriotism and of a divided allegiance, to point to the example of this leader in thought and action—with him love of country amounted to a passion. . . . [R]arely did a statesman who made laws or a soldier who defended his flag love our country as much as did Bishop Spalding."[1]

The first years of Mundelein's Chicago tenure were devoted to demonstrating, in word and deed, that the predominantly foreign constituency of his Church was, like Spalding, thoroughly American.

On December 5, 1915, the *New World* had announced George W. Mundelein's appointment to the vacant episcopal seat in an article "An American for Americans." "Noted as a linguist of an old American family," the paper reported, "he is fitted for Archbishop of Chicago where the Gospel is preached in twenty-five languages, but where Catholics are all Americans in the making." That same day an interview with the appointee appeared in the city's daily papers, clearly indicating that the Brooklyn auxiliary did not believe in hyphenated Americanism. Either the people of the United States were American or something else, for they could not, as he explained to the reporter, serve two nations. By way of example, he proudly recounted the story of his German immigrant grandfather, who volunteered to serve in the Union Army and subsequently gave his life for his adopted country.[2]

The 43-year-old churchman, who had been the pride of the

German Catholic societies of New York State, who had been "kind and benevolent" to their organizations, who treasured his membership in Brooklyn's Lokal-Verband, and maintained a lively interest in German culture and history,[3] considered himself an American Catholic. By birth, experience, and predilection, he was an American, not a German, and by baptism, education, and conviction a Catholic. Americanness and Catholicism were fused together in his person and shaped his perceptions of and responses to the demands placed upon him when he came to Chicago. His goal was to make the same identification and central force in the lives of his Chicago flock. Illustrative was his reply to a reporter for a German newspaper who queried him on his trip to Chicago: "Have you any special message, your grace, for the German Catholics of Chicago?" Mundelein promptly answered: "None other than the message to all Catholics of Chicago. I have no separate message for any particular nationality. . . . I shall not speak to the Germans as Germans, or the Italians as Italians, or any other class of people. My message will be to all Catholics of whatever nationality."[4]

On that same train, his patron, Bishop Charles McDonnell, told another newsman that although the archbishop-elect spoke German fluently, he "is not what you seem pleased to term out here a 'hyphenated' American. He is a genuine, true blue American, and will be loved by all nationalities in Chicago."[5]

Most Catholics agreed with Rev. Thomas V. Shannon, Quigley's last editor of the *New World*, who wrote an article for the *Chicago Tribune* on the occasion of Mundelein's arrival. In that article he emphasized the Americanism of Chicago's Catholics:

> He [Mundelein] comes among people typically American. The cosmopolitan character of our city has been widely commented on, when in reality its very cosmopolitanism is its chief claim to Americanism.
>
> The people of this great city are not bound by the traditions that have clung so steadfastly to eastern cities. The air of freedom here has a better chance to sweep away the chaff of the old world. Under these conditions men become Americans in the west more rapidly than in any other part of our country. Chicago is the most American of cities.
>
> The statistics as to the number of Poles, Germans, Bohemians, Lithuanians, Italians, etc., in Chicago merely emphasize our contention. The fact that many of these still use the language of the country from which they came is no argument that they are not already absorbed by their adopted home.

Shannon concluded his article saying that nationality traits would pass into "the great current of American life," and, while this process worked itself out, the Catholic administrator, by respecting these traits, would form a "splendid" citizenry.[6]

As an American, Mundelein hoped to see his flock enjoy his country's blessings, participate in its government, and grow in devotion to it. However, the differences between his hopes and reality caused him persistent tension. Resurgence of the nativist spirit, which questioned the loyalty of the Catholic Church and the undivided allegiance of its members, who clustered in ghettos about national parishes, accentuated the differences. As Chicago's Catholic administrator and chief shepherd, he was mindful of the universality of the Church's mission and cognizant of the heterogeneity of his flock's interests and affections. When he first addressed the laity, he acknowledged that they were "a people gathered from the nations of the earth; speaking many tongues, but united in their faith to God."[7] To be true to himself and to his Church and nation, he would assume the role of mediator. He would try to explain his Church to non-Catholic America and America to his charges.

Mundelein believed that the Roman Catholic Church had a place in America—that it was not, as many critics contended, unsuited to a democratic republic. He conceived his Church to be the guardian of American liberty and preserver of the social order. In his mind, Catholicism was "the greatest conservative force for law and order, the great bulwark against anarchy, the great preventative agency against crime in our cities." Without its schools and charitable institutions, America would have to ready itself for the "cyclone of crime, the reign of terror that would sweep our city, raze its walls, blot out its people." As archbishop, he hoped to show "decent" citizens who were not members of the faith that Catholicism inspired devotion to the United States and enriched society through its mission to lead men along the paths of a moral life.[8]

The country's youngest archbishop, who recognized the existence of prejudice, sought to eradicate it by service to Chicagoans.[9] But despite his intention of countering prejudice with convincing deeds of Catholic citizenship, the Chicago Catholic Church generally assumed a traditional stance; as before, it denied all allegations of un-Americanism and attacked its critics. Between 1915 and 1916, the *New World*, under the archbishop's watchful eye, spoke out against religious bigotry preached under the guise of patriotism. The *New World*'s work of exposing the false premises of anti-American rhetoric and the irrationality of prejudgments were nonetheless fruitless. The deeply rooted anti-Catholic traditions remained an important prop to assuaging the anxiety that flowed from the uncertainty of social and economic conditions in the United States and the possibility that the country might be drawn into the European war.

Archbishop Mundelein realized that bigotry had practical aspects that could not be dealt with by a stroke of a pen. For example, he was concerned for the many Catholic girls who taught in the city's public schools and whose future seemed jeopardized by the absence of Catholic support on the school board. Shortly after his arrival, he discussed the need for favorable representation with Charles Ffrench, a Catholic member of the Chicago Board of Education. From Ffrench, Mundelein learned that only five of the twenty-one members were Catholics and that many of the non-Catholics were hostile to Romanism. "I had no idea that in a city like this," the archbishop wrote Ffrench, "in which the population is more than half Catholic, we should have so little and so poor representation on the Board of Education, which controls the schools in which so many of our girls are teaching." The serious absence of power, "in case we should ever get to a pinch regarding educational matters," greatly disturbed him. In the hope of averting trouble in the future, Mundelein promised to consult with Ffrench again.[10]

Even though the archbishop never experienced trouble from the school board, he soon saw Catholic child-care institutions threatened by what he perceived as anti-Catholic bigotry. In January 1917, Judge Jesse Baldwin of the Circuit Court of Cook County ruled that the county's financial aid to Catholic institutions which received wards of the state was unconstitutional. Public funds, although they were not adequate for the complete maintenance of the institutions, were complemented by the generous support of the laity and made it possible to build new and better facilities—more than $1.5 million had been spent in six years at the Feehanville complex.[11] The court's enjoiner created a serious financial problem for the archdiocese, and threatened the continuance of its institutions.

Addressing his flock on the ruling through a pastoral letter, read in every church on February 11, 1917, Mundelein tried to create a sentiment of righteous anger. He stressed that the court decision would throw 2,000 children into the streets, "unless our institutions were to have pity on them and take them without any compensation whatever." He reminded the faithful that the Juvenile Court of Cook County had contracted with Catholic institutions "in perfect good faith," and now the Circuit Court had betrayed that covenant. He had planned better opportunities and special training[12] "to show our fellow-citizens irrespective of creed or position how these children could later be counted among the most desirable element of our citizenship." Now the realization of these plans was jeopardized by society's "general unappreciative, cold and unresponsive" attitude toward the good done by Catholics.

Caustically, he noted that Catholics, who already paid a double tax for their schooling, could ill afford the "rather expensive luxury in this city to be a Catholic." Only the prejudiced denied that "the most powerful influence for good in Chicago is the Catholic Church, the one organization under whose roof twenty-six nationalities dwell in harmony, where rich and poor, learned and ignorant, Daughters of the American Revolution and immigrant laborers sit side by side in the pews of nearly three hundred churches." "Nobody denies," he continued, "that neither the laws of man nor the punishment of the State exert a fractional part of the restraint on the one-half of the population of this city as those of the simple 'thou shalt not' of the Catholic priesthood." Yet, despite this gift of an educated and law-abiding citizenry, the state had forbidden blameless children to receive and appreciate the one thing their parents' had left them—their religion.

Rather than directly attack Judge Baldwin's decision, the archbishop called for a new state constitution. He explained that the writers of the document could not have foreseen the poverty, congestion, and disease of a city and 2.5 million persons, or the tremendous asset religious training would be for the common good. Therefore, he argued, a constitution with provision for the religious welfare of such children was absolutely necessary. In the meantime, he pledged he would not abandon children to the "cold soulless care of the state."[13]

Compared to his privately expressed sentiments, the pastoral letter was gentle. Writing to a Brooklyn friend, he attacked the court decision and explained his strategy for victory.

Shortly after I came, I found that the Constitution here of the State of Illinois was drawn up by a lot of bigots and that it contained an anti-religious clause of which I was very much afraid. Before I had come, one mentally afflicted man with latigious [sic] mania had begun a suit against the City of Chicago and the county of Cook to cut off these appropriations to our institutions on the grounds that they were unconstitutional. The case went before a very narrow, puritanical judge. He rendered his decision in accordance with the Constitution.

The purpose of my letter to the people was rather in order to create public sentiment and this has already had its effect. As a result, the case against the House of the Good Shepherd last week was decided in our favor. The atmosphere that was created because of the publicity given to this matter by me, I am quite sure penetrated into the court and had its affect on the ruling. As a result, I have begun a number of other suits, the first being in behalf of the German Catholic Orphan Asylum Angel Guardian which will come up shortly, and of course you know me well enough to know that I will not ly [sic] down very easily on these cases. As long as I have got a slim chance at all, I am going to battle right ahead even until I get to the United States Supreme Court. We are living in an age of bigotry, the age of materialism, in which anti-Catholic and anti-Christian forces have a great deal of money. Now the only thing for us to do is to keep our people united and combat against this all the time, and I feel sure we are going to win out in the end. However, we are not calling anybody names here; we are simply going to fight this case to the finish on its merits.[14]

In his first year in office, Mundelein responded to anti-Catholic sentiment with self-righteous anger and a will to fight for the rights of his people. Like the pragmatic authors of the pastoral letter against the Edwards Law, he realized that political strength and public relations were as important in their way as prayer. Constitutional reform and court battles, however, receded in importance within days of the above letter. America's entrance into the European conflict demanded the archbishop's immediate attention.

As the spirit of anti-Catholic sentiment plagued Archbishop Mundelein's first year in office, so too did the growing anti-foreign sentiment, much of which was obliquely directed toward the character of the Church's membership. The possibility that the United States would become involved in Europe fueled the demand for uncompromising unity. The *Chicago Tribune* declared: "We must and will destroy every nationalism except Americanism. We do not want German societies here, nor Polish societies, nor Swedish societies."[15]

For Mundelein, who prided himself on his Americanism, such sentiment must have caused great pain. As head of a cosmopolitan Church, he had to respect all members of that institution, and as a loyal American, he had to exert his influence to ensure that his people were truly American.

He did not seek to obliterate the identities of his polyglot flock. Furthermore, he knew that such action would produce bitterness and hatred. In his first years as archbishop, he went out of his way to manifest his respect for the origins of his people. He addressed the Irish on St. Patrick's Day, the Poles on the 125th anniversary of the proclamation of the Polish Constitution, and even the diminishing number of French-Canadians.[16] His warmest words were reserved for German Catholics in a speech delivered in September 1916, when anti-German sentiment was gaining strength. "Two years ago," he told his audience, "it was a distinction to be known as a German-American. Today one almost mentions it under his breath." The new atmosphere grieved him because it was "rather late in the day to ask the German-American to prove his patriotism." Many German-Americans, like his grandfather, had demonstrated their love for America during the Civil War, and if necessary, he insisted they were ready in 1916 to do the same. However, preparedness to defend America did not preclude their expressions of sympathy for relatives and friends who remained in the homeland. If a war that pitted the United States against Germany should come, he believed all Americans would see that German-Americans' love for their newly taken spouse was stronger than that for their mother.[17]

The former member of the country's first German national parish realized the importance of national parishes and the role they played in preserving the faith of newcomers, and when he came to Chicago, Mundelein made no effort to disestablish these parishes. They were, he knew, the best safeguard of the Catholic faith among the thousands of persons who were experiencing the trauma of adapting to a new culture. However, he did nothing to encourage erection of new national parishes; rather, he favored a moratorium on creation of parishes for particular national groups. When new parishes were needed, he generally established territorial parishes and installed pastors who were representative of the dominant group within the parishes' boundaries.

One hundred and eighteen of the 211 parishes in Chicago were for foreign-language congregations when Mundelein became archbishop. That same year, the Holy See issued its revised Code of Canon Law and put special emphasis on the territorial parish. The previous version, promulgated after the Council of Trent in the sixteenth century, made no provision for national parishes; the authors had not anticipated the possibility of large colonies of Catholics of diverse tongues living side by side. National parishes evolved in response to the needs of Catholic immigrants in America. Canon 216, paragraph 1 of the revised code, stated that every diocese was to be divided into "distinct territorial parts," with an assigned church and pastor for the population, within specific boundaries. However, the fourth paragraph of the canon legitimized and ensured the preservation of existent national parishes:

> Distinct parishes for the people of various tongues or nationalities dwelling in the same city or territory . . . cannot be created without special apostolic indult; as regards parishes already in existence, no change is to be made without consulting the Holy See.[18]

The new law, however, manifested a "certain disfavor" toward the future establishment of national parishes, the plain territorial parish being the preferred type because its government was less subject to confusion and difficulties. However, the law gave "particular protection" to the rights and privileges of existent foreign-language parishes. A third type of parish, the "mixed" parish, also was given legitimacy; it was defined as "one whose population is determined by both territorial and personal criteria."[19] For example, Assumption parish, which was given territorial boundaries in 1904 but served an Italian congregation drawn from a region larger than its designated limits, was a mixed parish.

Unlike Archbishop Quigley, Mundelein balked at creation of mixed parishes. As long as a congregation manifested concern to preserve the national character of its parish and supported the church's maintenance, he did not assign territorial boundaries. Two instances demonstrate the confusion caused by national and territorial boundaries and manifest Mundelein's thoughts on the sticky question. When a woman wrote the archbishop to inquire whether she and her German-descent husband could attend St. Martin's German parish rather than the territorial parish in whose boundaries they resided, he answered in the affirmative. He explained that they might assist at St. Martin's, for it was still a German church, and added: "Later on the status of this parish may be changed to take all the people within a certain boundary; however, the time for that has not yet come. A lot of these difficulties with regard to language and nationality only time can straighten out, and the best way is to do the best we can in each individual case."[20] When an Irish-surname Catholic asked if he might attend St. George's Slovene Church, which was convenient to his South Chicago home, the archbishop replied in the negative:

> As St. George Church is a church that was founded and is intended solely for the use of the Slovenian people, and as its status has not been changed by the diocese or the diocesan authorities, we could not allow any English-speaking people who do not make use of the Slovenian language to affiliate themselves

with that parish. And you readily understand that, were we to make any exception to a rule of this kind, in the course of time it would work untold harm in the discipline of the people of Chicago. Moreover, St. Francis Parish which is located at 102nd Street and Ewing Ave. [the addressee lived at 9832 Ave. H] is not purely a German church, but is supposed to take care of all the English-speaking people in the neighborhood. It would certainly injure the future of this parish were there any other church placed close to it, for the Catholic population of that section is hardly able to support more than the present church.[21]

Pastors also found territoriality and nationality frustrating. The pastor of St. Boniface German parish complained to Mundelein that the only way to ensure the financial health of the parish was to convert it to a territorial parish. Poles, who had moved into the formerly German neighborhood, were legally bound to go to the Polish church or a more distant territorial parish.[22] In another instance, the pastor of a territorial parish complained that the Polish and Bohemian pastors in his area were usurping his jurisdiction by ministering to people other than their own nationality. In 1918 the vicar general for the German clergy wrote the chancellory office about the confused state of affairs and lamented that "no definite settlement has yet been made" on the jurisdictional issue.[23]

Although Mundelein was willing to maintain existing national parishes, he objected to the creation of new ones—a radical change in the policy that had been adhered to by every previous bishop. In July 1916 the archbishop informed a Polish priest that the rumor of establishment of a Polish national parish in his neighborhood was to be ignored because "my purpose in the formation of these new parishes is to make them largely territorial, i.e., to give them certain limits." He explained that the contemplated territorial parish would be predominantly Polish, though mixed, and for that reason the "principal language used there will be the Polish language."[24] This parish was probably St. Constance, erected in 1916 on the Northwest Side. Its pastor was an American of Polish descent, and the parish sponsored Polish societies, such as the Polish Roman Catholic Union and Alma Mater. Yet the parish was not, canonically speaking, a Polish parish.[25]

The new policy did not meet with universal approval, but Mundelein held fast and refused to be intimidated. When a delegation of Poles came to the episcopal office to request a meeting with the archbishop, relative to establishment of a new parish specifically for Poles in a suburban region, Chancellor Edward F. Hoban put them off. He must have sensed the group's determination and communicated it to the archbishop, for Mundelein wrote a forceful letter to the delegation's representative, Michael Piwowar, telling him he would not meet with the group because it would be a mutual waste of time, "as there is no change contemplated in the immediate future on the matter of the Summit-Argo parish." He reminded the spokesman that his present parish had a pastor and an assistant who spoke English and Polish perfectly, "a blessing that some districts long for and had to do without." "I advise you, therefore," he concluded firmly, "that you allow the matter to rest where it properly belongs, in the judgment of the Archbishop, who has his own reasons for action, for which he is responsible to Almighty God."[26]

The archbishop's "reasons for action" were never directly stated in his correspondence, but several factors seemed to have shaped his policy. Although canon 216 might appear to have dictated his course of action, he never appealed to it as a reason for diocesan policy; rather, the law was an additional reason for carrying out a line of action dictated by immediate problems. Mundelein's near mania for order (he used the epigram "Order is heaven's first law")[27] would have been challenged by continuation of the jurisdictional confusion that attended the creation of national parishes. Through the proper selection of personnel, a territorial parish could meet the varied needs of a mixed population and, at the same time, obviate the boundary problem. Equally important, people in the areas where new parishes were needed were of various national backgrounds, and these new settlements (compared to older sections of the city where newcomers still lived, in very limited space) were sparsely populated. To set up a church for each group would mean that the national parish would have to draw from a wide range — miles not blocks. In this period, when a car was a luxury, such a system would probably have failed. The wisest course was to adjust to demands of the new population distribution.

Changes in constituency were also evident to the archbishop. The war had interrupted the arrival of non-English-speaking Catholics who needed special ministration, and the Americanization of people who moved to the regions where churches were needed was different from that of inhabitants in older settlements. Those who moved to the perimeter of the city were generally native born, or more acclimated to the American environment, than those who lived in the original immigrant settlements. They valued the blessings of space, privacy, and independence more than the social organizations of the immigrant ghetto. To be sure, some of the settlements were still of one predominant ethnic group, but the Old World flavor was not as strong. Again, the territorial parish, with the flexibility of using English and some other tongue, was a reasonable solution.

Finally, Mundelein desired no more national parishes because they would limit the horizons of people who might gather around them. He did not object to continuance of foreign languages and customs among the old—he even encouraged the publication of several Catholic newspapers in foreign languages for those who did not know and were not likely to learn English.[28] However, he saw that to Americanize meant social mixing and coming to know others— breaking down prejudices that each group may have brought with it. When a French-Canadian priest offered his services to the Chicago see in January 1918, Mundelein replied that he would probably need his help in caring for emigrants from war-torn France. Although the four French parishes would not be able to handle the projected French population, Mundelein said he would build no more churches for them; rather, he would assign French-speaking priests to the various parishes where they might settle.[29]

Despite the archbishop's determination to stop the founding of national parishes, he recognized the need to preserve some of the original ones, even when their congregants had moved away from the old settlements. Some of them, still desiring a liturgy surrounded by Old World trappings, went to churches in their former neighborhoods. Furthermore, the early national churches were important as religious and historical symbols to old immigrants and their children. When Notre Dame parish, the mother church of French Catholics of the city, was threatened with financial ruin because of the dispersion of its parishioners, Mundelein saved it by engaging a religious order of priests to make the church a center of religious devotion. In a rare expression of sentiment, Mundelein acknowledged the "deep pride that the children of the French people here in Chicago held in this church." To Rev. Achille L. Bergeron, who had served as pastor of the parish in its declining years, Mundelein wrote:

> Many of the Old French inhabitants of the city still attend Mass there occasionally on Sundays and Holy Days, and I know it was one of their dearest wishes that their last requiem might be sung in that church that was so dear to them. I am glad that this hope of theirs was not in vain. But with the coming of the Fathers of the Blessed Sacrament they will still have the opportunity of occasionally hearing the Word of God in their mother-tongue and in worshipping at the altar where perhaps they received the Sacraments for the first time. Moreover, the priest in charge will be able to administer to their wants, particularly in the tribunal of penance, and it is, therefore, a matter of satisfaction for all that the old French church has not passed into other hands.[30]

Able to identify with the old and immigrant members of his flock, the archbishop also was able to understand the younger element, the sons and daughters of the immigrants, whose future was in America, who had no knowledge of "the homeland" except through their parents. Reflecting on his childhood, he knew that his grandmother dearly loved her Germanness, but *his* experience had made him more American than German. It was with the young that the new archbishop most identified, and it was with them, he realized, that the future of Catholicism in America rested. The chief instrument to help them was the parochial school.

Mundelein agreed with his predecessors' conviction that preservation of a child's faith was contingent upon a complete system of Catholic education. Additionally, he realized, the parochial school strengthened a parish by providing a focus for interested involvement.[31] Illustrative of his concern for the young was his response to the pastor of St. Stanislaus Bishop and Martyr parish, who desired to build a new and "great" church. The archbishop investigated the needs of the parish and found the school in terrible disrepair and overcrowded, and that the nuns who worked in that school had to live in horrible quarters. Even if the precarious financial condition of the parish permitted erection of a monumental church, Mundelein told the pastor, "other things are much more badly needed."

> Your children need a new school and they need it as soon as you can provide it for them. They need it so much that for their sake I would even take more of a chance than I would for a church. And it would not do to say that when a new church is built the present church and auditorium would be released for school purposes, for that would put off the necessary improvement at least three years, to the great detriment not only of religion, but also of the children's physical health and intellectual progress, both of which must surely suffer under present conditions. I deem it prudent, therefore, that you at once plan to relieve the unsanitary and unsatisfactory surroundings of the children by the erection of an additional school building. . . . *Please remember, I shall insist on the children being cared for first, the older people can wait.* There is another circumstance which I must call to your attention, the discomforts under which the Sisters live are such that were it known outside, it would be characterized as disgraceful. Religious cannot give satisfaction if they are crowded in sleeping quarters as are the Sisters teaching in your school. This condition must necessarily be remedied by the erection of a convent or by providing more decent accommodations for the Sisters.[32]

The nature of the education imparted by the schools also received the archbishop's attention. Before his arrival, the administration and curriculum of each school were determined by the pastors. Their predilections and whims were reflected in the classroom; there were no norms for evaluation, no unified programs of study. Increased mobility among Chicago Catholics caused frequent movement from one parish to another, and diversity of curriculum made the students' transition difficult and caused extra burdens for parents, who had to buy new sets of textbooks. Mundelein saw the weakness in the 176 autonomous parish schools and promptly acted to correct the problem. In the first months of his arrival, he appointed a school board to supervise education and begin the work of unifying the curricula of the parish schools. Teachers' meetings were held to gather information, set policy, and establish a common curriculum for all of the diocese's schools. The new program went into effect for the four lower grades in September 1916 and for the other levels the following year.[33]

Besides dictating unity and encouraging a new professionalism, the archbishop dealt with the need to prepare parochial school children for life in the United States. There was a validity to the nativist charge that Catholic schools too often segregated children and kept them from becoming independent citizens. In 1915, a Chicago Catholic wrote the Jesuit weekly, *America,* and expressed his embarrassment that Polish and Italian schools (as some Protestant critics had recently argued) failed their students "because such schools allowed them to reach the higher grades without a knowledge of the English language, an essential in the world of business." The writer held that all children must learn English in the first years, but added that this did not mean the language of the mother country should not be preserved.[34] Mundelein pursued a course that would prepare the students for America, mute the criticism of nativists, and avoid alienating most immigrant parents.

The archbishop's personally selected school board—composed of one descendant of Irish, German, and Polish nationality—ruled that, beginning September 1, 1916, all textbooks for basic subjects were to be the same. This meant that English would be the medium of instruction. The *New York Times* stated that the Chicago archbishop had decided on a "radical departure in the education in parochial schools of foreign parentage which in substance means Americanization."[35] Rev. James J. Jennings, the Irish representative on the board, explained the meaning of the decision:

> It is the purpose of this order to thoroughly Americanize the catholic school system of Chicago. We propose to teach our youth that there shall no longer be Irish-American, German-American,

or Polish-Americans in our city, but only real Americans. In other words, we intend to take the hyphen out of the parochial schools in Chicago.[36]

Questioned about his textbook policy, Mundelein stressed that his prime motive was to unite the school system "because of the many people moving to and fro from one parish to another and [the] constant necessity of purchasing new textbooks under the past arrangement."[37] However, some believed he intended to destroy the heritage of the national groups. M. l'Abbe V. Germain of *L'Action Catholique* in Quebec, in a letter to an influential Chicago priest, objected to the new program and sent a clipping from the Rhode Island *La Tribune* (a French-language paper) that criticized the archbishop for being more American than the Yankees. Its author recounted the sacrifices of the French, who discovered the area and colonized Chicago, and pointed out that the Apostles, through the Pentecostal gift of tongues, evangelized people in their native languages. Why, the New England journalist asked, did Mundelein, a successor of the Apostles, demand a single language?[38] Despite this broadside, Chicago's small French-speaking community did not seem to object to the English-language stipulation.

Some Poles, however, vigorously opposed the new regulation. Polish dailies announced that the archbishop intended to eradicate Polish from the parochial schools, and they mobilized opposition to the plan.[39] Fr. Jennings' remarks were too harsh for many nationalistic groups to accept, and Mundelein seems to have been forced to make a partial retreat. The following month he amended his plan, saying: "Provisions will be made to give all nationalities in the archdiocese opportunity to teach such branches as catechism and reading in their own tongue, but only supplementary to the unified English course."[40] While recognizing the desires of immigrant parents, priests, and newspaper editors, he did not deviate from his goal of preparing Catholic youth for life in America. Furthermore, he asserted his power by requiring that all books for foreign-language classes and catechism be the same in the respective national parish schools.[41]

To placate nationalists, the archbishop tried conciliation. He "co-opted" superiors of the numerous religious teaching orders into the diocesan school administration. He also (as James Sanders noted in his study of the city's Catholic schools) "at first overcompensated by giving disproportionate voice in the school administrative structure to the Polish priests."[42] To counter the rumor that he had commanded Polish pastors to ban their language in the schools, he had Rev. Louis Grudzinski, a diocesan consultor, and Rev. Thomas Bona, the Polish representative on the school board, publish articles in the Polish press stating that he did not intend to eradicate their language.[43]

The archbishop's new program for American education, implemented when the nation was engaged in a vigorous America First program, achieved results. The following year, when University of Chicago and Northwestern University debaters argued that the parish schools of Back of the Yards taught English as an "ornament," a Polish pastor from that district accused the debaters of ignorance and bigotry because they had not bothered to get the facts. Were they to investigate, he said, they would find that English was the basis of instruction. He admitted that catechism and topics related to the mother country were taught in a foreign tongue, but he stressed that the children spoke English fluently, even if their parents did not, and that their education was as thoroughly American as that in the public schools.[44] Although some of the teachers may have had great difficulty adjusting to the new program (especially members of Slavic religious orders),[45] effective efforts were made to implement the school board's directives.

Mundelein's centralizing tendencies also affected the wide network of charity work by Chicago's Catholics. Because of limited resources in men and money, the new archbishop endeavored to create a more effective system. To the Knights of Columbus he gave the mission of caring for delinquent boys, to the Women's Catholic Order of Foresters the protection of working girls, and to the German Catholic Societies the operation of an employment bureau. He believed that organizations would die of "dry rot" if they did not have a specific mission to aminate their members, and his goal was to entrust a specific work of charity to each Catholic organization. No longer could an organization look solely after the good of its membership; it must, he contended, attempt to solve a current problem—do its share to bring improvement to the households in the city. Like a conductor, the archbishop sought to orchestrate the various societies to achieve the greatest good with simplicity and efficiency.[46]

This desire for efficiency and centralization led Mundelein to create Associated Catholic Charities, whereby all charity institutions would receive funding from a central treasury. Ever sensitive to the feelings of national groups, which previously had supported charity work directly, he retained the board-of-trustees system, composed of priests of each nationality (e.g., German priests formed the Angel Guardian Orphanage Board of Trustees); however, the archbishop made them directly responsible to him.[47] Indirectly, the centralization of Catholic charity made people more aware of their coreligionists of other nationalities: their money was used to support all—not just Polish, Bohemian, German, or Italian—activities. Additionally, the expansion of charity work, through increased efficiency, Mundelein believed, would "produce more . . . respect on the part of non-Catholics for our religious and charitable institutions."[48]

The anti-Catholic and anti-foreign hostility that Mundelein encountered upon assuming the Chicago episcopacy provoked an Americanizing response. Though he firmly believed that Catholicism was not antagonistic to, but supportive of, the country's democratic system, he realized that many Catholics, because of their immigrant heritage, were not fully American. To meet this challenge, he established policies in parish formation, education, and charity work that would broaden the horizons of newcomers and their children. In the process, he assumed power formerly delegated to the individuals and institutions and thereby brought greater order and unity to the polyglot archdiocese. Despite his centralizing and Americanizing, however, he was not insensitive to the spiritual and emotional nuances of immigrant members of his flock.

When the United States entered World War I on the side of the Allies in April 1917, Mundelein's newly acquired power was an asset. From his archiepiscopal throne, he exerted great influence that helped America in the war effort and, simultaneously, enhanced the respectability of all Chicago Catholics, whatever their origin. Before Mundelein came to Chicago, his predecessor had espoused neutrality; however, the neutrality of the nation (which leaned toward the Allied cause) was quite different from the Catholic stance.[49]

The New World, whose readership was largely Irish-American and English-speaking German-American, tended to support the Central Powers (Germany and Austria), and although the basis of this sympathy might be attributed to the ethnic identity of its readers, the archdiocesan weekly stressed Catholic interests as a basis of judgment. In an August 14, 1914, editorial, "The War and the Church," the paper had provided material for consideration in choosing sides. Because Germany, since the death of Chancellor Bismarck, had been friendly to Catholicism and because Austria-Hungary had refused to recognize Italy's usurpation of the Papal States, they were considered allies of the Church; the opposing forces were sketched as enemies of Catholicism. Russia persecuted Catholic Poland; England abused the Catholic Irish; and France had expelled religious orders and fallen into moral and religious lethargy. "To see the noble edifice of Catholic Germanic thoroughness crumble," the editor wrote, "would be a calamity beyond the power of expressing. . . . Catholics might well keep these facts in mind in the bestowal of their sympathy."

The paper called for a free and independent Poland, but disagreed with the majority of Poles, who accepted Russia's promise of Poland's reunification at the war's end. The Catholic Church had suffered much under the Russians: Polish bishops and priests had been arrested, imprisoned, and sent to Siberia. In light of Russia's record, therefore, the czar's sincerity was doubted. If Russia won, her policies of suppression, the archdiocesan paper feared, would be extended to the territories occupied by her armies.[50]

Editor Shannon manifested a German and Irish bias. When America's neutrality seemed jeopardized by Anglophiles, he declared:

> There is one danger to American neutrality, the Anglomaniac. Whenever we have faced a crisis in the past England has ever turned her hand against us. . . . Our debt is greater to many other European nations than England. America can ill afford to lend its sympathies to England at the cost of time-honored friendship with the other great nations.[51]

The *New World* agreed with President Wilson's initial plea for calmness in America's effort to restore peace in Europe. After the sinking of the *Lusitania,* it supported Wilson's warning to the kaiser that America would not tolerate unrestricted submarine warfare, but it added that the United States must demand English respect for the rights of neutral vessels.[52] The *New World*'s support for Wilson, however, soon faded. After the Princeton president and professor surrendered to the nativists and denounced the "divided loyalty" of immigrants as a security threat, Shannon wrote:

> Are you greatly enthralled with the sprightly romance of our sixty-year old President? Neither are we. Mr. Wilson waxes eloquent against Hyphenated-Americans. And all this before the Daughters of the Revolution. But if America had depended on the Daughters of the Revolution it would be as barren as Puritan New England. We doubt very much if there are many Irish-Americans or German-Americans, because it is against these two races the thrust is made, who are not ready to put America first as is Mr. Wilson.

President Wilson's undertaking to speak as an American for Americans was considered a "foolish prepossession that takes hold of a college professor in his modest role of omniscience." "We do not believe," the editor continued, "nor have we ever believed that there was in America the menace of the bogey which looms so large in the imagination of Mr. Wilson."[53]

When Mundelein came to Chicago, he supported neutrality, as his predecessor had, but in February 1917 the German government resumed unrestricted submarine warfare, forcing Wilson to sever diplomatic relations. As the city's dailies warned of imminent American entrance into the war, the *New World* was forced to backpedal and search for favorable qualities in America's prospective allies. Even more, it felt a necessity to assert Catholic patriotism and explain that Anglophiles did not have a corner on such a virtue.[54] In this period of crisis, Mundelein asked all Catholics to refrain from verbosity and to pray for God's guidance for the president and members of Congress. In March, as the likelihood of war increased, the archdiocesan weekly counseled that loyalty to America meant former antipathies must be transformed: "To continue at this time a bitter condemnation of any power that chance may make our ally, is of the same brand of disloyalty as clinging to a motherland that may be hostile to us."[55]

The declaration of war, on April 6, ended the dispute as to where sympathies and loyalties must rest. Chicago's Catholic population — Irish and Germans, as well as Poles, Lithuanians, Bohemians, Slovaks, and other Slavic people — supported the United States in war. Only four days after the declaration of war, Archbishop Mundelein pledged Catholic loyalty: "One thing is certain, and I speak for myself, for 880 priests and 1,000,000 Catholics — the moment the President of the United States affixed his signature to the resolutions of Congress, all differences of opinion ceased. We stand seriously, solidly, and loyally behind our President and his Congress."[56]

The following week the archbishop attended a meeting of the American hierarchy at the Catholic University of America and the bishops drew up a letter, addressed to the people of America, pledging Catholic loyalty to the nation in its hour of crisis:

> Inspired neither by hate nor fear, but by the holy sentiment of truest patriotic fervor and zeal, we stand ready, we and all the flock committed to our keeping, to cooperate in every way possible with our President and our national government to the end that the great and holy cause of liberty may triumph and that our beloved country may emerge from this hour of test stronger and nobler than ever.[57]

Mundelein's address and the hierarchy's letter, however, conveyed Catholic defensiveness as well as Catholic loyalty. Members of the Roman Church were acutely aware that, as a minority group accused of un-Americanism, they would be carefully watched, and Mundelein, because of his ancestry, was doubly aware. Knowing that patriotism demanded more than well-turned phrases ("By our acts we will be judged, not by our words"),[58] the youthful archbishop used his great influence to stimulate patriotic deeds. His work and that of his flock fell into three categories: military service, financial support, and home support. In their service, they were fighting not only for the United States but also to make manifest the loyalty of all Catholics, native and foreign born.

Little encouragement was necessary to spur the Slavic peoples, especially the Poles and the Czechs, who had well-organized associations and had already sent young men to join the Canadian forces. If Irish-Americans and German-Americans had reservations about enlisting, the *New World* sought to diminish them through its editorials. Shannon advised Catholic youth: "Go to the front if you can, young man. You are a coward if, seeing your duty, you fail to do it." Mothers and fathers were counseled: "Give your sons—do not say: 'War is terrible!' Lost honor is worse."[59]

Archbishop Mundelein knew that, for devout Catholics, love of country is not an isolated virtue but is bound up with love of God and love of home. In light of this reality, he released priests, who were sorely needed for parochial work, that they might go with the troops. In the week that war was declared, two young priests were "practically released and ready to go within an hour's notice," and Mundelein had arranged for another priest to work at the Naval Training Station at Lake Bluff, Illinois.[60] In June, he wrote to Rev. Lewis J. O'Hern, C.S.P., who headed the Catholic Army and Navy Chaplain Bureau, to promise more priests.[61]

However, Chicago priests were not needed. Changes in the number of chaplaincies for Catholics declined from 128 to 46 because the New National Army conformed to the European plan of fewer but larger regiments. O'Hern explained that unless the War Department established new procedures, there was no need to file further applications, as the number on hand was more than sufficient.[62] However, when the archbishop learned of the situation he immediately wrote Archbishop John Ireland, because O'Hern was "not of sufficiently heavy calibre." He asked Ireland, who had distinguished himself as a Civil War chaplain and was highly regarded by the secretary of war, to intervene.

> With only 46 Catholic Chaplains accompanying this vast national army of a million men, it would probably mean the spiritual and moral ruin of the vast number of men—young men it must be

remembered — who are being drafted or have volunteered for the service. Figuring that 40% of the new army are Catholics, and that it's not an exaggerated estimate, it would mean one priest to 10,000 Catholic soldiers, an impossible task.

Thus Mundelein asked Ireland to use his influence so that the chaplain of each regiment could appoint assistant chaplains. Mundelein also sent one of his diocesan consultors to discuss this suggestion with Cardinal Gibbons.[63]

Archbishop Ireland, who responded immediately, explained that the proposal would not work, because Congress, not the Secretary of War, had the power to change the system. The veteran chaplain said he intended to go to Washington in October and would "consult with the Secretary of War and other officials to see what may be done." "I wish," he said, "it were possible for you to be in Washington while I am there. Your influence with the Senators and Congressmen from Illinois, and others, would be a strong argument in favor of the action we may wish to have taken."[64] Ten days later, the aged archbishop wrote Mundelein that he had learned "it may be an easy thing to bring Congress to our views. Let us do our share to this intent."[65]

Upon receipt of the letters, Mundelein replied that he was very happy at the news of the Washington trip, and added: "Your presence on the ground will be able to adjust some of the matter which now seems to be in a snarl." He informed Ireland that he would not be able to accompany him, but that he had already conferred with several congressmen from Illinois and had scheduled a meeting with Senator James H. Lewis. Lewis was described as a very valuable man because of his position as "whip," as one who had helped secure the clergy-exemption amendment in the conscription law, and as "very anxious to help me in every way that he possibly can."[66] Mundelein also told Ireland he already had five chaplains in the service and, at his own expense, had furnished several chaplains to the Naval Training Center near Chicago. Furthermore, he was willing to supply more.

> I am candid in telling Your Grace that my sole purpose is because I recognize that we have a wonderful opportunity at the present time to show the people at large in the country that there is no institution which is more patriotic than is the Catholic Church, and I feel that if we will only seize this opportunity now, we are going to reap golden fruit in the years to come.[67]

As a result of a special Washington conference, at which statistics showed that Catholics comprised an unusually large proportion of the U.S. Army, the Catholic chaplain quota was raised from 24 to 48 percent. Mundelein released forty priests from parish work to serve in the army and navy and, before the war ended, offered to supply twenty-two more whenever necessary.[68] Significantly, he made a special effort to supply Polish priests, for the Poles were fully behind the war effort and would willingly serve in the armed forces if they had priests who could confess them in their own tongue.[69] Irish-descent clergy, who were most numerous in Chicago, supplied the most chaplains, but the list of priests who served in the army and navy mirrored the ethnic character of the Chicago see: names like Donovan and Harrington, Lauermann and Hartke, Danokowski and Grembowicz, Girard and Moissant, Bubacz and Retzek.[70]

Thousands of Chicago Catholics went to war, but many did not return. The city's first casualty was a Polish-American who had received his education at St. Adalbert's, and Mundelein used the young man's death to praise the loyalty of Catholics:

> We are proud that the first hero slain on the battlefield from the citizens of this, America's second largest city, was a boy of Catholic family, educated in our Catholic schools, who had been among the first to volunteer even before the country entered the war. It is likewise a cause for congratulation that his heroic death is a conspicuous proof of the loyalty and patriotism of the children of those of our people who have come from other lands and who form such a large and such a desirable element of our citizenship of this city.[71]

Catholics' willingness to sacrifice, demonstrated by those who entered the armed services, was matched by their fellows who remained at home. The American hierarchy's appeal that Catholics supply whatever the government asked of its citizens was well received by Chicagoans,[72] who did their share to meet the financial needs of a nation at war.

On May 28, 1917, a representative of the Liberty Loan Committee of Chicago approached the archbishop to enlist the support of the Catholic clergy in the sale of government bonds. Mundelein pledged the cooperation of the clergy and their willingness to speak on behalf of the new Liberty Loan from the pulpit. That afternoon, he told a meeting of the clergy that he was subscribing $10,000 as a first installment, and he instructed the pastors of the diocese's 350 parishes to subscribe $100 or more of the parishes' money immediately, "so that every Catholic parish in Chicago, no matter what the nationality may be, would take an active co-operation in the floating of the new war loan." He told the chairman of the Liberty Loan Committee that he hoped to show all Chicagoans, especially "our Catholic people, that the

Church feels it is a positive duty at this time to aid the nation in every way that it possibly can in return for the peace and the liberty that the Church has always enjoyed in these United States."[73] In bold headlines, the *New World* of June 1, 1917, proclaimed Church Subscribes for Liberty Bonds, and throughout the ensuing year and a half gave much space to promoting their sale.

Much more important was the work of parish priests, who induced Catholics to provide financial support. Their effect is not measurable, but their influence as community leaders was crucial in breaking down the distrust of government that was characteristic of immigrants' Old World experience; and the people's response appears to have been generous. In his Christmas greeting of 1917, Archbishop Mundelein remarked that his people's willingness to sacrifice demonstrated "a deeply-rooted patriotism on the part of a united people formed out of varied elements, a loyalty not only on the part of the native, but just as much on the part of the foreign-born, that gives splendid promise for the future of this republic." In the same breath he added: "The year has brought with it a gradual decline in bigotry, a growth of better understanding among all people, a truer estimate of the devotion of our Catholic people to this land of their birth and adoption."[74]

In March of 1918, when the government initiated its third loan drive, Mundelein was requested to use the various parishes to help make the campaign successful, and he again reminded his priests of the blessings of liberty and the benefits that would accrue to Catholics by a proper display of patriotism.[75] Under the direction of Rev. Thomas V. Shannon, bond-sale booths were erected in the vestibule of each church of the diocese. Although numerous pastors objected to turning the temples over to money changers, Shannon persisted because he realized that Sunday sales were necessary for many national parishes (especially Slovak, Croatian, and Hungarian), whose congregations were drawn from great distances. Further, he did not want critics to say that Catholics did not cooperate as fully as non-Catholics, who also sold bonds in their churches.[76]

The response was impressive: $8,686,250 were subscribed to the Third Liberty Loan by Catholics of the archdiocese.[77] Most impressive was the participation of recent immigrants, and Shannon reported to Mundelein that the cooperation of Slovaks, Croatians, and Hungarians would make

> excellent copy for [the] public press. In certain sections of the city of Chicago the news came in yesterday that many Catholic foreigners who had put their money in safety deposit vaults, were withdrawing the money in such great numbers that they had to

have a special detail of police so that only forty at a time could get into the vaults.[78]

To demonstrate the government's appreciation, Treasury Secretary William Gibbs McAdoo visited Mundelein and publicly praised Chicago Catholics' response. By the time the war ended, they—through the instrumentality of the Church—had subscribed to nearly $13 million in loans.[79]

On the home front, Catholics sacrificed for the men who carried the flag into battle and for the families they left behind. Again, Archbishop Mundelein set the example; he accepted membership on the local committees of the American Red Cross and the Illinois State Council of Defense to demonstrate Catholic involvement. But besides serving on committees and offering invocations at public rallies, he committed the Church to the cause of victory, offering the buildings, equipment, and services of every Catholic hospital to the government. He directed that the St. Vincent DePaul conferences bring "quick relief" to households with men at war and he pledged the services of the Church's welfare institutions. He supported and encouraged the financial backing of the war effort by the Knights of Columbus. His newspaper publicized the sacrifices of Catholics and directed readers to conserve the food, energy, and materials needed to wage the war.[80]

Mundelein's pledge of loyalty was not compromised. When the war ended, in November 1918, the *New World* boasted that although Catholics comprised but 18 percent of the nation's population, they contributed 35 percent of the volunteers; that the first gunner to fire upon German trenches with an American salvo was a Catholic; that the first American to die in France was a Catholic; and that the first Chicagoan to give his life for the country was a Catholic. In an editorial, the paper declared that Catholics had done "their full share in men and means as they have always done at every crisis in our history," and their blood flowed as freely as that of fellow citizens of other beliefs.[81] Catholics earnestly hoped that, being "first in war," they might, like George Washington, be "first in peace, and first in the hearts of our countrymen."[82]

The young archbishop had played a significant part toward realizing his prayer that the nation, "formed from the flesh and blood of many nations and tribes and peoples," would stay "united as a people loyal to our flag, devoted to our country and country's cause."[83] Through his leadership and example, all of Chicago's Catholics had exhibited the virtue of loyalty, so that, as Fr. Shannon informed the secretary of the treasury, Chicago's foreign-born poor "took more bonds per capita than in any other city in America," because of

Mundelein's "patriotic impulse." Shannon observed: "From the beginning of the war, his quota was not alone to keep the foreign-born contented, but to actually make them sterling Americans. As a consequence of this we have had in Chicago not a single instance of a Catholic guilty of treasonable talk against our Government."[84]

United States participation in World War I was thus a test for American Catholics. In Chicago, where Mundelein had initiated Americanizing policies, his flock manifested a remarkable patriotism. Under their archbishop's leadership, Catholics gave their lives, savings, and energy to defend America and "make the world safe for democracy." Their response was characterized by a clear and consistent desire to prove they were loyal to America, that their religion and origins did not conflict with their devotion to the principles for which the country stood.

Mundelein's wish to demonstrate that the words he spoke of Bishop John Lancaster Spalding applied to all Catholics — "with him love of country amounts to a passion" — was realized. Nonetheless, even after the war, Catholics still had to contend with nativist animosity, even more virulent than before.

9. Toward Ethnic Homogeneity

THE ALLIED VICTORY OF 1918 did not usher in a new era of peace and harmony for American Catholics; rather, the postwar decade was a time of increasing tensions. Native Americans found adjusting to a new and rapidly changing society difficult. The erosion of social, economic, and political structures, which had previously guaranteed security, bred anxiety. In response to their phobias, many Americans acted to reestablish (or "preserve") the nation as it had been. The Red Scare, the Americanization campaign, immigration restrictionism, and the rebirth of the Ku Klux Klan were manifestations of their insecurity. All of these nativist movements directly affected the Catholic Church in Chicago. Under Archbishop Mundelein, the Church increased its efforts to harmonize its polyglot membership with the host society. Although his policies ruffled many recent immigrants, they were generally successful.

The first incident of postwar nativism to affect the Church was the Red Scare—the cry that foreign radicals planned to substitute Bolshevism for the American way of life. During the war, organized labor had benefited greatly through government intervention, and it nourished the hope that after the war it might improve and consolidate its position. While some unions *did* call for an end to capitalistic control and a continuation and broadening of government regulation, their demands were not revolutionary. The Communist and anarchist contingents of the labor movement, though constituting a small minority of labor, attracted great attention because of their aggressive evangelization among the urban poor. Management united to crush unionism. To destroy public sympathy for union demands, employers and commerce associations used their economic control of the press to link radicalism to labor and they created the impression that the nation's welfare was imperiled. Frenzy and irrationality, whipped up by respected leaders, such as Attorney General A. Mitchell Palmer, carried the day.

During the Red Scare, the Chicago Catholic Church repeated its injunctions against socialism, communism, and anarchism. In so doing, Mundelein followed the course set by his predecessors. The radicalist endeavor to make socio-economic class the basis of political organization prompted the *New World* to call such alignment "a lamentable pollution of the American political arena." The archdiocesan weekly admitted that while political parties might require "reorganization or even banishment with the formation of new parties," these lines should not be drawn on the basis of class consciousness. "The general mingling of public life," the paper believed, "opposes any segregation of the various classes in the polling-booth." The Church, composed largely of the working masses, also repeated its earlier counsel to labor:

> The real future of American labor does not lie in any union with the element of radicalism under a cover of political activity, but rather in the direction which the American Federation of Labor has taken in a sharp divorce from Socialism and Bolshevism, and in a healthy, active participation in national affairs.[1]

The Chicago Church sided with labor in the postwar labor strife. Thoroughly aware of the tensions in his country and his Church, Mundelein tried to prepare his priests to deal with the possible worsening of the conflict between capital and labor. In his 1919 retreat address, he devoted his attention to riots, strikes, labor's demand for reasonable wages, and the prospect of an economic crisis, and outlined the role the Church should play in the event of a crisis:

> It seems to me that a line is being drawn sharply and men are gathering in two great camps preparing for a struggle that may turn out to be gigantic and the cost thereof staggering to humanity. On the one side are the great corporations with their tremendous wealth, their hold strengthened even more by the help the government gave them during the war. Grouped with them are their clerical help and employees, none of them protected by unions or brotherhoods, for the most part educated, but unable to do anything much but what they are doing. Together with them are the small army of men and women who have their wealth, their savings, sometimes their all invested in the bonds and shares of these corporations. Together with them finally will be practically all of the newspapers of the country. On the other side will be the trades, labor, skilled and unskilled,

unionized as they were never before, conscious of their strength, unafraid of competition, now that immigration has almost ceased. If these two gigantic forces come to a clash, to a contest of strength, to a clinch, then God help the country. But for us there can be no question as to what side we must be on. In a crisis of this kind the Church must be on the side of the workingmen, on the side of the poor. They are our people, they have built our churches, their children fill our schools, we ourselves are the sons of workingmen. That does not mean that we must enter into any controversy, that we must espouse their side from the pulpit or the platform; on the contrary the less haranguing we do on the social question just now the better. But the workmen must feel that we are in sympathy with them, that when it is a question of their rights, even though sometimes crudely put we agree with them, that when they are in want, we are going to help them if we can, that we are not controlled by big interests to be used as watchmen over them.

Mundelein gave an example of a recent meeting he had had with an official of a company that employed many workers in Chicago and other cities. The official explained that he came on behalf of the directorate of his firm to ask the archbishop for the Church's help in the event of hostilities. In other cities the company's workers had gone on strike, and in Chicago they were preparing to do so. He asked that, if trouble broke out, the archbishop use his influence with the workers, who were largely of a particular Slavic nationality. Mundelein had answered:

Will you kindly tell me what your company has ever done for the Catholic Church that we should act as the policeman for you now. I happen to know that some of your directors have given large sums to the Y.M.C.A. organization and to different secular universities. I would suggest that they go to the Y.M.C.A. and to these institutions to quiet their men now.

Concluding his address, the archbishop stated that the Chicago Church must stand with the laboring man, the striker, and advise him "against lawlessness, to a peaceful settlement of the question, to arbitration, if the arbitration is just and fair and not like loaded dice." Then he directed his clerical listeners to seek his advice and guidance before responding to a call to act in the public arena, in order that the Church present a united front.[2]

His directives were not startling; they were consistent with the position taken earlier that year by the Administrative Committee of the

National Catholic War Council, the national voice of American bishops. Its brief study of the economic and social problems facing the United States, titled "Social Reconstruction: A General Review of the Problems and a Survey of Remedies," was written largely by Rev. John A. Ryan and called for a moderate program of social reconstruction. The document (signed by Bishop Peter J. Muldoon, chairman of the committee, and his three associates) advocated a government program to settle returning service men on vacant land, creation of a national employment service, continuation of the National War Labor Board, maintenance of wartime pay levels, more and better housing for workers, reduction in the cost of living, minimum-wage legislation, workmen's compensation, labor participation in industrial management, vocational training, and stringent child-labor laws. The bishops also outlined a program for future reforms that included cooperative productive societies and copartnerships, increased income for labor, and abolition or control of monopolies.[3]

Significantly, Chicago was already supporting labor experimentation aimed at effectuating the recommendations in the bishops' study. The Chicago Federation of Labor, guided by its president, John Fitzpatrick, had formed the Independent Labor Party, which was committed to reforms "closely resembling" those proposed by the NCWC.[4] There is no record that Mundelein gave official approval to the Independent Labor Party, but he did nothing to impede its growth.

The timing of the Church's endorsement of workers' rights was noteworthy. The pastoral letter of 1919 was issued when labor unions were losing much public support and when (as the *New World* noted in retrospect) "cowardice counseled silence."[5] Mundelein, as well as his episcopal colleagues, realized that the unrest posed a "serious menace to the future peace of every nation and the entire world."[6] By supporting labor's cry for justice, the Catholic Church pursued a conservative course, one that might preserve the good and eliminate the bad in the social order. "It is not a visionary program, it is not the picture of Utopia to be realized in the far distant future," the president of the Chicago Federation of Labor said in defense of the NCWC study, which had been attacked as socialistic. "It is what labor demands now, and those who wish to avoid the excesses and dangers of a violent and bitter upheaval can do nothing better than acknowledge its true conservatism and aid organized labor in putting it into practice."[7] By advocating workers' rights, the Chicago Church reinforced the traditional, warm relationship that had kept its members in the Church and out of socialistic and communistic movements.

Though advocating a conservative course, the Church did not endorse reactionism. The *New World* supported efforts to check radicals but it objected to abridgment of civil liberties and deportation of foreigners. Freedom of speech and press should not be denied, the paper's editor wrote, "save on special permit."[8] Acutely aware of minority rights, the *New World* strenuously objected when, in 1920, the New York state legislature prohibited the seating of several duly elected socialists.

> The exclusion of five Socialists from the New York legislature has all the appearance of patriotic duty. Yet patriotism has been put to strange uses. If elected representatives can be put out at the will of the majority excuses will not be lacking. In Georgia, Florida, and Alabama it is not beyond possibility, that the legislature may decide that Catholics cannot sit in that body.[9]

The Catholic Church's antiradical heritage proved a bulwark against antiradical nativists, but its cultivation of national parishes and immigrant societies to prevent leakage was vulnerable to attack by "100 percenters." Americanization programs and legislative measures proliferated after the war and gained wide public support, and the Catholic Church felt great pressure because its membership was the object of the Americanizing crusade. Previously, officials of the Chicago Church had responded to charges of un-Americanism by calling for its members to be good citizens, but had taken little direct action to assimilate its immigrant membership into the American mainstream. George W. Mundelein, more thoroughly acculturated than his predecessors, broke from tradition.

Responding to the Red Scare, many Americans advocated deportation of foreign radicals; however, most citizens chose a more moderate course, Americanization. Initiated before World War I by patriotic societies and settlements, efforts were made to educate newcomers in American ideals and ways so that they might become loyal citizens. During the war, Americanization gained additional advocates, who feared the "hyphen" and sought the security of national solidarity. The social objective of helping immigrants, which characterized many programs, was eclipsed by preoccupation with undivided loyalty—100 percent Americanism. Uncompromisingly, jealous nationalism supplanted the concepts of cosmopolitan democracy; immigrants were prodded to initiate citizenship procedures, adopt the English language, and proclaim unquestioning reverence for American institutions. When the war ended, immigrants, despite their demonstrated loyalty, remained suspect,[10] and postwar immigrant nationalism and fear of radicals produced an even greater demand for Americanization programs. The *Chicago Tribune* attacked the nationalist spirit of immigrant groups as "madness" because it affected domestic peace. "Let there be no mistake," the paper said, "Americanism and foreign attachments cannot co-exist." In 1919 and 1920, as a result of 100 percenters' lobbying efforts, state legislatures passed laws to implement Americanization.[11]

In 1916, while the United States government was devising its America First campaign, the *New World* declared that Americanization was the "greatest work before the Catholics of America at the present time."[12] Because the interruption in trans-Atlantic transportation produced an ebb in the immigrant tide, the paper's editor wrote that conditions were favorable "to catch up with the work we are so far behind in, the assimilation of those arrived in the past two decades."[13] To procrastinate, he believed would, cause "damage which . . . will be absolutely impossible to repair."[14] The paper had not ventured to outline a program of action, and when the country went to war, victory, rather than Americanization, became its highest priority.

When the war ended, the Church again confronted the problem of Americanization. Although Mundelein's editor had endorsed Americanization, and said there was no reason to link it to the sinister purpose of the past, when Americanizers had sought to destroy immigrants' faith,[15] he developed serious reservations about such programs. The people who most fervently called for assimilation were generally Protestant or irreligious, and the activities they managed reflected their beliefs. Moreover, to many Catholic immigrants, becoming American meant not only immersion in the culture of the host society but acceptance of the nation's Protestant heritage. Catholic officials, of course, were acutely aware of the dangers Americanization held for immigrants who came under the influence of many well-intentioned social settlement workers and, specifically, the Young Men's Christian Association.

To win the Church's endorsement, a program had to be uncompromisingly respectful of Catholicism, and few could meet the standard. The *New World* feared that Jane Addams, who tolerated anticlericalism, or other "women of this ilk, though possibly sincere in their purpose yet entirely warped in their political, economic and religious beliefs will be called upon to formulate and administer the national Americanization program." Existing ventures, conducted by wealthy women who volunteered their services to settlements, were harshly criticized:

A piece of news that might have been written as a skit on

busybodies narrates the fact that, whilst certain ladies were devoting an amazing amount of energy to Americanizing the children of foreign-born parents, their own were appearing with monotonous regularity before the Juvenile Court. The temptation of this new manifestation of social conscience about the foreigner is the danger of overlooking all lapses except grammatical English. . . . The endeavor of half-baked enthusiasts to interpret America to the alien may mean driving him back to indifference, or worse, towards this country. There is a real danger, therefore, in undertaking the task of Americanization. It is too sacred to entrust to the amateur or zealot. Indeed, it will require tact decidedly different from that shown by the average busybody.[16]

No less dangerous was the nonsectarian YMCA, which operated on the "smug assumption that Protestantism and Americanism are one and the same thing" and tried to proselytize new immigrants, especially Lithuanians.[17]

An additional reason for skepticism about the Americanization program was subversion of its intent. When the Division of Social Action of the National Catholic War Council undertook a study of Americanization programs to determine how Catholic agencies might enlist in unifying the country and deepening patriotic sentiment, it discovered attempts to manipulate programs so as to promote special interests and thwart social justice. "Americanization" had become a cover for reactionaries who sought to discredit progressive social-reform measures and, particularly, destroy organized labor. The dollar sign, rather than patriotism, motivated many well-publicized schemes, and the Church would have nothing to do with them.[18]

Because of its distrust of many Americanization projects, the Church, under the leadership of the National Catholic War Council, struck out on its own. Rather than "Americanization," a term that had come to mean a chauvinistic attempt to destroy immigrants' heritage and faith, or make them tools of capitalistic enterprise, the Church called its work a "campaign for Civic Instruction."[19] It sought to teach civic duties and responsibilities to native-born adults, as well as millions of immigrants beyond school age, and its programs, conducted under the guidance of the NCWC's Social Action Bureau, were moderate.

John A. Lapp, who directed the campaign from his Chicago office, realized that any attempt to enforce English or citizenship upon newcomers would be a "flat failure." The only reasonable method was to enlist immigrants in a common cause—not to force English and social companionship upon him; to give evidence of sincerity, in belief and practice, concerning the ideal of the nation—not to prattle about liberty, justice, and fair play; to teach English as a tool for economic benefit and the mastery of citizenship—not as an end in itself. Americanization, properly understood, he said, was for all persons.

> Let us utilize the democratic strivings of the immigrant peoples to strengthen our own and mutually develop enthusiasm for the practical realization of the ideals of Democracy. Let us encourage every nationality to find in America the opportunity which they longed for at home, and which they could not attain. Let us remove illiteracy from the ranks of our own native-born. Let us Americanize ourselves. Let us see that every child grows into citizenship with a holy purpose to strive for fair play, justice and the common good. We shall not fail in the process of Americanization if we think and act in terms of solving mutual problems.[20]

Even before NCWC initiated its citizenship project, the Chicago archdiocesan weekly had endorsed such programs. In May 1918 the *New World* called upon pastors to make their parish halls and school rooms available for Americanization work, if they had not already done so, declaring that the adult immigrant was too often left to himself to form his views on the ideals of the government of the land he had adopted.[21] Work among the newly arrived, the paper told its English-speaking readers, was a patriotic duty as well as a work of charity.[22]

When the National Catholic War Council began its citizenship work in March 1919, Mundelein's paper praised the campaign and again noted that too many persons used Americanization as a veil for proselytism and "perversion," and pointed out that the haphazard manner in which campaigns were carried out favored the ill intentioned. The editor wrote, referring to volunteer Americanizers who had no credentials other than zeal:

> the viewpoint to which they seek to bring the working man may be far more foreign to American ideals than that which the immigrant himself holds. Individually we must be constantly watchful for such perversion. . . . This watchfulness, together with a hearty seconding of the War Council endeavors, is the price demanded of us so that in the Americanization process millions are not irretrievably lost to both the Church and State.[23]

The extent of Chicago parishes' affiliation with the NCWC civic instruction program is not clear. A 1920 civic organization's survey of

Americanization in Chicago reported: "The Catholic Church has already under way a plan for a very broad education campaign making use of motion-pictures, lectures and distribution of literature."[24] However, in the first three years of the War Council's citizenship work the *New World* made no mention of parochial undertakings and the *National Catholic War* (later *Welfare*) *Council Bulletin* recorded but one: St. Stephen Slovenian parish's program, begun in 1922. The only other references to Chicago's use of NCWC services were letters, published in that organization's monthly, expressing satisfaction with the *Civic Catechism*.[25] Although he endorsed and provided financial support for the national agency, Mundelein appears to have left participation to the discretion of each pastor.[26]

Other citizenship activities were initiated to instruct the city's Catholic aliens. In four widely separated districts, adult men and women of Polish origin attended English and civics classes conducted under the auspices of their parish churches. Instead of having people go to classes conducted by the Chicago Board of Education, parishes made arrangements to have the city supply teachers free of charge. At SS. Peter and Paul, on the Southwest Side, five teachers instructed nightly classes with a combined enrollment of nearly 100. In St. Barbara's parish, an average of 14 attended, and at Holy Trinity, in the heart of the oldest Polish settlement, 36 men and women came to classes. At the recently founded South Chicago parish of St. Mary Magdalene, morning and evening classes were held to accommodate steel workers, assigned to alternating shifts. In this parish, which had an average attendance of 15, the students learned their lessons well; they organized a drive for more and better street lights, and won city council approval.[27]

Catholic settlements and day nurseries also provided educational programs for neighborhood residents. The Knights of Columbus, which had served Allied soldiers in war, found a new mission; it used DePaul University and St. Ignatius College facilities, and leased a twenty-classroom building from the Chicago Board of Education, to teach (without charge) honorably discharged servicemen. Ranging from accounting to oxyacetylene welding, the courses tried to advance veterans in their daily work or provide them with the basics for a more satisfactory type of employment. Among the courses offered were "citizenship," "English to foreigners," and "civics." The enrollment of the three branches for the 1920/21 academic year was 4,900.[28]

In spite of the efforts of the parishes and Church-affiliated institutions and societies, their influence was quite limited. The Chicago Community Trust, a civic group which sought to coordinate

Americanization activities, estimated that the public and semipublic agencies and religious and patriotic societies reached less than 8 percent of the city's non-naturalized population.[29]

Wisely, however, Mundelein took other measures to ensure the Americanization of his flock. As the administrator of the Catholic Church, he was able to reach more than half the city's population and a much greater percentage of its immigrants. Although his contact was generally indirect, it was not thereby less influential. Through policy decisions, implemented by his army of priests, sisters, brothers, and lay societies, and the ideas expressed in pastoral letters and the columns of the *New World*, he touched the lives of all.

The Associated Catholic Charities of Chicago bore witness to the brotherhood of man: money collected in national parishes was spent for the welfare of peoples of other races. In appealing for funds, the archbishop invoked the Apostle Paul's admonition to the Galatians: "Therefore, whilst we have time, let us work good to all men, but especially to those who are of the household of the faith."[30] Not only would their generosity provide for the needy, it would win public esteem. "Our non-Catholic fellow citizens," he wrote, "may not understand or appreciate . . . the sacrifices we bring for the Church or school, for religion or education, but all of them understand and surely must appreciate what we do for the relief of the suffering, for feeding the hungry, for helping those who cannot help themselves."[31] Succoring thousands of needy families through Associated Catholic Charities, Catholics practiced citizenship as well as charity, for their gifts "added to the contentment of this community."[32]

More than the charitable work of the Church, Mundelein's policy of restricting creation of national parishes added to the Americanization efforts. Despite the agitation of foreign-language groups, he held to his position, when immigration increased after the war. When Rev. Martin F. Schmidt was commissioned to establish a parish in a predominantly German area, the archbishop emphasized that the new institution was to be territorial and American. Schmidt was told that all functions were to be performed in English, even if the Germans, Austrians, and Luxemburgers of his congregation protested. However, without permission, the pastor took a middle course in order to prevent defections: he preached in English, but added German prayers after Mass. Gradually, he dropped them, until the service was entirely in English and Latin.[33]

For the Poles, the most recent but least Americanized, the policy had greater impact. Unlike the Germans, who had been forced to give up much of their Teutonic identity during the war, the Poles gained greater group consciousness through erection of the Polish state. A new nationalism affected them and they wanted, more than ever, to have their own institutions. Despite this development, Mundelein tried to remain firm. In 1921, when a group of Poles in the western suburb of Bellwood sent $25,000 to the archbishop, with a request for a priest and a parish to care for 100 families of Polish origin, the money was returned and the people were told to see their own pastor.[34]

Some Poles, disturbed by the new departure, threatened schism. They declared that if Poles were not given their own church, they would join the Polish National Church, whose schismatic bishops and priests preserved Polish culture in church services, and the pastor of St. Domitilla's territorial parish in suburban Hillside faced such a problem. A Polish portion of the congregation, "under the influence of nationalistic agitators," erected their own church without episcopal approval. They hoped to "scare" Mundelein into recognizing them by threatening to leave the Catholic Church. According to Oscar Strehl, the Polish-descent pastor, this was "a common trick with Polish agitators."[35]

In a lengthy letter to Chancellor Edward F. Hoban, Strehl requested Mundelein's help in ending the discord and bringing the nationalistic element back to his church. He asked that the archbishop offer a High Mass at St. Domitilla's to demonstrate that it was the only parish for the people of the region. Strehl wanted Mundelein, who had earlier told him, "Ignore their church . . . I forbid you to say Mass there," to remain firm in the face of the agitators' threat of schism:

> Only a firm policy can save the situation; after the storm has passed there will be quiet, order, discipline and obedience to the Church authorities. . . . Obedience to lawful ecclesiastical authorities is here at stake and therefore we must remain cool-headed and firm, otherwise more Poles will move out here and fall into the hands of those agitators and then there would be a great commotion. This small number can be assimilated into the English-speaking parish and the newcomers will then follow their example.

Rev. Strehl, who had learned Polish from his parents and claimed he could "pass for a Pole," believed he could weaken the nationalists by a tactic similar to that followed by Rev. Schmidt:

> In order to give no chance to agitators, I read the Epistle and Gospel in Polish, I preach in Polish, sing and pray with them in Polish. But I have *no* special services for them as I want them to

take in *all* the English reading, praying, singing and preaching. I only add a little Polish after the English services are over. Would I have special services for them they would not unite with the rest, but remain separate and then there would be about 100 families . . . would want a Polish Church and we should have the same trouble. But now they listen with profit to the English and are glad also to hear a little in their own mother-tongue, their sentiment for the Polish is thus satisfied and *unconsciously* they learn and appreciate the English services. As the Polish is only *added* to the services, in time it can fall away entirely without creating hard feeling. There would be by far not so much difficulty if all our parishes would have limits.[36]

Although he did not accede to the demands of the Hillside nationalists, Mundelein gave in to the pressure of highly organized groups, but only after a waiting period. The Bohemians of Berwyn, who, according to the archbishop, had an "exaggerated spirit of nationalism that is rampant today among these various Slav races, amounting almost to a mania in some cases," supported by the Bohemian clergy, won a national parish in 1919. When another group of Bohemians appealed for an additional parish six years later, they were refused.[37] The Poles of the Brighton Park district of Chicago, failing to receive a favorable hearing from the archbishop, appealed to the apostolic delegate to intercede on their behalf. When Mundelein learned of the actions of the "Polish nationalist agitators," he was incensed and determined to "let these people wait a while longer [the matter had been under consideration for several months] before they would get what they were after as a punishment for their impatience." However, he relented, forgave them, and divided the crowded parish of Five Holy Martyrs.[38]

Between 1916 and 1929, Archbishop Mundelein commissioned the foundation of only nine national parishes in a total of 42.[39] Although 21 percent of new parishes were listed as national, this was a significant change, compared to Archbishop Quigley's policy.

The national parishes created by the Americanizing archbishop reflected the needs of his constituency. Parishes were permitted for the most recently arrived groups, which had not been able to build enough churches to prevent leakage in the early years of adjustment. Illustrative of his concern to safeguard the immigrants' religion was Mundelein's solicitude for Mexicans. Not only did he encourage spiritual work among Mexicans, he endeavored to supply priests and parishes for them. He converted St. Francis Assisi, the old German parish on the Near Southwest Side, into a Mexican parish and blessed a Spanish-speaking priest's use of storefront centers to celebrate Mass, hold missions, and teach catechism.[40]

Because Chicago was the United States city with the fourth largest Mexican population, it was considered appropriate that these people have their own, special church. In 1925 in South Chicago, a little wooden church, Our Lady of Guadalupe, named after the patroness of Mexico, was opened, thanks to Mundelein's efforts on behalf of "these strangers in our midst."[41] Later, when the congregation grew too large, the archbishop offered to sponsor a $100,000 loan for erection of a more fitting church and to devise a definite plan to help the struggling congregation defray its expenses. In 1928, work was begun on a brick structure to serve the growing Mexican population of the region.[42]

The new church and hall complex of Our Lady of Guadalupe provided a respectable neighborhood meeting place; previously, pool rooms, barber shops, and restaurants were their only gathering sites. The hall was to be used as a "center of Americanization work among the 8,000 Mexicans of the Calumet district, the scene of entertainments and classes in citizenship." The Spanish-born pastor, Rev. James Tort, C.M.F., boasted of his American citizenship and urged his flock to "learn the language and adopt the customs of the United States."[43] Also, the parish was to be the base for settlement work by Spanish-speaking nuns, lest Protestant proselytizers rob the Mexican of his religion, "a wholly contemptible affair."[44]

Thus even when Mundelein seemed to deviate from his declared intent to limit new national parishes, he saw to the civic as well as the spiritual welfare of his charges. In his mind, they were inseparable, and his territorial policy was complemented by use of the parish school to educate the children of immigrants in the American way.

Although some of the foreign-born sisters who conducted Slavic parish schools had difficulty with English, implementation of the 1916 program was thorough. The superintendents, appointed by the archbishop, saw to the unification of school programs and encouraged professionalism, and the consolidation and Americanization of the school system apparently had an impact. By 1924, the pastor of St. George's Lithuanian parish had to give sermons in English at the children's Sunday services, over the protests of the nationalist members of his congregation.[45]

In 1919 the Illinois General Assembly, responding to the Americanization crusade, passed a modified version of the Edwards Law. The statute required that the "elementary branches of education shall be in the English language." The legislators reasoned that Eng-

lish, as the common as well as official language of the United States, was
"essential for good citizenship."[46] This law caused no serious problem
because Mundelein had used his influence to see that a more extreme
bill, which would have excluded all foreign-language use, was
defeated. His goal was that all students be prepared for life in America,
not that their ethnic heritage be destroyed.[47]

Mundelein's final but equally important step was also educational in
nature: development of a thoroughly American clergy. Even though it
had more seminarians than any other United States diocese prior to his
arrival, Chicago did not have a seminary system.[48] Bishop William
Quarter had established St. Mary of the Lake Seminary and College,
but his successors failed to promote its growth, and in 1866 the
seminary had been closed by Bishop Duggan. Thereafter, the diocese
sent its young men to seminaries of other dioceses in the United States
and abroad, while its bishops tried to secure immigrant clergy to
minister to their polyglot flock. The absence of a seminary system of its
own was a serious drawback for a diocese the size of Chicago, as it was
impossible to create an *esprit de corps* among a clergy so widely diverse in
background and experience. Archbishop Quigley realized the urgency
of fostering an indigenous clergy, and to this end, in 1905, he had
opened Cathedral College for high school youths intent upon a priestly
vocation. At the time of his death, this preparatory seminary had 175
students;[49] but it remained for his successor to develop a complete
training system for Chicago's clergy.

Six months before his death, Quigley had met Mundelein, the
Brooklyn auxiliary, at the funeral of a mutual friend and told him of
his plans to improve Cathedral College.[50] But before he could
implement the project, he died. Mundelein, recalling this conversation
when he learned of his appointment to Chicago, determined to carry
out Quigley's plans and expand the facilities for priestly training. "If
the Lord spares me long enough," he told a reporter, before leaving
New York, "Chicago will have a seminary."[51] In May 1916, he
announced that the "inadequate, unsuited and insufficient" buildings
of Cathedral College would be replaced by a new structure that would
be a fitting monument to his predecessor's "silent, zealous self-
sacrificing" devotion to Chicago's Catholics. He secured property and
began erection of a twelfth-century French Gothic facility (a deliberate
replica of Ste. Chapelle, Paris) that would become an architectural
landmark. Quigley Preparatory Seminary, composed of three
buildings—chapel, college, and gymnasium-library—and resembling a
medieval structure, with rose window, sculpture, high-pitched roofs,

courtyard, and flying buttresses, rose in the heart of the architecturally progressive city (on the Near North Side). Although costly, Mundelein believed the project was a splendid investment for the future.

On the occasion of his announcement, he shared his hope to provide "a Theological Seminary for this diocese, as complete, as beautiful, as monumental, as any in this country."[52] Two years later, he purchased an extensive tract of land in Area, Illinois,[53] about 45 miles northwest of the city, and over a period of years erected a major seminary that was "complete," "beautiful," and "monumental." From 1920 to 1934, the archbishop built an educational complex of fourteen buildings which expressed his esthetic tastes and Americanizing tendencies. The seminary, dedicated in 1924 as St. Mary of the Lake, perpetuated the name of Bishop Quarter's pioneer undertaking. As its name linked it to the past, so did its architecture; instead of choosing a European style, Mundelein selected American Colonial. The chapel, the hub of the campus, was a reproduction of a Puritan meeting house in Lyme, Connecticut. The archbishop's villa, on a hill overlooking the lake, was a brick reproduction of George Washington's Mount Vernon on the Potomac River.

Archbishop Mundelein selected native diocesan priests to oversee the spiritual and physical development of the young men and contracted with the Society of Jesus to provide the philosophical and theological foundations for the ministry — a new and realistic approach to seminary training. Traditionally, American seminaries were conducted by diocesan priests or other religious orders. For example, the seminary of the Archdiocese of St. Paul was staffed by diocesan clergy and that of the Archdiocese of Baltimore by Sulpicians. Mundelein realized that he did not have clergymen adequately prepared to train seminarians; however, he did not wish to turn their formation over to a religious order whose animating spirit was not akin to his own. By dividing the various tasks, he kept control over priestly formation and discipline, yet provided excellent academic training.

The seminarians were Mundelein's special pride. The young Rev. J. Gerald Kealy, the seminary's first rector, made weekly trips to Chicago to report to the archbishop on the progress of the students. When possible, the archbishop visited the seminary to observe his future clergy, and no costs were spared for his future priests. Besides providing "luxurious" surroundings — private bath for each student, gymnasium, and a golf course — he tried to enrich them culturally. Works of post-Renaissance masters adorned the halls, and original editions of literature classics, the correspondence of world-renowned artists, and the signatures of all signers of the Declaration of Independence were available for their inspection and study. The students were also encouraged to take music lessons and play in the seminary's orchestra.[54]

When (by then) *Cardinal* Mundelein dedicated the chapel in honor of a Chicagoan who had given his life for his country in the Great War, he explained the special significance of the seminary:

> Until now, let us confess it, without our seminary we were unable to accomplish much as we would; isolation, varied training, differences of custom due much to different seminary training, left us less united than we cared to admit, and if continued, it would have left a widening breach in our armour, which the enemy could easily have found. But with the oneness of their preparation, the newer clergy of the diocese will be a much more formidable force to attack, a much more unified body of officers and leaders to safeguard the interests of the Church for your children's eternal welfare.[55]

Indeed, much of the archbishop's correspondence dealt with conflicts of priests who would not or could not accept his demands for unity. They frequently resisted his Americanizing directives and his authoritative way and fought among themselves for leadership within their national groups. Although he despised such behavior, he could hardly discharge such priests, especially those of religious orders. Instead, he met the challenge by creating a more loyal and unified clergy.[56]

By 1924, his hope to be free of dependence on European priests was realized. "Our clergy has heretofore been drawn from countries all over the world," the cardinal explained to a reporter, "but now we will take only boys born and raised in Chicago, and all of them are given eleven years of training in the same courses under the same teachers."

> St. Mary's seminary is therefore a school which takes the cosmopolitan and turns it into the American. These boys who learn there how to be good priests will be the leaders in the process of Americanization in the future.[57]

Indirectly, Mundelein hoped to make each parish a "citizenship center." However, he did not ignore the sensibilities of immigrants who did not know English or felt uncomfortable confessing and praying in that language. Seminarians, according to their ethnic heritage, were required to study the language of their ancestors from the time they entered the preparatory seminary. As late as 1938, the archbishop fostered the teaching of foreign languages. He counseled a priest assigned to the seminary to teach Polish: "Those boys who don't know much Polish, be sure to teach them enough to be able to hear confessions in Polish."[58]

To carry out his Americanizing, the archbishop of Chicago needed the cooperation of his flock, and his actions appear to reflect the sentiment of his constituency. It is impossible to gauge the real support he received; however, the generosity with which fund drives for the seminary and Associated Catholic Charities were met, as well as the lavish reception accorded Mundelein on his elevation to the cardinalate, indicate that he had the backing and confidence of the majority of the city's Catholics.

Although the Chicago metropolitan won the favor of most of his people, some Catholics, especially among the Slavs, rejected him. They protested his policies as attempts to strip them of their identity. Participation in the Great War, the redrawing of the boundaries of eastern Europe, and the unity born of working for a common cause made them less malleable in the hands of the German-descent archbishop.

Within the immigrant communities, Mundelein's assimilationist policies were openly criticized and challenged. While Bohemians, Slovaks, and Lithuanians registered dissatisfaction with his administration, no resistance surpassed that of the Poles. The largest group of recent immigrants, they went furthest in their protestations and fomented a twentieth-century movement akin to Cahenslyism. The resistance was led by societies and individuals who would lose their grip on the community were Poles to give up their Old World language and traditions. Generally, they were supported by the uprooted, who sought to find comfort and security in the familiar patterns of a New World Polish village.

Dziennik Zwiakowy, the organ of the Polish National Alliance, perceived the Americanization programs instituted during the war as devoid of the "smallest particle of the true American spirit, the spirit of freedom, the brightest virtue of which is the broadest possible tolerance." Instead of promoting the source of unity, which was love of the ideals of liberty and honor, for which the nation stood, Americanizers fostered dissension and discontent by focusing on "superfluous" changes in language. The editor approved of Americanization that was based upon "mutual understanding, broad-mindedness and tolerance, a conviction that, on the opposite side, there is friendliness and a real concern for the welfare of one's fellow man." The Poles felt they were best qualified to Americanize their own.[59]

Mundelein's English-language stipulation for all parish schools was a chief source of irritation. To the editor of *Dziennik Zwiakowy*, it was an ignoble aspect of the Americanization movement. He believed that "Catholic bishops of other nationalities" were as dangerous to true Americanization as the strong anti-Catholic current emanating from other religious groups:

> Can such Americanization [that tends toward the elimination of foreign languages from national schools and the limitation of freedom to organize on national grounds] reach its goal even if it abandons the American spirit of tolerance, and adopts the Prussian system and methods, that is, violence? No, definitely not! Such Americanization must fail; it will create unrest and race hatred, and it will spoil the possibilities of mutual understanding and ideal Americanization. . . . Let the nation and the government turn their attention to the ideal Americanization, to education, to raising and ennobling those neglected, unknown, often hated or scorned "foreigners," and the rest will take care of itself. . . . But all violent, intolerant attempts upon the religio-nationalistic schools, upon the freedom of organization, upon the souls and traditions of those who were born elsewhere, will only spoil the really noble work of Americanization and we will stand as one man against them.[60]

Denials that the Church sought to destroy their identity, made by Mundelein's Polish lieutenants, did not assuage the fear of nationalists. At St. Michael's parish, where Bishop Paul Rhode had previously served as pastor, fund raising for the Associated Catholic Charities failed. The new administrator, Rev. John M. Lange, reported that despite the efforts of his three assistants, "the drive . . . proved unsuccessful on account of the campaign launched against the Most Rev. Archbishop regarding his supposed opposition with respect to our polish [*sic*] schools by a certain polish [*sic*] daily."[61]

But Mundelein was not beset simply by a hostile Polish press, he was also pressured by the clergy. In 1917 a petition of grievances, signed by more than 100 Polish priests, was delivered to him. When he failed to acknowledge the petition, he was again requested to consider the "spiritual welfare of the Polish-speaking Clergy and laity of the Chicago Archdiocese."[62] This second letter prompted him to make a sharp reply: "You won't mind me saying that I consider it rather indelicate for a portion of the clergy, unasked, to direct the head of the diocese as to his action with regard to some of his people, for it would argue that he had not the welfare of [their] Polish birth and descent at heart, which I do not think you for a moment would admit."[63] Such questioning and militancy in the ranks greatly agitated the archbishop.

The priests who signed the petition appear to have been members of the Chicago chapter of the Association of the Polish Clergy, founded by Bishop Rhode in 1912. The organization's primary aim was to strengthen the faith of immigrants, endangered by adjustment to a new way of life and by the schismatic Polish National Church. Secondarily, it sought to further the Polish language and culture in the churches and parochial schools. Because of its insistence on maintenance of Old World ways, the group threatened the archbishop's Americanizing and centralizing plans. According to Msgr. Dominic Szopinski, a leader in Polish nationalist activities, Mundelein, unlike Quigley, disapproved of the group. The archbishop replaced the organization's leader because the latter would not bend to his will, and—with Polish clergy eager to please him—infiltrated it. "For fear that their attendance at the meetings of the Group might be reported," Szopinski recalled, "many quit the ranks of their fellow priest. The work of the Chicago Group was thus paralyzed."[64]

Before Mundelein, the Polish clergy, often referred to as the "Polish League" by priests of other nationalities, had had its own way. One Polish-descent priest, who when asked by the future Pope Pius XI if Mundelein was not a German name, responded: "*Er is nicht nur ein Deutcher, er is sogar ein Preusse* (He is not only a German, he is a Prussian)." He said, however, that some of the League's leaders employed czar-like tactics to exercise control over Poles and gain financial benefits for themselves. Appalled by their deceit and greed, the priest told Mundelein of their trickery and asked him to act in behalf of the Poles. He added in a postscript: "Your Grace fully realizes that should the other priests find out that I have informed you of these things, I would be 'stoned to death'—therefore . . . I would like this to be a letter of confidence."[65]

In 1920 the General Union of the Polish Clergy of the United States, in collaboration with the Polish legate to the Vatican, drew up a thirteen-page memorial. The document, *I Polacchi Negli Stati Uniti Dell'American Del Nord* (The Poles in the United States of North America), outlined grievances against the American hierarchy. The joint memorandum rested on the conviction that bishops—in particular the Chicago metropolitan—were not only neglectful of Polish interests but intent upon destruction of their nationality. The memorandum was submitted to the Holy See by the Polish legate.

First, the authors petitioned for more Polish bishops, explaining that they were necessary to keep the faith alive and to maintain the national sentiment, which contributed to preservation of the faith in Poland. Only two Poles had ever been elevated to such a rank in the United States, and only one, Bishop Paul Rhode of Green Bay, was still living. Because of the large Polish population, they argued, there was an urgent need to raise more Poles to the episcopate in order to watch over immigrants who did not know English.

To support their contention, the memorial presented "the religious situation of Poles in America." The people had made supreme sacrifices to erect churches for the exclusive use of Poles for their religious, national, and social life. Further, they had built schools because the "American school separated the children from the family and language." These schools were not, the writers explained, simply to preserve the spirit of family and national customs, but also "to instruct them well enough to ready themselves for life in America, to introduce them to the American spirit, in order to better understand and capture its best aspects, and to prepare them adequately for opportunities in the field of labor." The schools taught English so that they might become good and intelligent American citizens and "penetrated with the Catholic and Polish spirit." Separated from these institutions, the immigrant, the authors believed, would be "lost to the nation and also to the Church."

The third section, "Serious Misunderstandings between Catholic Poles and the American Episcopate," accused the American bishops of lacking a "clear understanding" of the condition of American Poles. In particular, it criticized the episcopate's "Americanism," which disposed administrators to be less benevolent toward Polish immigrants, insensitive to the cultural needs of Polish seminarians, and overly rigid in implementation of canon law regarding territorial parishes and trustee control. Further, the position of pastors was weakened and their moral authority eroded by the financial demands of bishops. Specifically, diocesan charity drives forced pastors to become bureaucratic administrators rather than shepherds tending to the personal needs of their flocks. Such programs seriously weakened the influence of the pastor and threatened the welfare of the Church among the immigrants. The Polish National Church, which had forty-seven parishes in the United States, would become, it argued, a more formidable rival.

Polish Catholics' needs, the memorial continued, were not taken seriously by American bishops. To illustrate this point, reference was made to a confidential letter Mundelein had written to the apostolic delegate to the United States that was critical of Poles. The Polish legate at the Vatican observed that the Chicago archbishop was "*American* to excess" and unreasonable in his opposition to a Polish auxiliary for Chicago.

In conclusion, the memorialists objected to the theory that, since the Polish state had been resurrected, Poles in the United States should be Americanized. Nor should the Catholic Church, through its bishops, become the "instrument of Americanization" among Polish immigrants. The Union of Polish Clergy advocated intervention by the Polish government in behalf of the Polish clergy and their congregations. In particular, they asked that Bishop Rhode be given an archdiocese, auxiliaries be appointed for cities with large Polish populations, seminaries institute curriculums reflecting the needs of Polish students, and the American hierarchy make exceptions in the application of canon law where needs of immigrants were involved.[66]

At the American hierarchy's annual meeting in September 1920, the bishops took up the Polish memorial. After thorough discussion, the archbishop of Detroit offered the resolution:

> In reply to the memorial of the Polish Legation, addressed to the Holy See, be it resolved that:
>
> We the members of the American Hierarchy unanimously enter protest as American citizens against the interference of any foreign government in the ecclesiastical affairs of the United States, and moreover, that we record our reprobation of the unwarranted assumption on the part of laymen to dictate the nomination of bishops;
>
> and, furthermore, we condemn most emphatically the conduct of any body of the clergy, who appeal to laymen or to a foreign government, for the purpose of coercing the Episcopate in the selection of candidates for episcopal office.[67]

A committee, composed of Archbishops Dennis J. Daugherty of Philadelphia, Sebastian Messmer of Milwaukee, and George W. Mundelein, was called upon to "formulate a strong and earnest letter" in answer to the controversy initiated by the Polish minister at Rome.[68]

Archbishop Mundelein proposed that Daugherty repudiate foreign meddling in Church affairs of the United States while he and Messmer took up the specific charges against the hierarchy.[69] The Milwaukee prelate discussed formulation of a response with Mundelein at a Chicago conference and sent his notes to Daugherty, in whose hands the letter rested.[70] In November, Mundelein wrote Cardinal James Gibbons that he was satisfied with the reply, and confided: "Personally I think the letter in its present form, while temperate and respectful, will constitute one of the strongest and most forceful documents ever presented to the Holy See."[71]

On November 18, 1920, Cardinal Gibbons, in the name of the American hierarchy, forwarded the lengthy letter to Cardinal Peter

Gasparri, secretary of state to the pope. It began with citation of the resolution passed by the American hierarchy, which was followed by Archbishop Daugherty's closely reasoned argument that interference by a foreign government in ecclesiastical affairs restricted the liberty of the Holy See. Such meddling was doubly intolerable because pressure would be exerted by a government that was not in a position to form an accurate judgment of the ecclesiastical needs of a nation thousands of miles away. "Indeed," the Philadelphian wrote, "the Hierarchy feel that political motives, and not the welfare of the Church, prompted the memorandum." Daugherty, who had nearly become archbishop of Chicago, explained:

> The American people in general, and the government of the United States in particular, have ever been jealous of outside interference in their affairs. They expect the various nationalities, which seek a home here, to become one people, one race, loyal to the government of this country, which welcomes them, protects them, gives them liberty, and affords them the means of an honest livelihood. For generations the Catholics of the United States have received the unjust accusation of disloyalty to the American Government and of subserviency to foreign potentates. Should it become known that the Polish priests of the U.S. appealed to the Polish Government to bring pressure on the Holy See in favor of their pretensions, and that the Polish Government acceded to their wishes, without doubt, the Poles of this country would be accused of unfaithfulness to our Government and the American Church would be charged with subjection to foreign powers. Non-Catholics would calumniate us as hindering the unification of the Nation, as co-operating in the political aims of foreign nations, with whom our country may one day be at war. The consequences would be serious for the Catholic Religion.

While condemning the intervention of the Polish government, Daugherty, speaking for the American hierarchy, blamed "still more severely" the Polish priests, who were working for selfish ends. These priests, he maintained, should "make themselves worthy of the episcopate honors, rather than seek them." To give in to their demands would lead to chaos. If the Poles were to have a bishop, he asked, why not have one for Indians, Negros, Irish, Germans, Italians, Lithuanians, Austrians, Slovenians, Croatians, French-Canadians, Spaniards, French, Belgians, Portuguese, Dutch, English, Swiss, Bohemians, Tyrolese, and the numerous other peoples who made

America their home? To follow such a course, he said, would create confusion surpassing "any discord recorded in history."

The Polish legate's prediction that "dire disaster" awaited the religious state of Poles unless such a plan were executed was, according to Daugherty, a mere fancy. Earlier cries had proved false. Recalling the Cahenslyism of the past century, he noted that such warnings "were employed by other nationalities for political and selfish purposes similar to those harbored by the Polish Government." "As in the case of other nationalities," he concluded, "their prophesies of evil have remained unfulfilled; so, we are confident that the forebodings of the Polish Legate will come to naught."

The second part of the reply, prepared by Mundelein and his Milwaukee colleague, sought to answer the particulars of the memorandum. Showing that the statistics in the Polish document were "padded," they said that their first concern was to disprove the "willful distortion of truth" regarding the American hierarchy's treatment of Poles. To this end, they listed, challenged, and disproved the allegations.

The major charge was discrimination, because of Polish origin or descent, against priest and laymen. "In fact, just because of this charge," the Midwesterners wrote, "many concessions were made in Polish parishes and more freedom allowed the Polish priests." Poles formed but one element in the Catholic population, and although there were more German priests and parishes, there were no "distinctly" German seminaries, nor were non-Polish students sent to special seminaries in Europe, as were Poles. Furthermore, some American seminaries (notably those of the Archdioceses of Chicago and Milwaukee) taught the Polish language to students of Polish descent, and to institute courses in the history and traditions of Poland would necessarily lead to charges of favoritism.[72]

The charge that bishops sought to Americanize Polish parishes was rejected outright. Mundelein and Messmer noted that there had "never been any attempt to interfere . . . to change the language used in any of the foreign language churches." Only upon "urgent and repeated demands on the part of pastors," as in the cases of German and French churches, were changes made, "and this because the pastors found their young people, American born, deserting their churches for the neighboring English-speaking churches." "What these other earlier immigrant populations experienced," the two German-descent archbishops contended, "is now happening to the Poles." Similarly, the American bishops did not seek to hasten the demise of national parishes, and there was no effort to "interfere in any way in what is a perfectly natural change here in the United States by emphasizing a spirit of foreign nationalism," because, due to the declining number of immigrants and the growth of a native population, it "would cost the loss of many souls and effect really nothing in the end."

The Polish clerics' request for greater control of parochial administration, a demand akin to trusteeism, was declared uncanonical. Indeed, canon law prohibited parishioners from administering parish property; only special concessions by the Holy See, or usurpation by civil authority, made such practice possible. Further, they argued, the major incidents of schism among Poles in the United States resulted from this tendency. To accede would confirm Polish people in wrong ideas "by giving them what might be called a separate church administration under a distinctly Polish bishop and would be a fatal step leading them to downright schism."

Messmer and Mundelein were not sympathetic to the request for Polish auxiliary bishops and ordinaries because it was "positively a movement toward the complete isolation of the Polish Catholics from their American Catholic Brethren." Polish administrators for Poles, they reasoned, would "preserve a distinct and separate Polish nationality . . . and would be absolutely injurious to the Church and Country."

On the issue of Polish bishops and the impact of specially appointed bishops, Mundelein and Messmer expounded at length:

> It is absolutely false to say that by isolation the Polish Catholics will be more surely kept in the Faith. The contrary is the case as shown by experience. By being kept away from religious intercommunication with Catholics of other nationalities, by being taught their religion exclusively in Polish, these young Polish Catholics become absolutely aliens among their own brethren in the faith, they feel like strangers in the other Catholic churches, they are unable to go to confession to non-Polish priests, and can neither express nor defend their religious belief among non-Catholics. All of which is evidently against the true interest of Catholic faith. It is asserted, not without good reason, that when such Polish Catholics move into places and districts where there is no Polish Church, they easily fall away from the practice of their religion.

Reiterating Daugherty's position, they argued that concessions would adversely affect the welfare of Catholicism in America:

> It is of the utmost importance to our American nation that the

nationalities gathered in the United States should gradually amalgamate and fuse into one homogeneous people and, without losing the best traits of their race, become imbued with the one harmonious national thought, sentiment and spirit, which is to be the very soul of the nation. This is the idea of Americanization. This idea has been so strongly developed during the late war that anything opposed to it would be considered as bordering on treason. The American people and government are today fully determined that nothing shall stand in the way of promoting in every section of the country and in every portion of the people, this work of Americanization. It will be a real disaster for the Catholic Church in the United States if it were ever to become known that the Polish Catholics are determined to preserve their Polish nationality and that there is among their clergy and leaders a pronounced movement of Polonization. Still more will it provoke mistrust and suspicion among our Protestant fellow citizens and our American government, should they hear that the Catholic Poles of the United States have appealed to a foreign government in support of their unAmerican endeavors at the Vatican. In the face of the continual hatred and hostility against the Church manifested by thousands of American citizens, the Polish movement is, to say the least, fraught with great danger to the present peaceful and happy relation between the Church and the American people and government.

The letter concluded with the assurance that the American bishops, in drawing up this response to the Polish memorial, were not "actuated by motives other than their concern for the best interest of Religion and by the desire to fully inform the Holy See of existing conditions and assist in disposing of this unpleasant difficulty."[73]

The Vatican seems to have accepted the American hierarchy's reply as an objective assessment of the Polish question.[74] Also, Mundelein's Americanization efforts and firmness with Poles won the endorsement of his colleagues.[75] However, the archbishop failed to convince many of the Polish clergy and laity that he was deeply concerned about their welfare, that he did not seek to strip them of their culture, that he did not regard them as unequal to their Catholic brethren. As archbishop, he had led a campaign to collect money, from *all* Catholics, for the Polish victims of war in 1916, and had netted $40,000.[76] When he was made a cardinal, he had sought, and received, a special papal award for Anthony Czarnecki, an influential Polish journalist and politician, as a "recognition of all Chicagoans of Polish descent."[77]

Yet broadside attacks by nationalists continued, especially by *Dziennik Zjednoczenia,* an organ of the Polish Roman Catholic Union. In 1925 Msgr. Thomas Bona, Mundelein's faithful liaison with the Poles, wrote a pamphlet to defend his superior. Printed in Polish and distributed in Polish parishes, it attempted to disprove the charges of episcopal discrimination. Bona gave examples of the cardinal's concern for Poles and asked his fellow Slavs to realize they were called to a broader vision. Quite plainly, he told them they had imagined themselves to be giants, when in reality they were a "negligible quantity" in the eyes of their neighbors. Because they concerned themselves only with Polish movements, they had little impact on their fellow citizens.

> We are under the impression that we are impressing the world, whereas the world hears very little about us. The world as a matter of fact hears of us when we make [a] laughing stock of ourselves by our attacks on the Hierarchy of the Church, or when the papers disclose some scandal. His Eminence insists that we take a broader view of life, and taking also an active interest in Church and nationalistic affairs, show who we are and assume our place among the various nationalities in America.[78]

Indeed, Bona clearly spoke the mind of the cardinal, whose goal as shepherd of the Chicago Catholic Church was to see his people join with their fellow citizens to keep America ever the land of the free and the home of the brave, and to thrust it forward as "leader of the countries of the world." When he returned from Rome in 1924, he addressed the city's Catholics, who crowded into the Auditorium Theatre or huddled around their radios. With them he shared his vision of the Church's role in America and his special mission in that drama. The future of the United States was to lead "not in the prowess of war; not even so much in the markets of commerce; rather in the field of charity, in the interest of decency, of gentlemanly conduct, of brotherly love."

> To see the hand of God in the destiny of the American people we need only consider how, from a mixture of emigrant races, we are forming a people that is the admiration of the world. The Lord surely must have some great mission in store for a people with whose formation he has taken so much care as with this nation of ours. And now comes our duty, yours and mine, to keep that people one and undivided; to keep it far from alien influences, and shield it against foreign propaganda. To repel from our midst those who would split up in parts, who would halt our

progress, who would hamper our mission for the peace, the happiness, and the real prosperity of our people and our country.

This is my part of this great purpose. All these races that are gathered here this evening, to unite in one great happy family; to rule them all impartially without fear or favor; to bring their children . . . the same opportunity for success in their work in this life, and the hope for happiness in the life to come. It is this work our schools succeed in accomplishing, and in an even greater measure, our seminaries will produce, where the future pastors are being trained under our own eyes, to be the real leaders of Americanization in this city, youths in whose veins run the blood of many lands, but in whose heart burns ardently, and undyingly, the love of but one country, the land of their birth, the land of the Star Spangled Flag.

He told his audience that, as archbishop of Chicago, his greatest honor and privilege was to form the leaders who would train a million and more citizens to be faithful to the Church and loyal, upright, and law-abiding citizens of their great nation. This work, he prophesied, "will last and keep known to men my name long after the scarlet robes I wear have moulded in the tomb, and the red hat of the Cardinal swung high in the vaulted heights of my Cathedral." To accomplish this mission, he sought the cooperation of all Chicagoans, irrespective of race and creed, so that "this city we all love may be known the world over, and live on history's pages, not only as the greatest industrial and commercial center, but the city that answered to every cry of distress with its characteristic response, 'I will.' "[79]

Conclusion

THE CATHOLIC CHURCH SHAPED, and was shaped by, the people and events in Chicago between 1833 and 1924. This study of its changing identity during that period leads to several conclusions about that institution, its leaders, its members, and the host society.

The membership of a multiplicity of peoples in the Chicago Catholic Church caused serious problems for its administrators from its origins, more than a quarter of a century before the Civil War, through the 1920s. Responding to the wants of immigrants was not a problem that suddenly appeared in the 1880s and vanished at the turn of the century. The hierarchy was called upon to acknowledge the uniqueness of each group as soon as enough people of one nationality existed to organize a lobby for special treatment or demand a voice in ecclesiastical affairs. The Irish petitioned that a fluent English-speaking priest be retained in Chicago as early as 1837, and the Germans, in the following decade, sought and received a German-speaking bishop.

The greater heterogeneity and numerical strength of national groups in the period 1880–1900 made the problems of nationalist aspiration more pronounced and acute. After the turn of the century, the growing number of second- and third-generation Americans began to have a greater impact on the Church, and nationalism lessened. However, the demands of particular national groups continued to be a serious challenge for ecclesiastical administrators.

That the Catholic Church survived the storm of immigrant nationalism is remarkable. At the time of the Church's origin in Chicago, it might have been unreasonable to expect that one institution could withstand the centripetal force generated by more than twenty distinct nationalities. Yet its bishops and archbishops, without benefit of successful models, brought unity out of potential chaos. The Polish National Catholic Church, established in 1895, was the only schismatic

226

break, and it made but limited progress. Unlike Lutheranism and the denominational crises that affected it, the Catholic Church maintained its oneness. Furthermore, it prospered.

In secular terms, the success and vitality of the Chicago Church rested on the intense faith and socio-psychological needs of the immigrants, the wise and flexible leadership of the bishops, and the persecution of the host society.

For European peasants, the Church was an integral part of life. It was their mediator with the supernatural and a center of community life. When these people came to America, they sought to transplant that institution in order to nourish their spirit, to preserve their culturally rich devotions and customs, and to establish a foundation for a cohesive community, capable of giving them a sense of belonging. The Church became a keystone of social networks and the conserver of treasured Old World ways. For an immigrant in Chicago to break with the authority of the Church would have been an extreme action, which would have meant ostracism and intensification of the trauma of uprootedness that was part of the immigrant experience. The sacrifices that immigrants made to build churches and schools reflect their commitment to and their need for the Catholic Church.

Equally important in transplanting the Catholic Church in Chicago was the leadership of the bishops. The hierarchy diligently endeavored to meet the religious and social needs of its polyglot constituency and thus preserved integrity of doctrine and authority. Each official was motivated by a keen desire to prevent the loss of souls and to strengthen the Catholic faith of the baptized. They achieved their goal, not simply because of their dedication but because they were flexible and sensitive men. They did not assume episcopal authority with the intention of forcing people to conform to a predetermined mold. The bishops respected the distinctness of each immigrant group in the diocese.

Chicago's bishops and archbishops relied on national parishes, parochial schools, Church and parish organizations, and an immigrant clergy to keep immigrants' faith intact. Aware that a newcomer's faith was deeply wedded to his culture, none of the hierarchy interfered with that relationship. They realized that to strip an immigrant of his Old World heritage could be done only at the expense of his religion. Parishes, schools, and numerous social and religious societies served to strengthen the immigrant's allegiance to the Church in the painful period of adjusting to a new land. Foreign clergy, whom the bishops recruited to guide the moral development of their charges, also functioned as influential leaders in the immigrant communities. In the latter role, priests further joined the peoples' social life to the Church. Only when a group's nationalist aspirations conflicted with the Church's mission to all Catholics did the hierarchy assert its authority to regulate.

The episcopate did not advocate perpetuation of a European Church in America. However, it did not believe that the process of Americanization should be advanced too rapidly. Furthermore, without an adequate number of native clergy who could facilitate the assimilation of newcomers, the bishops had little option in converting the churches into Americanizing institutions. Despite the absence of systematic programs of Americanization prior to World War I, they held that the Church should be an active Americanizing agent. They used the Catholic press, the pulpit, and parochial schools and organizations to introduce American customs and ideals. National parishes were to conserve the faith until the immigrant could feel comfortable in his and her new environment; they were not designed to create a world apart.

Unlike Cardinal James Gibbons, Archbishop John Ireland, and Bishop John J. Keane, Chicago's prelates before George W. Mundelein did not engage in public discussion of the ideological aspects of Americanization. They concerned themselves primarily with diocesan affairs. By nature and training, Archbishops Patrick A. Feehan and James E. Quigley were pastors who were appreciative of the immigrants' plight and, by commission, administrators who were all but overwhelmed with the responsibility of maintaining a complex and rapidly growing institution. Both men were eminently capable of intellectual formulations; however, they did not have the luxury of time that was available to their Americanizing colleagues in smaller and less dynamic sees. More importantly, they did not see the need to discuss their administrative courses. Both men practiced pluralism, saw that it worked, and had no reason to pursue a course designed to please outsiders whose interests were not sympathetic to the welfare of Catholic immigrants. To alienate the majority of their flock for the sake of a vocal minority, even within the Church, was not in the best interests of Catholicism, the archbishops believed. Experience had taught them the meaning of the doctrine of catholicity and the need to be blind to the accidental differences of nationality.

In large degree, the Church's prosperity in Chicago resulted from the temperate leadership of the Irish and those of Irish descent. Bishops William Quarter and Thomas Foley and Archbishops Feehan and Quigley were exceptional men who, through pastoral experience, had learned to appreciate the richness of humankind. They were skilled in the art of reconciling differences and building coalitions. Sensitive but pragmatic, they chose pluralism as the surest means to preserve the faith and make certain the Church's growth in Chicago. This selection or choice was based on their knowledge of the complex relationship between religion and culture, not on espousal of a particular social theory. Whether men of another nationality might have succeeded as well as the Irish is moot. That one ethnic group produced such capable leaders is remarkable.

Because the Irish predominated in the American hierarchy, Continental immigrants often made the charge—which has been uncritically repeated by historians—that efforts were made to "Irishize" the Church in America. At the turn of the century, Chicago's Irish immigrant clergy had resorted to intrigue and outright lies to prevent elevation of an Irish-American to the auxiliary bishopric and, through their spokesman, Jeremiah Crowley, had attacked Archbishop Feehan's disregard for Irish interests. This clearly indicates that the foreign-born Irish considered themselves as sharing the lot of non-English-speaking immigrants. The indictments made by these irate priests illustrate that the hierarchy was adapting the Church to America and not to one particular group of people.

The Chicago Church not only responded to its immigrant membership but reacted to the pressure exerted by nativists and others whom it considered hostile. External antagonists who called on the Church to conform to the customs of the Anglo-Saxon Protestant majority made Catholics aware of their minority status, strengthened Catholic unity, and aided the hierarchy in creating a Catholic body that was supranational in identity. Assaults by members of the host society provided the Church leaders a tool for fostering cooperative action that led the diverse Catholic populace to unite.

Know Nothings and common-school advocates, who called for a homogeneous society in the 1850s, caused Catholics to develop a defensive, victim-like mentality and to pursue courses that would protect their rights. To preserve their faith, Catholics established schools and institutions that would be fortresses against the onslaughts of hostile hosts. The American Protective Association and Edwards Law campaigns of the 1890s, which attacked the Church and the "foreign" character of its institutions and members, increased Catholics' self-consciousness and further unified the polyglot institution. While it is possible that nativists caused some Catholics to give up their faith, in order to be accepted by the dominant society, their assaults seem to have made the immigrants "more Catholic." Simultaneously, nativist pressure forced Catholics to participate in the political process to safeguard their constitutional rights. Catholicism brought people together whose Old World antipathies had previously held them apart.

In fulfillment of its intent to prevent "leakage" (loss of faith among newcomers), the Chicago Catholic Church involved itself in the battle for social and economic justice. Through its contact with the urban poor and the pervasive influence of Progressives and Social Gospellers, the Church broadened its traditional approach to social problems. By the second decade of the twentieth century, the Church had begun to promote legislation designed to cure social ills. Yet, despite the new awareness, Catholics did not formally join hands with Progressives. The Church was still too wary of reformers because of their past alliances with nativists and their apparent disregard for spiritual values.

As a Church of the laboring class, it defended the interests of its constituency, and the spirit of Pope Leo XIII's *Rerum Novarum* was evident in Chicago even before 1891, when the encyclical was published. Bishop Foley, Archbishop Feehan, and their priests had endorsed unionization. Their successors, Quigley and Mundelein, did the same. These men realized that supporting the workers' struggle for a "living wage" was not only a moral responsibility but the best means to counteract the influence of radical organizations whose economic theory was based on atheistic materialism. Wishing to conserve the best elements of the American economic system, the hierarchy and clergy counseled moderation to labor leaders and called on capital to correct its abuses to prevent a socialist revolution. The Church's course won the respect of the laborers (who composed it) and made it a powerful force in preserving order in Chicago.

Unlike its counterparts in European nations, the Chicago Church was not bound by a self-serving commitment to a repressive governmental social and economic policy. The conservatism of the Church was not reactionary, but progressive. Because its membership was largely drawn from the unskilled and semiskilled, and because it owed no allegiance to the barons of industry, it pursued a course untypical of European Catholicism. These reasons also explain its success at a time when urban Protestant churches failed to attract members from the working class.

World War I was a watershed for the Catholic Church in Chicago, as the immigrant Church assumed a new identity, American Catholicism. The majority of the Catholic constituency was American by birth, and the decline in immigration, due to the war, ensured continuance of this fact. The appointment of George W. Mundelein, a third-generation American, made it certain that a specifically American character would be imprinted upon the Chicago archdiocese. For the first time in four decades, more territorial than national parishes were established. Although many immigrants militantly resisted following the new direction taken by the Church, the numerically superior natives ensured the emergence of an American Catholic identity.

Cardinal Mundelein, the architect of American Catholicism, unlike his predecessors, was more a businessman than a pastor. Since his ordination, the latter role was always secondary to the former. He came to Chicago with designs to make the local Church a financially solvent institution, to make it a model see, and to win the respect of the host society; then he initiated programs to Americanize his charges. The creation of territorial parishes, the use of English as the language of instruction in parochial schools, the unification of Catholic charity work, and the erection of a seminary to train a corps of native-born clergy were the concrete foundations of his undertaking.

Although Mundelein's administration was not characterized by the cultural pluralism of earlier administrators, he manifested flexibility. The old, who would not or could not adjust to the New World, were permitted to practice their faith as before. However, their influence was progressively limited. Newer groups, in particular Mexicans and Yugoslavs, were given special consideration. He commissioned the establishment of national parishes for newcomers so they might preserve their faith during the period of transition.

Mundelein, Chicago's third archbishop, realized that the children of immigrants were no longer satisfied with the old ways of the ghetto churches, and therefore he tried to make the Church responsive to them. Because Americanism and Catholicism were their primary identities, he endeavored to join them more closely together by making the Church more American. Had he failed, he would have destroyed his inheritance: vital faith among all Catholics. His course, though necessarily different from his predecessors', was a completion of their work.

By 1924 Cardinal Mundelein had initiated his strategies to Americanize the immigrant Church, but his goal, that Americans accept Catholics as equals, was not immediately realized. While his constituents were assuming an American Catholic identity, Congress passed national-origin immigration legislation, which implied that the Church's newest members could not be Americanized.

In 1928, the bid for the presidency by Alfred Smith, a Catholic New Yorker and second-generation American, rekindled anti-

Catholic hostilities. Even Mundelein, who in 1915 had declared that a Catholic could be elected president "because Americans are at heart a just and generous people,"[1] was shaken by the prejudice that surfaced during the campaign. The *New World* declared that American society told Catholics they were only half Americans, because it granted them "the power to vote and not the right to be voted for." Catholics would not go hat in hand and beg for favors. "Twenty million people," it said, "are too many to all kneel in prayer supplicating those rights that the Constitution confers on them." In a way "best determined by themselves," it pledged, Catholics would change their petitioner status.[2]

Earlier optimism vanished. More than a decade after Smith's defeat, when James A. Farley, a Catholic and chairman of the Democratic party, considered running for the presidency, Mundelein counseled him: "James, I do not believe that a Catholic can win."[3]

The bitter experiences of the 1920s had made Catholics aware of their minority status. Insecure in their Americanism, they more than ever submerged their foreignness and sought to conform to the standards set by the host society. Not until 1960 and John F. Kennedy would Chicago Catholics demonstrate that Catholics were neither beggars nor petitioners, but equals who had the right to vote and be voted for.

The progress of the Catholic Church in Chicago was marked by adjustment and identity transformation. Because of constant changes in the Church's constitutency, its exact identity was always elusive. Nonetheless, there was clear movement, from a national Catholicism to a supranational Catholicism and then to an American Catholicism. In the process of adjusting to a new environment and defending itself against internal and external foes, the Church changed its outward identity and that of its members. Never monolithic, but one from many, it moved toward being one with America while remaining one with Rome.

Tables

TABLE 1

CHURCHES ESTABLISHED FOR IMMIGRANT GROUPS
BY CHICAGO BISHOPS (1844–1880)

BISHOP		IRISH	GERMAN	FRENCH	BOHEMIAN	POLISH	TOTAL
Quarter	(1844–49)	3	2	0	0	0	5
Van de Velde	(1849–53)	0	2	1*	0	0	3
O'Regan	(1854–57)	3	0	0	0	0	3
Duggan	(1859–69)	10	1	1	1	1	14
Foley	(1870–79)	6	4	2	2	2	16

*Destroyed by the Fire of 1871 and not rebuilt.

Source: Based on Joseph J. Thompson, *The Archdiocese of Chicago, Antecedents and Developments* (Des Plaines: St. Mary's Training School Press, 1920), pp. 161–475, passim.

TABLE 2

NUMBER OF CHURCHES FOR EACH IMMIGRANT GROUP
UNDER CHICAGO BISHOPS (1844–1880)

BISHOP		IRISH	GERMAN	FRENCH	BOHEMIAN	POLISH	TOTAL
Quarter	(1844–49)	3	2	0	0	0	5
Van de Velde	(1849–53)	3	4	1*	0	0	8
O'Regan	(1854–57)	6	4	1	0	0	11
Duggan	(1859–69)	16	5	2	1	1	25
Foley	(1870–79)	22	9	1	3	3	38

*Destroyed by the Fire of 1871 and not rebuilt.

Source: Based on Thompson, *The Archdiocese of Chicago,* pp. 161–475, passim.

TABLE 3

Population of Native- and Foreign-born
Persons in Chicago (1833–1880)

YEAR	NATIVE AMERICAN	IRISH	GERMAN-AUSTRIAN	FRENCH AND FRENCH-CANADIAN	BOHEMIAN	POLISH
1833	c.200	—	—	c.150	—	—
1843	5,324	773	816	—	—	—
1850	13,693	6,096	5,093	—	—	—
1860	54,636	19,889	22,230	—	—	109
1870	154,420	39,988	59,229	10,379	6,277	1,205
1880	298,326	44,411	75,205	14,755	11,887	5,536

Source: Based on Robert Fergus, *Fergus Directory for Chicago for 1843* (Chicago: Robert Fergus, 1843), p. 14; *United States Statistical View . . . Being a Compendium of the Seventh Census, 1850,* p. 399; *The Eighth Census of the United States, 1860,* p. 613; *Ninth Census of the United States, 1870,* I:386–391; and *Tenth Census of the United States,* I:538–541.

TABLE 4

National Parishes Established under
Archbishop Feehan's Administration

NATIONAL PARISHES	1880–1884	1885–1889	1890–1894	1895–1899	1900–1902	TOTAL
Irish	9	11	11	2	8	41
German	5	6	4	2	2	19
Bohemian	—	2	3	—	—	5
Polish	3	2	6	3	1	15
Italian	1	—	—	2	—	3
Croatian	—	—	—	—	1	1
Slovak	—	—	—	1	—	1
Slovene	—	—	—	1	—	1
Dutch	—	—	—	—	1	1
French	—	2	1	—	—	3
Lithuanian	—	—	1	—	2	3
Negro	—	1	—	—	—	1
TOTAL	18	24	26	11	15	94

Source: Based on Joseph J. Thompson, *The Archdiocese of Chicago, Antecedents and Developments* (Des Plaines: St. Mary's Training School Press, 1920), pp. 161–597, passim.

TABLE 5

National Parishes Established by
Archbishop Feehan and His Predecessors

NATIONAL PARISHES	ARCHBISHOP FEEHAN (1880–1902)	PREDECESSORS (1833–1880)	TOTAL (1833–1902)
Irish	41	22	63
German	19	9	28
Bohemian	5	3	8
Polish	15	3	18
Italian	3	—	3
Croatian	1	—	1
Slovak	1	—	1
Slovene	1	—	1
Dutch	1	—	1
French	3	1	4
Lithuanian	3	—	3
Negro	1	—	1
TOTAL	94	38	132

Source: Based on Thompson, *The Archdiocese of Chicago, Antecedents and Developments*, pp. 476–597, passim.

TABLE 6

Population of Chicago according to Origin and Parentage
(1880–1910)

	1880	1890	1900	1910
Total Population	514,420	1,099,850	1,698,575	2,185,283
Native Born	309,561	649,184	1,111,463	1,401,855
Foreign Born	204,859	450,666	587,112	783,428
Foreign Parentage*	—	855,523	1,315,307	1,693,918**
Native Parentage	—	244,327	383,268	445,193**

*Includes all persons of native or foreign birth, who had one or both parents who were foreign born. This classification was first recorded in 1890.
**Includes whites only.

Sources: Based on *Tenth Census of the United States, 1880*, I:538–541; *Eleventh Census of the United States, 1890*, I:cxxvi and clxix; *Twelfth Census of the United States, 1900*, I:651, 796, and 866; and *Thirteenth Census of the United States, 1910*, I:173, 208.

TABLE 7

Chicago Foreign-Born Population for Specified Groups
(1880–1900)

	1880	1890	1900	1910
Irish	44,411	70,028	73,912	65,963
German	75,205	188,232*	182,553*	182,281
Bohemian	11,887	25,105	36,362	50,063**
Italian	1,357	5,685	16,008	45,169
Polish	5,536	24,086	59,713	126,059

*Includes Austrian born
**Includes Moravian.

Sources: Based on *Tenth Census of the United States, 1880,* I:538–541; *Eleventh Census of the United States, 1890,* I:670–672; *Twelfth Census of the United States, 1900,* I:796–799 and *Thirteenth Census of the United States, 1910,* I:942, 989.

TABLE 8

Chicago Foreign-Parentage Population
for Specified Groups (1890–1900)

	1890	1900
Irish	149,795	180,991
German	293,338	381,263*
Bohemian	41,014	72,862
Italian	7,924	26,043
Polish	—	107,669

*Includes persons of Austrian parentage.

Sources: Based on *Eleventh Census of the United States, 1890,* I:708–709, and *Twelfth Census of the United States, 1900,* I:878–879.

TABLE 9

CHICAGO FOREIGN BORN, NATIVE OF MIXED OR FOREIGN PARENTAGE, AND FOREIGN STOCK FOR SPECIFIED GROUPS (1910)

	FOREIGN BORN	NATIVE OF MIXED OR FOREIGN PARENTAGE	FOREIGN STOCK
Irish	65,963	138,858	204,821
German	182,281	319,551	501,832
Bohemian & Moravian	50,063	60,673	110,736
Italian	45,169	29,774	74,943
Polish	126,059	104,073	230,132
Slavic	20,273	6,082	26,355

Source: Thirteenth Census of the United States, 1910, I:942, 989.

TABLE 10

NATIONAL PARISHES ESTABLISHED BY ARCHBISHOP QUIGLEY AND HIS PREDECESSORS

NATIONAL PARISHES	1833– 1902	1903– 1905	1906– 1910	1911– 1915	TOTAL 1903– 1915	TOTAL 1833– 1915
Irish	63	8	11*	7**	26	89
German	28	2	—	—	2	30
Bohemian	8	1	—	—	1	9
Polish	8	3	6	6	15	33
Italian	3	5	1	1	7	10
Croatian	1	—	—	3	3	4
Slovak	1	1	2	1	4	5
Slovene	1	1	—	—	1	2
Lithuanian	3	4	1	2	7	10
Dutch	1	—	—	—	—	1
French	4	—	—	—	—	4
Negro	1	—	—	—	—	1
Syrian	—	—	1	—	1	1
Belgian	—	—	1	—	1	1
Chaldean	—	—	—	1	1	1
Hungarian	—	1	—	—	1	1
Total	132	26	23	21	70	202

*Mixed: St. Clare of Montefalco.
**Mixed: St. Sebastian (German and Irish) and St. Pascal (European).

Source: Based on Joseph J. Thompson, *The Archdiocese of Chicago, Antecedents and Developments* (Des Plaines: St. Mary's Training School Press, 1920), pp. 599–660, passim.

TABLE 11

YEAR	DIOCESAN PRIESTS	RELIGIOUS ORDER PRIESTS	TOTAL
1835	1		1
1845	4		4
1855	13		13
1865	18	11	29
1875	41	39	80
1885	92	44	136
1895	220	80	300
1905	259	107	366
1915	347	137	484
1925	422	172	594

TABLE 12

PARISHES STAFFED BY DIOCESAN AND RELIGIOUS ORDER PRIESTS
(1835–1925)

YEAR	DIOCESAN STAFF	RELIGIOUS ORDER STAFF	TOTAL
1835	1		1
1845	1		1
1855	8		8
1865	12	2	14
1875	25	7	32
1885	42	12	54
1895	82	19	101
1905	128	27	155
1915	171	42	214
1925	179	52	231

Notes

1. TRANS-NATIONAL FOUNDATIONS

1. Cited in Harold M. Mayer and Richard C. Wade, *Chicago: Growth of a Metropolis* (Chicago: University of Chicago Press, 1969), p. 3.

2. Cited in Bessie Louise Pierce, *A History of Chicago* (3 vols.; New York: Alfred A. Knopf, 1957), I:49.

3. Mayer and Wade, p. 35.

4. See table 1.

5. October 11, 1871.

6. Cited in Mayer and Wade, p. 3.

7. For the missionary period of Chicago's religious history, see Gilbert J. Garraghan, S.J., "Early Catholicity in Illinois," *Illinois Catholic Historical Review,* I (July 1918): 8–28, and Joseph J. Thompson, "The Illinois Missions," *Illinois Catholic Historical Review, 1 (July 1918): 38*–63.

8. The records of the Old Cathedral of St. Louis show that baptismal services were rendered for Chicagoans in 1799. Garraghan, "Early Catholicity in Illinois," p. 19.

9. Cited in A. T. Andreas, *History of Chicago from the Earliest Period to the Present Time* (3 vols.; Chicago: A. T. Andreas, 1884–1886), I:289. The petition was signed by thirty-seven persons. It should have been addressed to the bishop of Bardstown, Kentucky, whose jurisdiction included Illinois. See also Gilbert J. Garraghan, S.J., *The Catholic Church in Chicago, 1673–1871* (Chicago: Loyola University Press, 1921), pp. 45–47.

10. Pierce, I:44, and Garraghan, *The Catholic Church in Chicago,* pp. 37–44.

11. St. Cyr to Rosati, June 4, 1833, cited in Garraghan, *The Catholic Church in Chicago,* p. 50.

12. St. Cyr to Rosati, June (n.d.) 1833, cited in ibid., p. 54.

13. Ibid., pp. 61–65. St. Cyr spent the first winter in St. Louis "begging" for funds to finish the church and obtain supplies.

14. St. Cyr to Rosati, January (n.d.) 1837, cited in ibid., p. 91.

15. Cited in ibid., p. 96. The great majority of the petition signers had Irish names. Andreas, I:249.

16. St. Cyr to Rosati, January (n.d.) 1837, cited in Garraghan, *The Catholic Church in Chicago,* p. 92.

17. Pierce, I:176–177.

18. Bruté to Rosati, May 7, 1837, cited in Garraghan, *The Catholic Church in Chicago*, p. 101.

19. Bruté to Rosati, June 29, 1837, cited in ibid., n. 21, p. 103.

20. Pierce, I:238; Garraghan, *The Catholic Church in Chicago*, pp. 105–107; Andreas, I:292.

21. James McGovern, *Souvenir of the Silver Jubilee of the Episcopacy of His Grace the Most Reverend Patrick Augustine Feehan* (1891), pp. 16–34.

22. Cited in John E. McGirr, *The Life of the Rt. Rev. Wm. Quarter D.D., First Catholic Bishop of Chicago* (Des Plaines: St. Mary's Training School Press, 1920), p. 87.

23. Quarter to Carrell, July 30, 1844, cited in Garraghan, *The Catholic Church in Chicago*, p. 111.

24. Bishop Quarter tried to keep the two priests as they desired to stay in Chicago; however, the bishop of Vincennes would not provide the *exeat.* Quarter to Purcell (bishop of Cincinnati), Chicago, September 18, 1844, University of Notre Dame Archives (hereafter UNDA).

25. Quarter's diary (in McGovern) provides a sketchy but valuable record of the first bishop's work. In a letter to the New Orleans prelate, Quarter lamented that he had only 22 priests for the 60,000 Catholics scattered about the state of Illinois. Quarter to Blanc, Chicago, September 2, 1844, UNDA.

26. Garraghan, *The Catholic Church in Chicago*, pp. 111–113; McGovern, p. 69; and Joseph J. Thompson, *The Archdiocese of Chicago, Antecedents and Developments* (Des Plaines: St. Mary's Training School Press, 1920), p. 673. In its 25 years of existence the university graduated 500 men, more than 25 of whom were ordained.

27. Quarter to Blanc, Chicago, January 17, 1845, UNDA.

28. Garraghan, *The Catholic Church in Chicago*, pp. 113–114.

29. McGovern, p. 75, and Thompson, *The Archdiocese,* pp. 235–237.

30. Quarter's diary, January 9, 1848, in McGovern, pp. 85–86. See Ruth Margaret Piper, "The Irish in Chicago, 1848–1871" (unpublished M.A. thesis, University of Chicago, 1936), for an account of the work and history of the Hibernian Benevolent Emigrant Society, pp. 10–14.

31. The protest was inspired by Fischer, who hoped that a strong protest would make it possible for him to remain in Chicago. Quarter to Purcell, Chicago, September 18, 1844, UNDA; and F. G. Holweck, "Rev. Gaspar Henry Ostlangenburg," *Illinois Catholic Historical Review,* III (July 1920):43–52.

32. Quarter to the archbishop of Vienna, Chicago, December 20, 1845, cited in Francis J. Epstein, "History in the Annals of the Leopoldine Association," *Illinois Catholic Historical Review,* I (October 1918):236.

33. Holweck, p. 53.

34. Quarter to the archbishop of Vienna, Chicago, December 20, 1845, cited in Epstein, p. 231.

35. Quarter to the archbishop of Vienna, Chicago, December 31, 1845, cited in ibid., pp. 227–228.

36. Loras to Blanc, Dubuque, July 26, 1844 (French), UNDA.

37. Lefevre to Purcell, Detroit, May 1, 1848, UNDA.

38. Fitzpatrick to Purcell, Boston, April 14, 1844, UNDA.

39. Kenrick to Purcell, St. Louis, May 2, 1848, UNDA.

40. Printed petition of the German Catholics of Illinois to the hierarchy of the United States (n.d.). Cited in Robert Frederick Trisco, *The Holy See and the*

Nascent Church in the Middle Western United States, 1826–1850 (Rome: Gregorian University Press, 1962), pp. 93–94.

41. Coleman J. Barry, O.S.B., *The Catholic Church and German Americans* (Milwaukee: Bruce Publishing Co., 1953), pp. 15–16.

42. Propaganda to Van de Velde, bishop-elect of Chicago, October 9, 1848 (Latin), cited in Trisco, p. 94.

43. Cited in Garraghan, *The Catholic Church in Chicago*, p. 141.

44. Ibid., pp. 148–149, and Thompson, *The Archdiocese*, p. 297. The land was donated by Michael Diversey, a member of the committee requesting a German speaking bishop.

45. Garraghan, *The Catholic Church in Chicago*, pp.148–149. In 1846 thirty families made up St. Peter's and in 1853, the date of its relocation, it had 150 families. The church was moved because it had become engulfed by the business district.

46. Ibid., pp. 146–149, and Thompson, *The Archdiocese*, pp. 235–236.

47. November 11, 1849, cited in McGovern, p. 136, and Garraghan, *The Catholic Church in Chicago*, p. 150.

48. J. O. Van de Velde, *Panegyric on St. Patrick: Delivered in St. Mary's Cathedral, March 17, 1852* (Chicago: Western Tablet, 1852), p. 12.

49. Van de Velde to Blanc, Natchez, March 2, 1854 (French), UNDA.

50. James Oliver Van de Velde's autobiographical sketch in the St. Louis University Archives, published as "Right Reverend James Oliver Van de Velde, D.D.," *Illinois Catholic Historical Review*, IX (July 1926):67.

51. Ibid., 67–68; *Western Tablet*, November 12, 1853; and John Rothenstiener, "Interesting Facts Concerning Chicago's First Four Bishops," *Illinois Catholic Historical Review*, IX (October 1926):155–157.

52. Kenrick to Purcell, St. Louis, November 9, 1853, UNDA.

53. Kenrick to Purcell, Baltimore, October 12, 1853, UNDA.

54. Van de Velde to Blanc, Natchez, March 2, 1854 (French), UNDA.

55. At the recommendation of the American bishops, the Holy See divided the Chicago diocese and created the Quincy diocese. The latter, however, was never occupied. In 1857 it was enlarged and became the Diocese of Alton. Because of the preponderance of Germans in southern Illinois, the diocese was entrusted to a German. McGovern, p. 195.

56. Garraghan, *The Catholic Church in Chicago*, pp. 167–168; Thompson, *The Archdiocese*, pp. 35–37; and McGovern, pp. 186–189.

57. Thompson, *The Archdiocese*, pp. 315 and 321–329.

58. O'Regan to Lefevre, Chicago, October 29, 1856, UNDA; O'Regan to Purcell, Chicgao, June 13, 1857, UNDA; *Boston Pilot*, July 18, 1857; Andreas, I:296–297.

59. *Boston Pilot*, July 18, 1857, and Thompson, *The Archdiocese*, p. 291.

60. O'Regan to Chaiselot, director of the Society for the Propagation of the Faith at Lyon, Chicago, March 25, 1857, Correspondence of the Society for the Propagation of the Faith (hereafter SPF).

61. O'Regan to Purcell, Chicago, January 20, 1855, UNDA.

62. Spalding to Purcell, Louisville, September 6 and 12, 1855, UNDA.

63. O'Regan to Chaiselot, Chicago, June 15, 1855, SPF.

64. Spalding to Purcell, Louisville, September 12, 1855, UNDA.

65. O'Regan to Chaiselot, Chicago, April 7, 1856, SPF.

66. O'Regan frequently appealed to Chaiselot for funds to build

ten churches. See his letters of January 25 and June 16, 1855, and March 5, 1857, SPF.

67. Spalding to Purcell, Louisville, September 12, 1855, UNDA.

68. O'Regan to Chaiselot, Chicago, March 25, 1857, SPF.

69. McGovern, p. 195; and Thompson, *The Archdiocese*, p. 38.

70. Spalding to Purcell, Louisville, September 12, 1855, UNDA.

71. McGovern, pp. 169–199; Thompson, *The Archdiocese*, p. 39; and Garraghan, *The Catholic Church in Chicago*, p. 180.

72. See Garraghan, *The Catholic Church in Chicago*, pp. 188–201, and Thompson, *The Archdiocese*, pp. 331–415.

73. O'Regan had secured the Jesuits to serve the Irish and the Holy Cross priests to staff the seminary. Andreas, I:295–296.

74. See Jay P. Dolan, *The Immigrant Church: New York's Irish and German Catholics, 1815–1865* (Baltimore: Johns Hopkins University Press, 1975), p. 82.

75. Thompson, *The Archdiocese*, pp. 355 and 377–379.

76. Duggan to Lefevre, Chicago, October 19, 1863, UNDA.

77. Joseph J. Parot, "The American Faith and the Persistence of Chicago Polonia, 1870–1920," (unpublished Ph.D. dissertation, Northern Illinois University, 1971), pp. 5–15.

78. J. M. Leur (bishop of Fort Wayne) to Purcell, Notre Dame, June 12, 1868, UNDA; W. McCloskey (bishop of Louisville) to Purcell, New York, February 5, 1869, UNDA; McCloskey to Purcell, Louisville, March 24, 1869, UNDA. Bishop Duggan sent a circular letter to all the priests of the diocese to defend himself against the charges made by Revs. McMullern, Dunne, Roles, and McGovern. Chicago Papers, box I, UNDA.

79. McGovern, p. 202; Garraghan, *The Catholic Church in Chicago*, pp. 219–220.

80. Cited in McGovern, p. 204.

81. Rev. Daniel J. Riordan to Richard H. Clarke, March 11, 1885, UNDA; McGovern, p. 201; and William J. Onahan, "Catholic Progress in Chicago," *Illinois Catholic Historical Review*, I (October 1918):181.

82. Foley to Bishop Francis McFarland, Chicago, November 6, 1871, UNDA, and Garraghan, *The Catholic Church in Chicago*, p. 211.

83. St. Louis Church (for the French) was not rebuilt after the fire. Prior to the fire, Foley saw to the organization of one new parish for the Bohemians. Thompson, *The Archdiocese*, pp. 271 and 417.

84. Thompson, *The Archdiocese*, pp. 271 and 417.

85. Ibid., p. 437.

86. Ibid., pp. 417 and 433.

87. Ibid., pp. 453 and 447.

88. Joseph Chada, *Czech-American Catholics, 1850–1920* (Lisle: Benedictine Abbey Press, 1964), pp. 35–36. Chada's account improperly ascribes the request for the deed to Bishop Duggan; Foley, as administrator, requested the deed in Duggan's name.

89. Parot, pp. 16–33.

90. McGovern, pp. 221–226, and *Chicago Tribune*, November 26, 1880.

91. Ray A. Billington, *The Protestant Crusade, 1830–1860: A Study of the Origins of American Nativism* (New York: Macmillan, 1938), chapters 1–3.

92. St. Cyr to Rosati, Chicago, May 1, 1833, cited in Garraghan, *The Catholic Church in Chicago*, p. 49, and Timothy Walch, "The Catholic Schools in Chicago

in Milwaukee: 1840–1890" (unpublished Ph.D. dissertation, Northwestern University, 1975), chapter I.

93. Quarter to Blanc, Chicago, September 2, 1844, UNDA.

94. "First Pastoral Letter from James Oliver Van de Velde, Bishop of Chicago, to the Clergy and Laity, June 4, 1849," cited by McGovern, p. 105.

95. *Western Tablet,* January 31, 1852.

96. Ibid.

97. Bruce McKitterick Cole, "The Chicago Press and the Know–Nothings, 1850–1856" (unpublished M.A. thesis, University of Chicago, 1948), pp. 2–15.

98. Daniel Kucera, *Church–State Relationships in Education in Illinois* (Washington, D.C.: Catholic University of America Press, 1955), p. 75.

99. See the pastoral letters for 1829, 1833, 1837, 1840, and 1843 in Peter Guilday, *The National Pastorals of the American Hierarchy* (Washington, D.C.: National Catholic Welfare Council, 1923).

100. "Pastoral Letter of 1843," in ibid., p. 152.

101. *Western Tablet,* February 21 and 28, 1852. Two German schools educated one-third of the Catholic students.

102. Ibid., April 3, 1852.

103. The letters by "Philaleteas" indicate uncanny knowledge of the bishop and never appeared when Van de Velde was out of the diocese. The first letters appeared in defense of a series of controversial sermons by the bishop that were challenged by the Protestant papers.

104. *Western Tablet,* March 5, 1853.

105. Ibid.

106. Ibid., March 17, 1853.

107. Ibid., April 30, 1853.

108. *Chicago Tribune*, April 2, 1853.

109. Ibid., May 11, 1853.

110. *Western Tablet*, July 23, 1853.

111. Kucera, pp. 76–77.

112. Walch, pp. 58–75.

113. Foley to Purcell, Chicago, September 17, 1875, UNDA.

114. *Chicago Tribune*, September 16, 1853.

115. Ibid., October 18 and 21, and November 5, 1853.

116. *Western Tablet* had earlier demanded that railroads force contractors to pay decent wages and discontinue the fraudulent methods used to secure laborers. See March 19, 1853.

117. *Chicago Tribune*, December 23, 1853.

118. Ibid. The paper made the same distinction between German Catholics and German Protestants (March 2, 1855).

119. Ibid., January 30, 1854. See also ibid., November 15, 1853.

120. *Western Tablet*, February 4, 1854.

121. *Chicago Tribune*, July 29 and September 2, 1854, and March 2, 1855.

122. *Western Tablet*, May 1, 8, 29, and October 30, 1852.

123. Cole, pp. 28–30.

124. *Chicago Tribune*, March 2, 1855.

125. Ibid., February 10, 1855. See also February 26, 1855.

126. Cole, p. 56.

127. Cited in *Chicago Tribune*, February 26, 1855.

128. Ibid., February 26, 1855.

129. Ibid., February 19, 1855.
130. Cole, pp. 61–63.
131. Cited in *Chicago Tribune*, March 13, 1855.
132. Cole, pp. 88–103.
133. Andreas, II:163–165 and 193–195.

2. *ARCHBISHOP FEEHAN, 1880–1902*

1. *Chicago Daily News*, November 26, 1880.
2. Pierce, III:64.
3. See table 7.
4. Pierce, III:53, and Ray Ginger, *Altgeld's America: The Lincoln Ideal versus Changing Realities* (Chicago: Quadrangle, 1965), chapter 1.
5. Cited by Ginger, p. 89. For a discussion of Chicago's social problems, see Jane Addams, *Twenty Years at Hull House* (New York: New American Library, 1961), chapters 7–14, and William T. Stead, *If Christ Came to Chicago! A Plea for the Union of All Who Love in the Service of All Who Suffer* (London: Review of Reviews, 1894).
6. Pierce, vol. III, chapter 12.
7. Cornelius J. Kirkfleet, *The Life of Patrick Augustine Feehan, Bishop of Nashville, First Archbishop of Chicago, 1829–1902* (Chicago: Matre, 1922), p. 1–22; Patrick J. Mannell, compiler, *Maynooth Students and Ordinations, 1795–1895* (available in Maynooth College Library); and Rev. Matthew Barry, C.M., president, Castle Knock College, to author, Dublin, January 4, 1976.
8. John O'Hanlon, *Life and Scenery in Missouri: Reminiscences of a Missionary Priest* (Dublin: James Duffy, 1890), pp. 261, 286.
9. *Vitae* of Patrick Feehan (photocopy), Archives of the Archdiocese of St. Louis.
10. Kenrick to Olin (bishop of New Orleans), St. Louis, May 2, 1865, UNDA. See also Kenrick to Purcell, St. Louis, November 8, 1865, UNDA.
11. *Sadlier's Catholic Almanac and Ordo,* 1864 and 1880 (New York: Sadlier, 1864 and 1880), pp. 176–177 and 315–316.
12. Cited by Kirkfleet, pp. 66–69.
13. By a decree of the Holy See, dated September 10, 1880, the Diocese of Chicago was elevated to the rank of archdiocese. McGovern, p. 237.
14. *Chicago Daily Times* and *Chicago Tribune*, November 26, 1880.
15. William J. Onahan, "Catholic Progress in Chicago—Personal Recollections of Catholic Progress and Activities in Chicago during Sixty-four Years," *Illinois Catholic Historical Review* I (October 1918):181.
16. Cited by the *New World*, July 19, 1902.
17. Bishop Bernard McQuaid of Rochester felt that Feehan was a weak man who feared to lose the favor of the Irish (McQuaid to Corrigan, January 3, 1883, cited by Frederick J. Zwierlein, *The Life and Letters of Bishop McQuaid* [Rochester: Art Print Shop, 1926], II:289). William T. Stead, the English journalist and reformer, believed Feehan was too "timid" in the cause of reform (pp. 257–258).
18. Cited by *Chicago Daily News*, July 14, 1902.
19. William Dillon to John Dillon, M.P., Chicago, January 8, 1901 (microfilm), John Dillon Papers, Trinity College Archives, University of Dublin.
20. Cited by Kirkfleet, pp. 289–290.

21. The analogy of the sun's control over the planets was used by Archbishop Ryan of Philadelphia and Rev. D. S. Phelan, editor of *The Western Watchman* (St. Louis), in speeches in honor of Feehan's twenty-fifth anniversary as a bishop. Cited by McGovern, pp. 280–283 and 284.

22. *Catholic Home Journal,* April 1895, cited in *New World,* April 6, 1895.

23. *Chicago Tribune,* July 13, 1902.

24. See James Sanders, "The Education of Chicago Catholics: An Urban History" (unpublished Ph.D. dissertation, Univesrity of Chicago, 1970), for an excellent account of the growth of the Catholic school system.

25. Cited by Kirkfleet, p. 229.

26. For a sketch of various eleemosynary institutions, see Thompson, *The Archdiocese,* pp. 721–762. John Patrick Walsh's "The Catholic Church in Chicago and Problems of an Urban Society: 1893–1915" (unpublished Ph.D. dissertation, University of Chicago, 1948) provides an account of the Church's institutional response to urban problems.

27. April 1895, cited by *New World,* April 6, 1895.

28. Ibid.

29. *Catholic Home,* July 17 and November 3, 1888, and November 13, 1889; and *New World,* November 9, 1895, May 26, 1900, and July 19, 1902.

30. *Chicago Tribune,* July 13, 1902.

31. *Western Catholic,* January 19 and February 23; McGovern, pp. 257–371; *New World,* July 19 and 26, and August 2, 1902.

32. "The Catholic Majority after the Americanist Controversy, 1899–1917: A Survey," *Review of Politics,* XXI (January 1959):57.

33. *New World,* October 15, 1892. As early as 1884, Feehan's name had been mentioned in this regard. *Western Tablet,* November 29, 1884.

34. *Chicago Daily News,* July 22, 1901.

35. Cited by Kirkfleet, p. 354.

36. *New World,* June 29, 1895; December 10, 1898; and July 14 and November 8, 1900.

37. Ibid., February 11, 1899, and July 19, 1902.

38. Thompson, *The Archdiocese,* pp. 65–71; *New World,* July 19, 1902; and *Chicago Tribune,* July 13, 1902.

39. Eulogistic editorials, reprinted in the Chicago dailies and numerous Catholic newspapers, were reprinted in *New World.* See ibid., July 19 and 26, and August 2, 1902.

40. *Chicago Tribune,* July 14, 1902.

41. Cited in *Chicago Times,* November 29, 1880.

42. See tables 4 and 5.

43. See tables 11 and 12.

44. *Official Catholic Directory,* 1889 and 1900.

45. John Clark Ridpath, "The Mixed Populations of Chicago," *Chautauguan,* XII (January 1889):47.

46. See tables 7 and 8.

47. III:24–25.

48. Emmet Larkin, "The Devotional Revolution in Ireland, 1850–1875," *American Historical Review,* LXXVII (June 1972):625–652.

49. See table 5.

50. Philadelphia: Lippincott, 1966, p. 23.

51. *Chicago Tribune,* December 1–3, 1881; June 29, 1882; August 19, 1886; and *New World,* November 17, 1894, and November 23, 1901.

52. *New World* August 11, 1893; March 24, July 7, September 1 and 15, October 6 and 13, 1894; February 23, 1895; September 26, 1896; December 4, 1897; November 12 and 19, and December 17, 1898; April 14 and May 19, 1900; January 19, 1901; and January 25, 1902.

53. The Danes and Germans erected statues to their heroes but the Irish failed in this regard, despite pleas to "bestir themselves to do honor to their great men." Ibid., October 3, 1896.

54. Barry, p. 7.

55. *Chicago Tribune*, August 4, 1892.

56. Ibid.

57. Pierce, III:22–24, and Andrew Jacks Townsend, "The Germans of Chicago" (unpublished Ph.D. dissertation, University of Chicago, 1927), pp. 1–23 and 198–214.

58. Barry, 9–11.

59. Thompson, *The Archdiocese*, pp. 725–726 and 729–731; *A History of Angel Guardian Orphanage, One Hundred Years of Service to Girls and Boys, 1865–1965* (Chicago: privately printed, 1965); and *Illinois Staats Zietung*, June 24, 1863, Foreign Language Press Survey, Works Project Administration, 1942 (microfilm of translations from Chicago foreign-language newspapers; hereafter FLPS).

60. Marion A. Habig, *The Franciscans at St. Augustine's and in Chicagoland* (Chicago: Franciscan Herald Press, 1961), passim, and *Souvenir of the Golden Jubilee of St. Peter's Friary, 1875–1925* (Chicago: privately printed, 1925), pp. 17–19.

61. *Illinois Staats Zietung*, September 7, 1887, and September 26, 1891, FLPS.

62. *Abendpost*, April 29, 1896, FLPS.

63. Miecislaus Haiman, "The Poles in Chicago," in *Poles of Chicago, 1837–1937* (Chicago: Polish Pageant Inc., 1937), p. 4.

64. Ridpath, p. 485. His estimate was based upon public school census data.

65. See table 8.

66. Emily Greene Bach, *Our Slavic Fellow-Citizens* (New York: Charities Publication Committee, 1910), p. 49; Julius John Ozog, "A Study of Polish Home Ownership in Chicago" (unpublished M.A. thesis, University of Chicago, 1942), pp. 19–29; and Joseph John Parot, "The American Faith and the Persistence of Chicago Polonia, 1870–1920" (unpublished Ph.D. dissertation, Northern Illinois University, 1970), pp. 1–3.

67. Thomas and Znaniecki, *The Polish Peasant in Europe and America* (Chicago: University of Chicago Press, 1918), III:203 and V:14–15.

68. *Dziennik Chicagoski*, November 28, 1893, FLPS. For a discussion of Polish messianism, see A. P. Coleman, "The Great Emigration," in *Cambridge History of Poland, 1697–1935* (Cambridge: Cambridge University Press, 1941), pp. 321–323, and Parot, pp. 105–108.

69. Parot, p. 108, and Thomas and Znaniecki, V:30–41.

70. Thomas and Znaniecki, V:41–42.

71. Ibid., pp. 42–43.

72. Thaddeus J. Lubera, "Hundred Years of Economic Contribution of the Poles to Chicago Progress," *The Poles in Chicago*, pp. 13–14; *Dziennik Chicagoski*, May 7, 1896, FLPS; and Thomas and Znaniecki, pp. 48–49.

73. *Dziennik Chicagoski*, September 29, 1894, FLPS. The editor also appealed to national pride, saying other nationalities had their own clerks in large firms because their people were not ashamed to speak their native language.

74. Polish Jews were not considered Poles.

75. *Dziennik Chicagoski*, February 13, 1891, FLPS. Poles from the German and Russian territories looked down upon Poles from Austrian Galicia.

76. For illustrations of rivalries, see *Dziennik Chicagoski*, March 5, 1891; February 29, 1892; January 10 and 28, and August 10, 1896, FLPS; *Chicago Tribune*, January 5, 1891. For illustrations of calls for peace and unity, see *Narod Polski*, August 15, 1897; and *Dziennik Chicagoski*, January 16 and February 29, 1892; and March 11 and 14, 1896, FLPS.

77. Kenneth D. Miller, *The Czecho-Slovaks in America* (New York: George M. Koran Co., 1922), pp. 44–45.

78. Ridpath, pp. 488–489. "Bohemian" was used interchangeably with "Czech." Americans did not distinguish between Bohemians and Moravians. Such distinctions, however, were made by Czechs.

79. Pierce, III:33–34; *New World*, April 14, 1900; and Jakub Korak, "Assimilation of Czechs in Chicago" (unpublished Ph.D. dissertation, University of Chicago, 1928), pp. 22–23.

80. The Czechs had a history of religious divisiveness since the time of John Hus, whose martyrdom in 1415 led to a religious-nationalist revolt. Miller, pp. 31–35. See also Eugene Ray McCarthy, "The Bohemians in Chicago and Their Benevolent Societies: 1875–1946" (unpublished M.A. thesis, University of Chicago, 1950), pp. 32–38.

81. The Free Thinkers considered religion a "clerical business" that enslaved believers to superstition and prejudice, instead of freeing them for "honorable work, honorable thoughts, good will, and sincere hearts . . . loyal to truth, liberty and humanity in all their endeavors." *Svornost*, May 29, 1899.

82. Chada, pp. 47–48.

83. Ibid., pp. 96–97, and Thompson, *The Archdiocese*, p. 681. The Benedictine Press also published textbooks for the Bohemian schools, and religious brochures and leaflets. The Benedictine Press was attacked by the Free Thinker paper *Svornost* (August 18, 1899, FLPS) and the moderate *Denni Hlastel* (January 4, 1902, FLPS). The former emphasized the Press's lust for mammon and not the service of religion, while the latter accused it of parochialism at the expense of the welfare of all Bohemians.

84. Miller, pp. 122–123.

85. "A Small Catechism of Czech-American Schools," cited in ibid., pp. 129–130. The Free Thinkers opposed use of the Bible in public schools. *Svornost*, May 8, 1896, FLPS.

86. *New World*, April 14, 1900.

87. See Chada, pp. 56–64; Thompson, *The Archdiocese*, pp. 679–681 and 762; *Svornost*, September 1, 1890; and *New World*, June 30, 1900.

88. Thompson, *The Archdiocese*, pp. 477–597, passim, and Alan Spear, *Black Chicago: The Making of a Negro Ghetto, 1890–1920* (Chicago: University of Chicago Press, 1974), pp. 94–95.

89. Thompson, *The Archdiocese*, pp. 575–576.

90. See table 7.

91. Pierce, III:42–43; Virgil Peter Puzzo, "The Italians in Chicago, 1890–1930" (unpublished M.A. thesis, University of Chicago, 1937), passim; and Humbert Nelli, *Italians in Chicago, 1880–1930: A Study of Ethnic Mobility* (New York: Oxford University Press, 1970), pp. 30–54.

92. "Prelates and Peasants: Italian Immigrants and the Catholic Church," *Journal of Social History* (Spring 1969), pp. 227–231.

93. Bernard J. Lynch, "The Italians in New York," *Catholic World*, XLVII (April 1888):72.

94. Cited in Henry J. Browne, "The 'Italian Problem' in the Catholic Church in the United States, 1880–1900," *Historical Records and Studies, United States Catholic Historical Society*, XXXV (1946):52.

95. Thompson, *The Archdiocese*, pp. 437–445 and 481–483, and *L'Italia*, April 30, 1887; March 15, 1890; and April 1, 1899, FLPS.

96. *New World*, May 7 and October 15, 1898, and February 10, 1900; and Thompson, *The Archdiocese*, p. 578.

97. *Souvenir of the Golden Jubilee of St. Peter's Friary*, pp. 27 and 72.

98. Jesuit priests at Holy Family parish ministered to the Italians before the establishment of Guardian Angel parish. Thompson, *The Archdiocese*, p. 578.

99. *New World*, March 18, 1899.

100. Ibid.

101. Ibid., June 17, 1899; also April 14 and September 15, 1890.

102. Joseph Krisciunas, "Lithuanians in Chicago" (unpublished M.A. thesis, De Paul University, 1935), pp. 5–7 and 21.

103. Ibid., pp. 5–6, and Thompson, *The Archdiocese*, pp. 518–519, 584–585, and 622.

104. *Lietuva*, December 10, 1892; May 20, 1893; March 24, 1894; and March 28 and May 30, 1896, FLPS.

105. Ibid., September 10, 1897; September 16, 1898; and June 10 and November 15, 1901, FLPS; and Krisciunas, pp. 32–33.

3. NATIVISM

1. *Catholic Home*, August 1 and 11, 1888.

2. Ibid.

3. Ibid., November 24, 1888.

4. Ibid., November 17, 1888. See also ibid., March 30, 1889. The *Chicago American*, however, was considered the chief anti-Catholic paper. Ibid., May 11 and 18, 1889.

5. John Higham, *Strangers in the Land: Patterns of American Nativism, 1860–1925* (New York: Atheneum, 1971), chapter 3; Samuel P. Hays, *The Response to Industrialism, 1885–1914* (Chicago: University of Chicago Press, 1968), chapter 2; and Robert W. Weibe, *The Search for Order, 1877–1920* (New York: Hill and Wang, 1967), chapter 3.

6. Margaret Shepherd, cited in *The Patriot, an Advocate of Americanism*, I, no. 1 (March 1891):15.

7. "The Pastoral Letter of 1884," in John Tracy Ellis, *Documents of American Catholic History* (2d ed.; Milwaukee: Bruce Publishing Co., 1962), p. 173.

8. Ibid., pp. 173–175.

9. *Synodus Diocesana Chicagienis Prima, Juxta Norma a Conc. Balt. III, Praestitutam Habita in Ecclesia Metropolitana S.S. Nominis* (Chicago: Cameron, Ambert and Associates, 1887), p. 6.

10. Ibid., pp. 6–7. The directive read: "Omnes parentes Catholici prolem suan ad scholas parochalies mittere tenentur nisi vel domi vel in aliis scholis Catholicius Christianae filiorum suorum educationi, quantum necesse est, consulant, aut ob causam suffiucientem, ab Archiepiscopo sive in communi sive in individuo approbatam, eos ad alias scholas mittere ipsis liceat."

11. Ibid., p. xvi. The territorial examiners were all Irish surnamed.

12. *Catholic Home,* September 8, 1888.

13. Ibid., April 13, 1889.

14. James Sanders, "The Education of Chicago Catholics: An Urban History" (unpublished Ph.D. dissertation, University of Chicago, 1970), p. 59. See also James McGovern, *Souvenir of the Silver Jubilee of the Episcopacy of His Grace the Most Reverend Patrick Augustine Feehan* (n.p., 1891), p. 253.

15. *Dziennik Chicagoski,* January 20 and 21, February 5, and June 2, 1891, Foreign Language Press Survey, Works Project Administration, 1942 (hereafter cited as FLPS).

16. *Chicago Tribune,* March 14, 1886.

17. Edith Abbot and Sophonisba P. Breckinridge, *Truancy and Non-Attendance in the Chicago Schools: A Study of the Social Aspects of Compulsory Education and Child Labor Legislation of Illinois* (Chicago: University of Chicago Press, 1917), pp. 53–57. The compulsory attendance law was one of three bills adopted by a citizens' meeting and presented to the Board of Education and later endorsed and forwarded to Springfield. The two other bills dealt with child labor and truant children.

18. Richard Edwards Papers, box I, Illinois State University Archives (hereafter cited as ISUA).

19. *Chicago Tribune,* May 12, 1889, and Abbot and Breckinridge, p. 55.

20. *Chicago Tribune,* May 24, 25, and 26, 1889, and November 7, 1892.

21. Cited in ibid., May 26, 1889 (emphasis mine).

22. Cited in ibid. Public schools were required to teach all subjects in the English language, according to legislation of 1845. Daniel W. Kucera, *Church–State Relationships in Education in Illinois* (Washington, D.C.: Catholic University of America Press, 1955), p. 112.

23. *Chicago Tribune,* May 11 and 26, 1889.

24. Kucera, pp. 112–113.

25. See Abbot and Breckinridge, pp. 66–68, and Ernest L. Bogart and Charles M. Thompson, *The Industrial State, 1870–1893,* vol. IV of *The Centennial History of Illinois* (Springfield: Illinois Centennial Commission, 1918–1920), p. 184. Both credit the agitation against the compulsory school law of 1889 to German hostility to the language provision.

26. *Catholic Home,* May 11, 1889.

27. For a study of the Bennett Law, see Louise Phelps Kellogg, "The Bennett Law in Wisconsin," *Wisconsin Magazine of History,* II (September 1919): 3–25, and William E. Whyte, "The Bennett Law Campaign," *Wisconsin Magazine of History,* X (June 1927): 363–390.

28. *Catholic Home,* July 13 and 20, 1889, and January 18, February 15, March 29, May 10 and 17, and June 7 and 28, 1890.

29. Ibid., March 8, 1890.

30. *Statistical Jahrbuch, 1889,* p. 74, cited by Walter H. Beck, *Lutheran Elementary Schools in the United States* (St. Louis: Concordia Publishing House, 1939), p. 180.

31. *Verhandlungen des Illinois Districts, 1889,* p. 115, cited by Beck, pp. 232–233.

32. Ibid., p. 233.

33. *Catholic Home,* July 31, 1889.

34. Ibid., November 23, 1889, and March 22, May 10, and October 25, 1890.

35. *Chicago Tribune,* January 12, 1890.

36. Ibid., December 2, 1889, and February 5, 1890.

37. Ibid., July 21, 1889.

38. Ibid., October 5, 1889. See also ibid., January 14 and February 19, 1890.

39. For the full text of the pastoral letter, see *Catholic Home,* March 22, 1890.

40. *Chicago Tribune*, March 14 and 22, 1890.

41. Ibid., March 15, 1890.

42. Ibid., March 8, 1890.

43. Ibid., April 3, 1890.

44. Ibid., March 27 and April 7, 1890.

45. Ibid., April 18 and 28, 1890.

46. Ibid., May 20 and 30, 1890. The special session was to make plans for the Columbian Exposition.

47. Cited by *Catholic Home*, June 14, 1890.

48. Cited by ibid., June 28, 1890 and *Chicago Tribune*, June 25, 1890. Richard Edwards was requested to draft a resolution to amend the compulsory education law so German Lutherans and Catholics would not be alienated from the party. A very close friend of Edwards suggested that the party soften the language issue, but to no avail. J. H. Freeman (public school superintendent of Aurora, Illinois) to Richard Edwards, May 5, 1890, Richard Edwards Papers, box 5, ISUA.

49. Newton Bateman, *Historical Encyclopedia of Illinois with Commemorative Biographies* (3 vols.; Chicago: Munsell Publishing Co., 1926), I:438.

50. See Kucera for a fuller treatment of the Protestant stand on the Edwards Law, pp. 117–120.

51. Donald L. Kinzer, *An Episode in Anti-Catholicism: The American Protective Association* (Seattle: University of Washington Press, 1964), p. 79.

52. Cited by *Chicago Tribune*, June 16, 1890.

53. Ibid., November 31, 1890.

54. Richard Edwards Papers, box I, ISUA. For similar reasoning, see "The Compulsory Education Law," tract no. I, issued by the Illinois Republican Central Committee and prepared by the office of the Superintendent of Public Instruction in 1890. The pamphlet contained a special appeal to Lutherans. Ibid.

55. *Catholic Home*, May 31, 1890.

56. Cited by McGovern, pp. 340–341.

57. Unmarked newspaper clipping, about October 20, 1890, in Richard Edwards Papers, box 2, ISUA.

58. *Abendpost*, October 30, 1890, FLPS.

59. Ibid., October 24, 1890.

60. *Chicago Tribune*, November 8, 1890. In Cook County, Raab received a plurality of 16,000.

61. John W. Cook to Richard Edwards, Normal, Illinois, November 6, 1890, Richard Edwards Papers, box 2, ISUA. Edwards denied that he was responsible for the objectionable form of the law that bore his name when corresponding with a leader of Illinois Germans. Richard Edwards to General W. C. Kueffner, Springfield, Illinois, September 12, 1890, ibid., box 6a.

62. George P. Brown to Richard Edwards, Bloomington, Illinois, November 6, 1890, ibid., box 2. Brown noted that priests' influence in Illinois was not as serious as in Wisconsin because there weren't as many foreigners in the state. See also J. W. Freeman to Richard Edwards, Aurora, Illinois, November 6, 1890, ibid.

63. *Chicago Tribune*, November 8, 1890. Partisan representation in the Illinois General Assembly was as follows:

	HOUSE	SENATE	TOTAL
Republicans	74	27	101
Democrats	76	24	100

64. *Chicago Tribune*, May 28, 1891, and November 6, 1892.

65. Ibid., June 14, 1891.

66. Ibid., May 7, 1892.

67. *The Patriot*, I, no. 1 (March 1891).

68. The most noted presiding officer was Henry F. Bowers, founder of the APA. Other officers who presided were the president of the Illinois APA Council, president of the Patriotic Order of the Daughters of America, president of the Patriotic Order of the Sons of Democracy, and Margaret Shepherd, foundress of the Loyal Women of American Liberty. (Mrs. Shepherd, like Murray, was not native born and had a Catholic father. In the late 1880s and early 1890s she achieved notoriety for her lectures and exposés of Catholic clerical immorality, but revelations about her own immorality destroyed her influence.) Ibid., I, nos. 1 and 4 (March and June 1891), passim, and *Chicago Tribune*, May 30, 1891.

69. *The Patriot*, I (March 1891):3.

70. Ibid., pp. 25, 33-34.

71. Ibid., p. 16.

72. Cited in ibid., p. 17.

73. Cited by *Chicago Tribune*, June 22, 1891.

74. Cited in ibid., May 25, 1891.

75. *Chicago Times*, September 15, 1892.

76. Pastoral letter of the bishops of Illinois, September 11, 1892, cited in *New World*, September 10, 1892.

77. Ibid. The pastoral was signed by Patrick A. Feehan, archbishop of Chicago; John Lancaster Spalding, bishop of Peoria; James Ryan, bishop of Alton; and John Jassen, bishop of Belleville. Its authorship is not clear, but John Tracy Ellis suggests that Spalding may have written it, as the pastoral "reads like him and [it] would be natural that he should have been chosen as the author since he knew much more about the subject of Christian education than the other prelates." *John Lancaster Spalding, First Bishop of Peoria, American Educator* (Milwaukee: Bruce Publishing Co., 1961), p. 57.

78. *New World*, September 17 and 24, 1892.

79. Beck, pp. 246-247.

80. *Chicago Tribune*, September 13 and 18, 1892.

81. Ibid., September 17, 1892. See also ibid., September 18, 1892, and *New World*, September 24, 1892.

82. *Chicago Tribune*, November 6, 7, and 8, 1892.

83. Cited by Andrew Jacke Townsend, "The Germans of Chicago" (unpublished Ph.D. dissertation, University of Chicago, 1927), p. 97. See also *Illinois Staats Zeitung*, June 25, 1892, FLPS. The paper was published by Washington Hesing, a German Catholic who was a staunch Grover Cleveland supporter.

84. John M. Allswang, *A House for All Peoples: Ethnic Politics in Chicago, 1890-1936* (Lexington: University Press of Kentucky, 1971), p. 218.

85. *Chicago Tribune*, November 9 and 12, 1892.
86. Ibid., November 12, 1892.
87. Cited in ibid., November 10, 1892.
88. Ibid., November 9, 1892.
89. *New World*, November 12, 1892.
90. *Illinois Staats Zeitung*, November 10, 1892, FLPS.
91. *Chicago Tribune*, February 18, 1893, and *The Illinois School Law, 1889–1895* (Springfield: State Printer, 1895), p. 96.
92. *Chicago Tribune*, November 9, 1892.
93. John Higham, "The Mind of a Nativist: Henry Bowers and the A.P.A.," *American Quarterly*, IV (Spring 1952):16–24, and *Strangers in the Land*, pp. 68–104.
94. Kinzer, p. 83, and *The Catholic Citizen*, April 8, 1893, cited by Humphrey J. Desmond in *The A.P.A. Movement* (Washington, D.C.: New Century Press, 1912), p. 66.
95. *New World*, December 23, 1893. Religion was not the only issue. Hopkins' Irish ancestry was played upon by the Republican press in order to woo nationalities who disliked the sons of Eire. The *Inter Ocean* was most strongly concemned by the *New World* for appealing to ethnic prejudices.
96. Pierce, III:279.
97. *New World*, December 23, 1893.
98. Ibid., October 20, 1894.
99. *Chicago Tribune*, November 4 and 5, 1894, and *New World*, November 10, 1894.
100. *New World*, February 8, 1896.
101. Ibid., November 7, 1896.
102. Ibid., March 2, 1895.
103. Ibid., December 26, 1896.
104. Ibid., October 22, 1892.

4. IMMIGRANT NATIONALISM

1. Cited in Kirkfleet, p. 295.
2. Cited in ibid., p. 296.
3. *Irish-American Nationalism, 1870–1890* (Philadelphia: Lippincott, 1966), p. 23. See also Joseph P. O'Grady, *How the Irish Became Americans* (New York: Twayne, 1973), pp. 38–42.
4. Brown, pp. 23–25, 38.
5. Michael Funchion, "Chicago's Irish Nationalists, 1881–1890" (unpublished Ph.D. dissertation, Loyola University, 1973), pp. 22–24.
6. Ibid., pp. 25–26.
7. *Chicago Tribune*, November 28, 1880.
8. *Chicago Citizen*, February 8, 1890, cited by Funchion, p. 66.
9. *Chicago Citizen*, October 10, 1885, cited ibid.
10. Ibid., pp. 68–71.
11. William D'Arcy, *The Fenian Movement in the United States: 1858–1886* (New York: Russell and Russell, 1947), and O'Grady, chapter 4.
12. Bishop Duggan condemned the Fenians because they were a secret, oath-bound society, and he claimed that the Church could not sanction revolution by violent means. The Fenians responded by publishing their oath.

Bishop Wood of Philadelphia also condemned the order; however, most American bishops feared to do so lest they lose Irish Catholic membership. D'Arcy, pp. 35 and 49n; Piper, pp. 19–20; J. M. Luers to Purcell, Ft. Wayne, March 23, 1864, UNDA; and H. D. Junker [bishop of Alton, Illinois] to Purcell, Alton, April 3, 1864, UNDA.

13. Piper, pp. 20–22, and D'Arcy, pp. 42, 145, 229.

14. Piper, p. 28; McCafferty, pp. 85–88; D'Arcy, pp. 330–331, 409–411; and Brown, pp. 40–41.

15. "Constitution of the United Brotherhood, 1877," cited in Funchion, p. 50.

16. Ibid., p. 53.

17. Sullivan supposedly stole federal funds while serving as a postmaster and collector of internal revenue in Santa Fe, and in Chicago, escaped conviction for the murder of Francis Hanford, a school teacher who slurred the womanly virtue of his wife. See ibid., pp. 55–56.

18. Ibid., chapters IV–VI, and Brown, pp. 155–168.

19. For a full treatment of the question of secret societies, see Fergus McDonald, *The Catholic Church and Secret Societies in the United States* (New York: United States Catholic Historical Society, 1947).

20. John Tracy Ellis, *The Life of James Cardinal Gibbons* (Milwaukee: Bruce Publishing Co., 1952), I:447–456, and McDonald, pp. 109–113.

21. Funchion, pp. 77 and 79; Kirkfleet, pp. 124, 126, 129, 181; Brown, pp. 155–156; *Chicago Tribune*, March 15, 1914, *Chicago Times*, March 18, 1884; *Western Catholic*, March 22, 1884.

22. *Western Tablet*, October 18 and June 2, 1884.

23. *Western Catholic*, n.d., cited by the *Irish World*, April 7, 1883, in Funchion, p. 80.

24. *Western Catholic*, February 23, 1884.

25. McDonald, pp. 109–113.

26. Cited by Kirkfleet, pp. 239–241.

27. Ibid.; McDonald, pp. 109–114; Ellis, I:456–457; and Zwierlin, II:378–379, 382–383, 436, 461, and 462. The conservative bishops of New York, especially Bishop McQuaid and Archbishop Corrigan, were opposed to Clan-na-Gael because it registered support for the refractory priest, Rev. Edward McGlynn.

28. For accounts of the murder and trial, see *Chicago Tribune*, May 23, 1889; Funchion, chapter VI; and Henry M. Hunt, *The Crime of the Century or the Assassination of Dr. Patrick Henry Cronin* (Chicago: Kochersperger, 1889).

29. *Chicago Tribune*, June 12 and 14, 1889.

30. Ibid., June 16, 21, and 25, 1889.

31. *Catholic Home*, June 29, 1889.

32. Hunt, pp. 364–378, and Funchion, pp. 236–238.

33. Zwierlin, II:378–379 and 382–383.

34. *Review,* June 27, 1895.

35. John A. Hawgood, *The Tragedy of German America: The Germans in the United States of America during the Nineteenth Century and After* (New York: Putnam, 1940), pp. 227–286.

36. "Memorial on the German Question in the United States Written by Rev. P. M. Abbelen, Priest of Milwaukee, Approved by Most Rev. Archbishop of Milwaukee, and Submitted to the Sacred Congregation de Propaganda Fide in November 1886," cited in Barry, pp. 289–296.

37. "An Answer to the Memorial on the German Question in the United

States Written by Rev. P. M. Abbelen, by Bishop John Ireland of St. Paul, and Bishop John J. Keane of Richmond to His Eminence, Cardinal Simeoni, Prefect of the Holy Congregation of the Propaganda, Rome, December 6, 1886," cited, ibid., pp. 296–323.

38. Ibid., pp. 62–84.

39. John J. Meng, "Cahenslyism: The First Stage, 1883–1891," *Catholic Historical Review,* XXXI (January 1946):400.

40. "Memorial Drawn Up and Presented to His Holiness Pope Leo XIII by the First International Conference of St. Raphael Societies, Lucerne, Switzerland, December 9–10, 1890," cited by Barry, pp. 313–315.

41. Barry, pp. 141–143.

42. Ibid., p. 93; *Illinois Staats Zeitung,* January 10, 1886, August 19 and September 7, 1887, FLPS; *Chicago Tribune,* August 4, 1892; *New World,* August 8, 1896; and interview with Msgr. Martin F. Schmidt, Wilmette, Illinois, March 5, 1974.

43. Cited by McGovern, p. 331.

44. *Review,* April 1 and May 1, 1894.

45. Ibid., April 10, 1895.

46. Ibid., November 7, 1894.

47. Ibid., August 1, 1894.

48. Feehan to A. J. Thiele, Chicago, March 30, 1884, cited in *The Seventy Five Years of St. Aloysius Parish* (Chicago: privately printed, 1959), p. 29. Rev. Thiele, pastor of St. Aloysius parish, saw to the erection of St. Elizabeth Hospital, a girls' academy, and a boys' high school. Ibid., pp. 25 and 33. Interview with Msgr. Schmidt, Wilmette, Illinois, March 5, 1974.

49. *Chicago Tribune,* September 8 and 9, 1887; *Illinois Staats Zeitung,* September 7, 1887, and January 30, 1893, FLPS; and Barry, pp. 106–107.

50. *Review,* cited in Kirkfleet, pp. 355–356. The probable reason for the efforts to muzzle the *Review* was its unstated policy of exposing the shortcomings of the Irish race and condemnation of Irish chauvinism. *Review,* June 20 and July 25, 1895.

51. *Review,* October 17, 1894, and March 27, 1895.

52. *Illinois Staats Zeitung,* April 21, 1898, cited in Walsh, p. 20, and the *Review,* August 15, 1895.

53. Parot, pp. 55–57 and 27–28.

54. Ibid., chapter II, and *Dziennik Chicagoski,* January 19, 1891, FLPS.

55. Parot, pp. 42–67.

56. *Dziennik Chicagoski,* January 19, 1891, FLPS.

57. Ibid., June 6, 1896. See also ibid., August 27, 1892, and June 22, 1897, FLPS, and *Narod Polski,* June 20, 1900, FLPS. The *New World* opposed teaching foreign languages in the public schools because it was "useless and impractical," unless languages were first taught at home, and because it placed an extra tax burden on Catholics and benefited Protestant groups. February 25 and March 4, 1893.

58. Cited by *Zgoda,* December 20, 1900, FLPS.

59. Ibid., and March 28, 1901, FLPS.

60. *New World,* December 8, 1900.

61. Vincent Barzynski's brother, Joseph, was pastor of St. Hedwig's parish.

62. Parot, pp. 67–84; *New World,* March 2 and June 22 and 29, 1895; and *Dziennik Chicagoski,* June 15, 17, 20, 22, 24 and August 12, 1895, FLPS.

63. Cited in *Review,* June 13, 1895.

64. *New World*, October 5, 1895.

65. "Letter of Excommunication," cited in ibid.

66. *Dziennik Chicagoski*, February 26, May 11 and 15, 1897, FLPS.

67. The *New World* disputed this figure and suggested that the number of schismatics was much smaller. January 1, 1898.

68. *Igoda*, July 4, 1901, FLPS.

69. The letter wisely noted that its authors did not propose a national bishop; they must have feared stirring up the Cahenslyism issue. "Memorial to the American Hierarchy of November 10, 1901," cited by Parot, pp. 137–139.

70. *New World*, June 23, 1900.

71. Funchion, p. 69.

72. Interviews with Msgr. William Owens, Matteson, Illinois, February 21, 1974; Msgr. J. Gerald Kealy, Chicago, April 1974; and Msgr. Martin F. Schmidt, Wilmette, March 5, 1974. Donna Merwick, *Boston Priests, 1848–1910: A Study of Social and Intellectual Change* (Cambridge, Mass.: Harvard University Press, 1973), p. 116–123, and *New World*, February 9, 1901.

73. *New World*, November 9, 1895, and Thompson, *The Archdiocese*, p. 69.

74. Thompson, *The Archdiocese*, pp. 71–72; Francis G. McManamin, "Peter J. Muldoon: First Bishop of Rockford, 1862–1927," *Catholic Historical Review*, XLVIII (October 1962):365–378.

75. "The Paul E. Lowe Affidavit," in *Chicago Daily News*, March 14, 1902.

76. Ellis, II:416, and David Francis Sweeney, *The Life of John Lancaster Spalding: The First Bishop of Peoria, 1840–1916* (New York: Herder and Herder, 1965), pp. 285–286.

77. This was the first time a Roman official presided at the consecration of an American bishop since James Gibbons had become a cardinal in 1888. *Chicago Daily News*, July 16, 1901.

78. "Lowe Affidavit," *Chicago Tribune*, July 19, 24, 25, 1901, and *Chicago Record-Herald*, July 21 and 23, 1901.

79. Cited by *Chicago Record-Herald*, July 23, 1901.

80. Ibid., and *Chicago Tribune*, July 19, 23, 25, 1901. To assure Muldoon's safety, members of various Catholic societies were scheduled to act as his bodyguard.

81. *Chicago Tribune*, July 25 and August 3, 4, 5, 1901. Crowley also took his case to the Freeport (Illinois) court to have the injunction dissolved, but lost. See ibid., September 14, 1901, and *New World*, October 19, 1901.

82. *Chicago Tribune*, October 27 and 28, 1901, and *New World*, October 26 and November 2, 1901. The letter of excommunication was posted on the doors of all the churches.

The Sunday after the excommunication, Crowley brazenly rejected the excommunication notice and attended services in the Cathedral of the Holy Name. Because it was rumored that he would attend, guards were posted at the doors before the services. Crowley waited until the services had begun and the guards retired and then entered the church. Slowly and dramatically, he walked down the aisle and took a seat in the front of the church. Msgr. William Owens, who served Mass that day, recalls that a "profound silence" fell over the congregation when Crowley made his appearance. The High Mass was ended, the altar boys directed out of the sanctuary, the candles extinguished, and the organ and choir silenced. A Low Mass followed, because Crowley refused to leave when confronted by Chancellor Barry.

Because Crowley continued to disrupt services, the rector of the cathedral filed a bill to restrain the refractory priest from entering the church when services were conducted. The bill declared that his presence caused "disturbance," "annoyance," and "scandal." Interview with Msgr. William Owens, Matteson, Illinois, February 21, 1974; *Chicago Tribune*, November 4, 1901; and *New World*, November 30, 1901.

83. Sweeney, pp. 289–294.

84. *Chicago Inter Ocean,* March 16, 1902.

85. Crowley tried to secure an interview with Archbishop Feehan but was directed to take the matter up with Bishop Muldoon. However, he refused to leave the archbishop's residence unless he had a person-to-person meeting with Feehan. He spent the entire day waiting, and only left when he was arrested. *Chicago Inter Ocean,* March 13, 1902.

86. Cited in ibid.

87. *Chicago Daily News,* March 14, 1902.

88. Ibid., March 28, 1902, and *New World*, April 4, 1902.

89. Crowley wrote a book, *The Parochial School, a Curse of the Church, a Menace to the Nation. An Exposé of the Parochial School—The Loss of Thirty Million Catholics in the United States, Etc.* (Chicago: published by the author, 1905), defending himself and attacking the Muldoon-Barry group as corrupters of the Catholic faith.

90. Cashman and Hodnett remained pastors of their respective parishes after Feehan's death. Thompson, *The Archdiocese*, pp. 331 and 413, and *New World*, February 5, 1910.

91. *Review*, June 20, 1895.

92. Ryan attended Castle Knock College with Feehan and they came to St. Louis together.

93. Cited by Kirkfleet, p. 334. See also *Chicago Tribune*, July 13, 1902.

94. *Chicago Inter Ocean,* July 19, 1902.

5. PERFECTING THE COALITION

1. U.S. Bureau of the Census, *Thirteenth Census of the United States: 1910 Population,* Part I (Washington, D.C.: Government Printing Office, 1913), p. 1023.

2. See tables 7 and 8.

3. See table 9.

4. See Sanders, pp. 67–95.

5. N. W. Ayer and Son, *American Newspaper Annual and Directory* (Philadelphia: N. W. Ayer and Son, 1903–1915), and interviews with Msgr. F. Schmidt, Wilmette, March 5, 1974, Msgr. Arthur Terlecke, Chicago, March 21, 1974, and Msgr. William Owens, Matteson, February 21, 1974.

6. McCarthy, chapter I, and *Chicago Tribune*, July 31, 1904.

7. *Thirteenth Census,* I:984.

8. Ryan to Marchetti, Alton, July 25, 1902, cited by Sweeney, pp. 299–300.

9. These rectors held their pastorates for life; they could not be removed by the ordinary.

10. *Chicago Daily News,* July 24, 1902.

11. Spalding to Gibbons, Peoria, July 25, 1902, Baltimore Archdiocesan Archives (hereafter cited BAA). The *Chicago Tribune* incorrectly reported that the suffragans agreed on the *dignior* choice for Muldoon (July 25, 1902).

12. Cited by *New World*, August 3, 1903.

13. *Chicago Daily News,* July 24, 1902.

14. *New World*, August 2, 1902. Only three of the fourteen irremovable rectors and consultors were of non-Irish descent.

15. *Chicago Daily News,* July 24 and December 15, 1902.

16. Smyth to O'Connell, Evanston, July 24, 1902, cited by Sweeney, p. 301.

17. Spalding to Gibbons, Peoria, July 25, 1902, BAA.

18. Cudhay to Gibbons, Chicago, October 1, 1902, BAA.

19. Ireland to Eminentisseme, St. Paul, August 5, 1902, cited by Sweeney, p. 303.

20. Ibid., p. 303. Archbishop Ireland's criticism of Muldoon may have been conditioned by his own ambition for the red hat. When the facts of the Muldoon controversy broke earlier that year, Paul E. Lowe suggested that some outside force encouraged Cashman and Hodnett, and he noted that Ireland might have been involved because he wanted to rule the Chicago archdiocese. As the second largest diocese in America, it would have been natural for the see's prelate to be honored with the dignity of a cardinalship. When the consultors and irremovable rectors voted, the *Chicago Tribune* mentioned that it was a well-known fact that the archbishop of St. Paul would like the appointment. That Ireland wanted the Chicago appointment is difficult to dismiss, for when Bishop Mundelein was appointed to Chicago in 1915, he wrote him a congratulatory letter and signed it "John Ireland, Archbishop of Chicago." *New World*, March 23, 1902; *Inter Ocean*, March 12, 1902; *Chicago Tribune*, July 25, 1902; and Ireland to Mundelein, St. Paul, November 30, 1915, Chicago Archdiocesan Archives (hereafter cited CAA).

21. Sweeney, pp. 303–305.

22. Gibbons to Ledochowski, Baltimore, August 15, 1902 (copy), BAA.

23. *Chicago Daily News,* December 15, 1902.

24. Sweeney, p. 308.

25. *Chicago Tribune*, December 16, 1902.

26. Ibid., and *Chicago Daily News*, December 15, 1902.

27. *Chicago Tribune*, December 16, 1902, and *Chicago Daily News*, December 15, 1902.

28. Thompson, *The Archdiocese*, p. 73; *Chicago Tribune*, December 16, 1902; *Chicago Daily News*, December 15, 1902, and March 10, 1903.

29. *Chicago Daily News*, December 15, 1902.

30. Ibid., March 9 and 10, 1903, and *Chicago Tribune*, December 15, 1902.

31. *Chicago Tribune*, March 11, 1903; *Chicago Daily News*, March 10 and 11, 1903; and *New World*, March 14, 1903 (author's emphasis).

32. Interviews with Msgr. William Owens, Matteson, February 21, 1974, Msgr. Martin F. Schmidt, Wilmette, March 4, 1974, and Francis C. Kelly, *Archbishop Quigley, a Tribute* (Chicago: published privately, 1915).

33. *Chicago Tribune*, March 12, 1903.

34. Prior to 1907, DePaul had been St. Vincent College. Patrick J. Mullins, "A History of the University," *DePaul University Magazine* (Winter 1975), pp. 7–11.

35. *Chicago Daily News*, July 10, 1915. The special article was written by Anthony Czarnecki, a staff correspondent for the *News* and a friend of the archbishop. See also Thompson, *The Archdiocese*, pp. 75–81.

36. Cited by *Chicago Daily News*, July 13, 1915.

37. *New World*, August 3, 1901. See also ibid., March 14, 1903.

38. *New World*, July 3, 1909. Even after he was appointed chancellor of the archdiocese, Dunne took time to attend language classes at Cathedral College. Interview with Msgr. William Owens, Matteson, February 21, 1974.

39. "The Church and the Immigrant," in *Catholic Builders of the Nation* (4 vols.; Boston: Centennial Press, 1923), II:4.

40. Ibid., pp. 4–7.

41. *New World*, February 11, 1916.

42. Ibid., July 16, 1904.

43. Ibid., January 2, 1931, cited by Sanders, p. 79. See also Thompson, *The Archdiocese*, pp. 599–660.

44. *New World*, February 9, 1907.

45. Ibid., October 24, 1908. See also ibid., August 20, 1904, January 20, 1906, January 16 and June 26, 1909, and August 6, 1910.

46. Ibid., July 3, 1909. In 1909 nearly 90 parishes were predominantly Irish.

47. Ibid., May 20, November 11, and December 23 and 30, 1905; March 3 and 10, 1906; March 16, October 26, and November 9, 1912. It is interesting to note that a Jesuit of German extraction, Rev. Henry J. Dumbach, initiated Gaelic classes at St. Ignatius College and, according to one student, "although of German extraction, he did more than probably a great many Irishmen would be willing to do." Cited in ibid., February 22, 1908.

48. William Dillon, former editor of the *New World*, was the treasurer of the fund. Ibid., January 27, 1906, and November 25, 1905.

49. Ibid., February 9 and July 13, 1907, September 12 and October 3, 1908, January 7, 1911, October 5, 1912, January 4, 1913, and March 27 and May 29, 1914.

50. Ibid., November 2, 1912.

51. Ibid., March 10, 1906.

52. Ibid., March 28, 1908. See also ibid., March 24 and June 2, 1906, and March 7, 14, and 21, 1908. The paper also criticized serious drama. J. M. Synge's *Playboy of the Western World* was reviewed as an "infamous libel" on all Catholic Irish, and Israel Zangwill's *Nurse Marjorie* was objected to because one character, an Irish woman, blasphemed confession. Ibid., April 24 and May 15, 1908.

53. *New World*, July 18, 1908, March 18, 1911, and July 13, 1912.

54. Thompson, *The Archdiocese*, pp. 694–695.

55. Ibid., pp. 614–618 and 623.

56. Townsend, P. 196.

57. Rev. Joseph Brons and Harry Gerardin, *Old St. Joseph's* (Chicago: privately printed, 1926).

58. Thompson, *The Archdiocese*, p. 903.

59. F. L. Kalvelage, *Annals of St. Boniface Parish* (Chicago: privately printed, 1926), p. 83. Relative to St. Peter's parish, see Thompson, *The Archdiocese*.

60. *The St. Gregory Story, 1904–1954* (Chicago: privately printed, 1954), p. 38.

61. *A Historical Sketch of St. Clement's Church, Chicago, 1905–1930* (Chicago: privately printed, 1930), p. 9.

62. *New World*, April 22, 1911.

63. *Seventy-Five Years of St. Aloysius Parish*, p. 41.

64. *New World*, February 27, 1909, and January 30, 1914.

65. Cited in ibid., May 8, 1909.

66. Ayer, 1903, p. 150; 1908, p. 155; and 1915, p. 187.

67. *New World*, September 3, 1904, February 8 and November 28, 1908, and April 23, 1909.

68. *Seventy-Five Years of St. Aloysius Parish,* pp. 35, 36, and 46, and interviews with Msgr. Martin F. Schmidt, Wilmette, March 5, 1974, and Msgr. William Owens, Matteson, February 21, 1974.

69. A. J. Thiele, "Tentative List of Appointments," CAA. The list has check marks by a different pen, presumably Quigley's, next to the priests and suggested assignments. All of these assignments were made as suggested by Thiele. *Official Catholic Directory,* 1913 and 1914.

70. The *New World* was criticized for its "Irishness." A letter to the editor by a Frank G. Hoeny explained that other people should be given fair treatment because they were Catholic and not because of nationality. "There are various nationalities that shed as great a lustre around the Church of God as the Irish," Hoeny wrote (July 31, 1909). In 1909, when the paper sought to increase its circulation, it sponsored a contest and offered ten tickets to Ireland as prizes.

71. Arthur Preuss's *Review* was moved to St. Louis in 1896. No record of its Chicago readership is available.

72. *New World*, August 20, 1910, March 30, April 6, 13, 20, and September 21, 1912.

73. Ibid., November 13, 1897.

74. Ibid., March 30, 1910. As early as 1907, AOH and the German National Alliance joined together to lobby against entangling alliances and immigration restriction, and called for appreciation of all races in the upbuilding of America. Ibid., February 16, 1907. See also ibid., May 20, 1911, May 3, 1913, and July 17, 1914.

75. Ibid., June 19, 1914.

76. Sanders, pp. 126–128, and *New World*, April 14, 1900.

77. *Narod Polski*, February 13, 1901, FLPS. See also ibid., August 14, 1901, FLPS.

78. Ibid., January 25, 1905; June 18 and October 23, 1912; July 29, 1914, FLPS; *Dziennik Chicagoski*, August 28, 1906, FLPS; and *Dziennik Zwiazkowy,* February 1, 1908, FLPS.

79. *Dziennik Zwiazkowy,* December 5, 1911, FLPS.

80. *Narod Polski,* October 23, 1912, FLPS.

81. *Dziennik Chicagoski*, December 11, 1905, and June 5, 1908, FLPS; and Thompson, *The Archdiocese*, pp. 601–659, passim.

82. The Polish National Alliance still opposed clerical domination of the schools, and secured the right to have Polish taught in the city's high schools in 1911. *Dziennik Chicagoski*, July 11, 1908, and December 12, 1911, FLPS; and *Dziennik Zwiazkowy,* November 2, 26, and December 2, 1910, and October 6, November 1, 4, 8, 17, 21, 27, and December 2, 1911, FLPS.

83. Sanders, pp. 114 and 123.

84. *Dziennik Chicagoski*, September 1, 1908, FLPS, and *Dziennik Zwiazkowy,* September 9, 1910, FLPS. For a discussion of the Polish parochial school system, see Thomas I. Monzelli, "The Catholic Church and the Americaniza-tion of the Polish Immigrant," *Polish American Studies,* XXVI (January 1969):9–13.

85. *Dziennik Chicagoski*, September 7, 1905, FLPS.

86. *St. Stanislaus Kostka Church Centennial, 1867–1967* (Chicago: privately printed, 1967), p. 38, and *Dziennik Chicagoski*, May 9, 1908, FLPS.

87. Cited in *Daily Calumet,* in *Immaculate Conception BVM Parish, South Chicago, 1882-1957* (Chicago: privately printed, 1957), p. 35.

88. Parot, pp. 139-151; M. J. Madaj, "The Polish Immigrant, the American Catholic Hierarchy, and Father Wenceslaus Kruska," *Polish American Studies,* XXVI (January 1969):16-29; Greene, pp. 130-137.

89. *New World,* September 12, 1903.

90. Ibid., May 14, 1904.

91. Parot, pp. 152-153, and Greene, pp. 134-135.

92. *New World,* July 25, 1908.

93. Auxiliary Bishop Alexander McGavick, who had fallen ill in 1901, remained in Chicago but did not participate in the administration of the archdiocese.

94. Parot, pp. 156-157.

95. Ibid.; Thompson, *The Archdiocese,* pp. 87-88; and *New World,* June 27, July 17, 25, and August 1, 1908.

96. *Dziennik Chicagoski,* July 18, 1908, FLPS. See also ibid., August 11, 1908, FLPS.

97. *New World,* June 27, 1908.

98. The *New World* supported Polish protests and condemned the Germanization and Russification of Poland (January 18 and May 2, 1908).

99. *Dziennik Zwiazkowy,* November 26, 1910, FLPS.

100. *Narod Polski,* September 28, 1910, and July 10, 1912, FLPS, and *Dziennik Zwiazkowy,* July 22, 1911, FLPS.

101. *Narod Polski,* May 28, 1913, FLPS.

102. *Lietuva,* May 21 and August 20, 1915, FLPS, and Krisciunas, pp. 56-57.

103. *Lietuva,* April 23, 1909, FLPS. See also ibid., June 5, 1903, February 17, December 11, 1908, August 6 and 20, 1909, and June 3, 1914, FLPS.

104. Ibid., September 11, 1908, and September 17, 1909; "Record Book" of St. Casimir Sisters' Convent, FLPS; Krisciunas, p. 48; and Mother Lurretta Lubowedska, superior general of Sisters of the Holy Family of Nazareth to Mundelein, Rome, 1922, CAA.

105. Icilio Felici, *Father to the Immigrants: The Servant of God John Baptist Scalabrini, Bishop of Piacenza* (New York: P. J. Kenedy and Sons, 1955), pp. 171-172.

106. Archbishop Quigley to Cardinal Lai, Chicago, March 21, 1913, cited by Sanders, p. 183.

107. *New World,* June 27, 1903, October 29, 1904, June 22, 1907, April 24, 1909, and September 13, 1913.

108. Felici, pp. 175-176; Thompson, *The Archdiocese,* pp. 578, 579, 599; and *New World,* March 31, 1906.

109. Thompson, *The Archdiocese,* pp. 578-651, passim, and *Chicago Tribune,* July 11, 1915.

110. In 1904, Archbishop Quigley made the Church of the Assumption a territorial parish; however, few non-Italians attended it or its school in the ensuing decade. *Calendario Della Parrocchia Dell' Assunta, Chicago,* April 1905, p. 17; March 1906, p. 20; January 1913, p. 13, and March 1913, p. 19.

111. Ibid., April 1907, pp. 14-17.

112. Sanders, p. 183. The parish school of the Church of the Assumption, founded in 1899, taught religion in Italian, as well as the Italian language, history, and literature. *Calendario Della Parrocchia Dell' Assunta, Chicago,* October, 1909, pp. 14 and 16.

113. *Calendario Della Parrocchia Dell' Assunta, Chicago,* November 1912, p. 13, and *New World,* April 11, 1912, and April 12, 1913.

6. SOCIAL CATHOLICISM

1. Cited in *New World,* July 16, 1915.

2. For a full treatment of changes in charity work in the United States, see Robert H. Bremner, *From the Depths, the Discovery of Poverty in the United States* (New York: New York University Press, 1956) and *American Philanthropy* (Chicago: University of Chicago Press, 1960); Blanche D. Coll, *Perspectives in Public Welfare: A History* (Washington, D.C.: U.S. Department of Health, Education, and Welfare, 1969); and Roy Lubove, *The Professional Altruist* (New York: Atheneum, 1972).

3. Jenkin Lloyd Jones (comp.), *A Chorus of Faith* (Chicago: Unity Publishing Co., 1893), p. 169.

4. Walsh, pp. 35–36; Robert Cross, *The Emergence of Liberal Catholicism in America* (Chicago: Quadrangle Books, 1968), pp. 106–111; and Abell, *American Catholicism,* chapter IV.

5. *New World,* September 16, 1911.

6. Walsh, p. 35.

7. *Second Annual Report of the Visitation and Aid Society, 1891,* cited in ibid., p. 98.

8. Ibid., chapters VI–VIII.

9. *Chicago Tribune,* March 15, 16, 1914, and *Chicago Daily News,* March 15, 16, 1914.

10. Riley, *The Higher Life of Chicago* (Chicago: University of Chicago Press, 1905), p. 87.

11. Addams, "The Subjective Necessity for Social Settlements," in *Twenty Years at Hull-House* (New York: New American Library, 1961), p. 98.

12. *New World,* December 21, 1895.

13. Thompson, *The Archdiocese,* p. 775; Walsh, pp. 130–134.

14. Walsh, pp. 147–148, *New World,* July 23, 1904, and July 19, 1914.

15. Walsh, pp. 144–147, and *New World,* December 24, 1910, May 20, 1911, March 29, 1913, and July 17, 1914.

16. St. Philip Benizi's St. Juliana Day Nursery and Kindergarten was opened under the auspices of the Catholic Women's League.

17. *New World,* June 13, 1903. The Catholic centers were located to compete with the secular and Protestant settlements. Guardian Angel Day Nursery was within a block of the University of Chicago settlement, St. Elizabeth Day Nursery was close to the Northwestern University settlement, and St. Juliana's Day Nursery was near Chicago Commons. When Harvey Carbaugh compiled his *Human Welfare Work in Chicago* in 1917, he listed seventeen "important" settlements, only one of which was Catholic ([Chicago: A. C. McClurg, 1917], pp. 199–209).

18. *New World,* April 14, 1906, and February 22, 1913.

19. Ibid., October 17, 1903.

20. Ibid. See also ibid., October 1, 1904, and May 18, 1907.

21. Ibid., September 29, 1906.

22. Ibid., October 17, 1903.

23. Cited in ibid., January 21, 1911.

24. Ibid.

25. Ibid., February 22, 1903.

26. Ibid., February 3 and April 18, 1912.

27. Ibid., November 26, 1910. See also ibid., March 9, 1912.

28. Interview with Jane Addams in *Chicago Record-Herald,* March 1, 1908.

29. Few Catholics understood that the anticlericals and the anarchist parties were quite distinct. Ibid.

30. *New World*, April 25, 1908.

31. Ibid., February 27, 1914.

32. Conwell became editor in 1913.

33. *New World*, February 27, 1914. See also ibid., March 6, 1914.

34. Ibid., December 7, 1912. See also ibid., October 26, 1911.

35. Ibid., June 25, 1904.

36. Ibid., June 8, 1907.

37. Ibid., November 7, 1906, and May 4, 1907.

38. Ibid., July 18, 1903, and February 25, 1911.

39. Ibid., April 20, 1912.

40. Ibid., February 14 and September 26, 1903; September 3, 1904; March 18 and September 23, 1905; November 17, 1906; March 9 and July 6, 1907; and May 7, 1910.

41. Ibid., April 20, 1912.

42. See ibid., May 26, 1894.

43. While the women discussed the appropriateness of the terms "suffragette" and "suffragist," the editor suggested they be called "insufferable."

44. *New World*, June 25, 1904.

45. Ibid., January 30, 1914.

46. Ibid., March 20, 1914.

47. Ibid., September 23, 1911.

48. "Obituary." *Chicago Provincial Chronicle* (Spring 1939); A. J. Murphy, "Father Siedenberg, S.J.," *Catholic Charities Review* (March 1939), pp. 85–86; and interviews with Rev. Robert C. Hartnett, S.J., Chicago, April 14, 1974, and Miss Mary McPartin, Chicago, April 18, 1974.

49. Cited in *New World*, June 13, 1913.

50. Ibid., October 30, November 20, December 4, 1914, and April 9 and 30 and May 7, 14, 21, and 28, 1915.

51. Ibid., August 23 and 30 and September 6 and 13, 1902.

52. Cited in Anne Fremantle, ed., *The Papal Encyclicals in Their Historical Context* (New York: Mentor-Omega Books, 1963), p. 187.

53. Cited in *New World*, December 11, 1897.

54. *New World*, July 7, 1900.

55. Weibe, pp. 63, 137, 139, and 207–208.

56. Abell, "The Reception of Leo XIII's Labor Encyclical in America, 1891–1919," *Review of Politics*, VII (October 1945):479.

57. McCloskey to Purcell, Louisville, March 17, 1873, UNDA.

58. Ellis, *Life of James Cardinal Gibbons*, II:215 and 448.

59. February 25, 1886, cited in Henry J. Browne, *The Catholic Church and the Knights of Labor* (Washington, D.C.: Catholic University of America Press, 1949), pp. 147–148.

60. His father, John Blake Dillon, and his brother, John Dillon, both served as members of Parliament. F. S. Lyons, *John Dillon: A Biography* (London:

Routledge & Kegan Paul, 1968), pp. 1–6, 32–33, 59, and 69–70. Both of Dillon's books, *The Dismal Science: A Criticism of Modern Political Economy* (Dublin: H. H. Gill and Son, 1882) and *John Mitchell* (2 vols.; London: Kegan, Trench and Company, 1888), reflect his sensitivity to the needs of the poor.

61. *New World*, July 16, 1900.

62. Ibid., August 10, 1901. See also ibid., August 3, 1901.

63. Ibid., June 3, 1899.

64. Ibid., September 7, 1901.

65. For letters to the editor by socialists and editorial responses, see ibid., March 2, 24, and September 15, 1900.

66. Ibid., October 12, 1901. See also ibid., October 26, 1901.

67. *Dziennik Chicagoski*, April 20, 1892, FLPS.

68. Theodore B. Thiele, "The Catholic Movement: Its Necessity and Its Aims," *New World*, November 23, 1901, and January 25, 1902.

69. Corrigan's series of sermons on socialism was carried in the *New World*. In his third sermon, on socialism's "vain promises," he condemned "seductive promises" of an "earthly paradise for mankind." The socialist pledges were despicable substitutes for the promise of happiness after death. "For me," he exclaimed, "the present contains a large possibility of happiness for the frugal, honest poor, and the future holds forth hope for more. Neither rich nor poor can be happy—each must taken his woe to Bethelehem. Christ is the only way." Cited in ibid., January 18, 1902.

70. Ibid., December 20, 1902, and *Chicago Tribune*, July 11, 1915.

71. Philip Gleason, *The Conservative Reformers: German-American Catholics and the Social Order* (Notre Dame: Notre Dame University Press, 1968), p. 76, and Marc Karson, *American Labor Unions and Politics, 1900–1918* (Carbondale: Southern Illinois University Press, 1958), pp. 231 and 240. In February 1903, Fr. Anton Heiter, one of the leaders of the Buffalo Catholic worker's movement, spoke at Chicago's St. Martin (German) parish hall. He discussed the fallacies of socialism and the need for Christian principles. "Let us," he declared, "stand on the ground of Christianity, let the workers and employers hold to the teachings of Jesus Christ, let the state go hand in hand with the hand of the Church and the social question shall be happily solved, without the Socialists." Cited in *Dziennik Chicagoski*, February 11, 1903, FLPS.

72. *Buffalo Evening News*, July 5, 1902, cited in Karson, p. 231.

73. *Chicago Tribune*, March 11, 1903, and *New World*, March 14, 1903.

74. *New World*, December 6, 1902.

75. Ibid., December 3, 1904.

76. Ibid., March 11, 1905. See also ibid., March 14, 1903.

77. Ibid., April 8 and July 8, 1905.

78. Ibid., March 30, 1907. See also ibid., November 24, 1906.

79. Ibid., April 4, 1908. See also ibid., February 1 and 15, and April 11, 1908.

80. Ibid., January 3, 10, 17, and 31, 1903.

81. Ibid., May 16, 1903, and November 19, 1904. The paper frequently criticized industrialists who donated millions to education and charity but failed to justly compensate their employees. Most harshly criticized was John D. Rockefeller, "who teaches the principles of Christianity to a catechism class on Sunday and acts out a system of satanic cruelty in crushing his fellow-men on Monday." Ibid., November 21, 1903, January 3 and 17, and April 14, 1904, March 11, 1905, January 20, 1906, and February 9, 1907.

82. Ibid., February 13, 1904.

83. Ibid., June 9 and 16, 1906; June 18, 1904; and March 23, 1913.

84. Ibid., August 24, 1907.

85. Ibid., February 14, 1903.

86. Ibid., December 24, 1903.

87. Ibid., May 16 and November 19, 1904.

88. Ibid., November 26, 1904. See also ibid., September 26, 1903, and February 6, 1914.

89. Ibid., May 16, 1903.

90. Ibid., October 17, 1903. See also ibid., June 13, 1903.

91. Ibid., April 15, 1905.

92. For coverage of the strike, see *Chicago Tribune* and *Chicago Daily News*, July 12 through September 9, 1904.

93. *Chicago Tribune*, July 31, 1904. Of the 20,000 members of the striking union, 15,000 were immigrants. Twelve thousand were unskilled and spoke little or no English.

94. *New World*, July 16, 1904.

95. *Chicago Tribune*, July 24, 1904.

96. Ibid., July 25, 1904. The *New World* noted, as did the police authorities, that various rumors of riots circulated in the daily papers were often false. Both the police and the Catholic paper praised the workers for avoiding saloons and staying indoors. "It is pleasant to see workingmen so orderly," the editor wrote. "The fact that a majority of them are Catholic Poles, Bohemians, Italians and Irishmen, unquestionably had much to do with the good order observable; and the fact that most of the strikers own homes also accounts for much." July 23 and July 30, 1904.

97. *Chicago Tribune*, August 8, 1904.

98. Ibid., August 14, 1904. Fr. P. M. Flanigan, who had helped to settle previous labor disputes, convinced the largest packer to agree to hire fewer workers in order to ensure constant employment and end the necessity of winter layoffs. Ibid., August 18, 1904. The strike was settled through the mediation of social settlement workers Dr. Cornelia de Bey, Jane Addams, and Mary McDowell. Ibid., September 7, 8, and 9, 1904.

99. *New World*, October 24, 1903. A partial survey of Catholic Sunday attendance indicated 75 to 80 percent attendance. Ibid., October 25, 1902.

100. Ibid., July 4, 1903. In 1897 the paper proudly cited the words of Dwight L. Moody: "The reason that the Catholic Church has such a hold on people is that it has one church and one service for rich and poor alike. Some Protestants might get a good lesson from this." May 1, 1897.

101. The editorial was based upon an article that appeared in *Catholic Columbian Magazine. New World*, July 1, 1911.

When Victor Berger, the Socialist congressman from Milwaukee, proposed an old-age pension, the *New World* supported the measure. February 4, 1911.

102. Chicago Public Library Omnibus Project, Works Project Administration, *Bibliography of Foreign Language Newspapers and Periodicals Published in Chicago* (Chicago: Chicago Public Library, 1942), passim, and Ayer, 1905–1915.

103. *Dziennik Ludowy*, June 30, 1908, FLPS. See also ibid., March 19 and November 3, 1908, FLPS.

104. Foreign-language Catholic periodicals and newspapers published in

Chicago, according to frequency of publication and language for the years 1903–1915, were the following*:

	MONTHLY	SEMIMONTHLY	WEEKLY	SEMIWEEKLY	DAILY
German	2		2		
Polish	1		3		1
Bohemian	1	1	2	1	1
Lithuanian			1		2
Slovak		1	1		
Slovenian			1		

*Not all of these papers were published for the entire period (Chicago Public Library, *Bibliography*, passim).

105. Cited in *New World*, March 9, 1912.

106. The *New World* was one of the first (if not the first) Catholic newspapers to review the book and praise the author's work. The editor's two-part review was featured on page 1. May 12, 19, 1906, and Francis L. Broderick, *Right Reverend New Dealer John A. Ryan* (New York: MacMillan, 1963), p. 46 n.

107. (New York: Macmillan 1906), p. viii.

108. Abell, *American Catholicism*, pp. 178–179.

109. *New World*, October 26, November 2, 1912, and April 26, 1913.

110. Ibid., July 27, 1912.

111. Ibid., July 25, 1913, and Walsh, p. 309.

112. *New World*, October 19, 1912; Marie Seahan, "The Catholic School of Sociology," *Catholic Charities Review*, V (June 1921):196; "A Catholic Lecture Bureau," *America* (October 12, 1912), p. 16; and "Catholic Courses of Social Philanthropy," *America* (October 18, 1913), p. 40.

113. *New World*, January 25, 1913.

114. Ibid., October 23, 1914, and February 5, 1915.

115. Dietz's columns appeared frequently throughout 1913 and occasionally thereafter.

116. *New World*, March 2, 1912.

7. FIRST AMERICAN-BORN ARCHBISHOP

1. Cardinal De Lai, "De Secreto Servando in Degnandis ad Sedes Episcopales in Foederatis Statibus Americanae Septentrionalis" (Rome, March 1910), BAA.

2. Muldoon to Gibbons, Chicago, July 17, 1915, BAA.

3. Ibid. Correspondence from the apostolic delegate included the names of a third choice. The selections of the bishops of the Province of Illinois were (1) Rt. Rev. John P. Carroll, bishop of Helena, (2) Most Rev. J. J. Glennon, archbishop of St. Louis, (3) Rt. Rev. Thomas F. Lillis, bishop of Kansas City. John Bonzano to Gibbons, Washington, D.C., August 18, 1915, BAA.

4. Bonzano to Gibbons, Washington, D.C., August 18, 1915, BAA.

5. Muldoon was not a native Chicagoan, but had lived in the city from the time of his ordination (1886) until his appointment to Rockford.

6. Gibbons to Bonzano, Baltimore, September 1, 1915, BAA.

7. Messmer to Gibbons, Milwaukee, September 4, 1915, BAA. McGavick was not a serious candidate because of poor heath.

8. Ibid.

9. Gibbons to Messmer, Baltimore, September 6, 1915, BAA.

10. *Chicago Tribune*, July 11, 1915, and *Narod Polski*, July 14, 21, and 28, 1915. Their regret was mixed with joy because Rhode's elevation would benefit all Polish Americans. (The author is indebted to Donna Haniak for translating material in *Narod Polski*.)

11. Cited in *Narod Polski*, July 28, 1915. The text of the letter was printed in English and accompanied by an introduction and translation of the text in Polish. The use of English in the paper was exceptional.

12. Of the total 102 ballots cast, 2 went for a German-American and 9 for Bishop Rhode. Muldoon to Gibbons, Chicago, July 17, 1915, BAA.

13. Interview with Msgr. William Owens, Matteson, February 21, 1974.

14. *Chicago Daily News*, November 30, 1915.

15. Recorded interviews.

16. Muldoon to Gibbons, Rockford, December 4, 1915, BAA.

17. *Chicago Tribune*, November 30, 1915.

18. Interview with Msgr. Martin F. Schmidt, Wilmette, March 5, 1974.

19. *New York Times*, December 1, 1915.

20. Telegram, Bonzano to Mundelein, Washington, D.C., November 29, 1915, CAA.

21. Interviews with Msgr. William Owens, Matteson, February 21, 1974, and Msgr. Harry Koenig, Mundelein, July 15, 1974.

22. Interview with Msgr. Harry Koenig, Mundelein, July 15, 1974, and "Notes and Comment," *America*, XIV, no. 9 (December 9, 1915):216.

23. The biographic material that follows was culled from numerous interviews and various printed sources. The most useful are Paul R. Martin, *The First Cardinal of the West* (Chicago: New World Printing Co., 1934); *Chicago Tribune*, November 30, 1915, and October 3, 1939; and *Chicago Daily News*, December 3, 1915, and October 4, 1939.

24. Interview with Msgr. Harry Koenig, Mundelein, July 15, 1974, and Rev. Leonard Schlemm, O.S.B., cited in *Chicago Daily News*, November 30, 1915.

25. Mundelein's ordination was unique. Bishop McDonnell used his influence to break age-old precedent in order that he could personally ordain his favored seminarian. Traditionally, the privilege of ordaining students of the College of the Propaganda had been reserved for the cardinal vicar.

26. "Farewell Address to the Clergy of the Diocese of Brooklyn, New York, February 2nd, 1916," in *Two Crowded Years, Being Selected Addresses, Pastorals, and Letters Issued during the First Twenty-four Months of the Episcopate of the Most Reverend George W. Mundelein as Archbishop of Chicago* (Chicago: Extension Press, 1918), pp. 23–27.

27. Msgr. F. J. Fitzsimmons, acting administrator of the Archdiocese of Chicago, to Mundelein, Chicago, January 13, 1916, CAA, and *Chicago Tribune*, February 11, 12, 13, 14, and 15, 1916.

28. "Address at the Noon Reception of the Clergy, February 9, 1916," in *Two Crowded Years*, pp. 38–42.

29. "Retreat Address, 1919," CAA.

30. For examples see Mundelein to Rev. Constantine Zajowski, Chicago,

February 22, 1918 (copy), CAA, and Mundelein to Most Rev. Joseph Weber, Chicago, February 15, 1918 (copy), CAA.

31. Interviews with Msgr. Arthur F. Terlecke, Chicago, March 21, 1974, Msgr. Martin F. Schmidt, Wilmette, March 5, 1974, and Msgr. William Owens, Matteson, February 21, 1974.

32. Interview with Msgr. Arthur Terlecke, Chicago, March 21, 1974.

33. *Official Catholic Directory*, 1915 and 1928.

34. *Chicago Tribune*, February 10, 1916, and October 3, 1939.

35. Mundelein to Rev. Achille L. Bergeron, March 22, 1918 (copy), CAA, and Mundelein to Fernando Gaudet, S.S.S., March 6, 1922 (copy), CAA.

36. Mundelein to James Pacelli, Chicago, March 12, 1919 (copy), CAA; Mundelein to Rev. P. Barbarino, C.S.C.B., Chicago, September 13, 1916 (copy), CAA; Chancellor Edward F. Hoban to Rev. D'Andrea, Chicago 6, 1921 (copy), CAA; *70th Anniversary of St. Anthony's Parish* (Chicago: privately printed, 1973); and interview with Rev. Joseph Chiminello, C.S., Chicago, March 19, 1974.

37. "Address on the Occasion When the Associated Catholic Charities of Chicago was Formed, April 10, 1917," in *Two Crowded Years*, pp. 142–145, and George W. Mundelein, "The Catholic Charities: Nine Letters," in *Letters of a Bishop to His Flock* (New York: Benziger Brothers, 1927), pp. 65–103.

38. Cited in *Chicago Tribune*, May 12, 1924.

39. Interview with Msgr. Arthur F. Terlecke, Chicago, March 21, 1974.

40. Francis C. Kelly to Alfred E. Burke, n.p., April 17 and 26 and July 26, 1916 (copy), Archdiocesan Archives of Oklahoma City.

41. Martin, pp. 128–137, and "The Bishops' Pastoral Letter," *National Catholic War Council Bulletin*, I (November 1919):25.

42. "Peter's Pence: Nine Letters," *Letters of a Bishop*, pp. 17–47, and Pius XI, "Address of Welcome," *Illinois Catholic Historical Review*, VII (July 1924):14–15.

43. Mundelein to Polk, Chicago (copy), CAA.

44. De Valera to Mundelein, Dublin, November 13, 1921, CAA.

45. *Chicago Tribune*, May 18, 21, and 24, 1937, and *Chicago Daily News*, May 18, 20, and 21, 1937.

46. Milton Fairman, "The Twenty-eighth International Eucharistic Congress," *Chicago History*, vol. V, no. 4 (1976).

47. U.S. Bureau of the Census, *Fourteenth Census of the United States: 1920, Population*, part I (Washington, D.C.: Government Printing Office, 1922), p. 51., and *Fifteenth Census of the United States: 1930, Population*, part I (Washington, D.C.: Government Printing Office, 1933), p. 74.

48. *Fourteenth Census: Population*, part I, p. 788.

49. Immigration to Chicago between 1901 and April 1930. *Fifteenth Census: Population*, part I, p. 541.

YEARS	IMMIGRANTS
1901–1910	252,965
1911–1914	129,813
1915–1919	27,801
1920–1924	104,624
(April) 1925–1930	63,314

50. Ibid., p. 248, and *Fourteenth Census: Population,* part I, p. 729.

51. *Thirteenth Census, Population,* part I, pp. 942 and 989; *Fourteenth Census, Population,* part I, pp. 51, 729–731; and *Fifteenth Census, Population,* part I, pp. 74, 316–319, and 248–250. The transient character of the Mexican population makes the tabulation of precise figures impossible. See Paul S. Taylor, "Mexican Labor in the United States: Chicago and the Calumet Region," *University of California Publications in Economics,* VII, no. 2 (Berkeley: University of California Press, 1932):26–280, and Louise Ano Nuevo de Kerr, "Chicano Settlements in Chicago: A Brief History," *Journal of Ethnic Studies,* 2, no. 4 (1975):22–32.

52. *Fourteenth Census, Population,* part I, p. 1014.

53. McCaffrey, pp. 151–168, and O'Grady, *Irish,* pp. 120–124.

54. *New World,* May 5, 1916. See also ibid., May 12 and 19 and June 2, 1916.

55. Ibid., June 9, 1916.

56. O'Grady, *Irish,* pp. 124–132.

57. *New World,* December 20, 1918, and July 18, 1919.

58. "Letter to the Ladies' Auxiliary of the Ancient Order of Hibernians, Commending the Study of Irish History," *Two Crowded Years,* pp. 310–311. In 1924 the archdiocesan school board discussed the Hibernians' advocacy of Irish history classes for parish schools and decided to leave the matter to the discretion of individual pastors. "Minutes of the School Board Meeting," n.d., CAA.

59. *New World,* July 21 and September 15, 1916, and *St. Thomas the Apostle Church: 1869–1969* (Chicago: privately printed, 1969), pp. 5–6.

60. Townsend, chapters V–VII.

61. Ibid., p. 23, and Paul Frederick Cressey, "Population Succession in Chicago: 1898–1930," *American Journal of Sociology,* XLIV (July 1938):65.

62. McCarthy, chapters I and III–IV; Jakob Harak, "Assimilation of Czechs in Chicago: A Sociological Analysis of the Process of Assimilation in the Czech Community" (unpublished Ph.D. dissertation, University of Chicago, 1928), pp. 22–57; and Cressey, pp. 66–67.

63. Cressey, p. 67; Parot, pp. 169–185; Ozag, pp. 39–48; and Edward R. Kantowicz, "American Politics in Polonia's Capital, 1888–1940" (unpublished Ph.D. dissertation, University of Chicago, 1972), pp. 288–296.

64. Krisciunas, passim, and Sanders, p. 166.

65. McCarthy, pp. 70–78, and Otakar Odlozilk, "The Czechs," in Joseph P. O'Grady, ed., *The Immigrants' Influence on Wilson's Peace Policies* (Lexington: University of Kentucky Press, 1967), pp. 204–223.

66. Parot, pp. 272–280; Kantowicz, pp. 241–248, and Luis Gerson, "The Poles," in O'Grady, *Immigrants' Influence,* pp. 272–286.

67. *Lietuva,* December 31, 1915.

68. Ibid., June 29 and October 19, 1917, FLPS.

69. Cited by Nelli, p. 240.

70. Ibid., p. 202.

71. One avenue of economic "success" was organized crime. Ibid., chapter V.

72. Giovanni E. Schiavo, *The Italians in Chicago: A Study of Americanization* (Chicago: Italian American Publishing Co., 1928), p. 118, and Nelli, p. 239.

73. (New York: Grosset and Dunlap, 1951), p. 244.

74. Louise Montgomery, *The American Girl in the Stockyard District* (Chicago: University of Chicago Press, 1913), pp. 57–61.

75. *Chicago Tribune,* April 2 and 6, July 17, and August 5, 1915, and *New World,* August 15, 1915.

76. Quigley was a member of the National Liberal Immigration League. *New World*, February 22, 1908.

77. *New World*, June 14, August 2 and 23, and October 4, 1913, January 16, 23, and 30, February 13, 20, and 27, April 3, May 1, and December 18, 1914, and January 8 and February 5 and 12, 1915.

78. *Dziennik Zwiazkowy,* December 15, 1914, and January 11, 1915, FLPS.

79. Cited in *Narod Polski,* January 27, 1915, FLPS.

80. *New World*, September 3, 10, 17, 1915.

8. DIVIDED, THEN UNITED

1. George W. Mundelein, "Funeral Oration over the Body of the Most Rev. Archbishop John Lancaster Spalding, Former Bishop of Peoria, Illinois, in the Cathedral, Peoria, August 29th, 1916," *Two Crowded Years,* pp. 134–135.

2. *Chicago Daily News*, December 3, 1915, and *Chicago Tribune*, December 4, 1915.

3. John Frey (president of D.R.K. Staatsverband of New York) to Mundelein, New York, July 6, 1900, CAA; Rev. A. Evers to Mundelein, Colorado Springs, April 5, 1917, CAA; and "Address to the Catholics of German Descent, Chicago, September 24th, 1916," *Two Crowded Years,* p. 108.

4. Cited by *Chicago Tribune*, February 9, 1916.

5. Ibid.

6. *New World*, February 10, 1916.

7. "Address in Reply to the Welcome of the Laity of the Archdiocese, Delivered in the Auditorium, Chicago, February 13th, 1916," *Two Crowded Years*, pp. 45–46.

8. Ibid.

9. *Chicago Tribune*, February 13, 1916.

10. Mundelein to Ffrench, Chicago, March 26, 1916 (copy), CAA.

11. *Chicago Tribune*, January 26, 1917, and Walsh, pp. 165–166 and 172–173.

12. Six months earlier, Mundelein had directed Catholic child-care institutions to offer courses that would prepare the children to earn a livelihood upon graduation. Mundelein to Rev. George Eisenbacher, Chicago, October 21, 1916 (copy), CAA.

13. *Pastoral Letter,* Chicago, February 9, 1917, CAA.

14. Mundelein to Rev. William F. McGinnis, Chicago, March 27, 1917 (copy), CAA.

15. Cited by *Narod Polski,* July 12, 1916, FLPS.

16. "Address at the Banquet of the Irish Fellowship Club, Chicago, March 17, 1916"; "Address at the Celebration of the One Hundred and Twenty-fifth Anniversary of the Proclamation of the Polish Constitution, Delivered in the Auditorium, Chicago, May 3rd, 1916"; and "Address to the Ancient Order of Hibernians, Chicago, March 17, 1917." *Two Crowded Years,* pp. 88–92, 93–98, and 99–104.

17. "Address to Catholics of German Descent," in ibid., pp. 105–111.

18. Cited by T. Lincoln Bouscaren, S.J., and Adam C. Ellis, S.J., in *Canon Law, a Text and Commentary* (Milwaukee: Bruce Publishing Co., 1957), p. 149.

19. Ibid., pp. 149–151. See also Nicolas P. Connolly, *The Canonical Erection of Parishes* (Washington, D.C.: Catholic University of America Press, 1938), and Joseph Edward Ciesluk, *National Parishes in the United States* (Washington, D.C.: Catholic University of America Press, 1944).

20. Mundelein to Mrs. David Rose, Chicago, March 31, 1917 (copy), CAA.

21. Mundelein to Edward McGrath, Chicago, March 6, 1917 (copy), CAA. Similarly, people were refused permission to attend their former parishes once they moved outside its boundaries. Chancellor Edward F. Hoban to Jacob Bryfczynski, Chicago, October 26, 1919 (copy), CAA.

22. Rev. C. A. Rempe to Mundelein, Chicago, August 3, 1917; Mundelein to Rempe, Chicago, August 25, 1917 (copy); and Rempe to Mundelein, Chicago, August 27, 1917, CAA.

23. Rev. Charles Erkenswick to Msgr. F. A. Rempe (vicar general), Cicero, January 4, 1918; and F. A. Rempe to Hoban, Cicero, January 15, 1918, CAA.

24. Mundelein to Rev. Francis Chicotzki, Chicago, July 10, 1916 (copy), CAA.

25. Thompson, *The Archdiocese,* pp. 661–665.

26. Mundelein to Michael Piwowar, Chicago, December 6, 1918 (copy), CAA. Four years later the archbishop received another request from Summit, but it was quite different. Three ladies wrote: "We the English-speaking people of Summit and Argo want a Church, an Irish American Pastor and a parochial school for our own." They were disturbed that Polish newcomers to the region had "usurped" their position in the parish. Mrs. Rall, Mrs. Scully, and Mrs. Allison to Mundelein, Summit, May 13, 1922, CAA.

27. Cited by Mundelein, "Millions for Charity," in *Letters of a Bishop,* p. 85.

28. Mundelein to Rev. Thomas Bona, Chicago, January 13, 1917 (copy), CAA, and Assistant Chancellor to Rev. F. Kudersko, Chicago, July 29, 1918 (copy), CAA.

29. Mundelein to Rev. Edgar Bourget, Chicago, January 11, 1918 (copy), CAA.

30. Mundelein to Rev. Achille L. Bergeron, Chicago, March 22, 1918 (copy), CAA.

31. "Address at the Church-School of Our Lady of Solace, Chicago, October 21st, 1917"; "Address at the Dedication of the Church-School St. Thomas Canterbury, Chicago, June 24th, 1917"; and "Address at the Dedication of the Church-School at Highland Park, Illinois, November 19th, 1916." *Two Crowded Years,* pp. 51–55, 56–59, and 67–68.

32. Mundelein to Rev. Stanislaus Swierczek, C.R., Chicago, December 19, 1919 (copy), CAA (italics mine).

33. *New World,* March 10, April 28, and June 23, 1916; *Chicago Daily News,* May 12, 1916; and Sanders, pp. 216–217. In 1915, 176 of the city's 216 parishes had schools, with an enrollment of 93,830. Sanders, p. 59.

34. S. A. Smyth to the Editor, Chicago, n.d., *America,* XIII, no. 16 (July 31, 1915):399.

35. May 12, 1916.

36. Cited by *Chicago Daily News,* May 12, 1916.

37. Mundelein to William Menger (general manager, *Southern Messenger*), Chicago, July 17, 1916 (copy), CAA.

38. L'Abbe V. Germain to Msgr. Francis Kelly, Quebec, August 2, 1916 (and enclosed clipping), CAA. Kelly responded to the letter, declaring that no one was inconvenienced "to the slightest degree" because English had been the basic language of instruction in almost all parochial schools. Further, he wrote that the national interests of the ethnic groups were not being jeopardized. Kelly to Germain, Chicago, August 11, 1916 (copy), CAA.

39. Thomas Bona, "His Eminence, George Cardinal Mundelein," CAA. Not

all Poles opposed Mundelein's action. A Polish home builder wrote the archbishop to express pleasure with the English-language directive. "As an American citizen of Polish decent [*sic*], I heartily approve of this action, and think that no service could be of greater importance to our country than this. It will help to make our coming generation better American citizens." William Zelosky to Mundelein, Chicago, July 25, 1916, CAA.

40. Cited in *New World*, June 23, 1916.

41. Ibid., August 11, 1916.

42. Ibid., March 10, April 28, and June 23, 1916, and Sanders, p. 219.

43. Bona, "His Eminence."

44. *New World*, January 19, 1917.

45. Sanders, p. 219.

46. "Address to the Knights of Columbus—Care of Delinquent Boys, February 22nd, 1916"; "Address at the Silver Jubilee of the Women's Catholic Order of Foresters, Auditorium, Chicago, April 28, 1916"; and "Address to the Catholics of German Descent." *Two Crowded Years*, pp. 180–187, 194–199, and 103–111.

47. Interview with Msgr. Arthur Terlecke, Chicago, March 21, 1974, and Mundelein to Eisenbacher, Chicago, July 9, 1920 (copy), CAA.

48. Address on the Occasion When the Associated Catholic Charities of Chicago Was Formed, April 10th, 1917," *Two Crowded Years*, p. 152.

49. Jerry Dell Gimarc's "Illinois Catholic Editorial Opinion during World War I" (*Historical Records and Studies, United States Catholic Historical Society*, XVIII [1960]:167–184) discusses the positions of four Illinois diocesan newspapers. They generally espoused the same line taken by the *New World*.

50. *New World*, August 14, 1914, March 19, and April 9, 1915.

51. Ibid., August 14, 1914.

52. Ibid., August 21, 1914, and May 21, 1915.

53. Ibid., October 15, 1915.

54. Ibid., February 2 and 9, 1917.

55. Ibid., February 15 and March 9, 1917.

56. "Address on the Occasion When the Associated Catholic Charities of Chicago Was Formed," *Two Crowded Years*, pp. 146–157.

57. Cited in Thompson, *The Archdiocese*, p. 119. See also *Chicago Tribune*, April 19, 1917, and *New World*, April 20, 1917.

58. "Address on the Occasion When the Associated Catholic Charities of Chicago Was Formed," *Two Crowded Years*, p. 147.

59. *New World*, June 8, 1917. Men with children were told they ought to ask for an exemption as there was a need for a father in the home; pacifists, however, were severely criticized. The paper told its readers that the latter should be made to feel like "men without a country." Further, it suggested that they be refused the "privileges of the civilized community in which they live" as the most effective means to limit their breed. Ibid., July 27, September 7, and November 9, 1917.

60. "Address on the Occasion When the Associated Catholic Charities of Chicago Was Formed," *Two Crowded Years*, pp. 147–148.

61. O'Hern to Mundelein, Washington, D.C., June 7, 1917, CAA.

62. O'Hern to Chancellor Hoban, Washington, D.C., August 25, 1917, CAA.

63. Mundelein to Ireland, Chicago, August 31, 1917 (copy), CAA.

64. Ireland to Mundelein, St. Paul, September 3, 1917, CAA.

65. Ibid., September 10, 1917, CAA.

66. When efforts were made to remove seminarians from the exempt status, the *New World* protested that the Church had already given many priests to the service and that to take away the source of replenishment would be a disservice to the moral life of the nation. May 3, 1918.

67. Mundelein to Ireland, Chicago, September 21, 1917 (copy), CAA.

68. George W. Waring *United States Catholic Chaplains in the World War* (New York: Ordinate Army and Navy Chaplains, 1924), pp. xiv–xv and 347.

69. Mundelein sent young Polish priests, who, besides knowing the Polish language, were much more strongly imbued with an American spirit than the older immigrant clergy. He believed "they will be of much assistance . . . in affecting a thorough amalgamation of the various elements in the camps to which they will be assigned." Mundelein to O'Hern, Chicago, November 1, 1917 (copy), CAA.

70. Waring, pp. 61–62, 237–238, 179–180, and Thompson, *The Archdiocese*, p. 669.

71. "Letter Directing Requiem Services for the First Chicago Soldiers Killed in War," *Two Crowded Years*, p. 308.

72. *New World*, April 20, 1917.

73. Mundelein to Charles W. Folds, Chicago, May 29, 1917, cited in ibid., June 1, 1917.

74. "Christmas Salutation to the People of the Archdiocese of Chicago, 1917," *Two Crowded Years*, p. 156.

75. Letter to the pastors of the Archdiocese of Chicago, March 22, 1918 (copy), CAA.

76. Shannon to the Pastors of the Archdiocese of Chicago, Chicago, April 8, 1918 (copy); Rev. J. Fitzsimmons to Mundelein, Chicago, April 17, 1918; and Shannon to Mundelein, Chicago, April 17, 1918, CAA.

77. Shannon to Mundelein, Chicago, n.d., CAA. The *New World* reported a different figure: $8,677,659. It is interesting to note that Shannon's predominantly Irish parishioners of St. Thomas the Apostle in Hyde Park subscribed for $174,800. The largest parish, St. Stanislaus Kostka, recorded bond sales of $114,450 (May 31, 1918).

78. Shannon to Mundelein, Chicago, April 7, 1918, CAA.

79. Martin, pp. 120–121, and *New World*, November 15, 1918.

80. "Letter in Favor of the Work of the Red Cross," *Two Crowded Years*, pp. 286–287; Insull to Mundelein, Chicago, September 10, 1917, CAA; "Address on the Occasion When the Associated Catholic Charities of Chicago Was Formed"; "Letter of Appeal for Aid to the St. Vincent de Paul Society"; and "Letter in Favor of the Knights of Columbus War Camp Activities," *Two Crowded Years*, pp. 148–150, 278–281, and 303–306; Thompson, *Knights of Columbus*, pp. 25 and 721–733; "The Columbus Hospital of Chicago," *National Catholic War Council Bulletin*, I, no. 5 (October 1919):26–27; and *New World*, November 30 and December 7 and 21, 1917.

81. *New World*, November 30, 1918.

82. Ibid., December 14, 1918.

83. "Prayer at the Great Rally under the Auspices of the State Council of Defense, Chicago, 1917," in *Two Crowded Years*, pp. 112–113, and Thompson, *The Archdiocese*, p. 120.

84. Shannon to Glass, Washington, D.C., March 22, 1919 (copy), CAA.

9. TOWARD ETHNIC HOMOGENEITY

1. January 3, 1919. When Gompers died, the *New World* praised him for restoring "self-respect, independence, and the rights of the workingman" and for laboring for the new dawn of cooperation between capital and labor (January 16, 1925).

2. "Retreat Address, 1919," CAA.

3. *Reconstruction Pamphlet No. 1* (Washington, D.C.: Committee on Special War Activities, National Catholic War Council, 1919), and Abell, *American Catholicism*, pp. 199–211.

4. John Fitzpatrick, "The Bishops' Labor Program," *National Catholic War Council Bulletin*, I, no. 2 (July 1919):1–10.

5. "Pastoral Letter of 1919," in Guilday, pp. 265–340, and *New World*, October 22, 1926.

6. "Social Reconstruction," p. 3.

7. Fitzpatrick, p. 9.

8. *New World*, July 11, 1919.

9. Ibid., April 16, 1920.

10. Higham, *Strangers in the Land*, pp. 195–221 and 234–254.

11. *Chicago Tribune*, December 17 and 23, 1919, and Higham, *Strangers in the Land*, pp. 254–263.

12. *New World*, November 3, 1916.

13. Ibid., May 19, 1916.

14. Ibid., November 3, 1916.

15. Ibid., May 24, 1918.

16. Ibid., November 28, 1918. See also ibid., February 25, 1916.

17. Ibid., September 24, 1920, and January 14 and February 18, 1921.

18. John A. Lapp, "Bogus Propaganda: Dollar Mark Shows Attempts to Control Americanization Programs," *National Catholic War Council Bulletin*, I, 11 (June–July 1920):9–10.

19. Lapp, "The Campaign for Civic Education," *National Catholic War Council Bulletin*, I, 1 (July 1919):11–12.

20. "Bringing Immigrants into Citizenship," *National Catholic War Council Bulletin*, III, 2 (July 1921):2–4.

21. *New World*, May 24, 1918. The editorial was a reiteration of the article "Instruction to the Immigrants Is a Catholic Duty," which had appeared in the Central Verein's *Central Blatt* and been reprinted in the *New World*, one and a half years earlier. November 3, 1916.

22. Ibid., July 5, 1918.

23. Ibid., March 7, 1919. See also ibid., August 15 and 29, 1919.

24. Chicago Community Trust, *Americanization in Chicago: The Report of a Survey* (Chicago: Chicago Community Trust, 1920), p. 28.

25. "N.C.W.C. Social Action Department Enlists Chicago Slovenians in Civic Education Campaign," "Widespread Demand for Civics Catechism," and "N.C.W.C. Catechism Popular in Chicago Industrial Plant," *National Catholic War Council Bulletin*, III, 10 (March 1922):21–22; II, 3 (November 1920):22–23; and II, 9 (May 1921):19.

26. Archbishop Edward J. Hanna (archbishop of San Francisco and chairman of the NCWC Administrative Committee) to Mundelein, Washington, D.C., December 12, 1920, CAA.

27. "Citizenship Activities in Chicago Parochial Schools," *National Catholic War Council Bulletin*, I, 11 (June–July 1920):24.

28. Chicago Community Trust, pp. 20 and 28, and Thompson, *Knights of Columbus,* pp. 865–868.

29. Chicago Community Trust, p. 3.

30. Cited in Mundelein, "The Advantages of Co-ordinated Effort," *Letters of a Bishop,* p. 83.

31. Ibid., p. 80.

32. "Charity Aid to the City Itself," in ibid., p. 97. See also "The First Register of Charities," ibid., pp. 65–69.

33. Interview with Msgr. Martin F. Schmidt, Wilmette, March 5, 1974.

34. Michael Gasior (and other members of St. Michael Archangel Society) to Mundelein, Bellwood, February 21, 1921, CAA.

35. Strehl to Hoban, Hillside, February 10, 1921, CAA.

36. Ibid.

37. Mundelein to Rev. Maurice McKenna (pastor of Queen of Heaven), Chicago, November 16, 1920 (copy); Ben Brozovsky (and others) to Mundelein, Cicero, March 12, 1917; Mundelein to Rev. A. J. Dedera (pastor of Mary Queen of Heaven), Chicago, January 25, 1919 (copy); "Bohemian Priests" to Mundelein, Chicago, February 25, 1920; and "Petition of 163" to Mundelein, Berwyn, n.d., CAA.

38. Rt. Rev. Paul Marella (auditor of Apostolic Delegation), Washington, D.C., February 21, 1924; Mundelein to Marella, Chicago, February 26, 1924 (copy), CAA; and *Five Holy Martyrs Church and School, Golden Jubilee: 1909–1959* (Chicago: privately printed, 1959).

39. Marvin R. Schafer, "The Catholic Church in Chicago: Its Growth and Administration" (unpublished Ph.D. dissertation, University of Chicago, 1929), pp. 15–16.

40. *New World,* January 15, 1926, and September 28, 1928; Rev. George Hindelang, C.PP.S., to Mundelein, Celina, Ohio, September 27, 1923, CAA; and Kerr, p. 24.

41. Mundelein to James Farrell, Chicago, April 11, 1925 (copy), CAA. Farrell, a New York friend of the archbishop, contributed $12,000 and offered to pay more in order to cover the full cost.

42. *New World,* February 10, 1928, and interview with Msgr. Arthur F. Terlecke, Chicago, March 21, 1974. Priests from both St. Patrick's and St. Francis de Sales parish (in South Chicago) helped to establish the parish.

43. *New World,* February 10, 1928. It is interesting to note that the cornerstone was laid by the bishop of Tabasco, Mexico, and that 10,000 persons — Polish, Irish, Germans, Slovaks, Croatians, Italians, Colombians, as well as Mexicans — participated in a prededication parade. Ibid., April 6, 1928.

44. Ibid., September 28, 1928, and January 26, 1926.

45. Rev. W. L. Kruszas to Mundelein, December 5, 1924, CAA. Several priests who were interviewed stated that many young Poles became dissatisfied with the "Polishness" of their parish services.

46. *School Laws of Illinois, Circular No. 138* (Springfield: State Printer, 1919), pp. 3–4.

47. Bona, "His Eminence."

48. *Chicago Tribune*, February 6, 1916.

49. Thompson, *The Archdiocese,* p. 75.

50. Mundelein, "Pastoral Letter in Favor of the Preparatory Seminary of the Archdiocese," *Two Crowded Years*, pp. 321–322.

51. *Chicago Tribune*, February 6, 1916.

52. "Pastoral Letter in Favor of the Preparatory Seminary of the Archdiocese," *Two Crowded Years*, p. 325.

53. Area was later renamed Mundelein in gratitude for the cardinal's gift of a fire engine to the village.

54. Interviews with Msgr. J. Gerald Kealy, Chicago, April 1, 1974, Msgr. Girard Picard, former prefect of discipline at St. Mary of the Lake Seminary, February 14, 1974; and Thomas Madigan to Mundelein, New York, April 18, 1925, CAA.

55. "Dedication of St. Mary of the Lake Seminary," in *Letters of a Bishop*, p. 304.

56. To prevent the "serious mistakes made in the past," Mundelein personally interviewed each seminary applicant. Mundelein to William Dillon, Chicago, April 29, 1916 (copy), CAA.

57. Cited in *Chicago Tribune*, May 11, 1924.

58. Cited in an interview with Msgr. Stanislaus Piwowar, Chicago, February 15, 1974.

59. *Dziennik Zwiakowy*, August 7, 1918, FLPS. See also ibid., May 13, 1922.

60. Ibid., August 7, 1918, FLPS.

61. Lange to Associated Catholic Charities, August 19, 1919, CAA.

62. Rev. Francis Wojtalewicz to Mundelein, Chicago, November 10, 1917, CAA.

63. Mundelein to Wojtalewicz, Chicago, November 13, 1917 (copy), CAA.

64. Msgr. Dominic Szopinski to author, Rumia, Poland, November 7, 1973. Szopinski edited a Polish ecclesiastical journal, *Prezglad Kościelny*, and in it attacked Mundelein for his treatment of the Polish clergy. See Bona to Mundelein, Chicago, n.d., CAA. Attached to the letter was a translation of an article from *Prezglad Kościelny* (April 1922), attacking Mundelein.

65. Szopinski to author, Rumia, Poland, November 7, 1973, and Rev. A. Furman to Mundelein, Chicago, January 10, 1917, CAA.

66. *I Polacchi Negli Stati Uniti Dell' American Del Nord* (Rome, June 28, 1920 (copy), Philadelphia Archdiocesan Archives (hereafter cited PAA). Translation from Italian by author.

67. Minutes of meeting of American hierarchy, note I, September 23, 1920, PAA.

68. Gibbons to Daugherty, Baltimore, October 2, 1920, PAA.

69. Mundelein was anxious to have the matter settled. Daugherty noted that the Chicagoan had already written his portion of the reply during the Washington meeting. However, the archbishop of Philadelphia believed that, "owing to the hurry and distraction . . . he has not done full justice in this answer to Polish accusations. Instead of sweeping denials in which he deals, I feel he ought to have submitted fuller information and statistics." Daugherty to Gibbons, Philadelphia, October 4, 1920, PAA.

70. Messmer to Daugherty, Milwaukee, November 11, 1920, PAA. Attached was a 5-page statement on the Polish question.

71. Mundelein to Gibbons, Chicago, November 16, 1920, PAA.

72. The Poles had their own seminary, Orchard Lake Seminary, in Michigan.

73. Gibbons to Gasparri, Baltimore, November 18, 1920 (copy), PAA.

74. In a letter to Daugherty, Messmer mentioned that a Vatican official had visited Mundelein and had tried to meet with himself on what appeared to be a secret mission. The mysterious Roman agent had been calling only on Polish priests. Milwaukee, November 19, 1920, PAA.

75. Most Rev. John T. McNicholas (bishop of Duluth) to Mundelein, Sinsinawa, Wisconsin, n.d., 1920, and Most Rev. Joseph Chartard (bishop of Indianapolis) to Mundelein, February 26, 1924, CAA.

76. Bona, "His Eminence"; Mundelein, "Letter Ordering a Collection for the Suffering People of Poland," *Two Crowded Years*, pp. 312–317; and "Relief for Central Europe," *Letters of a Bishop,* pp. 198–200.

77. Interview in *Chicago Tribune*, May 11, 1924.

78. Bona, "His Eminence."

79. Cited in "Momentous Moment in the American Church," *Illinois Catholic Historical Review,* VII, 1 (July 1924):72–73. See also *Chicago Tribune*, May 13, 1924.

CONCLUSION

1. Interview in *Chicago Tribune*, November 30, 1915.

2. *New World*, November 9, 1928.

3. Cited in James A. Farley, *Jim Farley's Story: The Roosevelt Years* (New York: McGraw-Hill, 1948), p. 176.

Bibliography

MANUSCRIPT SOURCES

The Archives of Assumption and St. Philip Benizi Parishes. Pastoral correspondence, parish records and bulletins of both parishes, housed at Assumption Parish, elucidate the Church's work among Italian Catholics.

Baltimore Archdiocesan Archives. The papers of Cardinal James Gibbons contain correspondence of the Chicago hierarchy and that of American priests and bishops relative to the condition of the Church in Chicago. Also, valuable correspondence with Roman officials relative to immigrant nationalism are contained in its holdings.

Chicago Archdiocesan Archives. Although the archives lacks the correspondence of Archbishop Patrick A. Feehan and contains few of Archbishop James E. Quigley's papers, the Cardinal George W. Mundelein correspondence is voluminous. Catalogued to 1926, at the time of research, the correspondence of the cardinal and his chancellors as well as pastoral letters and parish reports are a rich source of information.

Illinois State University Archives. The Richard Edwards Papers, containing the writings and correspondence of the Illinois Superintendent of Public Instruction and unpublished biographic material and newspaper clippings provide a broader dimension to the Edwards Law controversy.

Maynooth College Archives. General records of matriculation and ordination are available in the archives; however, a serious fire destroyed Patrick A. Feehan's records.

Philadelphia Archdiocesan Archives. The archives contains valuable information on the Polish question. However, because the archives had not been catalogued at the time of research, the potential worth of the Philadelphia holdings could not be utilized.

University of Notre Dame Archives. The correspondence of many American bishops has been collected and catalogued and made available for research. Also, the archives possesses microfilms of the correspondence of early missionary societies. Both of these sources contain numerous references to the Catholic Church in Chicago as well as letters by Chicago's first bishops.

NEWSPAPERS AND JOURNALS

Calendario Della Parrocchia Dell' Assunta, Chicago (monthly), 1905–1915.
Catholic Home (Chicago).
Chicago Daily News, 1890–1939.
Chicago Tribune, 1850–1939.
Chicago Record-Herald, 1890–1902.
Chicago Inter Ocean, 1899–1902.
New World (Chicago), 1892–1928.
New York Times, 1902–1916.
The Patriot: An Advocate of Americanism (Chicago), 1891.
Review (Chicago and St. Louis), 1894–1896.
Western Catholic (Chicago).
Western Tablet (Chicago), 1852–1854.

REPORTS, PROCEEDINGS, AND PUBLIC DOCUMENTS

Bateman, Newton, ed. *School Laws and Common School Decisions of the State of Illinois.* Urbana, Ill.: Pillsbury and Freeman, 1889.
Burgess, E. W., and Charles Newcomb. *Census Data for the City of Chicago, 1920.* Chicago: The University of Chicago Press, 1931.
Debates and Proceedings of the Constitutional Convention of the State of Illinois. Springfield, Ill.: E. L. Merrit and Brother, 1870.
The Illinois School Law, 1889–1895, An Act to Establish and Maintain a System of Free Schools, Approved May 21, 1889, Including Additional Acts Relative to Schools. Springfield: State Printer, 1895.
Illinois Supreme Court Reports, 1918, Vol. 280. Bloomington: Pantagraph Printing and Stationery Company, 1918.
Proceedings of the Constitutional Convention of the State of Illinois, Convened January 6, 1920. Volumes I–V. Springfield: State Printer, 1920 and 1922.
The School Laws of Illinois, Circular No. 138. Springfield: State Printer, 1919.
Synodus Dioecesana Chicagiensis Prima, Juxta Norma, Conc. Balt. III, Praestitum Habita In Ecclesia Metropolitana S.S. Nominis. Chicago: Cameron, Amberg and Associates, 1887.
Synodus Dioecesana Chicagiensis Secunda. Chicago: Cameron, Amberg and Co., 1902.
Synodus Dioecesana Chicagiensis Tertia. Chicago: Cameron, Amberg and Co., 1906.
U.S. Bureau of the Census, *Census of the United States, Population, 1880, 1890, 1900, 1910, 1920, and 1930.* Washington, D.C.: Government Printing Office.
———. *The United States Statistical View . . . Being a Compendium of the Seventh Census, 1850.* Washington, D.C.: Government Printing Office, 1850.
U.S. Congressional Senate Report of the Immigration Commission, XXVI, XXVII. *Immigrants in the Cities.* 61st Congress, 2nd Session, 1911. Washington, D.C.: Government Printing Office, 1911.

————. Report of the Immigration Commission, XXIX, XXXIII. *Children of Immigrants in Schools.* 61st Congress, 3rd Session, 1911. Washington, D.C.: Government Printing Office, 1911.

BOOKS

Abell, Aaron I. *American Catholicism and Social Action: A Search for Social Justice.* Notre Dame, Ind.: University of Notre Dame Press, 1960.

Abbot, Edith, *The Tenements of Chicago, 1908–1935.* Chicago: The University of Chicago Press, 1936.

Abbot, Edith and Sophonisba P. Breckenridge. *Truancy and Non-Attendance in the Chicago Schools.* Chicago: The University of Chicago Press, 1917.

Addams, Jane. *Twenty Years at Hull House.* New York: The New American Library, 1961.

Allen, Frederick Lewis. *Only Yesterday: An Informal History of the Nineteen-Twenties.* New York: Perennial Library, 1964.

Allswang, John M. *A House for All Peoples: Ethnic Politics in Chicago, 1890–1936.* Lexington: University Press of Kentucky, 1971.

Andreas, A. T. *History of Chicago from the Earliest Period to the Present Time.* 3 vols. Chicago: A. T. Andreas, 1884–1886.

Andrews, Theodore. *The Polish National Catholic Church in America and Poland.* London: S.P.C.K., 1953.

Bach, Ira J. *Chicago on Foot: An Architectural Walking Tour.* Chicago: Follett Publishing Company, 1969.

Balch, Emily Greene. *Our Slavic Fellow Citizens.* New York: Charities Publication Committee, 1910.

Barnard, Harry. *Eagle Forgotten: The Life of John Peter Altgeld.* New York: The Bobbs-Merrill Company, 1938.

Barry, Colman J. *The Catholic Church and German Americans.* Milwaukee: Bruce Publishing Company, 1953.

Beck, Walter H. *Lutheran Elementary Schools in the United States.* St. Louis: Concordia Publishing House, 1939.

Benson, William S., James J. Walsh, and Edward J. Hanna, eds. *Catholic Builders of the Nation: A Symposium of the Catholic Contribution to the Civilization of the United States.* 4 vols. Boston: Continental Press, Inc., 1925.

Billington, Ray Allen. *The Protestant Crusade, 1800–1860: A Study of the Origins of the American Nativism.* New York: Atheneum, 1971.

Bogart, Ernst L., and Charles M. Thompson. *The Industrial State: 1870–1893, vol. IV, The Centennial History of Illinois.* Springfield: Illinois Centennial Commission, 1920.

Bouscaren, T. Lincoln, and Adam C. Ellis. *Canon Law: A Text and Commentary.* Milwaukee: Bruce Publishing Company, 1957.

Bremner, Robert H. *American Philanthropy.* Chicago: University of Chicago Press, 1960.

————. *From the Depths, The Discovery of Poverty in the United States.* New York: New York University Press, 1956.

Broady, David. *The Butcher Workmen: A Study in Unionization.* Cambridge, Mass.: Harvard University Press, 1964.

Broderick, Francis L. *Right Reverend New Dealer John A. Ryan.* New York: The Macmillan Company, 1963.

Brown, Thomas N. *Irish-American Nationalism, 1870-1890.* Philadelphia: J. B. Lippincott, 1966.

Browne, Henry J. *The Catholic Church and the Knights of Labor.* Washington, D.C.: Catholic University of America Press, 1949.

Bürgler, F. C. *Geschite der Katholische Kirche, Chicagos.* Chicago: Wilhelm Kuhlmann, 1889.

Bushnell, Charles J. *The Social Problems at the Chicago Stock Yards.* Chicago: University of Chicago Press, 1902.

Cada, Joseph. *Czech-American Catholics, 1850-1920.* Lisle, Illinois: Benedictine Abbey Press, 1964.

Carbaugh, Harvey C., ed. *Human Welfare Work in Chicago.* Chicago: A. C. McClurg and Company, 1917.

Ciesluk, Joseph Edward. *National Parishes in the United States.* Washington, D.C.: Catholic University of America Press, 1944.

Coll, Blanche D. *Perspectives in Public Welfare: A History.* Washington, D.C.: U.S. Department of Health, Education and Welfare, 1969.

Connolly, Nicholas P. *The Canonical Erection of Parishes.* Washington, D.C.: Catholic University of America Press, 1938.

Copek, Thomes *Czechs in America.* Boston: Houghton-Mifflin Company, 1920.

Corey, Lewis. *Meat and Men: A Study of Monopoly, Unionism and Food Policy.* New York: Viking Press, 1950.

Cross, Robert D. *The Emergence of Liberal Catholicism in America.* Chicago: Quadrangle Books, 1968.

Crowley, Jeremiah J. *The Parochial School, A Curse to the Church, A Menace to the Nation. Priestly Graft, Immorality and Sacrilege — The Loss of Thirty Million Catholics in the United States, Etc.* Chicago: Published by Author, 1905.

D'Arcy, William. *The Fenian Movement in the United States: 1858-1886.* New York: Russell and Russell, 1947.

David, Henry. *The History of the Haymarket Affair: A Study in the Social-Revolutionary and Labor Movements.* New York: Russell and Russell, 1958.

Desmond, Emmett. *Fabulous Chicago.* New York: Random House, 1935.

Desmond, Humphrey J. *The A.P.A. Movement.* Washington, D.C.: The New Century Press, 1912.

Dillon, William. *The Dismal Science: A Criticism on Modern English Political Economy.* Dublin: H. H. Gill and Son, 1882.

————. *The Life of John Mitchell,* 2 vols. London: Kegan, Trench and Company, 1888.

Ellis, Elmer. *Mr. Dooley's America: A Life of Finley Peter Dunne.* New York: Alfred A. Knopf, 1941.

Ellis, John Tracy. *American Catholicism.* Chicago: University of Chicago Press, 1956.

————. *John Lancaster Spalding, First Bishop of Peoria, American Educator.* Milwaukee: Bruce Publishing Company, 1961.

————. *The Life of James Cardinal Gibbons, Archbishop of Baltimore, 1843-1921*. Milwaukee: Bruce Publishing Company, 1952.

————, ed. *Documents of American Catholic History*. Milwaukee: Bruce Publishing Company, 1956.

Farrell, James T. *Studs Lonigan, A Trilogy Containing Young Lonigan, The Young Manhood of Studs Lonigan, Judgment Day*. New York: The Modern Library, 1963.

Felici, Icilio. *Father to the Immigrants: The Servant of God John Baptist Scalabrini, Bishop of Piacenza*. New York: P. J. Kenedy and Sons, 1955.

Fremantle, Anne, ed. *The Papal Encyclicals in their Historical Context*. New York: Mentor-Omega Books, 1963.

Fox, Paul. *Poles in America*. New York: George H. Dorn Company, 1952.

Garraghan, Gibert J. *The Catholic Church in Chicago, 1673-1871*. Chicago: Loyola University Press, 1921.

Ginger, Ray. *Altgeld's America: The Lincoln Ideal Versus Changing Realities*. Chicago: Quadrangle Paperbacks, 1965.

Gleason, Philip. *The Conservative Reformers: German-American Catholics and the Social Order*. Notre Dame, Ind.: The University of Notre Dame Press, 1968.

Guilday, Peter, ed. *The National Pastorals of the American Hierarchy*. Washington, D.C.: National Catholic Welfare Council, 1923.

Handlin, Oscar. *Al Smith and His America*. Boston: Little, Brown and Company, 1958.

————. *Boston's Immigrants, 1790-1865: A Study in Acculturation*. Cambridge, Mass.: Harvard University Press, 1941.

————. *Race and Nationality in American Life*. Boston: Little, Brown and Company, 1957.

————. *The Uprooted*. New York: Grosset and Dunlap, 1951.

Hawgood, John A. *The Tragedy of German America: The Germans in the United States During the Nineteenth Century and After*. New York: G. P. Putnam's Sons, 1940.

Higham, John. *Strangers in the Land: Patterns of American Nativism, 1860-1925*. New York: Atheneum, 1971.

Hofstadter, Richard. *The Paranoid Style in American Politics and Other Essays*. New York: Alfred A. Knopf, 1965.

Hoyt, Homer. *One Hundred Years of Land Values in Chicago, 1830—1930*. Chicago: University of Chicago Press, 1933.

Hunt, Henry M. *The Crime of the Century of the Assassination of Dr. Patrick Cronin*. Chicago: Kochersperger, 1889.

Iwicki, John. *The First One Hundred Years: A Study of the Apostolate of the Congregation of the Resurrection in the United States, 1866-1966*. Rome: Gregorian University Press, 1966.

Jackson, Kenneth T. *The Ku Klux Klan in the City, 1915-1930*. New York: Oxford University Press, 1968.

Jones, Jenkin Lloyd. *A Chorus of Faith*. Chicago: Unity Publishing Company, 1893.

Jones, Maldwyn Allen. *American Immigration*. Chicago: University of Chicago Press, 1965.

Karson, Marc. *American Labor Unions and Politics, 1900–1918*. Carbondale: Southern Illinois University Press, 1958.

Kinzer, Donald L. *An Episode in Anti-Catholicism: The American Protective Association*. Seattle: University of Washington Press, 1964.

Kirkfleet, Cornelius J. *The Life of Patrick Augustine Feehan*. Chicago: Matre and Company, 1922.

Kucera, Daniel W. *Church-State Relationships in Education in Illinois*. Washington, D.C.: Catholic University of America Press, 1955.

Leuchtenburg, William E. *The Perils of Prosperity, 1914–1932*. Chicago: University of Chicago Press, 1966.

Lichliter, M. D. *History of the Junior Order of United American Mechanics of the United States of North America*. Philadelphia: J. B. Lippincott Company, 1908.

Lubove, Roy. *The Professional Altruist: The Emergence of Social Work as a Career, 1880–1930*. New York: Atheneum, 1972.

Lyons, F. S. L. *John Dillon, A Biography*. London: Routledge and Kegan Paul, 1968.

McAvoy, Thomas T. *The Great Crisis in American Catholic History, 1895–1900*. Chicago: Henry Regnery Company, 1957.

————. *A History of the Catholic Church in the United States*. Notre Dame, Ind.: University of Notre Dame Press, 1969.

McCaffery, Lawrence J. *The Irish Question, 1800–1922*. Lexington: University of Kentucky Press, 1968.

McDonald, Fergus. *The Catholic Church and Secret Societies in the United States*. New York: The United States Catholic Historical Society, 1947.

McGirr, John E. *Life of the Rt. Rev. Wm. Quarter, D.D., First Bishop of Chicago*. Des Plaines, Ill.: St. Mary's Training School Press, 1920.

Martin, Paul R. *The First Cardinal of the West*. Chicago: The New World Publishing Company, 1934.

Merwick, Donna. *Boston's Priests, 1848–1910: A Study of Social and Intellectual Change*. Cambridge, Mass.: Harvard University Press, 1973.

Mickells, Anthony Bernard. *The Constitutive Elements of Parishes, A Historical Synopsis and a Commentary*. Washington, D.C.: Catholic University of America Press, 1950.

Miller, Kenneth D. *The Czecho-Slovaks in America*. New York: George M. Doran Company, 1922.

Montgomery, Louise. *The American Working Girl in the Stockyards District*. Chicago: The University Press, 1913.

Mowry, George E. *The Era of Theodore Roosevelt and the Birth of Modern America: 1900–1912*. New York: Harper Torchbooks, 1962.

Moynihan, James H. *The Life of Archbishop John Ireland*. New York: Harper and Brothers Publishers, 1953.

Mundelein, George W. *Letters of a Bishop to His Flock*. New York: Benziger Brothers, 1927.

————. *Two Crowded Years, Being the Selected Addresses, Pastorals, and Letters Issued*

During the First Twenty-four Months of the Episcopate of the Most Reverend George W. Mundelein as Archbishop of Chicago. Chicago: Extension Press, 1918.

Nelli, Humbert S. *Italians in Chicago, 1880–1930: A Study in Ethnic Mobility.* New York: Oxford University Press, 1970.

O'Grady, Joseph P. *How the Irish Became American.* New York: Twayne Publishers, Inc., 1973.

———, ed. *The Immigrants' Influence on Wilson's Peace Policies.* Lexington: University of Kentucky Press, 1967.

Pierce, Bessie Louise. *A History of Chicago.* 3 vols. New York: Alfred A. Knopf, 1958.

Putz, Louis J., ed. *The Catholic Church, U.S.A.* Chicago: Fides Publishers, 1956.

Reddaway, S. F., and J. H. Penson, O. Halecki, and R. Dyboski, eds. *The Cambridge History of Poland, 1697–1935.* Cambridge: Cambridge University Press, 1941.

Reichman, John J. *Czechoslovaks in Chicago.* Chicago: The Czechoslovak Historical Society of Illinois, 1937.

Riley, Thomas James. *The Higher Life of Chicago.* Chicago: University of Chicago Press, 1905.

Rothman, Emmet H. *The German Catholic Immigrant in the United States: 1830–1860.* Washington, D.C.: Catholic University of America Press, 1946.

Schiavo, Giovanni E. *The Italians of Chicago.* Chicago: Italian American Publishing Company, 1928.

Shaughnessy, Gerald. *Has the Immigrant Kept the Faith? A Study of Immigration and Catholic Growth in the United States, 1790–1920.* New York: MacMillan Company, 1925.

Shuster, George N. *The Catholic Spirit in America.* New York: The Dial Press, 1927.

Soloman, Barbara Miller. *Ancestors and Immigrants: A Changing New England Tradition.* Cambridge, Mass.: Harvard University Press, 1959.

Stead, William T. *If Christ Came to Chicago.* Chicago: Laird and Lee, 1894.

Sweeney, Francis David. *The Life of John Lancaster Spalding: The First Bishop of Peoria, 1840–1916.* New York: Herder and Herder, 1965.

Thomas, William I., and Florian Znaniecki. *The Polish Peasant in Europe and America.* Chicago: University of Chicago Press, 1918.

Thompson, Joseph J. *A History of the Knights of Columbus in Illinois.* Chicago: Universal Press, 1921.

Trisco, Robert Frederick. *The Holy See and the Nascent Church in the Middle Western United States, 1826–1850.* Rome: Gregorian University Press, 1962.

Vanderbosch, Amry. *The Dutch Communities of Chicago.* Chicago: The Knickerbocker Society of Chicago, 1927.

Waring, George J. *United States Catholic Chaplains in the World War.* New York: Ordinate Army and Navy Chaplains, 1924.

Wiebe, Robert W. *The Search for Order, 1877–1920.* New York: Hill and Wang, 1967.

Wendt, Lloyd, and Herman Kogan. *Bosses in Lusty Chicago: The Story of Bathhouse John and Hinky Dink.* Bloomington: Indiana University Press, 1967.

Woodham-Smith, Cecil, *The Great Hunger.* New York: Harper and Row, 1962.

Zglenicki, Leon, ed. *Poles of Chicago, 1837–1937.* Chicago: Polish Pageant Incorporated, 1937.

Zorbaugh, Harvey W. *The Gold Coast and the Slums, A Sociological Study of Chicago's Near North Side.* Chicago: University of Chicago Press, 1929.

Zwierlein, Frederick J. *The Life and Letters of Bishop McQuaid.* 3 vols. Rochester: The Art Print Shop, 1926.

ARTICLES

Abell, Aaron I. "Origins of Catholic Social Reform in the United States: Ideological Aspects." *Review of Politics* XI (July 1949):294–309.

————. "The Reception of Leo XIII's Labor Encyclical in America, 1891–1919." *Review of Politics* VII (October 1945):464–495.

"The Bishops' Pastoral Letter." *National Catholic War Council Bulletin* I (November 1919):25.

"Catholic Courses of Social Philanthropy." *America* XII (October 18, 1913):40.

"A Catholic Lecture Bureau." *America* XI (October 12, 1912):16.

Cavanaugh, John. "Personal Tribute to William J. Onahan." *Illinois Catholic Historical Review* I (April 1919):480–483.

"Citizenship Activities in Chicago Parochial Schools." *National Catholic War Council Bulletin* I (June–July 1920):24.

"The Columbus Hospital." *National Catholic War Council Bulletin* I (October 1919):26–27.

Cressey, Paul Frederick. "Population Succession in Chicago: 1898–1930." *American Journal of Sociology* XLIV (July 1938):59–69.

Cross, Robert D. "The Changing Image of the City Among American Catholics." *Catholic Historical Review* XLVIII (April 1962):33–52.

Epstein, Francis J. "History in the *Annuals* of the Leopoldine Association." *Illinois Catholic Historical Review* I (October 1918):225–233.

————. "History in the *Annuals* of the Leopoldine Association." *Illinois Catholic Historical Review* I (January 1919):372–379.

Fitzpatrick, John. "The Bishops' Labor Programme." *National Catholic War Council Bulletin* I (July 1919):9–10.

Gallery, John Ireland. "The Chicago Catholic Institute and Chicago Lyceum." *Illinois Catholic Historical Review* II (January 1920):303–322.

Garraghan, Gilbert J. "Early Catholicity in Illinois." *Illinois Catholic Historical Review* I (July 1918):8–28.

Girmarc, Jerry Dell. "Illinois Catholic Editorial Opinion During World War I." *Historical Records and Studies, United States Catholic Historical Society* XLVII (1960):167–184.

Girter, Michael. "The Relation of Educational Legislation in Illinois to Catholic

Interests." *Educational Association Bulletin* IV (November 1907):89–94.

Gladden, Washington. "The Anti-Catholic Agitation." *Harper's Weekly* LIX (September 12, 1914):255–256.

Higham, John. "The Mind of a Nativist: Henry Bowers and the A.P.A." *American Quarterly* IV (Spring 1952):16–24.

Holweck, F. G. "Rev. Gaspar Henry Ostlangenburg." *Illinois Catholic Historical Review* II (July 1920):43–60.

Hubbard, Elbert. "A New Disease." *Arena* X (June 1894):76–83.

Kellogg, Louise Phelps. "The Bennett Law in Wisconsin." *Wisconsin Magazine of History* II (September 1918):3–25.

Kelly, Francis C. "The Anti-Papal Panic, What Catholics Think of It." *Harper's Weekly* LIX (December 5, 1914):535–536.

Lapp, John A. "Bogus Propaganda: Dollar Mark Shows Attempts to Control Americanization Program." *National Catholic War Council Bulletin* I (June–July 1920):9–10.

———. "The Campaign for Civic Instruction." *National Catholic War Council Bulletin* I (July 1919):11–12.

Larkin, Emmet. "The Devotional Revolution in Ireland, 1850–75," *American Historical Review* LXXVII (June 1978):625–652.

Larkin, Helen M. "Catholic Education in Illinois." *Illinois Catholic Historical Review* IV (April 1922):339–354.

McAvoy, Thomas T. "The Catholic Minority after the Americanist Controversy, 1899–1917: A Survey." *Review of Politics* XI (January 1959):53–82.

———. "The Irish Clergyman in the United States." *Records of the American Catholic Historical Society of Philadelphia* XXXV (March 1964):6–38.

McMahon, Charles A. "Bishop Muldoon's War and Reconstruction Service." *Illinois Catholic Historical Review* X (April 1928):295–300.

———. "Education and Good Citizenship." *National Catholic War Council Bulletin* I (March–April 1920):14–17.

———. "The N.C.W.C. Program for Better Citizenship." *National Catholic Welfare Council Bulletin* III (July 1921):6.

McManamin, Francis G. "Peter J. Muldoon: First Bishop of Rockford, 1862–1927." *Catholic Historical Review* XLVIII (October 1962):365–378.

Madaj, M. J. "The Polish Immigrant, the American Hierarchy, and Father Wenceslaus Kruszka." *Polish American Studies* XXVI (January–June 1969):16–29.

Meng, John J. "Cahenslyism: The First Stage, 1883–1891." *Catholic Historical Review* XXXI (January 1946):398–413.

———. "Cahenslyism: The Swecond Chapter, 1891–1910." *Catholic Historical Review* XXXII (October 1946):302–340.

Monzell, Thomas I. "The Catholic Church and the Americanization of the Polish Immigrant." *Polish American Studies* XXVI (January–June 1969):1–15.

Murphy, A. J. "Father Siedenburg, S.J." *Catholic Charities Review* XXIII (March 1939):85–86.

"N.C.W.C. Catechism Popular in Chicago Industrial Plan." *National Catholic Welfare Council Bulletin* II (May 1921):9.

"N.C.W.C. Social Action Department Enlists Chicago Slovenians in Civic Education Campaign." *The National Catholic Welfare Council Bulletin* III (March 1922):21–22.

Nolan, J. Allen. "Right Reverend Peter James Muldoon, D.D., First Bishop of Rockford, 1863–1927." *Illinois Catholic Historical Review* X (April 1928):291–294.

"Notes and Comments." *America* XIV (December 9, 1915):216.

"Notes and Comments." *America* XIV (February 12, 1916):431–432.

Onahan, William J. "Catholic Progress in Chicago—Personal Recollection of Catholic Progress and Activities in Chicago during Sixty-four Years." *Illinois Catholic Historical Review* I (October 1918):176–183.

Prescott, W. W. "The Pro-Papal Program." *Harper's Weekly* LIX (October 3, 1914):321–322.

Ridpath, John Clark. "The Mixed Population of Chicago." *Chautaugan* XII (January 1891):483–493.

Riordan, D. J. "The University of St. Mary of the Lake." *Illinois Catholic Historical Review* II (October 1919):135–160.

Rothenstiener, John. "Interesting Facts Concerning Chicago's First Four Bishops." *Illinois Catholic Historical Review* IX (October 1926):151–161.

Sheahan, Marie. "The Catholic School of Sociology." *Catholic Charities Review* V (June 1921):196–197.

Swastek, Joseph. "The Contribution of the Catholic Church in Poland to the Catholic Church in the U.S.A." *Polish American Studies* XXIV (January–June 1967):15–26.

Sweet, Frederick A. "Putting Over a Civic Education Program." *National Catholic War Council, Bulletin* I (August 1920):10–11.

Taylor, Paul S. "Mexican Labor in the United States: Chicago and the Calumet Region." *University of California Publications in Economics* VII (1932):26–280.

"Textbooks for Civics." *National Catholic War Council Bulletin* I (July 1919):16.

Thompson, Joseph J. "The Illinois Missions." *Illinois Catholic Historical Review* I (July 1918):38–62.

———. "The Irish in Chicago." *Illinois Catholic Historical Review* II (April 1920):458–473.

———, ed. "Momentous Moment in the American Church." *Illinois Catholic Historical Review* VII (July 1924):3–94.

Whyte, William F. "The Bennett Law Campaign." *Wisconsin Magazine of History* X (June 1927):363–390.

"Widespread Demand for Civic Catechism." *National Catholic Welfare Council Bulletin* II (November 1921):2–4.

(Van de Velde, James Oliver). "The Right Reverend James Oliver Van de Velde, D.D." *Illinois Catholic Historical Review* IX (July 1926):56–70.

MEMORIALS, SOUVENIRS, AND PARISH HISTORIES

All Saints' Parish (Lithuanian) Golden Jubilee, 1906–1956. Chicago: Privately printed, 1956.

Archdiocese of Chicago Centennial, 1843–1943. Chicago: The New World Publishing Company, 1943.

Assumption Church, Diamond Jubilee, 1881–1956. Chicago: Privately printed, 1956.

Brons, Joseph, and Harry Gerardin. *Old St. Joseph's.* Chicago: Privately printed, 1926.

Catholic Educational Exhibit at the World's Columbian Exhibition, Chicago, 1893. Chicago: J. S. Hyland and Company, 1896.

Chronological History of St. Augustine's Church, Chicago, Illinois, 1879–1936. Chicago: Privately printed, 1936.

Diamond Jubilee of St. Alphonsus Church, 1882–1957. Chicago: Privately printed, 1957.

Gallery, Mary Onahan. *Life of William J. Onahan, Stories of Men Who Made Chicago.* Chicago: Loyola University Press, 1929.

Golden Jubilee: Five Holy Martyrs Church and School, 1909–1959. Chicago: Privately printed, 1959.

Golden Jubilee of Holy Cross Lithuanian Roman Catholic Parish Chicago, 1904–1954. Chicago: Privately printed, 1954.

Habig, Marion A. *The Franciscans at St. Augustine's and in Chicagoland.* Chicago: Privately printed, 1961.

Healy, John. *Maynooth College: Its Centennial History, 1795–1895.* Dublin: Browne and Nolan Limited, 1895.

A Historical Sketch of St. Clement's Church, Chicago, 1905–1930. Chicago: Privately printed, 1930.

A History of Angel Guardian Orphanage, One Hundred Years of Service to Girls and Boys, 1865–1965. Chicago: Privately printed, 1965.

Holy Trinity: Fifty Years, 1910–1960. Chicago: Privately printed, 1960.

Illustrated Souvenir of the Archdiocese of Chicago. Chicago: R. M. Fleming Publishing Company, 1916.

Immaculate Conception B.V.M. Parish, South Chicago, 1882–1957. Chicago: Privately printed, 1957.

Kalvalage, F. L., ed. *The Annals of St. Boniface Parish, 1862–1926.* Chicago: Privately printed, 1926.

Kelley, Francis Clement. *Archbishop Quigley, A Tribute.* Chicago: Privately printed, 1915.

McGovern, James J. *Souvenir of the Silver Jubilee in the Episcopacy of His Grace the Most Rev. Patrick Augustine Feehan, Archbishop of Chicago.* Chicago: Privately printed, 1891.

100 Hundred Years, The History of the Church of the Holy Name. Chicago: The Cathedral of the Holy Name, 1949.

St. Boniface Diamond Jubilee, 1865–1940. Chicago: Privately printed, 1940.

The St. Gregory Story, 1904–1954. Chicago: Privately printed, 1954.

St. John Berchmans Church, Chicago, Illinois, Golden Jubilee, 1905–1955. Chicago: Privately printed, 1955.

St. Mary Magdalene, 1910–1960, Souvenir Book. Chicago: Privately printed, 1960.

St. Michael Diamnetes Jubilam, 1852–1927. Chicago: Privately printed, 1927.

St. Stanislaus Kostka Church Centennial, 1867–1967. Chicago: Privately printed, 1967.

St. Thomas the Apostle Church, 1869–1969. Chicago: Privately printed, 1969.

St. Wenceslaus Parish Golden Jubilee, 1912–1962. Chicago: Privately printed, 1962.

70th Anniversary of St. Anthony's Parish. Chicago: Privately printed, 1973.

Seventy-Five Years of St. Aloysius Parish, 1884–1959. Chicago: Privately printed, 1959.

Souvenir of the Golden Jubilee of St. Peter's Friary, 1875 — 1925. Chicago: Privately printed, 1925.

Thompson, Joseph J. *The Archdiocese of Chicago, Antecedents and Developments.* Des Plaines, Illinois: St. Mary's Training School Press, 1920.

DIRECTORIES AND ALMANACS

Chicago and Cook County Official Directory and Sketch Book, 1900. Chicago: R. P. O'Grady, 1900.

Chicago Daily News Almanac and Year Book. Chicago: The Chicago Daily News Company, 1890–1928.

Fergus, Robert. *Fergus Directory for Chicago for 1843.* Chicago: Robert Fergus, 1843.

The Official Catholic Directory, 1890–1928. Publisher varies: New York: D. J. Sadlier and Company; Milwaukee: M. H. Wiltzius Company; New York: P. J. Kenedy and Sons.

PAMPHLETS

The Committee on Special War Activities, National Catholic War Council. *The Church and Reconstruction.* Reconstruction Pamphlet No. 10. Washington, D.C.: National Catholic War Council, 1920.

———. *The Fundamentals of Citizenship.* Reconstruction Pamphlet No. 6. Washington, D.C.: National Catholic War Council, 1919.

———. *Land Colonization: A General Review of the Problems and Survey of Remedies.* Reconstruction Pamphlet No. 2. Washington, D.C.: National Catholic War Council, 1919.

———. *A Program for Citizenship.* Reconstruction Pamphlet No. 5. Washington, D.C.: National Catholic War Council, 1919.

———. *Social Reconstruction: A General Review of the Problems and Survey of Remedies.* Reconstruction Pamphlet No. 1. Washington, D.C.: National Catholic War Council, 1919.

———. *Speakers' Outline of Talks on Citizenship.* Reconstruction Pamphlet No. 11. Washington, D.C.: National Catholic War Council, 1920.

Loomis, Frank D. *Americanization in Chicago.* Chicago: The Chicago Community Trust, 1920.

National Catholic Welfare Council. *Catechismo Civile De Diritti e Doveri dei Cittadani Americani.* Reconstruction Pamphlet No. 13. Washington, D.C.: National Catholic Welfare Council, 1920.

———. *Katechizm Obywatelski: Pouczacy o Prawach I Powinnosciach Ameryanskiego Obywatela.* Reconstruction Pamphlet No. 13. Washington, D.C.: National Catholic Welfare Council, 1920.

———. *Obacianšky Katekizm o Právach A Povinnstiach Amerikánskych Obcánov.* Reconstruction Pamphlet No. 13. Washington, D.C.: National Catholic Welfare Council, 1920.

The Proposed New Constitution for Illinois to Be Voted upon December 12, 1922. Chicago: Chicago Bureau of Public Efficiency, 1922.

UNPUBLISHED SOURCES

Chada, Joseph. "A Survey of Radicalism in the Bohemian-American Community." Unpublished paper, 1954.

"The Chicago Foreign Language Press Survey." Chicago Public Library Omnibus Project, Works Project Administration, 1942.

Cole, Bruce McKitterick. "The Chicago Press and the Know-Nothings, 1850–1856." Unpublished Master's thesis, University of Chicago, 1948.

Felter, Eunice. "The Social Adaptations of the Mexican Churches in the Chicago Area." Unpublished Master's thesis, University of Chicago, 1941.

Funchion, Michael F. "Chicago's Irish Nationalists, 1881–1890." Unpublished Ph.D. dissertation, Loyola University of Chicago, 1973.

Horak, Jakub. "Assimilation of Czechs in Chicago." Unpublished Ph.D. dissertation, University of Chicago, 1920.

Kantowicz, Edward R. "American Politics in Polonia's Capital, 1888–1940." Unpublished Ph.D. dissertation, University of Chicago, 1972.

Krisciunas, Joseph. "Lithuanians in Chicago." Unpublished Master's thesis, DePaul University, 1935.

McCarthy, Eugene R. "The Bohemians in Chicago and Their Benevolent Societies: 1875–1946." Unpublished Master's thesis, University of Chicago, 1950.

Ozog, Julius John. "A Study of Polish Home Ownership in Chicago." Unpublished Master's thesis, University of Chicago, 1942.

Parot, Joseph John. "The American Faith and the Persistence of Chicago Polonia, 1870–1920." Unpublished Ph.D. dissertation, Northern Illinois University, 1970.

Piper, Ruth Margaret. "The Irish of Chicago, 1848 to 1871." Unpublished Master's thesis, University of Chicago, 1936.

Puzzo, Virgil Peter. "The Italians in Chicago, 1890–1930." Unpublished Master's thesis, University of Chicago, 1937.

Sanders, James. "The Education of Chicago Catholics: An Urban History." Unpublished Ph.D. dissertation, University of Chicago, 1970.

Schafer, Marvin Reuel. "The Catholic Church in Chicago: Its Growth and Administration." Unpublished Ph.D. dissertation, University of Chicago, 1929.

Townsend, Andrew Jacke. "The Germans of Chicago." Unpublished Ph.D. dissertation, University of Chicago, 1927.

Walsh, John Patrick. "The Catholic Church in Chicago and Problems of an Urban Society: 1893–1915." Unpublished Ph.D. dissertation, University of Chicago, 1948.

INTERVIEWS

Chicago, Illinois. Rev. Joseph Chiminello, S.C. February 19, 1974.

Northfield, Illinois. Rev. William Dorney. March 18, 1974.

Chicago, Illinois. Rev. Thomas Fiorruci, O.S.M. April 29, 1974.

Chicago, Illinois. Msgr. James Hardiman. January 31, 1974.

Chicago, Illinois. Rev. Robert C. Hartnett, S.J. April 15, 1974.

Evergreen Park, Illinois. Msgr. Patrick J. Hayes. January 29, 1974.

Chicago, Illinois. Msgr. J. Gerald Kealy. April 1, 1974.

Mundelein, Illinois. Msgr. Harry Koenig. July 15, 1974.

Chicago, Illinois. Mary Lou McPartlin. April 18, 1974 (telephone).

Madison, Wisconsin. Most Rev. Cletus O'Donnell. May 13, 1974 (telephone).

Matteson, Illinois. Msgr. William Owens. February 21, 1974.

Chicago, Illinois. Msgr. Girard Picard. February 14, 1974.

Chicago, Illinois. Msgr. Stanislaus Piwowar. February 15, 1974.

Chicago, Illinois. Rev. Edward Przybyliski. February 19, 1974.

Wilmette, Illinois. Rev. Martin F. Schmidt. March 5, 1974.

Chicago, Illinois. Msgr. Arthur F. Terlecke. March 21, 1974.

CORRESPONDENCE

Rev. Dominic Szopinski to Author, Rumia, Poland, November 7, 1973.

Index